A HISTORY OF NORWEGIAN MUSIC

BY NILS GRINDE

A History of Norwegian Music

TRANSLATED BY WILLIAM H. HALVERSON & LELAND B. SATEREN

University of Nebraska Press: Lincoln & London

Copyright 1991 by the University of
Nebraska Press
All rights reserved
Manufactured in the United States of America
Originally published in Norway as *Norsk
musikkhistorie*, 3rd ed., copyright 1981
Universitetsforlaget AS

Library of Congress Cataloging-in-Publication Data
Grinde, Nils.
[Norsk musikkhistorie. English]
A history of Norwegian music / by Nils Grinde;
translated by William H. Halverson and
Leland B. Sateren.
p. cm.
Translation of: Norsk Musikkhistorie. 3rd ed.
Includes bibliographical references
and index.
ISBN 0-8032-2135-5 (alk.)
1. Music—Norway—History and criticism.
I. Title.
ML312.G7513 1991 780'.9481—dc20 90—44907
CIP MN

Publication of this volume has been assisted by a
generous grant from the Andrew E. and
G. Norman Wigeland Fund and the American
Scandinavian Foundation.

Contents

Illustrations

Translators' Preface

Non-Norwegians, including many who are generally knowledgeable about art music, often find it difficult to name a single Norwegian composer other than Edvard Grieg. Some who have been piano students may remember that the composer of the well-known "Rustle of Spring" was a Norwegian named Christian Sinding, but few are likely to recall such names as Ole Bull, Halfdan Kjerulf, Rikard Nordraak, or Johan Svendsen. The general impression, one fears, is that Grieg is something of an anomaly—a composer with no predecessors, no contemporaries, and no successors in his own land, a solitary master who miraculously sprang forth in a cultural wasteland like the proverbial root out of dry ground.

We hope that the publication of Nils Grinde's *A History of Norwegian Music* will help to demonstrate that the reality is quite different from the perception. Although it is true that throughout most of its history Norway has been a follower rather than a leader in the realm of music, Grieg was by no means the solitary genius that he is often perceived to have been. He was indeed an especially gifted composer, so much so that his gifts elevated him to a position of special prominence among his contemporaries. But Grieg's genius could not and would not have emerged in a cultural void. The lesser figures who preceded him prepared the way for him, and during his lifetime he shared center stage in his own country with an equally illustrious contemporary, Johan Svendsen. Nor did serious music writing and music making come to an end in Norway with the death of Grieg in 1907. Indeed, the magnitude and diversity of music life in contemporary Norway are truly astonishing—a tribute, no doubt, to the foresight of a people and a government that have long made it a policy to provide generous public support for their creative artists.

As one would expect, there are many references in the text to folk songs and compositions as well as to books, journals, newspapers, and articles whose original titles are in Norwegian or some other language other than English. Our policy regarding the translation of such titles is as follows. The titles of books and articles are always given in English translation, regardless of the language of the original and irrespective of whether or not they are available in English. Except as otherwise noted in the text or the Selected Bibliography it should be assumed, however, that these works are not available in English. Because the titles of newspapers and periodicals constitute proper names, we have in these instances retained the original languages. Folk-song titles are usually given in English (although few such songs have been translated into English) except when the title is a proper name or is so idiosyncratic that we have deemed it impossible to provide a translation that would not do violence to the original. With respect to compositions, when the original title is in Norwegian, Swedish, or Danish we give an English equivalent; when the original title is in some other language (usually German, French, or Latin), we retain the original title.

The Norwegian language employs three vowels in addition to those used in English: æ (pronounced like the "a" in "man"), ø (pronounced like the "u" in "fur"), and å (pronounced like the "o" in "more"). When these vowels occur in proper names we transliterate as follows: æ = ae, ø = ö (the German umlaut), and å = aa.

We have found it advisable to retain a few Norwegian terms—primarily those denoting uniquely Norwegian dance forms—in the body of the text. These terms appear in italics each time they occur and the meaning of each is explained at its first occurrence. A glossary is also provided to obviate the need to repeat the explanation each time the italicized term recurs.

The titles of major-length works appear in italics; the titles of all other works (including the subsections of larger works except those with standard designations, such as Allegro and Minuet) are in quotation marks.

The harmonic analysis used in this book is based on the system of "functional harmony" developed by Hugo Riemann (1849–1919) which, with some modifications, is generally employed today in Germany and northern Europe. The system, which was adapted to analyze harmonic properties in music written from ca. 1630 to ca. 1900, regards all harmonies as belonging to one of three functions: tonic, dominant, and subdominant. Chords based on scale degrees II, III, and VI are regarded as the relative minors of IV, V, and I, respectively, and their respective functions are, therefore, subdominant, dominant, and tonic. Scale degree VII is regarded as having a dominant function.

We express our gratitude to the Lutheran Brotherhood Life Insurance Company of Minneapolis for a travel grant that enabled us to confer with the author on two different occasions in the course of our work; to Professors Finn Benestad and Dag Schjelderup-Ebbe of the University of Oslo, whose considerable bilingual expertise has helped us avoid many pitfalls in the translation of this book; and to Professor Grinde himself, who has given generously of his time to make this edition of his book maximally useful to non-Norwegian readers. The successive Norwegian editions of Professor Grinde's book have long been regarded in Norway as the definitive modern history of Norwegian music. We are confident that this English-language edition of his book will quickly earn a place of equally high esteem among British and American readers.

WILLIAM H. HALVERSON, LELAND B. SATEREN

To the Reader

This survey of Norwegian music from ancient times to the present is based on the third edition (1981) of my *Norsk musikkhistorie*, which was published in Oslo by Universitetsforlaget. The text has been revised to some extent, however, in deference to the needs of non-Norwegian readers for explanations of place names and references to events in Norwegian history. The last chapter, "Music Since 1950," has been thoroughly rewritten to reflect, among other things, developments in Norwegian music since 1981.

The book presents an overview of the history of Norwegian music with emphasis on art music. An entire chapter is devoted to folk music, however, and other types of music—church music, jazz, popular music, film music—are also discussed. For more detailed information regarding each of these types, however, the reader is referred to the relevant literature in the Selected Bibliography and to the various institutions and agencies listed at the end of the book.

The Selected Bibliography includes only the most important works, especially those giving a general survey of Norwegian music. It is also limited for the most part to books and articles in English.

The preparation of this book was greatly facilitated by the cooperation of the staff of the Norwegian Music Information Center, especially Jostein Simble and Hilde Holbaek-Hanssen. I hereby thank them for their valuable assistance. I also wish to thank Dr. Dag Schjelderup-Ebbe, who read an early draft of the translation and made many helpful suggestions that have enriched the final result. Lastly, I want to express my deep gratitude to the translators, Dr. William H. Halverson of The Ohio State University and Dr. Leland B. Sateren of Augsburg College, for their splendid work in the preparation of the English text. Without their great interest and commitment this edition would not have been possible.

NILS GRINDE, OSLO, NORWAY

From the Stone Age to the Iron Age
(to ca. A.D. 800)

Anthropologists think that human beings have lived in Norway for more than 10,000 years. Discoveries of hunting and fishing gear made of bone and stone tell us something about the daily life of the hunters and fishermen thousands of years ago, but we have no information about their music. The modern study of primitive cultures makes it tempting to suppose that primitive types of songs as well as simple musical instruments were in use during the Stone Age in Norway as well. We have no firm proof of this, however, as no such instruments from this period have been found in Norway. Although a bone flute discovered on the Danish island of Bornholm may date from the late Stone Age (about 2000 B.C.), the date is widely disputed. Nor do the oldest rock carvings of the third and fourth centuries B.C. shed any light on the instrumental or vocal music of the ancient Norsemen.

THE BRONZE AGE
The Bronze Age in Norway extended from ca. 1500 B.C. to ca. 500 B.C. An impressive number of musical instruments—the so-called bronze *lurs*—dating from this period have been preserved. Approximately fifty such *lurs* have been found in northern Germany, Denmark, southern Norway, and Sweden. Most were found in Denmark. Four were found in Norway: two in excellent condition were discovered in a marsh near Stavanger, and fragments of two others in Brandbu (north of Oslo).

The name *lur*, given to these instruments when the first specimens were discovered in Denmark in about 1800, is actually misleading, for they bear little similarity to the *lurs* of the saga or later periods. The bronze *lurs* are impressive instruments, however. The modern instrument to which they are most similar in tone as well as pitch production is the tenor trombone. The body of a fully fashioned *lur* may be from 1.5 to 2.25 meters in length. It

Bronze lurs *found near Stavanger in 1894. (Arkeologisk Museum, Stavanger, Norway)*

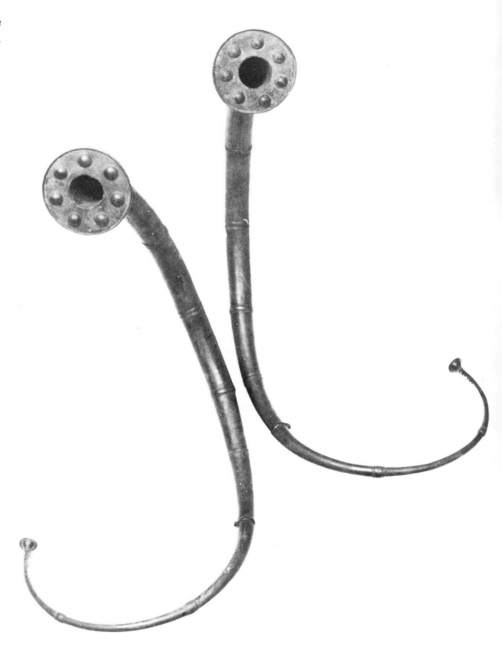

is conical in shape and curved in such a way as to create a modified S. The instruments were cast in bronze in sections of varying length, which were then coupled. The larger instruments consist of two separable parts and the connection is so constructed that the two parts can be joined in only one way (i.e., the connection is not revolving). Surrounding the bell of many *lurs* there is also a round, decorative plate that has no acoustic significance. Some *lurs* also have a carrying chain. The instruments are decorated with orna-

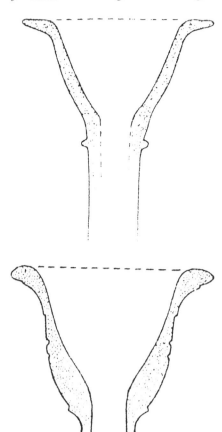

Cross section of lur *mouthpiece (top) compared with that of a mouthpiece for a modern brass instrument (bottom). (From Broholm, Larsen, and Skjerne,* The Lures of the Bronze Age*)*

ments and in most cases are excellently crafted. They are undoubtedly some of the finest specimens of handicraft that have come down to us from Bronze Age culture. The best of the *lurs* have mouthpieces that are well designed for good tone production and are astonishingly similar to those of the modern trombone.

Most of the bronze *lurs* were found in matched pairs of equal length; the two instruments in each pair, therefore, have the same fundamental tone. They are bent in opposite directions, each *lur* thus being a mirror image of the other (see picture on p. 2). Traces of wear on some of the instruments show that they were carried with their decorative bells upright and facing forward, a fact that is also confirmed by figures appearing in Bronze Age stone carvings. It must have been an impressive sight when two such instruments were carried at the front of a procession.

It would appear that these *lurs* were used principally in connection with worship. This is indicated by the fact that the instruments have almost always been found in bogs near ancient places of sacrifice. It is further confirmed by the fact that portrayals of *lur* players appear in the stone carvings, for these always had religious significance. The large decorative plate that adorned most *lurs* also confirms their cult function; it presumably symbolized the sun god. It does not appear, however, that *lurs* were used as military instruments. No such instruments have been located in Bronze Age graveyards, where so many articles constituting a chieftain's equipment, including weapons, have been found. Clearly, *lurs* did not belong in that category.

With today's performance technique the first eight to ten partial tones can be sounded on the bronze *lurs*, and in a few cases it is possible to sound up to the twelfth partial tone. It is difficult to form any opinion about what the Bronze Age performer could produce on the instrument. The fact that the instruments are typically found in pairs, and that they are mirror images of each other, suggest that they were played together. Some researchers have inferred from this the possibility of some kind of two-part music, but this seems very unlikely as early as the Bronze Age. Comparison with the practice of other cultures at a corresponding stage of development suggests either an antiphonal use of the two *lurs* or, at most, a type of heterophony. The excellent construction of the mouthpieces on the best *lurs* indicates, in any event, that the Bronze Age *lur* players knew how to make the most of the instrument's capabilities.

THE FIRST CENTURY OF THE CHRISTIAN ERA

Apart from the Bronze Age *lurs*, we have no firm information about music activity in Norway through many centuries. A billy goat's horn fashioned like a wind instrument and dating from the latter part of the Iron Age has been found in Sweden, but nothing of the sort has been found in Norway despite some fairly rich grave finds containing a large quantity of home furnishings. We do, however, encounter for the first time during these centuries literary accounts regarding music life among the Teutons. It is primarily Latin writers who have given us these accounts, and, as one might expect, the picture they provide is fairly superficial and, to some extent, negative. These lines by Bishop Venantius Fortunatus (530–609) are often quoted:

> Romanusque lyra plaudat tibi, Barbarus harpa,
> Graecus achilliaca, chrotta Britanna canat.

Here the several peoples are exhorted to sing praise to the accompaniment of various instruments, and when the "barbarians"—which in this case clearly means the Teutons—are exhorted to use the harp it is certainly because the harp was known to be the instrument of the Teutons. Gregory the Great described a Teuton victory celebration in 579 in which a goat's head was sacrificed. The people danced around it, wrote Pope Gregory, and "sang loathsome songs." We have similar reports from other writers. To be sure, most of the Latin sources from this period describe the southern Teutonic peoples—those who most frequently came in contact with the Romans— but the songs of the people from further north certainly sounded no better to the ears of foreigners. An Arab traveler, Ibrahim ibn Ahmad at-Tartushi, who visited Schleswig in the tenth century, reported that he had never heard uglier singing than he heard there. He wrote: "It consists of a growling that comes from their throats like the barking of dogs, only even more bestial." The music sung at the sacrificial rituals in Uppsala, Sweden, is described in negative terms in so late a source as the chronicle of Adam of Bremen (ca. 1070), who wrote: "Many are the songs that are sung at these offerings, but they are so shameful that it is best that their contents be concealed."

If we look at the literary sources within the Scandinavian cultural circle, the picture is quite different. Unfortunately, we have only a single work that in some degree gives us information from the period. This is the Anglo-Saxon epic poem *Beowulf*, which is thought to date from the eighth century and reflects conditions in both Denmark and Sweden. Here both vocal and instrumental music are given a positive evaluation. The instrument that is named is the harp ("hearp"):

> He heard happy laughter loud in the hall,
> the thrum of the harp, melodious chant,
> clear song of the scop.[1]

1. *Beowulf* 88–90. This and later quotations from *Beowulf* are from the translation by Howell D. Chickering, Jr. (Garden City: Anchor Books, 1977).

Thus the epic tells about the celebrations in the "Heort" hall. We are told nothing about how this harp looked, but we know that it was often used. When Beowulf's victory over the monster Grendel was to be celebrated, the epic reports:

There was tumult and song, melodious noise,
in front of Healfdene's battle-commander;
the harp was plucked, good verses chanted
when Hrothgar's scop in his place on the mead-bench
came to tell over the famous hall-sport
[about] Finn's sons when the attack came on them.[2]

It is interesting to note that the Old English word for "harp" used in the passage just quoted is not "hearp" but "gamen-wudu," which means "the wood of gladness." That tells us something about how the people of that time thought of the instrument. It was not only on festive occasions that song was employed, however. Beowulf's death, according to the epic, was an occasion for song of a different kind:

In the same fashion a Geatish woman,
her hair bound up, [wove] a grief-song,
the lament [for Beowulf].[3]

Later, after Beowulf's ashes were laid in the barrow, the epic reports:

Then round the barrow
twelve nobles rode, war-brave princes.
They wanted to mourn their king in their [grief],
to weave a lay and speak about the man:
they honored his nobility and deeds of courage,
their friend's great prowess.[4]

Despite distances of time and culture, this portrait of the twelve men who rode around the funeral mound and sang their dirges comes to life in a marvelous way as we read of it in this old epic poem. Like us, the people of that period used song to express both joy and sorrow.

2. *Beowulf* 1063–66.   3. *Beowulf* 3150–51.   4. *Beowulf* 3169–74.

The Viking Expeditions and the High Middle Ages (ca. 800–1350)

The Viking period in the history of Norway began shortly before A.D. 800 and continued until shortly after A.D. 1000. It was a time of significant expansion as Norwegians, Danes, and Swedes launched expeditions of varying size and spread out over large portions of Europe. There were many reasons for these expeditions, including population growth, the need for more land, and stronger social organization. The most important reason, however, was a technological development: the Nordic peoples learned at this time how to build good seagoing vessels, with both sails and oars, that could traverse great distances. The Norwegian Vikings sailed primarily westward and southward, sometimes to ravage and plunder the richer and more developed countries they encountered, sometimes to settle down and become permanent residents in lands far removed from their homeland. "Viking kingdoms" both large and small sprang up in various parts of western Europe and on the islands out in the Atlantic Ocean. The Faroe, Orkney, and Shetland Islands, as well as Iceland and Greenland, were all colonized during the Viking period. Expeditions reached as far as the lands bordering the Mediterranean Sea and (as has now been confirmed) even to the eastern coast of North America.

Shortly before A.D. 900 Norway was united into a single kingdom by Harald Fairhair. Harald defeated his last remaining enemies at the battle of Hafrsfjord, which is usually said to have occurred in the year 872. The date given for that decisive battle is probably not accurate, but it is clear that by 890 or so Harald was the undisputed ruler of most of the territory that comprises modern Norway.

By the end of the Viking period Christianity officially had triumphed over the old Norse religion. The death of Olaf Haraldsson ("Saint Olaf") at the battle of Stiklestad in 1030 is regarded as the decisive event in the Christianization of Norway. The development of a permanent organization to govern the new kingdom and the Catholic Church in Norway took many years, however.

The twelfth century saw many years of bitter civil strife in Norway, and not until the following century was there a brief period when Norway emerged as a major power in northern Europe. King Haakon Haakonsson (reigned 1247–63) was able to extend his power not only over mainland Norway but over Jemtland (now part of Sweden), the Shetland and Orkney islands, Iceland, and Greenland.

During this time Nordic cultural life developed rapidly, while gradually becoming strongly influenced by the culture of the lands to the south. This cultural flowering was suddenly halted by the Black Death plague of 1349–50, the paralyzing effect of which was felt in Norway for over a century. Even the efforts of the Catholic Church to sustain what was possible of the cultural life of the people were severely limited. Only in the sixteenth century did it rise again to contribute new cultural impulses. Outside the Church we can also discern traces of creative impulses from this period in Norwegian folk music and folk poetry. Both of these areas will be discussed in separate chapters later.

Historical sources regarding vocal and instrumental music now become much richer, notably in literary materials, drawings, and instrument finds. Additionally, a few surviving melodies are thought to date from this period.

The literary sources can be divided into four groups:

1. *The Eddas (old Icelandic poems) and skaldic lays.* The oldest poems of both types presumably date from the ninth century, but most date from the tenth and eleventh centuries. It appears that the creation of Eddic poems virtually ceased by the twelfth century, while skaldic lays were cultivated into the thirteenth century, albeit in somewhat stilted forms.

2. *The sagas.* The most important of these date from the thirteenth century, though the writing of sagas continued into the following century. It is especially the more legendary sagas that were created at this time. All of the sagas are presumed to have been written in Iceland, but many of them reflect Norwegian conditions. In this group we must also mention old Norse translations of medieval European literature. Several of these include information regarding the state of music that may reflect the situation in Norway as well.

3. *The Latin chronicles and other Latin writings.* The oldest of these are from the same period as the sagas. Most of them were written by clerics and thus represent more accurately than the other sources the Church's view of the cultural life.

4. *The statute books.* The old Norse statutes contain very little information about music conditions, but read in conjunction with other Scandinavian statutes they constitute a valuable supplement to our other material.

The pictures dating from this period consist, for the most part, of wood carvings on the stave churches (elaborately crafted wooden structures built during the twelfth and thirteenth centuries) but there is also one piece of stone sculpture in the Nidaros cathedral in Trondheim that includes a representation of a musical instrument. These pictorial remains, in addition to our very limited instrument finds, give us a fairly clear idea of how the instruments of that time must have looked.

Gunnar in the snake pit. Wood carving on the Uvdal stave church. Gunnar is playing a three-cornered harp. (Riksantikvariatet, Central office of historic monuments and sites, Norway)

HOW MUSIC WAS REGARDED BY THE VIKINGS

With one important exception, the literary sources give music a very high rating. When the writers of the period mention the performing musicians—the players—of the high Middle Ages, it is generally with disdain and derision. Except for these passages, however, the literature of the period always discusses music and musicians with great respect. One could say that this is simply a continuation of the view reflected in *Beowulf*. In the *Orkneyinga* saga, when Earl Ragnvald Kali counts among his nine accomplishments the art of playing the harp and fashioning verse, this seems to be nothing more than a commonplace expression of the twelfth-century Norse ideal of the educated man. We see, too, that the harp continues to be the "classical" instrument. As early as in "Voluspaa," the poetic Edda about the gods and creation, we read:

> Happily, Egde,
> the giant shepherdess of trolls,
> sat on the knoll
> and strummed the harp.[1]

Supernatural power was often ascribed to music. One of the most popular stories in Viking literature seems to have been the tale of King Gunnar who, according to legend, was thrown into a pit of snakes. It is recounted in several places and is given here as it appears in chapter 37 of the *Volsung* saga:

> Now King Gunnar was placed in a snake pit. There were many snakes, and his hands were tightly bound. Gudrun [his sister] sent him a harp, and he demonstrated his ability by playing it most artistically with his toes, performing so exceedingly well that many thought that they had never heard anyone play as well even with their hands. He continued playing in this manner until all the snakes were asleep except for one

1. "Voluspaa," verse 39, from a Norwegian paraphrase by Ivar Mortensson-Egnund.

Gunnar in the snake pit. Wood carving on the Hyllestad stave church from ca. 1200. Here the harp is shaped like a lyre. (Universitets Oldsaksamling)

large, evil lizard. It crawled toward King Gunnar and thrust its snout into him until it pierced his heart. And there he died a courageous death.[2]

The fanciful Icelandic *Bosa* saga of the fourteenth century ascribes to music a power over both people and inanimate things. The legendary Sigurd must have been an extraordinary performer, for in chapter 12 we find the following account of his playing at a wedding:

King Gudmund sat in the seat of honor with the bridegroom at his side. Rörek waited on the bridegroom. Nothing is said about how the chieftains sat, but it is reported that Sigurd played the harp for the bride. And when the bowls were brought in, Sigurd played in such a way that people said he was virtually without equal; but at first he paid

2. From the Norwegian translation by Torleiv Hannaas and Magne Myhren.

little attention to this. The king bade him not to hold back. And when the bowl dedicated to Thor was brought in, Sigurd changed the tune, and everything that was loose—knives, dishes, and everything that people didn't hang on to—began to move about. Many people rose from their seats and began to dance, and this lasted awhile. Next came the bowl that was dedicated to all the gods. Again Sigurd changed the tune and began to play so loudly that the echo sounded throughout the hall. Then everyone stood up except the bridegroom, the bride, and the king, and the hall was filled with carousing and revelry, and this continued for some time.

Then the king asked Sigurd if he could play other *slaatter*, and he answered that there were still a few small pieces, but he requested that people first take a little rest. Then the men began to drink. Sigurd played [the *slaatter*] "Gygreslag," "Drömbud," and "Hjarrandeljod." Next came the bowl dedicated to Odin, whereupon Sigurd opened the harp. It was so big that a man could stand up inside it and looked as if it was made of gold. Sigurd donned white, gold-embroidered gloves. He played the *slaatt* called "Faldaföykar," and the kerchiefs were torn from the heads of the women and flew up to the rafters. All the women and men stood up, and everything was in commotion. When this bowl was emptied, the bowl dedicated to Frey was brought in; this was to be the last one. Then Sigurd grasped the string that lay across the other strings, and bade the king prepare himself for "Rameslaget." The king was so startled that he jumped to his feet, as did also the bride and groom. No one danced more beautifully than they, and this continued for some time.[3]

The account is so laden with fantasy that it can hardly be intended as an accurate report of individual details. It is impossible for us to understand, for example, the account of Sigurd taking "the string that lay across the other strings." Nonetheless, it is interesting to note all the *slaatt* titles that are mentioned. The name "Rameslaget" is especially interesting, for it has been preserved as a *slaatt* title to the present day. Now, as then, this *slaatt* represents a high point of both dancing and musical frenzy.

In these and other sources the harp is referred to as a solo instrument, but nowhere in old Norse literature is it said that it was used as an accompanying instrument. This point needs to be stressed, for there is reason to believe that the southern Teutonic peoples used it for accompaniment. Although it has been a popular belief that the Viking skalds also performed their songs with harp accompaniment, it is extremely doubtful, for neither literary nor other

---

3. From the Norwegian translation by Magne Myhren.

sources support such a conclusion. So far as is known, the skalds sang—or, more accurately, recited—their lays without instrumental accompaniment.

HARP, LUR, AND HORN

The literature contains many references to instruments, but very little information is given about how they looked. Some accounts—those in the *Bosa* saga, for example—are so fanciful that we can draw no conclusions from them. We must look elsewhere for such information, i.e., to the iconography and instrument finds.

The instrument most frequently represented pictorially is, as might be expected, the harp. All these representations are related to the account of Gunnar in the snake pit (see p. 8). They show that two different instruments have been called by the same name, "harp." Most of the representations depict an instrument shaped like a lyre. In only two instances is it depicted as a three-cornered harp—i.e., a harp in the usual sense. Examples exist of both types of instruments. A partial specimen of a lyre was found on the farm Kravik, northwest of Oslo. Its shape is somewhat different from the pictures, but it appears to be the same kind of instrument. It evidently was made in the late Middle Ages, and it gives some idea of how an indigenous harp from that period looked. It presumably had seven strings and was almost certainly played by plucking. We do not have a specimen of a three-cornered harp dating from the Middle Ages, but it has been a part of Norwegian folk culture until as recently as the nineteenth century. A number of such folk instruments from more recent times are preserved in various Norwegian museums. The oldest dates only from the seventeenth century. It is likely, however, that the three-cornered harp has its roots in the type that was widely used throughout Europe in the Middle Ages.

The horn is mentioned as early as in "Voluspaa." Here it appears as a purely mythical instrument, so it is difficult to know how people conceived of it. In many other sources, however—especially in Norse statute books—the horn is referred to as an everyday instrument used for giving signals. Such horns probably were of the same general type as the animal horns still used today as herding instruments. Some have finger holes and some do not (see page 88). Both types were in use in Norway in the Middle Ages.

The *lur* also appears in the literary sources as a signaling instrument. It undoubtedly resembled the herding instrument that we know today by the same name. The similarity has been confirmed by the discovery in a mound near Oseberg (south of Oslo) of an instrument dating from ca. 850. It is about a meter long, and has many similarities to the *lurs* of today. The most important difference is that the Oseberg *lur* to all appearances was not covered with birch bark (or anything of the kind) as is the modern herding *lur*.

Front view of lyre found on the Kravik farm in Numedal. (Norsk Folkemuseum)

The two halves were held together by five rings made of willow or some similar material. The literature indicates that the *lur* was used as, among other things, a military instrument.

PERFORMERS AND THEIR INSTRUMENTS

The players of instruments hold a unique position in Norse literature: they are almost always spoken of with contempt and abhorrence. A passage from Saxo Grammaticus's thirteenth-century *Denmark Chronicle (Gesta Danorum)* is a good example:

> It was not Hugleik's custom to honor worthy people with gifts, but toward clowns and minstrels he was generous enough. No doubt it was also in this way that a rogue sought the company of other rogues, and that he who covered himself with shame and disgrace took good care of others like himself through thick and thin.[4]

This attitude toward performers is the common one in the literature, and it is confirmed in the old Norse statute books, which generally depict instrument players as people who had virtually no legal rights. The low estimate of performing musicians is strange in view of the high opinions one finds regarding music itself. There are perhaps several reasons for this anomaly. The performers were a motley international group whose job it was to entertain at celebrations of various kinds. Although they played primarily for the nobility, at times they certainly appeared before a broader audience. They were versatile performers with many talents including, as a rule, the ability to play several instruments. They traveled from place to place and likely were looked upon as tramps. Although they were not well regarded, they were nonetheless indispensable to all celebrations, and on such occasions they usually received large gifts. The earliest reference to them in Norse literature is in a bard poem about Harald Fairhair dating from ca. 900, but they apparently did not achieve much importance until the twelfth and thirteenth centuries. They appeared in the aftermath of the strong cultural influences of the lands to the south that pushed northward into Scandinavia during the high Middle Ages. The fact that they may have been perceived as a foreign element may well have contributed to the low opinion of them.

Performers came from abroad, then, bringing with them the instruments that were in general use in Europe at that time, including several that were not indigenous to Norway. Didrik's saga tells of a renowned fiddler named Isung who, when he appeared before King Osantrix, said: "I can sing and

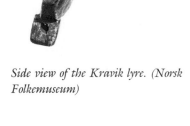

Side view of the Kravik lyre. (Norsk Folkemuseum)

4. From the Norwegian translation by Hans Olrik.

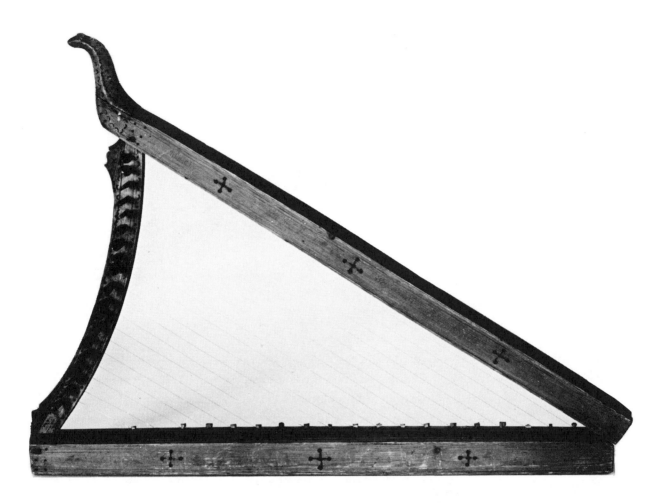

Three-cornered harp from Stor-Elvdal, dated 1776. Several such harps are still in existence but they are no longer played in Norway. (Norsk Folkemuseum)

I can play the harp, the fiddle, the *gige* [see below], and all kinds of stringed instruments." Although the harp is mentioned here, the fiddle and *gige* were more typical of the instruments played by these performers. Didrik's saga also cites other instruments, notably pipes and trombones. This is in itself a fairly complete list of instruments mentioned with any frequency in the old Norse literature, although there are scattered references to a few others. One can conclude from what is known about these traveling performers in other countries that still other instruments were in use.

Though it is very difficult to determine their exact configuration, the instruments mentioned most frequently in old Norse literature are the fiddle and *gige*. They are mentioned together so often that one must conclude they were two different instruments, but it is not clear exactly what the difference was. Both were stringed instruments. The fiddle appears in the literature as early as the twelfth century, and in the oldest sources the playing of the instrument is referred to as "strumming the fiddle." From the thirteenth

The lur *from Oseberg. (Norsk Folkemuseum)*

Stone sculpture on the Nidaros cathedral in Trondheim depicting a musician playing on a stringed instrument.

century the *gige* also appears, frequently coupled with the fiddle as in the Didrik saga: "bow the fiddle and the *gige*." This may indicate that the fiddle was originally a plucked (and only later a bowed) instrument, whereas the *gige* appears to have always been bowed. The chief difference between them, however, probably was their shape. Through comparison with continental bowed instruments it has been conjectured that the *gige* had a pear-shaped back while the fiddle had a flat one, but no definite conclusions on this matter are possible.

Nor is it certain if the Finnish "bowed harp" (*jouhikantele*) was in use in Norway during the Middle Ages. There is an interesting twelfth-century stone sculpture in the great cathedral in Trondheim that shows a musician playing a stringed instrument, and some scholars have suggested that it might be a kind of *jouhikantele*. This lone piece of statuary, however— which, for all we know, may have been hewn by a foreign sculptor— provides slight basis for such a conclusion. It is equally uncertain whether there is a connection between any of these instruments and the later Hardanger fiddle.

Pipes and trombones are mentioned frequently in old Norse literature. The term "pipes" apparently included two instruments: the recorder and the shawm (an antecedent of the modern oboe). That recorder-type instruments were used is confirmed by an instrument find in Norway. A fourteenth-century bone flute with five finger holes and in good playing condition was found in the German wharf area of Bergen. Whether it belonged to a trav-

Bone flute found during excavation in Bergen in 1957. It was in playable condition. (Norsk Folkemuseum)

eling performer is uncertain, but we can nonetheless safely conclude that similar instruments were used by both performers and the general populace.

The shawm was a common performing instrument in other European countries, and despite the lack of direct evidence it seems likely that it was in use in Norway as well. We also have no concrete evidence that trombones were used in Norway, but comparisons with neighboring countries suggest that brass wind instruments were in use—first, perhaps, the straight type and then the coiled. The closely related trumpet was certainly known, and it can be assumed that various kinds of drums were in use. Bagpipes, barrel organs, and keyed harps were also well known in neighboring countries during the Middle Ages, but there is nothing to indicate that they were used in Norway.

MELODIES FROM THIS ERA

Vocal and instrumental music had, then, an important place in old Norse culture, both in everyday life and on festive occasions. Unfortunately, it is unusually difficult to ascertain the character of this music, for there is no written record of the secular music of the Middle Ages. The oldest melodies in Norway of which we have any record are examples of church music. The surviving melodies of the oldest folk ballads—for example, those for the "Dream Ballad"—date from a much later period. The roots of these melodies are certainly old, but it is doubtful that they, like the texts, go back to the fourteenth century.

The same may be said of five melodies that appear in a book published in 1780 by the French author J. B. de La Borde, *An Essay on Ancient and Modern Music*. It contains three melodies for a bard poem, one melody for "Haavamaal," and one for "Voluspaa"—"as they are still [in 1780] sung in Iceland," according to the author. The melody for "Voluspaa" is given in example 1. La Borde had gotten these melodies from the Dano-German musician Johann Ernst Hartmann, who settled in Copenhagen in 1762. Hartmann had no doubt written them down as they were sung by Icelanders visiting Copenhagen. Thus they were transcribed during the latter part of the eighteenth century. Because "Voluspaa" probably dates from the tenth century, it is very unlikely that these melodies are the original ones, though the fact that they are built on simple melodic formulas may indicate that they are quite old.

Some scholars have pointed to a certain similarity between the "Voluspaa" melody and the Gregorian Lamentations used in the Good Friday liturgy of the Roman Catholic Church. Whether the similarity is merely accidental or a case of actual influence is uncertain. It is thought that the "Voluspaa" text came into being under the influence of—and possibly as a

Example 1. "Voluspaa"

defense against—advancing Christianity. Thus the melody may have been influenced by the Church as well. In any case, it is reasonable to suppose that the song of the Roman Catholic Church heard in Norway's churches for centuries had some influence on the musical language of the people of the Middle Ages. There is evidence of this in Norway's folk songs (see p. 76). That there might have been some influence in the opposite direction is more questionable. There does appear to be evidence of such an influence in a non-liturgical church melody, however, in the so-called "Magnus Hymn" (see p. 22). The two-part idiom that we find here may reflect a similar manner of "folk singing" common in certain sections of northern Europe.

For over a century after the plague, the sources are mute with respect to information about the music life of Norway. While it is true that the Black Death plague struck most of Europe, it appears that its paralyzing effects were of longer duration in Norway than in, for example, its neighboring countries. This could be owing to several factors. Harsher climatic conditions made it more difficult to reclaim the fields that had become overgrown. Also, the political decline and subsequent union with Denmark deprived Norway of its culturally productive court milieu. Finally, even after the Black Death plague, Norway was repeatedly assailed by powerful epidemics of various kinds. It is difficult, therefore, to follow the history of Norwegian music during the fifteenth century. The few traces we have are to be found for the most part in the church music of the period.

3

The Music of the Roman Catholic Church (ca. 1000–1536)

With the establishment of Christianity in Norway came the music of the Roman Catholic Church, Gregorian chant. Christian missionary activity in Norway got seriously under way in the tenth century, and one could say that externally, at least, Christianity was officially victorious by the year 1030 when Olaf Haraldsson, the country's patron saint, lost his life at the battle of Stiklestad. There was, in any case, no organized opposition to the Christian Church in Norway thereafter—though how much may have remained of the old heathen beliefs is another matter. The foundation for the administration of the Church probably was laid by Olaf's bishop, Grimkel. In the course of two or three generations after Olaf's death the Church progressively established itself in Norwegian society. Its organizational expansion may be said to have been completed with the establishment of the archbishopric of Nidaros (now Trondheim) in 1153.

Gregorian chant was already highly developed, and its character was substantially the same throughout the Roman Catholic Church. The only new elements that were admitted were the sequences. These songs, which were usually appended to the Alleluia of the Mass on major religious holidays, came into being over a period of several centuries (ca. 900–1300). They too were for the most part common throughout the Roman Catholic Church, but because different saints were venerated in different countries there was an opportunity for the development of fairly independent sequence melodies. Apart from Gregorian chant, those aspects of church music that were more or less unique to Norway include, especially, the music for the St. Olaf celebration—the so-called "St. Olaf music."

Olaf was Norway's foremost saint, and his memory was celebrated annually with great festivities centered in Nidaros from July 28 to August 5, the climax being a High Mass on St. Olaf's Day, July 29. The festival played an important role not only in Norway but throughout Scandinavia and in

The sequence "Lux illuxit." These pages contain the text and melody of the first six stanzas and a portion of the seventh.

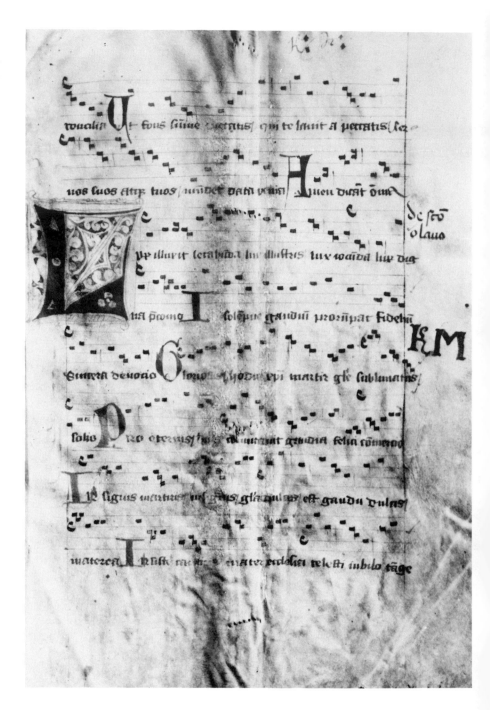

several other European countries as well. During the Middle Ages, throngs of pilgrims made their way to Nidaros to participate in the solemn ceremony and to seek healing from the holy relics thought by the faithful to have

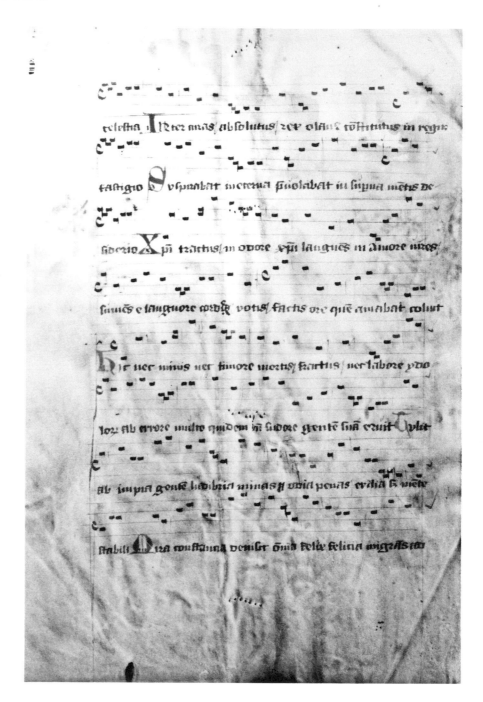

miraculous powers. Belief in King Olaf as a saint appears to have spread with surprising rapidity after his death. An officially approved text for St. Olaf's Day dating from 1050 or earlier has been found in England. Thus it would appear that the church celebration of his sainthood was widespread as early as twenty years after his death.

The complete texts (in Latin) for the worship services for the St. Olaf celebration are contained in the *Missale Nidrosiense* and the *Breviarium Nidrosiense*, both dating from 1519. Neither book contains the melodies,

Example 2. "Lux illuxit."

1. Lux il-lux-it   læ-ta - bun-da, lux il-lu-stris, lux ju-cun-da, quæ dig-na præ-co - ni-o.

2. In so-lem-ne gau-di-um   pro-rum-pat fi - de-li-um   sin-ce-ra de - vo - ti - o.

3. a. Glo-ri - o-sus ho-di-e Chri-sti mar-tyr glo - ri-æ su - bli-ma-tus so - li-o,
   b. Pro æ-ter-nis bre-vi-a com-mu-ta - vit gau-di-a, fe - li-ci com - mer-ci-o.

4. a. In - sig - nis mar-ty - ris in - sig - nis glo - ri - a,
   b. In - si - ste can - ti - cis, ma - ter ec - cle - ci - a,

   dul - cis est gau - di - i, dul - cis ma - te - ri - a.
   cæ - le - sti ju - bi - lo. Tan - ge ce - le - sti - a.

5. a. In-ter cu-ras ab-so - lutus rex o - la-vus con-sti-tu-tus in re-gni fa - sti-gi-o.
   b. Su-spi-ra-bat in æ - terna præ-vo-la-bat in su-per-na men-tis de-si - de-ri-o.

6. a. Chri-sti trac-tus in o - do - re Chri-sti lan-guens in a - mo-re vi-res su-mens
   b. Hic nec mi - nis nec ti - mo - re mor-tis frac-tus, nec la - bo-re I - do-lo-rum

however, so these must be derived from other sources. With the help of various finds housed in the Norwegian State Archives, and through comparison with sources from other Scandinavian countries, it has been possible to reconstruct the melodies that were used. Stylistically they have the same character as Gregorian chant.

The same may be said of the sequences associated with the St. Olaf celebration. Of greatest interest is the sequence that was used in the High Mass on St. Olaf's Day, "Lux illuxit" (example 2). The sequence, which came into being around 1200, is presumed to have been written by a Norwegian cleric who was well acquainted with French sequence poetry as shaped by Adam of St. Victor in Paris. The melody of the sequence is unique, and may also have been created in Norway, but stylistically it is similar to the melodies of the French sequences. "Lux illuxit" contains nine rhymed stanzas that share a fairly common metrical pattern. Each of stanzas 3–9 consists of two distinct halves, with the same melody for each. The resulting melodic form, which is fairly common for sequences, is AB CC DD EE FF GG HH II.

The other sequence from the St. Olaf music is usually called the "Wednesday Sequence" because it was sung on the Wednesday celebrated as the anniversary of St. Olaf's death. It has come down in two forms. The older version survives in an early fourteenth-century manuscript that contains text and melody for three stanzas in the form A BB CC. The first words of the text in this version are "Predicasti Dei care." The melody is taken from a French sequence from which just the first, third, and fifth phrases are used. In the *Missale Nidrosiense* the text of the "Wednesday Sequence" is preserved in another form. Here it consists of five stanzas and begins with the words "Postquam calix Babilonis." It is thought that this latter form of the sequence came into being in the fifteenth century. It is possible that the older form, such as we have it, is only a fragment.

Other national saints were venerated as well. The veneration of St. Halvard, for example, was centered in Oslo. This celebration was much more local in character than the one honoring St. Olaf, but on St. Halvard's Day (May 15) a sequence was sung that has survived. In both text and melody it is closely related to "Lux illuxit." The text begins with the same words and is similar at many subsequent points. It consists of twenty stanzas, some of which have been only partially preserved. Fourteen of the twenty repeat the same melody with slight variations as necessary to accommodate the text.

We also have a secular song from this period that, musically speaking, belongs in the same group. It is a wedding song that was sung in Bergen in 1281 at the marriage of King Erik Magnusson and Margaret of Scotland. A manuscript containing this song is preserved in the library of the University of Uppsala, Sweden. Its form is that of a sequence with ten stanzas.

Of even greater interest is the so-called "Magnus Hymn" (example 3). Magnus was honored as a saint in the Orkney Islands, at that time a Norwegian territory, and the hymn was written there. It is preserved in a manuscript from 1280, but it may go back as far as 1140. Both its dating and its original function are, however, a matter of some dispute. The melody is

Example 3. The "Magnus Hymn."

No - bi - lis,   hu - mi - lis,   Mag - ne mar - tyr sta - bi - lis,   Ha - bi - lis,

u - ti - lis,   co - mes ve - ne - ra - bi - lis,   et tu - tor lan - da - bi - lis

Tu - os sub - di - tos   ser - va car - nis fra - gi - lis   mo - le po - si - tos.

simple, but it is interesting that it survives in a two-part setting. The "Magnus Hymn" is the oldest example in Scandinavia of a pluri-voiced song. Moreover, the part writing is different from that current elsewhere in Europe, characterized by the organum of the school of Notre Dame and the *ars antiqua*, in which thirds sounding simultaneously were generally avoided. The two-part setting of the "Magnus Hymn," consisting mainly of parallel thirds, does not appear, therefore, to reflect the influence of the polyphonic music of the Church but rather a folk tradition that may have existed in the Orkney Islands and elsewhere in Scandinavia.

In this connection it is interesting to quote briefly from the British author Giraldus Cambrensis (also known as Gerald of Wales), writing around 1200. Giraldus reported a remarkable manner of singing in Wales in which there were as many voice parts as there were singers. He continued:

Also in the northern part of Great Britain . . . the English inhabitants who live there employ a similar manner of singing, albeit with just two different voice parts, the lower humming while the upper sings softly and pleasingly. And it is not by artifice, but through use since ancient times and by well-established custom that these people [i.e., in Wales and northern England] have acquired this ability as second nature. And so thoroughly has this manner of singing gained a foothold and taken root among both peoples that no music is usually performed alone, but either many-voiced as with the Welsh, or in two parts as with the people of northern England. Even more admirable is the fact that boys and children in general, as soon as they stop crying, use the same manner of singing. Inasmuch as the English generally do not sing

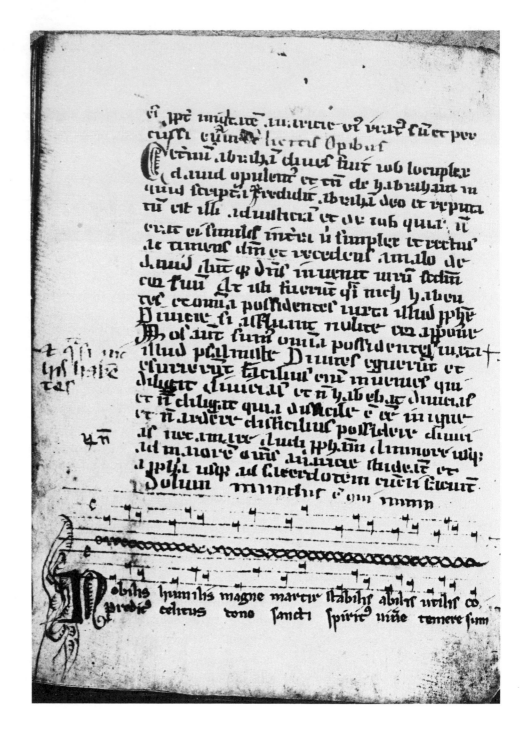

Thirteenth-century manuscript of the "Magnus hymn."

in this way, but only those in the north, I think they acquired it—as they have also the similarity of speech—from the Danes and Norwegians who often used to invade that part of Britain and remain there for some time.

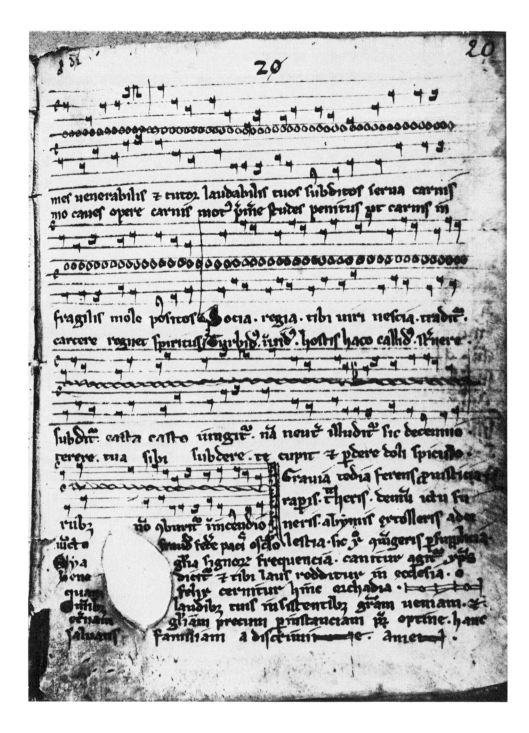

Although this information is not as precise as one might wish, it is conceivable that the "Magnus Hymn" is built on the same folk tradition as that to which Giraldus referred. We have no evidence of a similar style of singing anywhere in Norway.

An Icelandic source may be of interest in this connection, however. In *Biskupa Sögur* it is reported that Bishop Laurentius, bishop of Holar from 1322 to 1331, forbade both two- and three-part singing in the churches because he considered it indissolubly linked with the tradition of the minstrels. It is not clear whether it was *ars antiqua* polyphony or a folk style of singing that had begun to make an inroad here. Bishop Laurentius's use of the word "minstrelsy" ("leikaraskap") could indicate that this type of singing was of folk origin, but in view of what is known of the situation in the Church at this time it is perhaps more natural to assume that an effort had been made to introduce the French polyphonic church song.

In any case, organum of the *ars antiqua* type was not unknown in Scandinavia. It is reported that organum was sung in the cathedral in Uppsala, Sweden in 1298, and the wording is such that the reference can only be to the French organum. Later there was opposition to the polyphonic church song in Sweden as well. In the 1462 statutes of the Lund cathedral choir the use of polyphonic songs is forbidden. We have no information concerning attitudes toward *ars antiqua* in Norway. Presumably such singing was known there too, but evidently it did not play a significant role. The general cultural decline resulting from the Black Death undoubtedly hindered any further adoption of the new cultural impulses moving on the continent.

The organ was introduced to Norway early in the fourteenth century. We read in Laurentius's saga of an Icelander by the name of Arngrim who came to Nidaros shortly before 1330 and learned from a local organ builder both to play and to build organs. It is clear, then, that by this time the Nidaros cathedral had an instrument, but it is not known whether other larger Norwegian churches had organs at this early date.

The cathedral schools must also be mentioned in connection with church song. After the creation of an independent archbishopric at Nidaros in 1153, schools were established under the auspices of the most important churches in Norway. We know that by the thirteenth century there were cathedral schools in Nidaros, Bergen, Stavanger, and Oslo. There were, of course, other schools as well. Some were associated with cloisters, and others may have been "municipal schools" of some kind, but the cathedral schools were the most important. Their principal mission was to recruit candidates for religious orders, although some students did not plan to pursue careers in the church. These schools were modeled after similar schools on the continent. The curriculum was based on the seven *artes liberales*: grammar, rhetoric, logic, music, geometry, arithmetic, and astronomy. Although the Norwegian cathedral schools may not have offered this entire curriculum, we can assume that music (i.e., Gregorian chant) held a relatively important place. Training in music was necessary both for students preparing for the priesthood and for the older students, who were expected to sing with the minor clergy in the cathedral choir.

A glimpse of the place of song in the school is given in Haakon Haakonsson's saga. Haakonsson, who was later to become king of Norway, was enrolled in the Nidaros cathedral school as a seven-year-old in 1211. After he had been there for some time the boy was asked by a nobleman, "What are you learning, Haakon?" "I'm learning song, my lord," he replied. "You should not learn song," said the nobleman, "for you are not going to be either a priest or a bishop."

University education was reserved for the privileged few throughout the Middle Ages. During the thirteenth century, when Paris had become the university center for the whole of Europe, a total of about twenty Norwegians studied there. It is quite certain that they also became acquainted with the polyphonic music of the school of Notre Dame. In succeeding years there were markedly fewer Norwegian students in Paris, and from 1300 to 1449 only two.

The university in Rostock (Germany) was established in 1419 and soon became a major attraction for Norwegian students. In the fifteenth century about a hundred students from Norway enrolled there, thus becoming the recipients of musical influences from another source. In the 1470s a university was founded at Copenhagen, and gradually this replaced the university in Rostock as the principal center of study for Norwegian students.

Gregorian chant has sounded in Norwegian churches for several hundred years. One might ask: What significance has this had for the musical development of the Norwegian people? What traces has it left? Presumably the chant has influenced Norway's folk music, but the extent of this influence is a matter of some dispute. Two somewhat conflicting facts need to be kept in mind. On the one hand, most people attended worship services more or less regularly, and in this way were exposed to the Gregorian chants that were sung at such services. On the other hand, the singing was done primarily by the clergy—supplemented, where possible, by the older students from the local cathedral school. The congregation's active participation in the chant probably was restricted to such musically simple elements as the sequences, the hymns, and possibly some of the more elementary Kyries. These circumstances make it difficult to determine to what extent the general population became familiar with Gregorian chant.

The Black Death struck the Church a heavy blow. The clergy was virtually annihilated in some areas, and although during the plague the Church was bequeathed large tracts of land its income sank because of the many vacant farms that produced nothing. Organizationally, however, the Church appears to have emerged relatively intact. The decimated ranks of the clergy

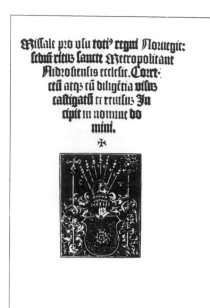

Title page of Missale Nidrosiense, *printed in Copenhagen in* 1519.

gradually were replenished, and it appears that by the end of the fourteenth century the Church had largely overcome the ravages of the plague. Nonetheless, the fifteenth century was not a time of strength for the Church in Norway. As in the rest of Europe, it was to some extent marked by moral decay, and it was also hampered by the weak political situation and ailing economy of the country. The sketchy sources available to us indicate a decline in sacred art and music, and it was not until the sixteenth century that it reawakened to new cultural efforts. As evidence of this new flowering, the publication of the *Missale Nidrosiense* in Copenhagen in 1519, and the *Breviarium Nidrosiense* in Paris that same year, serve as milestones in the cultural history of Norway. That they did not achieve the significance that might have been anticipated was owing to the advent of the Reformation in 1536, an event that created a new situation for church music.

Title page of Breviarium Nidrosiense, *printed in Paris in* 1519.

4

Late Renaissance and Baroque Music
(ca. 1500–ca. 1750)

During the century of the Lutheran Reformation, Norwegian society began to show signs of renewed progress. The economy grew little by little, and cultural life slowly emerged from the torpor brought on by the Black Death plague.

Similar progress did not occur in the political arena, however. The plague had dealt a hard blow to both the nobility and the governmental organization, and during the fifteenth and sixteenth centuries it became more and more difficult for Norway to survive as an independent political entity. During the first part of the fourteenth century all of the Scandinavian countries were for a time united in a single kingdom called the Kalmar Union. The union was dissolved around 1350 and was succeeded by two kingdoms, one Danish-Norwegian and the other Swedish-Finnish. Norway was clearly subordinate to Denmark, however—a fact that was made official in 1536 when, contemporaneous with the introduction of the Reformation, Norway was declared a Danish province and ceased to exist as a kingdom in its own right.

Norway's union with Denmark resulted in increased contact with the cultural life of the continent. Thus the various styles in European art and music found expression in Norway as well, albeit as pale and somewhat delayed reflections of the genuine article.

The cultural and economic progress was not at the outset a result of the Reformation. Actually, very little had been done to prepare Norway for the Reformation when it was imposed by decree of the state council in 1536. In Denmark and Sweden, clergymen sympathetic to the Reformation had worked in many places, and members of the middle class—the Reformation's firmest adherents—were broadly distributed throughout society. In those countries, therefore, the new teachings took hold quite rapidly in wide areas. In Norway, however, the emerging middle class played only a minor role, and Reformation-inspired preaching was relatively unknown. As a matter of fact, it appears that at first the Reformation edict had very little impact on the Church in Norway. To be sure, the possessions of the big churches and cloisters were placed under the king, and the prelates were removed, but the common clergy remained in their positions throughout the country.

Only in the latter half of the sixteenth century, as one by one the Catholic priests died and were replaced by Protestant pastors, was the populace exposed to the new doctrine. Indeed, there is evidence of considerable opposition to the new pastors and their teachings. It appears that at first the Reformation in Norway was more a tearing down of the old than a building of something new. Evidently it was not until the beginning of the seventeenth century that opposition to the Reformation was overcome. By then the Protestant clergy had established itself and the Lutheran Church had secured a firm foothold in the country.

Under these circumstances it is understandable that the break with Catholic church music was not a violent one. Moreover, while the Reformers were at great pains to purge the worship service of everything they regarded as "unevangelical" in word and deed, they were considerably more tolerant with respect to Catholic church music. Luther himself was the model in this matter, and he wanted to retain Gregorian chant (with Latin text) where feasible. The most important changes that Luther made in the High Mass were altering the ritual for Communion, deleting the sacrifice, and giving the sermon a more prominent place. These changes did not require extensive alterations in the music. However, the vernacular was supposed to be used much more than previously. What actually happened, therefore, was that various Latin elements of the Mass were replaced by hymns sung in the vernacular. Other elements were sometimes sung in Latin, sometimes translated into Norwegian and sung to Gregorian melodies adapted to the vernacular text. Luther himself did not advocate the latter practice, for it was his opinion that Latin texts should be used with Gregorian melodies.

The magnitude of the role played by hymns in the worship service varied greatly from place to place. In some places many of the Latin elements were replaced with hymns, creating what might be called hymn-based services. In others, many of the Latin elements were retained with their Gregorian melodies. The latter was possible, however, only where there was sufficient singing talent to handle them—i.e., where Latin school choirs were available to participate in the services. In the smaller communities, which is to say in most of Norway, the hymn-based services were used of necessity.

Title page of Hans Thomissön's Danish Hymnal *of 1569. (Universitetsbiblioteket i Oslo)*

Immediately following the initial establishment of the Reformation in Denmark and Norway, there was a great deal of variety in the form of the worship service from one locale to another. Some directives regarding this matter were embodied in the Danish Church Ordinance of 1539, an ordinance that was also applied to the Church of Norway until it was able to develop its own—which did not happen until 1607. The ordinance of 1539 gave few detailed rules for an order of worship, however, and it was of little help with respect to the musical elements of the worship service. People simply continued to use the old Catholic missals. It was not until late in the century that two books appeared that were to lay the foundation for Protestant church music in both Denmark and Norway: Hans Thomissön's *Danish Hymnal* of 1569, and Niels Jesperssön's *Gradual* of 1573. Thus it is evident that the destruction of the Catholic liturgical music books in Denmark and Norway did not start until 1573, when the publication of Jesperssön's *Gradual* made them superfluous.

THE CONGREGATIONAL HYMN OF THE LUTHERAN CHURCH

The congregational hymn played a pivotal role in the Reformation. Luther saw the possibility of influencing the ordinary layman with his German hymns, and he used them for that purpose. "Luther has damned more souls with his hymns than with his writings and preaching," wrote one of his opponents. Musically, too, the hymn tunes—i.e., the chorales—were of great importance. They were widely sung by the people, and composers employed them as the basis for larger compositions. In Norway they also had a profound influence on religious folk music (see p. 85).

Most of the Protestant chorales came from one or another of the following sources:

1. *Secular folk songs.* In some cases new texts were provided for the melodies; in others the old texts were "Christianized," i.e., revised in such a way as to give them an explicitly Christian content.
2. *Old Catholic folk songs,* such as those used on religious pilgrimages, processionals, and songs to or about the Virgin Mary. The texts had to be altered to make them suitable for use in the Lutheran Church.
3. *Gregorian melodies.* Suitable chants, sequences, and hymn melodies were often employed. Some required only minor alterations, while others had to be reworked from beginning to end. These melodies were frequently used with a vernacular translation of the original Latin text.
4. *Newly composed melodies.* These gradually found their place in Protestant hymnody. Luther himself may have composed original tunes (e.g., "A Mighty Fortress Is Our God"), and contemporary and later Protestant

Page from Thomissön's Danish Hymnal *introducing the section containing Christmas hymns. (Universitetsbiblioteket i Oslo)*

composers little by little made their contribution to the growing repertoire.

Thomissön's *Danish Hymnal* of 1569 was the first official Dano-Norwegian hymnal. Upon its publication a royal decree was issued specifying that this hymnal, and none other, was to be procured for all churches and used in all schools. It included, in addition to hymns, a calendar of the church year and a liturgy for the principal worship service. The order of worship contained here was for a hymn-based service, a simple liturgical form that could be used everywhere. This was a hymnal designed for the people. It was the largest collection of Danish hymns published up to that time, and it became the most important hymnal in Denmark and Norway for over a century. Thomissön himself had written some of the hymns, but for the most part the book consisted of translations and arrangements. Most of the melodies came from the German hymn collections, but Thomissön used a number of Danish secular folk tunes as well. He also imitated the German hymnists by revising—"Christianizing"—the original texts. In addition, there were several hymns by contemporary and earlier Danish hymnists. The format was text and tune only.

A number of chorales that to this day are among the most frequently sung hymn tunes in Norway appear in Thomissön's hymnal. The well-known hymn "We Now Implore the Holy Ghost" is given here (example 4) in the form in which it appeared in the *Danish Hymnal*. Another example is "Come Now to Me God's Son Doth Say," which is given in two versions in example 5. Example 5*a* is the one that appeared in Thomissön's *Danish Hymnal*; example 5*b* is a German version of the same hymn published in Nuremberg in 1534. The note values in both examples have been halved.

These melodies from the Reformation period have a characteristic, often syncopated, rhythm. The use of varying note values gives them a singularly lively rhythm that in later years was lost. The tunes varied considerably from place to place, and Thomissön often made significant changes in the German melodies that he adopted. The difference in the concluding phrases of examples 5*a* and 5*b*, for example, may indicate that Thomissön built on the indigenous Danish tradition.

Example 4. The chorale "We Now Implore the Holy Ghost" as it appeared in The Danish Hymnal *of 1569.*

Example 5. Two versions of the chorale "Come Now to Me God's Son Doth Say."

a

Kom - mer til mig sag - de Guds Søn / som ere be-sva - ret hver oc en /

met syn-den hart be - la - den / un - ge oc gam - le / quinde oc

Mand / ieg vil e-der veder - qvege for-sant / oc he - le e-ders ska - de.

b

Jerspersson's *Gradual* is an impressive book of 450 pages. Like the Catholic missal of the same name, it contains the music required for the worship services on all of the Sundays and ecclesiastical holidays of the church year. It retains a number of Gregorian melodies; the texts are sometimes in Danish, sometimes in Latin. It also includes a number of Danish hymns, but not as many as Thomissön's hymnal.

Both the texts and tunes of the hymns were taken from Thomissön. Although the *Gradual* provided for a number of options in the liturgy for the worship service, allowing the use of more Danish "in the rural villages," it was a fairly demanding order of worship. It probably was used only in larger communities where a church choir was available to provide the necessary musical support.

These two books were the only guides for Protestant church music in Norway for over a century. So far as the liturgy for the worship service was

Page from Jespersson's Gradual *showing the beginning of the liturgy for the first Sunday in Lent.*

concerned, the next step in its development was *Denmark and Norway's Church Ritual* of 1685. The most important new feature of this volume was the complete elimination of Latin from the service. The few Gregorian melodies that remained employed Danish texts. For all practical purposes the service had become totally hymn-based. It is also noteworthy that attention was paid to the role of the organ. It was stated that "in churches where there is an organ, the organist shall begin playing immediately . . . but only briefly so as not to delay the service." This was perhaps a necessary reminder that the service should not be lengthened unduly, for it already consumed three hours from beginning to end! It was also stated that the hymn preceding the sermon should be sung "according to the lead and sound of the organ." It is evident, therefore, that by this time the organ had begun to replace the choir in leading the congregational singing.

A change in times and styles had begun. The hymnist of the new age was Thomas Kingo who, even before the new church ritual had been issued, had published a collection of hymns, *Spiritual Songs*. The two volumes of this work appeared in 1674 and 1681, respectively. In 1689 Kingo published the first part of a *Hymnal*. It was initially authorized for use in the services of the Church, but shortly after its publication the authorization was withdrawn. Ten years were to pass before Kingo published *A New Church Hymnal*, containing texts and melodies only. The same year (1699) saw the publication of his *Gradual*, consisting largely of old chorale melodies, and both books were officially authorized for use in the Church.

Kingo's importance as a writer of hymn texts is indisputable, but his contribution to church music has been the object of fairly harsh criticism on grounds that he indiscriminately followed the fashions of the period. This criticism applies both to his handling of the old melodies borrowed from Thomissön's collection and to the new tunes employed, many of which he clearly derived from contemporary dance tunes. Although the latter practice had its parallel in the Reformation-era use of secular folk tunes, from a stylistic point of view the secular music of Kingo's day was much less similar to church music than was the Renaissance folk music sometimes adapted for church use by the Reformers.

An example of Kingo's recasting of an old melody may be seen in his handling (in the *Gradual* of 1699) of "Come Now to Me God's Son Doth Say" (example 6).

A comparison with Thomissön's version of the same hymn (example 5*a*) reveals considerable differences between the two. Kingo's rhythmic—and, to a lesser extent, melodic—changes in every phrase of the hymn make it much less lively than Thomissön's version.

Example 6. The chorale "Come Now to Me God's Son Doth Say" as it appeared in Thomas Kingo's Gradual of 1699.

An example of Kingo's use of a secular tune is the hymn "Sorrow and Gladness Journey Together" (example 7), which appeared in the second volume of *Spiritual Songs*. It was perhaps an old courante that Kingo here adapted to his purpose.

LATIN SCHOOLS

The Latin schools were the successors of the Catholic cathedral schools with respect to both the education of clergymen and training in church music. Indeed, throughout the sixteenth century clergymen in Norway commonly had to be content with nothing more than a Latin school education; the demand for a university education for clergy could not be met until after 1600. The responsibility of the Latin school choirs was even greater than that of the Catholic cathedral school singers had been, for unlike the larger Catholic churches, the Protestant churches had no corps of minor clergy to form the nucleus of a church choir. The school choir, led by its director, had to provide all the choir music for the worship services.

It is understandable, therefore, that the schools were of great interest to the Church. The Church Ordinance of 1539 states: "In each town there shall be a Latin school." It was not possible to implement this directive throughout Norway, but a number of Latin schools were established there. In addition to the large cathedral schools in Nidaros, Bergen, Oslo, Stavanger, and later Kristiansand, there were, at various times, Latin schools in Tönsberg, Fredrikstad, Halden, Skien, Drammen, and Kongsberg. The most important subjects taught in these schools were Latin, Christian theology, and singing. Because of the importance of choirs in the worship

Example 7. The hymn "Sorrow and Gladness Journey Together" as it appeared in Thomas Kingo's Spiritual Songs, *vol. 2 (1681).*

services, considerable emphasis was given to singing; indeed, rehearsals were held daily.

Actually, the importance of music in the Latin schools was even greater than might be supposed. In addition to their regular participation in the worship services—usually twice each Sunday—the school choirs also took part in all funerals and weddings, and for these they were paid fixed rates. This gave a much-needed boost to the schools' coffers, which were often in need of funds. The schools were largely dependent on gifts solicited by the students from local citizens and people in the surrounding districts. In the rural areas this occurred by means of the so-called "parish visitation," a semiannual undertaking in which the students were sent throughout the district in pairs to "beg money" for their school.

These parish visitations had several results. On the positive side, personal contact was thereby established between the students and the general population. The solicitations also had great musical significance, for the traveling students had to demonstrate their talents as singers and, on occasion, as instrumental performers. We can assume that through such visits the people in these isolated communities had some contact with the music life of the

Latin schools that they otherwise would not have had. The negative consequences for the schools were more serious, however. Each such trip usually took the students away for a minimum of a month (thus a total of two months each year) and trips through the larger districts often took even longer. The result was a serious reduction in the time available for teaching. There is also no doubt that these trips, in which the boys traveled about unsupervised for weeks at a time, had unfortunate moral consequences as well.

In the cities where the schools were located, the solicitation of gifts was carried out in a unique way: the students and their teachers paraded singing through the town. Such processions occurred on the evenings preceding various church holidays, especially on Martinmass Eve (November 10), Christmas Eve, New Year's Eve, and Epiphany Eve. Gradually, however, they were restricted to just one or two of these occasions. The processions undoubtedly were very popular with the townspeople, and the gifts streamed in. Among school officials, however, the singing parades and parish visitations were unpopular because of the inconveniences and injurious consequences they occasioned for the students. Both activities were, therefore, gradually restricted. Parish solicitation was finally forbidden by the Norwegian Church Ordinance of 1607, the singing procession in 1739. The income that the schools thereby lost was replaced in part by fixed levies from the various districts.

The school choirs were well regarded by the townspeople, and were sometimes called upon to sing at private parties. We get a glimpse of this in a brief entry of January 6, 1563, in the diary of Bishop Absalon Pedersson Beyer. On that day a Rev. Matz, pastor of the Bergen cathedral, hosted a dinner party for Beyer and several other people. Beyer wrote: "There he had the 'Descanters' and 'David's Deacons' and plenty of wine and beer, and he had Karl—who played both the harp and the shawm—play for us." At this lively party, then, the guests were entertained with both instrumental and choral music. "Descanters" was the common name for the school choir. "David's Deacons" appears to have been a select group of student singers, at least in Bergen. In other places the whole choir was apparently given that name.

The director of the school's music activities was called the cantor. It was his responsibility to supervise the music education of the students and conduct their singing in the churches, at least on important occasions. Because most of the Latin schools in Norway were rather small, it was not always possible to support a full-time cantor. In such cases the duties of cantor were assumed by one of the teachers. In Bergen, for example, the position of cantor was established in 1671, and it was filled by Peder Mogenssön

Wandel—one of several Norwegian cantors of the Baroque period whose names are known to us.

What did the Latin school choirs sing? This question is not easily answered, primarily because their libraries were destroyed in the numerous fires that devastated Norway's cities and towns. In attempting to get an overview of the church choirs' repertoires, therefore, we must resort to guesses and comparisons with similar choirs in other countries.

First, the school choirs sang any unaccompanied Gregorian melodies that were a part of the divine worship service—those, for example, found in Jespersson's *Gradual*. The choir also sang polyphonic music, however. The oldest music in the repertoire likely included the *Piae cantiones*, a collection of Latin songs that played a large role in Swedish and Finnish Latin schools and presumably was also known in Norway. It was first printed in 1582, with a new edition following in 1625. In addition to unison melodies, the collection contains some two-part, three-part, and four-part settings. Some of these reflect the old *ars nova* style, but most display simple Renaissance-type choral settings.

Pratum spirituale, a collection of five-part choral works by the Danish composer Mogens Pederson, was of greater importance. Published in Copenhagen in 1620, it contains mainly arrangements of chorales, but also three Latin motets, a few pieces derived from the Latin Mass, and some Danish choral responses. The title page states that the collection contains "Masses, Hymns, and Motets suitable for use throughout Denmark and Norway." The preface notes that the collection is for "the further training of youth in the schools." Thus it is clear that Pederson also had in mind the Norwegian Latin schools, so it is reasonable to suppose that the collection was used in Norway. The hymn melodies in *Pratum spirituale* were taken largely from Thomisson's hymnal. The settings are in the late Renaissance choral style and demonstrate that Pederson was both a skillful and a sensitive composer. His motets are polyphonic, making frequent use of imitative passages. His arrangements of chorales, however, generally employ a fairly simple, homophonic idiom, as in example 8.

Knud Jeppesen, in his introduction to the *Collected Works of Mogens Pederson*, offers the following evaluation of the musical importance of *Pratum spirituale*:

Hans Thomisson's *Danish Hymnal* and Niels Jespersson's *Gradual* were the first two works, and Mogens Pederson's *Pratum spirituale* is the third and last, in the series of works that contributed significantly to the musical shaping of the older Lutheranism in Denmark. While the *Danish Hymnal* was addressed to the ordinary church-goer, and the

Gradual was designed, one could almost say, for the clergy and the choir, the *Pratum*—which, unlike the other two collections, contains pluri-voiced music—constitutes an artistically more richly developed supplement to both of them. Its influence was owing partly to the fact that its five-part arrangements of chorales had an impact on congregational singing (which it was the task of the choir to support, even as was the singing of these arrangements), partly in that the Latin

Example 8. Mogens Pedersön's setting of the chorale "We Now Implore the Holy Ghost" (from Pratum Spirituale, *1620).*

pieces (and perhaps also some of the more elaborate compositions with Danish texts) familiarized people with a repertoire intended exclusively for the choir.

We can safely assume that the repertoire in general use throughout Europe was also used to some extent in Norway. It is reported that the compositions of Josquin des Prez and Clemens non Papa were sung in Denmark's Latin schools. It is likely that the works of such German masters as Johannes Eccard, Hans Leo Hassler, and Michael Praetorius were sung as well. Later in the Baroque period newer compositions probably found their way into the Norwegian repertoire—those, for example, of Heinrich Schütz, who at two different times during the Thirty Year's War (1633–35 and 1642–45) was attached to the Danish court, and who brought with him the new monodic style.

As will be seen later, one of the duties of town musicians was to participate in some of the services in the church. These, together with their assistants and possibly some instrumentalists from among the Latin school students, could form an orchestra capable of performing middle and late Baroque cantatas and smaller oratorios. Although we know that such music was quite often performed in various places, specific compositions are difficult to ascertain. Norwegian cantors and organists of this period also composed or arranged music for various occasions, but none of it has been preserved.

TOWN MUSICIANS AND ORGANISTS

In addition to the Latin schools, the town musicians and organists were the principal shapers of the music life of Norway throughout the Baroque era. The work of the organists is fairly well known, but the role of the town musicians requires a somewhat more detailed discussion. On the continent the history of town musicians can be traced back to the late Middle Ages, while they evidently appeared in Denmark for the first time in the sixteenth century. There is no evidence of their appearance in Norway until the beginning of the seventeenth century, but it is possible that some Norwegian cities had them at an earlier date.

Town musicians had two functions: a) to provide instrumental (dance) music as needed for private and public festivities in the town and the surrounding district, and b) to provide instrumental music for the church services on major religious holidays. These functions were both the duty and the right of the town musician. Nobody else had the right, except as authorized by him, to play for a dance or any other similar event in the town or district under his jurisdiction. Of course, the task of providing music for all of these events was more than one person could handle alone. A town musician, therefore, needed assistants and apprentices to help him and to replace him in his absence. The more distant villages in the district were often assigned to local musicians who paid the town musician a fee for the privilege of representing him in that community. The town musician was also paid an annual salary for his work in the church.

The oldest extant contract for a Norwegian town musician is from Bergen. Dated November 20, 1620, it specifies the details of both his secular and his ecclesiastical responsibilities. The contract does not give the impression that the arrangement being set forth is new or unusual. His duties included playing from the church tower after the principal service each Sunday, and on weekdays from the watchman's tower. Church responsibilities probably became increasingly important as Baroque music required more and more instrumental participation. We know the names of a number of the town musicians who served throughout Norway. Several of them were important musicians who will be discussed later.

Norway's lack of a royal court and, therefore, of the culture associated with such a court tended to restrict the music life of the country. It should be added, however, that the Dano-Norwegian kings visited Norway quite frequently, and these visits were of some musical importance. For example, King Christian IV, who was an inveterate traveler, visited Norway no fewer than thirty times during his reign. As the royal visit was celebrated from place to place throughout the country, local musicians were called upon to perform. The royal party occasionally also included members of the court chapel or other musicians associated with the royal court. The most famous of these visits was that of King Frederik V in the summer of 1749, when his entourage included an Italian opera company, formed by the impresario Pietro Mingotti, which performed in Oslo. It is noteworthy that the previous leader of the opera company was none other than C. W. Gluck, later to become famous for his opera reforms. Though he had come with the group to Copenhagen, it is quite certain that he did not accompany them to Norway.

All things considered, the brief taste of court music provided by these royal visits probably was not of great importance. It was the Church that served as the chief provider of serious music in Norway throughout the Renaissance and Baroque eras. Gradually, after 1700, public and semi-public concerts were offered, but they did not acquire much significance until the latter half of the century.

The prominence of church music in Norway naturally implies a certain restriction of the country's music life, but on the other hand there are many indications that the range of such activity was considerably greater than once supposed. There is much evidence to show that the obligation of Latin school students and town musicians to participate in the church services was not merely a statement on paper, but an essential part of their respective tasks. We also know the names of a number of the organists of this period, and it appears that they were comparatively well paid. It is evident that an effort was made to secure capable people to serve as organists in the leading churches.

Unfortunately, sources describing Norwegian music activity in the Baroque period are sketchy, but one account throws some light on the customs of the time. It describes some "netherworldly music" that town musician Heinrich Meyer claimed to have heard in a rural area near Bergen (see page 94 for the complete account). Meyer wrote: "In the year 1695, after I had been an apprentice for about three months, it happened that before Christmas we were rehearsing the music that was to be played during the holidays . . . They all laughed at the farmer—my teacher, the cantor, and the organist, all of whom were present at the rehearsal." It is clear from the context that Meyer was an apprentice to Bergen's town musician and that the rehearsal was held in the latter's home. Nothing is said about the Latin school choir or singers from the choir being present, but since the cantor was there it seems likely that vocal music with instrumental accompaniment was being rehearsed. It must, therefore, have been some of the middle Baroque cantata-like compositions that were to be performed in the churches during the forthcoming Christmas season.

Music in these larger forms presumably was performed during the services only on the most important religious holidays. In any event, the responsibility of the town musician to participate in worship services was in many locales limited to the holidays. Rev. Christen Staffensön Bang confirmed this in his tract, *Music and Song of the Christian Church*, printed in Oslo in 1662. Bang wrote as follows:

> In our Lutheran churches a goodly number of musical instruments are used, especially on major holidays and whenever people of the upper class hold their wedding service. On these occasions instrumental music is played using organ, trumpets, trombones, zithers, violins, etc. And in this way singers and instrumentalists alike join together in praising and serving God as best they can.

In another place Bang listed several instruments used in the church: "Organ, trumpets, trombones, violins, drums, flutes, zithers, and other instruments." Evidently, then, a wide variety of instruments was employed in the churches of Norway as early as the middle of the seventeenth century.

It is also known that there were church concerts. The most famous account of such an event comes from Bergen and is contained in a 1764 report by Hildebrandt Meyer entitled *A Description of Bergen*:

> During Bishop Randulf's time, when Sören Lintrup was rector of the Bergen cathedral school (1695–1703), a weekly concert used to be

given in the cathedral. These were excellent, well-planned concerts of vocal and instrumental music. Not only did the students during Lent present the Passion story in song using Danish texts, but at other times as well they presented a number of other Bible stories. Their presentations of the stories about the rich man and the prodigal son were especially applauded and praised—by those best qualified to judge— for the extraordinary quality of the performances. Each of the singers had a specific role to perform, and the roles were assigned as if each singer was especially suited by talent and temperament to represent a particular person in the biblical story, as was also the music, at times melancholy and deeply moving, at other times cheerful and heroic. It is said that of the many fine singers in the choir, two were especially renowned. One presented the story of the prodigal son—how finally, in his miserable condition, he returned to his father and begged forgiveness—and he did it in such an excellent way, and with a voice so well suited to the material, as to stir profoundly the hearts of the listeners. The other one generally portrayed persons of high rank—for example, Pontius Pilate, when he sang the words, "What I have written, I have written." He had such an unusual bass voice that the listeners were compelled to admire him no less than the first singer. Throughout the time these concerts were given, they were diligently attended not only by the people of Bergen, but by others who came to the city, so the church was always filled. In fact, a reasonable, reliable, and trustworthy man living at that time has assured me that during the summer many people traveled to Bergen just to hear this performance. He has also told me that qualified critics, both Bergensers and others, had high praise for the concert and acknowledged that it was better than anything of the kind that they had heard elsewhere. That is evidence that this fair science [singing] was not only cultivated in Bergen, but was brought to a high level of perfection.

Behind this somewhat patriotic account one nonetheless senses a flourishing music life in Bergen around 1700. It is possible that these church concerts were inspired in part by Buxtehude's famous *Abendmusiken* in Lübeck: Sören Lintrup, rector of the Bergen cathedral school, had correspondence with people in Lübeck and thus probably knew something of the music life there.

Bergen was not the only city in Norway with significant church music activity. Although we have no detailed description of the church music itself in Trondheim, it appears that at the beginning of the seventeenth century the Latin school there was famed for its singers. A letter in 1618 from

Christian IV to the authorities of the Trondheim cathedral requested that a few good singers be sent from the cathedral school to Copenhagen:

> It is our wish and we hereby request that from your city's school you select three students—one of the best basses, a tenor, and an alto—who would be suitable for use in our *cantorei* [royal chapel choir], and send them to Copenhagen to our assistant director, Mogens Peders-sön, at your earliest convenience.

Christian IV was in the process of reorganizing his *cantorei*, and a similar letter was sent to the bishop of Aarhus in Denmark.

There were several able musicians in Oslo, so at times its music life must have been fairly rich. Johan Fredrik Clasen (1697–1775) was the best known of many organists who served in Oslo. The son of a Danish organist, Clasen was invited to Oslo in 1720 at the urging of Georg von Bertuch (who will be discussed later). He was engaged as an organ repairman, but was soon appointed both organist and cantor at the Latin school. In 1720 he presented a concert on Good Friday consisting of two cantatas that he himself had composed. On later occasions, too, he presented cantatas and other vocal music of his own composition, none of which has been preserved. During his tenure, Our Savior's Church procured a splendid new organ, built by the famous Danish organ builder, Lambert Daniel Carstens. It was dedicated by Clasen in 1729, and its façade remains in the church, now the Oslo cathedral.

It appears that even before 1750 there were fairly regular concerts in Oslo, presumably under the leadership of the town musician, Heinrich Meyer. No detailed information about these concerts exists, just a terse statement to the effect that they took place. Meyer was an able musician who certainly was capable of providing concerts of acceptable quality. It was reported, in any case, that "music was reestablished on a very solid footing" after he came to the city shortly before 1715. He served as town musician from 1715 to 1758, but (probably because of illness) was unable to fulfill his duties adequately in his later years.

Through these scattered accounts of the music milieu in Norway during the Baroque era, one glimpses the contours of both ecclesiastical and secular music life. Its development moved in waves. At times the quality was very low, but there is evidence that at other times the music—church music, in any event—reached a high level.

COMPOSERS

Very little is known of the Norwegian composers who lived during the early part of this period. Indeed, only two names remain. In the royal archive in

Stockholm there is a composition for four-part chorus *a cappella* on the text "Cor mundum crea in me Deus" (Psalm 51:10–11). The composer, identified as a Norwegian, was Caspar Ecchienus. Reproduced here in its entirety (example 9), the work begins with imitation but for the most part is quite homophonic. The style is late Renaissance, so the piece probably dates from around 1600 or a little earlier. The numerous instances of parallel motion suggest that the composer's training was somewhat deficient. Ecchienus, whose name is thought to be the Latinized form of the Norwegian name "Ormestad" (or "Ormsen"), may have been a cantor or organist in Norway around the year 1600, but nothing further is known about him.

We do know that another Norwegian composer, Johan Nesenus, was a cantor in Göttingen (Germany) from 1598 to 1604. He was born in Bergen, but it is not known if he was ever professionally active in Norway. A single surviving motet composed by him, "The Lord God Spoke," was printed in 1594. Portions of *Liebgärtlein*, a collection of secular choral works (villanellas) that he published in 1598, have also been preserved.

Only in the latter part of the Baroque period do we encounter composers about whom the record is somewhat more complete. Two German-born musicians—Georg von Bertuch and Johann Daniel Berlin—played particularly important roles in the development of music in Norway at this time.

Georg von Bertuch (1688–1743) was born in Helmershausen and received formal training as a musician. He later became a military officer and was engaged by the Danes, but he continued to cultivate music as an amateur. In 1719, as a reward for long and faithful service, he was named commander of the Akershus fortress in Oslo. He lived in the city until his death, taking an active part in its music life. He was personally involved, for example, in securing the services of F. Clasen as organist at Our Savior's Church.

There is reason to believe that some of Bertuch's compositions were performed in Norway. Those that have been preserved include a large choral cantata, "God the Lord, the Almighty Ruleth," two solo cantatas, and a collection of trio sonatas (1738). Originally there were twenty-four sonatas in the set, each in a different key as in Bach's *Well-tempered Clavier*. Of the set, the first six unfortunately have been lost.

Bertuch was a well-known composer in his time. He was a personal friend of Johann Mattheson of Hamburg (it was Bertuch who conveyed to Mattheson town musician Meyer's account of the "netherworldly music" in Bergen reproduced in part on p. 94), and he also had contact with Johann Sebastian Bach and a number of other important masters. His compositions show that he was well trained in the late Baroque style. The sonata collection bears this characteristic title (translated from the French): *Twenty-four Orig-*

Example 9. Caspar Ecchienus, "Cor mun-dum crea in me Deus."

inal Sonatas employing canons, fugues, counterpoint, and polyphony according to the system of twenty-four modes and the precepts of the famous musician, composer, and historian Jean Mattheson, with thoroughbass. It was with legitimate pride that Bertuch drew attention to the fact that he had employed both canon and fugue technique in his sonatas. Several movements are in strict canon, and fugal passages occur frequently. The number of movements in each sonata varies from three to five, and the sequence of tempos is also varied. The old *sonata da chiesa* form (slow–fast–slow–fast) appears only rarely. Somewhat more frequently Bertuch used the tempo sequence common in many late Baroque solo concertos (fast–slow–fast), but he used other sequences as well. Only rarely did he insert the descriptive title of a dance—as, for example, in the fourth movement of *Sonata No. 7*, where he wrote: "Allemande in canone." Some of the sonatas cannot correctly be called trio sonatas, for they contain movements written for a solo instrument with continuo.

The third movement of Bertuch's *Sonata No. 18* in A-flat major is given as a representative sample of his music (example 10). This little Vivace is a fine example of Bertuch's style. The structure is imitative. The imitations occur at the octave or unison, and once adjusted at the fifth. The relatively simple harmonic foundation is clear and correctly handled. As is often the case with Bertuch, the movement is in the usual Baroque binary form.

The same style marks Bertuch's vocal compositions. The cantata "God the Lord, the Almighty Ruleth" is for four-part chorus, three soloists, string orchestra, and continuo. It is a large-scale composition in eight movements based on Psalm 50:1–6 and the chorale "Zion's Watchman." It begins with

Example 10. Georg von Bertuch, "Vivace" from Sonata no. 18.

a sonata in French overture form. The choral sections are largely fugal. The last movement is a fugue built on the third stanza of the chorale, with the several phrases of the chorale being used as fugal themes.

The two solo cantatas are of more modest dimensions. "My Heart Is Prepared" is for alto solo and continuo; "Rejoice, O Daughter of Zion" is for bass solo, string orchestra, and continuo.

Bertuch's compositions show that he had considerable imagination and a good sense of sound. The concluding movement of his choral cantata, for example, captures many of the sonorities typical of the late Baroque period. Simple harmonies occasionally bordering on monotony and a tendency to overwork the same melodic material are the principal weaknesses in what are otherwise technically well crafted compositions. In Bertuch, Norway had imported a composer of high quality, and there is no doubt that he was a significant force in the music life of his adopted city.

Johann Daniel Berlin (1714–89), another German-born Baroque composer who spent much of his professional life in Norway, was born in Memel. His early music studies were with Copenhagen's town musician, Andreas Berg. In 1737, at the age of twenty-three, he was appointed town musician of Trondheim. In 1741 he became organist at the city's famed Nidaros cathedral, and in 1763 he became—oddly enough—the city's fire chief. The latter position required him in 1767 to relinquish his duties as town musician, but he continued as cathedral organist until his death.

Perhaps Berlin's chief contribution to music life in Norway was a textbook in elementary music that appeared in 1744—the first book of its kind in the Dano-Norwegian language. Its rather pompous title, given here in translation, was a kind of summary of the contents and objectives of the book: *The elements of music, or an introduction to the understanding of the basic principles of music including the musical signature as commonly used, also the fingering on some of the so-called stringed and wind instruments, and other matters relating to music, briefly and clearly set forth for those who cherish the desire to lay a correct foundation for understanding music; written and published by Johann Daniel Berlin.* Several copies of the book are extant, and it is clear that it was an excellent instructional book for its time. It was widely used, and was especially important for the amateur musicians who were to play such an important role in the music life of Norway in the latter half of the eighteenth century.

Berlin was also interested in the tempered tuning of keyboard instruments, a new development that was the subject of much discussion at that time. He constructed a monochord (a one-stringed instrument with a movable bridge used for the mathematical determination of musical intervals) for use in tuning an instrument in equal temperament. In 1765 he published a treatise on the monochord and the calculation of equal temperament. Its title, in translation, was: *An introduction to the measurement of sound, or how one with the help of logarithmic calculation can easily and quickly determine by geometric reasoning the so-called equal temperament. Also information about the monochord invented and constructed in 1752 by Johann Daniel Berlin, cathedral organist and town musician in Trondheim.* Two years later this treatise was also published in a German translation.

Berlin was an active composer, firmly anchored in the music of the late Baroque period. There is no way of knowing how much of his work has been lost, but what has been preserved includes a violin concerto, three symphonies, and a sonatina and several dances for the keyboard. There is reason to believe that he also composed cantatas for various special occasions, but none has been found.

The sonatina is the only composition by Berlin that was published during his lifetime. The printed publication bears the title (in German): *Musical Divertissement, consisting of a sonatina based on a simple tuneful melody and set for keyboard in accordance with modern tastes.* It is a standard dance suite in five movements, marked Capricetto, Arietta, Gavotte, Minuet, and Gigue. All are in the usual Baroque binary form, and nothing in them points toward early Classicism. The "modern taste" that Berlin mentioned in the title alludes to little more than the liberal use of the ornamentation then in fashion. Example 11 is the Arietta from this dance suite. Note that the binary form is employed in a completely standard manner, with a cadence to F major at the end of the first part and a return to D minor near the end of the second part. In another composition—a minuet for keyboard—Berlin used the customary ternary minuet form with trio.

The symphonies are in three movements ordered as in the late Baroque concertos (fast–slow–fast). In *Symphony No. 2* in D major, for example, the three movements are marked Allegro, Andante, and Allegro. The first two movements are in binary form, and the third suggests a ternary scheme: |:a:||:ba':|. The third section (a') is so altered, however, that the basic binary form—reinforced by the repeat signs—is strongly felt. The ensemble consists of string orchestra and continuo.

Thanks to his strong connections with several leading musicians in Germany, Berlin stayed well informed about developments in music on the continent. His large library of music literature and scores attests to this. As a composer, he nonetheless adhered to the relatively conservative style typical of the late German Baroque period. Within this style, however, he displayed a sure technique and fine musical taste.

The foremost Norwegian-born composer during this period was Johan Henrik Freithoff (1713–67). He was born in Kristiansand, but lived most

*Example 11. J.D. Berlin, "Arietta" from
the* Sonatina *for piano.*

of his life in Copenhagen and made his greatest contribution there. His first education in music came from his father, town musician Balthazar Freithoff. When he was twenty he set out on a long journey abroad; in later years he reported that he had traveled in Europe, Asia, and Africa. How extensive this journey was can only be conjectured, but we do know that he studied music in Italy. In 1742 he returned to Kristiansand. By this time he apparently had had enough of the life of a musician, for he sought a position as a civil servant. He was not immediately successful, however, and he went to Copenhagen where, in 1745, he became a violinist in the royal chapel orchestra. Finally, in 1746, he received a civil service appointment in Copenhagen. He continued as a member of the royal chapel orchestra, but performed only as a soloist on special occasions. He remained in Copenhagen until his death.

Freithoff's extant compositions include a trio sonata for two flutes and continuo, two trio sonatas for two violins and continuo, a violin sonata, and a flute sonata. There are also some shorter works, including a "Notturno" in E major for two violins and continuo and some arias for comic operas.

Freithoff's compositions reflect his Italian training. While his solo sonatas are rather conservative, in his trio sonatas one can observe the Rococo style breaking through. Some of his quick movements employ the polyphonic style characteristic of the Baroque period, wherein fairly equal importance is given to the several parts. In general, however, polyphony is replaced by a homophonic style in which the upper voice attracts most of the interest and the other voices, including the bass, are reduced to the role of mere accompaniment. Most of the sonatas consist of two movements; of the trio sonatas, only the sonata for two flutes has three movements. All the trio sonatas have a minuet as the last movement.

Example 12 is the third movement of Freithoff's *Trio Sonata* in A major for two flutes and continuo (1735). Note that it is in the usual ternary form, with the Trio in the parallel minor key (A minor). In this example, the dominating role of the upper voice is obvious. The two-measure motivic construction throughout is evidence of the emerging galant style.

Freithoff's vocal music is of less importance; indeed, he himself evidently regarded it as mere occasional music. It is marked by the airy, galant style of the Rococo.

It is a peculiar fact in the history of music in Norway during the Baroque era that the most important Norwegian-born composers of the period (Nesenus and Freithoff) did their work abroad, whereas the most important composers in Norway (Bertuch and Berlin) were foreigners. That the ablest Norwegian composers pursued careers abroad is perhaps not so strange, for conditions in Norway were rather difficult throughout the entire period. It is more surprising that so important a composer as Johann Daniel Berlin remained in Norway for so long. When he and other able foreign musicians settled in Norway, notwithstanding the difficult circumstances, other factors must have played a significant role. They liked Norway, felt at home there, and made their contributions under conditions as they found them. Without the contributions of so many able non-Norwegian musicians, music life in Norway during both this and later periods would have been substantially poorer.

Example 12. J.H. Freithoff, "Menuet" from the Trio Sonata.

Menuet D.C.

Rococo Music and Music Societies
(ca. 1750–ca. 1800)

The latter half of the eighteenth century was a time of rapid development in Norway, with continued economic growth and a marked increase in population. Now, for the first time in a long while, a spirit of nationalism infused the people. A tide of "Norwegian-ness" surged through both the upper and the lower classes; indeed, some of the civil servants of Danish origin working in Norway became as enamored of this movement as native-born Norwegians. What the people wanted above all was more independence for Norway, greater equality with Denmark, and more respect for special Norwegian circumstances and needs. Hardly anyone thought seriously about the possibility of a dissolution of the Dano-Norwegian union at this time, however; it was accepted without question that Copenhagen, the Danish capital, was the center of Norway's cultural life as well.

It is not surprising, therefore, that the Norwegian Society—Norway's most important cultural institution—was located in Copenhagen. It really was a literary club that served as a gathering place for Norwegian students (who had to go to Copenhagen to obtain a higher education) and other Norwegians living in the Danish capital. Characteristic of the spirit of the society is the song "For Norway, Homeland of the Brave":

> For Norway, homeland of the brave,
> We drink this sweet libation;
> When first we taste the glass we crave
> We'll dream of liberation.
> But one day we shall wake again
> And burst our bonds and break our chain.
> For Norway, homeland of the brave,
> We empty this libation.

The song was written shortly after 1770 by the clergyman (later bishop) Johan Nordahl Brun and was hailed with great enthusiasm. Indeed, it became almost a national song, especially for Norwegians living in Denmark. It was only a drinking song, however, and few who sang it felt obliged to take it seriously once the party was over. Culturally, there was no desire at this time to sever the ties with Denmark. The clearest proof of this is that the society's most prominent poet, Johan Hermann Wessel (1742–85), wrote in Danish rather than Norwegian. Wessel was a typical representative of the common culture that then prevailed throughout Denmark-Norway.

The music life of Norway at this time was characterized by two diverse currents. One was the continuation of the Baroque tradition: the town musicians, the cantors, and the Latin school choirs that played such important roles in the music of the Church. They continued to play their respective roles until about 1800. The stirring of a new age was evident, however, in the emerging interest in secular music that found expression in public concerts and—perhaps most importantly of all—in the creation of music societies whose orchestras gave public or semi-public concerts.

In these societies we encounter for the first time a group of musicians who were to be of great importance in Norway's music life for a full century thereafter: the amateurs, or "music dilettantes" as they often were called. They were recruited primarily from the upper class, i.e., government officials and families operating the large business firms that flourished at this time. Music and the theater were popular leisure-time interests for them. When one describes the music of this period as "society music," however, it is not primarily because the music was frequently performed by these new music "societies." The meaning goes deeper: "society music" connotes the underlying popular attitude at that time toward music as art. Music was a favored "pastime," a pleasant diversion after a tiring day at work and an important part of social life. Thus it was simply assumed that an "educated person" could carry a part in a choral piece or play an instrument in an orchestra.

This view of music as primarily a diversion had an influence on the attitude toward all art. It helps to explain, for example, why the title "divertissement" was popular at this time both in Scandinavia and on the continent. This "societal" outlook on music among music dilettantes did not necessarily imply inferior quality in performance. Their technical training was often quite good, frequently every bit as good as that of the professional town musicians, and the best of them were outstanding artists. Generally there was little competition between the amateurs and the professionals. The local music society was the place where the two groups met and worked together to produce an orchestra large enough to perform the new music.

Before this time such orchestras had not been necessary, for Baroque music does not require a large ensemble. Most Baroque music—both purely instrumental and vocal with instrumental accompaniment—could be performed by smaller groups (although larger orchestras were sometimes used when they were available). These small instrumental groups could for the most part be manned by the town musicians and their apprentices. Now, however, there was a dramatic change, for Rococo and early Classical music requires a larger orchestra. An ensemble of twenty to twenty-five musicians is needed to perform a symphony of Wagenseil or Haydn, and the town musicians lacked the resources to put together an orchestra of that size. It was possible only with the help of the local amateurs, and it appears that the orchestras of the music societies were of approximately this size. The leader of such orchestras, as a rule, was a professional musician. Often it was the local town musician who was engaged as "leader and instructor"—and usually also as a member of the first violin section. "Conductors" in the modern sense of the term (i.e., as leaders of public performances) did not become common until well into the nineteenth century.

The programs for the concerts of music societies were not limited to instrumental music; they also included vocal selections, usually in the form of arias from well-known grand operas or comic operas. The latter type of music was popular, and when the resources were available some of the lighter and more easily performable comic operas were staged in cooperation with the drama societies.

CHORALE BOOKS

Norway's cultural dependence on Denmark at this time is especially evident in the sphere of church music. Until the late 1800s, the only hymnals in Norway came from Denmark and were identical to those used in the Danish churches. After the publication of Kingo's hymnal of 1699 (see chapter 4), no new hymnal of importance appeared until the publication of Erik Pontoppidan's *New Hymnal* of 1740. Although not officially authorized for use in public worship, it was introduced in the palace chapels and was also used extensively in family devotions and various other ways. Of the new hymns to appear here, those of Hans Adolf Brorson (1694–1764) were especially important. Musically it was heavily dependent on German Pietism, especially as reflected in Anastasius Freylinghausen's *Spiritual Songs* of 1704. A number of new melodies—some folk-like, some reflecting the aria style of the late Baroque period—were also included.

Like earlier hymnals, the first editions of Pontoppidan's book included texts and melodies. By this time, however, the organ had come to the fore

Title page of Frederik Christian Breitendich's Complete Chorale Book *of 1764.*

as the leader of congregational singing, and it seemed appropriate to assemble the melodies in a book designed specifically for organists: a chorale book. Even before this time, organists had begun making handwritten chorale books. The oldest such book in Norway comes from Bergen, and evidently was assembled in the years just before and after 1600. The first printed Dano-Norwegian chorale book was F. C. Breitendich's *Complete Chorale Book*, published in 1764. It was not officially authorized either, but apparently was rather widely used. The melodies in Breitendich's book were provided with a figured bass, and the organists had to supply the inner voices. This should not have been difficult, for the harmonization was on the whole quite simple and it can be assumed that the hymns were sung in a slow tempo.

Example 13 shows the chorale "We Now Implore the Holy Ghost" as it appeared in Breitendich's hymnal. The fact that the melody was given in quarter notes does not imply a faster tempo. The frequent use of

Example 13. The chorale "We Now Implore the Holy Ghost" as it appeared in F.C. Breitendich's Complete Chorale Book *(1764).*

embellishments—for example, on the word "Hellig" in the first phrase— shows the influence of the popular operatic aria. This naturally necessitated a slower tempo as well: the congregation needed time to negotiate the embellished melodic line.

If one compares Breitendich's version of this hymn with the older form that appeared in Thomissön's *Danish Hymnal* of 1569 (see p. 33), the difference in rhythmic form is striking. In the original form of the melody the various syllables of the text were assigned to notes of varying duration, whereas in Breitendich every syllable (except the penultimate syllable in each phrase and occasionally the one preceding it) is given a quarter note. The second and fourth phrase endings, on the other hand, are considerably drawn out. Nothing remains of the lively rhythmic drive of the original.

The last part of the eighteenth century is usually called the Enlightenment or the Age of Reason. It was a period in which human reason, often rather narrowly conceived, set its stamp on the cultural life of the period: everything was to be reasonable, useful, and practical. The first Dano-Norwegian hymnal reflecting this cultural environment was that of Ove Höeg Guldberg, published in 1778. A new chorale book then became a necessity, and it was supplied by Niels Schiörring (1781). It too reflected the sober realism of the Enlightenment. The melodies were purged of all rhythmic and melodic "irregularities" with virtually every syllable of every hymn being assigned a half note.

Example 14 shows the chorale "We Now Implore the Holy Ghost "as presented by Schiörring. All that remain of the melodic embellishments are the mordents on the penultimate note of each phrase and two solitary quarter notes in the last phrase. The isometric chorale had completely superseded

Example 14. Isometric version of the chorale "We Now Implore the Holy Ghost" as it appeared in Niels Schiörring's Chorale Book *of 1781.*

earlier hymn forms. Schiörring was an able musician, however, and his harmonizations, in the form of a figured bass, were fresh and appropriate.
Within the natural limitations of the isometric chorale, the melodic form of
his settings is also admirable. Indeed, many of the older melodies included
in the 1926 *Chorale Book for the Norwegian Church* were adopted without
change from Schiörring.

The next hymnal in the series, the *Evangelical Christian Hymnal*, appeared
in 1798. It reflects the Enlightenment in every way, and later became the
object of rather severe criticism. The companion chorale book was Hard-
enack Otto Zinck's *Chorale Melodies*, published in 1801. The melodic form
of most of Zinck's chorales is virtually identical to Schiörring's. One important exception is the chorale "Only God in Heaven" (example 15).
Schiörring retained the triple rhythm of this old chorale, whereas Zinck

Example 15. H.O. Zinck's isometric version of the chorale "Only God in Heaven" as it appeared in Chorale Melodies *(1801).*

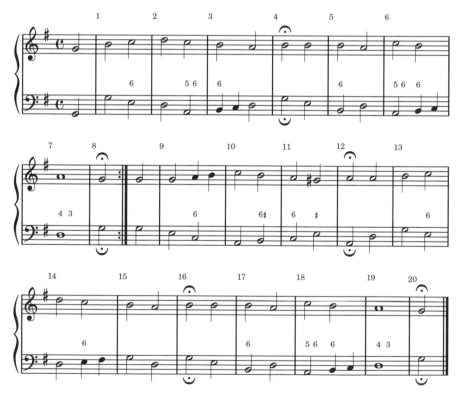

forced even this one into a rigid duple rhythm. It stands as an almost symbolic illustration of the absolute triumph of the isometric chorale. Nonetheless, it must be said that Zinck, too, was an excellent musician in his time. His harmonizations were uniformly good, and somewhat simpler than Schiörring's. He also composed several fine melodies, including such gems as "Now Rises Up the Sun" and "On God Alone." Although in the style of the period, their musical quality is such that they have become a vital part of Norway's hymnody.

Zinck's chorale book was published in two formats: one with the traditional figured bass, the other with three- or four-part settings. It was the last of the chorale books used by the churches in both Denmark and Norway. In 1838 O. A. Lindeman published a Norwegian chorale book, which will be discussed later (see p. 133ff.).

MUSIC SOCIETIES

The first known music society in Norway was in Bergen. Organized in 1765 as the Harmonic Society, it was the predecessor of the modern Bergen Philharmonic Orchestra. It is clear from the names of the founders that the leading families of the city were the driving force in this society. The goal was to cultivate music through concerts and various other means. The first leader of the society was a professional musician named Samuel Lind, but very little is known about him. At the turn of the century the leader was the Bergen town musician, Ole Rödder. Concerts were given at regular intervals, but in general they were open only to the members of the society.

A Society of Music Enthusiasts was established in Trondheim in 1768. For a time it gave a series of what might be called "subscription concerts," but it apparently did not survive for long. It was revived in 1786 as the Trondheim Music Society. Its orchestra presumably numbered about twenty-five musicians, and regular concerts were given. Both Johan Henrich Berlin and Otto Jacob Grundt (the town musician) were members of the society, but it is uncertain who was the leader of the group. Berlin withdrew after the first year, but concerts evidently continued to be given until near the end of the century.

Information regarding music societies in Oslo is somewhat sketchy. Concerts had been given fairly regularly before 1750, and these continued throughout most of the remainder of the century as well. From the 1780s onward an organization called the Music Society sponsored the performances, usually with the town musician as leader. In some years, however, the leadership was taken over by itinerant foreign musicians. In the winter of 1784–85, for example, the concerts were led by the Swedish court musician Johan Gottfried Zaar, who was living in Oslo at the time. Peter Höeg, the town musician, was then an elderly man and probably unable to exercise the leadership duties.

In addition to these performances, which usually were given weekly during the concert season, there was a significant increase in the number of solo concerts. Most of these were performed by traveling foreign musicians who were assisted, as a rule, by Norwegian artists or the music society's orchestra. Among the better-known solo performers were J. G. Zaar and the famous German musician Georg Joseph Vogler, often referred to as Abbé Vogler because he was an ordained Catholic priest. Vogler gave several organ recitals in Our Savior's Church in Oslo during the 1790s, and he gave recitals in Trondheim as well. During one of his stays in Norway he composed a set of variations on the Norwegian folk tune "The Lonely Sunday Evening"—possibly the first time a Norwegian folk tune was employed in a larger composition.

Although the system of town musicians continued throughout this period, the tradition began to decline. Claus Fasting, who attended a 1781 performance by Bergen's town musician and his assistants, wrote an imaginative critique of the performance that provides at least a glimpse of the quality of their music at that time:

> On the occasion of a friend's birthday recently I was invited to listen to a concert played by these poor devils. Considering the torment he thereby subjected me to, I wish this friend had never been born! Six fellows with spears and bows tramped into the room and readied themselves for battle. They tuned each instrument—that is to say, they dragooned it . . . Every note was like the grunt of a pig, the howl of a wolf, etc. Only the bass player had a prominent role and he played to the very end so as not to forget the smallest part of his repertoire.

Although the account exhibits a certain amount of poetic license, the criticism undoubtedly had some foundation. A 1780 royal decree pertaining to the town musicians pointed in the same direction. It asserted that "the music that prevails everywhere in the towns is mediocre, and in most places it is remarkably poor," and prescribed that in the future the town musician posts should be filled by members of the royal chapel orchestra in Copenhagen—provided the positions were sufficiently attractive to persuade these musicians to accept them. The decree had little effect, however. The institution of town musician was already becoming obsolete, and during the first decades of the nineteenth century it was abolished altogether.

Nonetheless, the decree did have one important result. After the death of town musician Höeg in Oslo in 1795, Frederik Christian Groth was appointed. A fine violinist, he came from the royal chapel orchestra and immediately took over the leadership of the weekly concerts supported by the Music Society. When an independent orchestra was organized in connection with the establishment of the Dramatic Society in 1799, Groth became its director as well. He was also one of the founders of the Music Lyceum in 1810.

Another of the fine town musicians of this period was Lorents Nicolai Berg, who worked in Kristiansand. In 1782 he published an instruction book entitled *First Lessons for Beginners in the Art of Instrument Playing*. It shows that, as a well-trained musician himself, he perceived the need for better training for others and wished to assist in bringing it about.

In addition to concerts by the music societies, programs consisting of Passion music were often presented during Lent. This was a continuation of an old tradition that prevailed in several of the larger cities. A German musician named Bendix Friedrich Zinck (a brother of H. O. Zinck) lived in Oslo in the 1760s and, among his other accomplishments, gave the first performance in Norway of the Passion oratorio *The Death of Jesus* by Carl Heinrich Graun (1701–59). Zinck later returned to Germany and became court musician in the little town of Ludwigslust. For many years the cantor Isak Andreas Flintenberg (1735–1813) presented the Passion concerts in Oslo. He was greatly respected in his time and evidently was an able musician. He composed music for several occasional cantatas, but none has survived.

The responsibility of the Latin school choirs to participate in the church services was terminated around 1800, by which time the practice had gradually become obsolete. Church music in general appears to have been on the decline in many places toward the end of the eighteenth century. The decline undoubtedly reflected the situation in the Church as a whole, which had been greatly weakened by the Rationalist trend that not only surrounded it but also to a considerable extent had penetrated its own ranks.

There is, however, one bright spot in the generally dark picture during this period: several of the larger churches in Norway acquired fine, large organs. Norway was fortunate to have at this time a most able organ builder, Gottfried Heinrich Gloger, a German craftsman whose training included an apprenticeship with the renowned Danish organ builder Lambert Daniel Carstens. In 1746 Gloger secured a license to build organs in Norway, and in succeeding years he produced a number of excellent church instruments. The most important example of his work still in existence is the splendid organ façade in the Kongsberg church. It is impressive proof of his skill.

Unfortunately, Gloger's financial sense was not as well developed as his talent as an organ builder. He earned little from his instruments and tried unsuccessfully to make a living as an organist. In his last years he was or-

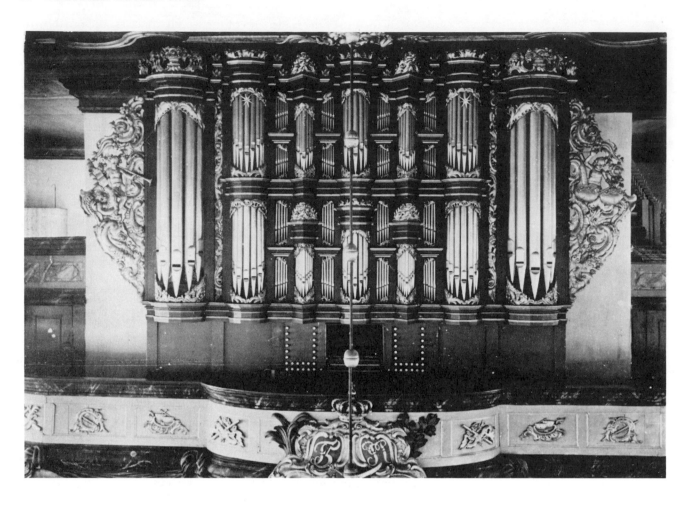

Façade of the organ in Kongsberg designed and built by Gottfried Heinrich Gloger. (Riksantikvariatet, Central office of historic monuments and sites, Norway)

ganist in the church at Stiklestad, playing the new organ he had built. Upon his death in 1779 a newspaper reported that he was "in such poverty that without the assistance of compassionate people he could not have been buried."

COMPOSERS BETWEEN THE BAROQUE AND CLASSICAL PERIODS
There were few composers in Norway during the latter half of the eighteenth century. Indeed, only one is worthy of mention: Johan Henrich Berlin (1741–1807). A son of town musician and organist Johann Daniel Berlin (see page 52), he was one of three brothers who became organists. He received his music education at an early age and soon began performing as a substitute organist. At the age of seventeen he was appointed organist of the Hospital Church in Trondheim, and in 1772 he moved to a similar position at Our Lady Church. In 1788, following the death of his father, he

became organist at the Trondheim cathedral and continued in that position until the year he died.

Berlin's life was relatively uneventful. He lived quietly and peacefully in the city of his birth, and evidently took no long journeys. The music education received from his father was augmented, no doubt, by the collection of books on music theory in his father's library. There he also found a fairly good selection of scores. We know, for example, that he became acquainted with some of Haydn's symphonies while he was still quite young.

Little is known of Berlin's activities other than his work as an organist. Although he gave organ recitals only occasionally, he must have been an industrious composer. In 1788 and 1791 he advertised that he had compositions for sale to anyone who might be interested, and both times he included a long list of works. On the basis of these lists and other sources, a comprehensive catalog of his works has been created comprising a total of fifty-nine compositions.

Unfortunately, only a few of these compositions have been preserved. Among them are two symphonies, one sonata for violin, cello, and keyboard, a sonata, a sonatina, and some smaller works for keyboard, and an occasional cantata. It is difficult to assign an exact date to any of these works; all may be relatively early compositions, with the sonatina for keyboard and the sonata for violin, cello, and keyboard appearing to be the most mature.

The sonatina is in two movements, both in B-flat major. It begins with a slow, Haydn-like introduction (example 16) that is thematically independent of the rest of the piece. One notes the "expressive" chromaticism, also the use of the Italian augmented sixth chord (measure 6) that was so characteristic of the Viennese Classicists. The introduction ends on a dominant seventh chord, thus preparing the way for the tonic of the Allegro that follows.

The Allegro has the characteristics of a Rococo sonata movement. It is rather short, but it has a principal and a secondary theme with the usual shifts of tonality, and a clearly identifiable exposition and recapitulation.

Example 16. J.H. Berlin, "Adagio" and beginning of "Allegro" from the Sonatina.

There is no development to speak of, however—just an eight-measure bridge between the exposition and the recapitulation. The last movement is also an Allegro; it has the character of a lively Rococo dance.

Judged by his surviving works, Berlin was a typical transitional composer who stood at the border of Viennese Classicism. Whether he moved ahead to a more mature Classicism in his later years is not known. His works occasionally appeared on the programs of the Music Society in Trondheim, but they do not seem to have been played much elsewhere. Berlin evidently received little encouragement as a composer. He probably felt rather isolated as an artist, and it is possible that his production waned accordingly in his later years.

Another Norwegian-born musician, Israel Gottlieb Wernicke (1755–1836), settled in Denmark, where he made an important contribution as a music teacher. Born in Bergen, he received his initial music education from his father, who was an organist. In the 1770s he went to Copenhagen, where he first gained attention as a keyboard virtuoso. Even at that early date he showed a then-unfashionable preference for the works of J. S. Bach. Later he received a stipend that enabled him to continue his music studies in Berlin, where he became a pupil of Johann Philipp Kirnberger. Kirn-

Manuscript of Wernicke's reversible canon.

berger, a former student of Bach, was also one of the foremost music theorists of his time. Thus Wernicke received a solid, traditional training in counterpoint.

After his return to Copenhagen he served for a short time as leader of the royal chapel orchestra. He was not successful in this position, however, because he had no interest in the music then in vogue. He was immersed only in Bach and had no appreciation for anything else—not even for the music of Haydn and Mozart, which was then beginning to gain an audience in Copenhagen. Following his release from this orchestral position in 1786, he settled in Kolding where he quickly became a famous music theorist and teacher. Through his teaching he conveyed the Bach tradition to Norway as well as Denmark, for O. A. Lindeman became one of his many students (see p. 133 ff.).

Wernicke was also a composer. During his brief tenure as orchestra leader he both arranged and composed music for the stage, but it must all be regarded as mere occasional music of no lasting importance. Of greater interest are a number of keyboard works that have survived. A fugue and some smaller pieces have been published, and there is an unpublished manuscript of a larger work obviously modeled on Bach's *Goldberg Variations*. Wernicke's compositions apparently did not enjoy wide exposure, however.

At the turn of the century, then, the music life of Norway appears to have been rather tepid. The Baroque tradition was virtually extinct, but the new trends that were to take its place were not yet well defined. Church music was at low ebb. With respect to secular music—i.e., concerts by professional artists and by the music-society orchestras—we can perhaps grant that in some places and at some times the performances were of reasonably high quality. We must add, however, that the quality of these performances was at best uneven and often poor. That the music societies were so dependent on amateur players also contributed to a kind of nonchalant attitude toward music. A glance at the repertoire performed at the concerts shows, however, that the Norwegian musicians of the late eighteenth century, both professional and amateur, followed what was happening in the concert halls on the continent surprisingly well. Symphonies of Haydn and Mozart appeared on the programs relatively early alongside the works of the best-known Rococo composers.

The intense interest in drama often led to cooperation between the music societies and the drama societies. A number of plays were performed with incidental music, but comic opera attracted the greatest interest. Imported from Denmark, where it was popular, this combination of comedy and music held a conspicuous place in Norway's music life at the end of the eighteenth century. Its light and entertaining character seems to have been ideally suited to the musical taste of the period, and it became in many ways the favorite form of expression for the music societies. Most comic operas were disarmingly simple and easily accessible, and their uncomplicated plots demanded little of the listeners. Understandably, the dominating role of this genre affected other types of music as well; indeed, the style put its stamp on Norwegian music well into the nineteenth century.

6

Folk Music

"Norwegian folk music" is a broad topic that includes many different types of vocal and instrumental music of highly varying ages and origins. It is difficult to draw precise boundaries between that which is and that which is not true folk music, but we can identify a few characteristic features.

In the folk-music tradition, the originator—the composer—is usually anonymous. This, however, is a rule with so many exceptions that it cannot be used to define the concept.

Folk music is often closely tied to its milieu, and it is preserved primarily through so-called "oral" transmission. That is to say, this music, whether vocal or instrumental, originally was learned and preserved from generation to generation simply by hearing, without the help of notation or other means. Only in modern times has this changed.

Such a method of transmission often produces a stylistic modification that, over time, transforms melodies ("foreign" melodies, for example) to make them conform to the stylistic principles of the tradition into which they are being incorporated. Through this process, several different variations may eventually develop from one original melody.

A folk-music tradition is often conservative, and thus can keep alive some very old musical features. Specimens of varying ages and with significant stylistic differences may commonly live side by side in the same tradition.

It is difficult to date the origins of Norwegian folk music. What can be said with some confidence is that its oldest parts have their roots in the late Middle Ages, i.e., in the thirteenth century when the old Norse culture was in full flower. Indeed, some elements may be even older. We cannot ascertain, however, whether any of these melodies in their present form have been handed down to us unchanged. The systematic gathering and notating of folk music did not get seriously under way until the 1840s, and on the basis of these and later sources one cannot confidently say anything about how the melodies were sung six or seven hundred years ago.

We can, however, distinguish to some extent between older and newer "strata" in Norwegian folk music. Both the age of the text (see p. 79) and the tonal and melodic characteristics of the music can tell us something about the age of the melody. Our present interest is primarily in the older stratum. That a living folk-music tradition can still be found in many places in Norway today is testimony to the surprising durability that such a tradition can have, especially when it is connected with certain functions of daily life. More often than not, when this connection is lost the tradition quickly dies out. An example of this phenomenon may be seen in the Norwegian *seter* melodies, the herding music used by shepherds and shepherdesses in the mountain meadows. Very few of these melodies remain. The methods of caring for farm animals have changed, and in most of Norway the way of life associated with the mountain meadows has given way to modernity. Thus the need for *seter* melodies has ceased, and they have quickly been forgotten. Some types of folk music, however, are still alive. One finds, for example, religious folk songs, lullabies, and *stev* (a type of monostrophic folk poetry in specific metrical patterns sung to traditional and mostly very old tunes). The best examples of instrumental folk music still flourishing are Hardanger-fiddle music and *slaatter* (dance tunes with certain distinctively Norwegian characteristics) for violin.

It is customary to divide folk music into vocal and instrumental categories, but one cannot make a hard and fast distinction between the two. It is not unusual to find *slaatt* tunes being sung, and the many examples of *slaatt-estev* associated with certain *slaatter* show that the music of the latter was also a part of the vocal repertoire. And of course it is not uncommon to play vocal melodies on instruments.

Norwegian folk music is associated for the most part with farm life, closely reflecting its various everyday facets. Some of it is specifically associated with *seter* life. This is true of the *lokk*, the *huving*, and the *laling*, all of which will later be discussed in detail. The instruments that are especially associated with the *seter* tradition are the *lur* (similar to an alpenhorn), the billy goat's horn, and the flute. In the farm homes one finds lullabies, whereas *stev*, folk ballads, and religious folk songs are used both in everyday life and on festive occasions. The same can be said about the jew's harp and the *langeleik* (an ancient stringed instrument of the zither type, with one fretted melody string and three to seven drone strings). Originally the *langeleik* was widely used at country dances. For this purpose, however, it has been supplanted by the fiddle—the Hardanger fiddle in some areas, the conventional violin in others.

VOCAL FOLK MUSIC

Norwegian vocal folk music is customarily divided into five groups as follows: a) *lokk*, *huving*, and *laling*; b) lullabies; c) *stev*; d) folk ballads; and e) religious folk songs.

Lokk, *huving*, and *laling* are related by virtue of the manner in which they are sung, but they serve different functions. A *lokk* ("call") is a herding song, a song or shout used to call the farm animals. One finds different kinds of herding songs corresponding to the different kinds of animals: cow calls, sheep calls, and goat calls. A *huving* or *laling*, on the other hand, is a song or shout the purpose of which is to make contact with other people—another herder some distance away, for example, or the milkmaid on the nearby mountain meadow. A *huving* may in some instances be associated with a particular herder. A *laling* is a type of *huving*, one in which the syllable "la" plays a prominent role in the text. In some parts of Norway (Österdalen and Trysil, for example) a *laling* is a kind of antiphonal song consisting of a short melody that is repeated over and over. Example 17 is a typical *laling* from Trysil, a district in eastern Norway.

Example 17. A laling from Trysil.

From a musical standpoint, the herding songs are of greatest interest. They are often on the boundary between a song and a shout, and do not have a definite musical form. One could say that they are improvisations on a group of selected musical motives (which is true of other types of Norwegian folk music as well). That is not to say that their structure is completely arbitrary, however. O. M. Sandvik, in his book on the music of Österdalen, gives an excellent description of a cow call:

That the herding songs are so difficult—and in some respects impossible—to write down in standard notation is owing to a number of things. First there is an introductory shout: "Oh, poor fellow!" or something of the sort, which is uttered in a deep, constricted, throaty voice. And one cannot characterize this sound any more closely than that: one cannot specify the precise *notes* on which the words are to be sounded. One wonders what these sounds are supposed to signify. Is it a mimicking of the cow's bellowing? Something similar to a mother's tender, awkward baby talk to a small child? Is it an attempt to talk "animal language"? After these sustained sounds, which are somewhat similar to the sounds of a horn, there follows a series of short, piercing shouts as the milkmaid calls the individual cows by name. These can begin in the highest pitch and leap up and down in intervals of a seventh, an octave, or a ninth. Last of all comes the part that is genuinely musical: the winding, coloratura-like run, sung in the finest voice the singer can muster. And the difficulty in reproducing this latter is owing partly to the often irregular intervals ("quarter tones") and partly to the peculiar, free rhythm. (*The Music of Österdalen*, p. 34)

What Sandvik is here describing is an old form of cow call. In later examples one often finds the cow call combined with elements derived from other types of folk music—such things as melodies that sound a bit like folk ballads, sometimes with words, or *slaatt* motives, usually sung without words. There is no doubt that the herding song goes back many, many years. Its close association with a form of animal husbandry that existed in Norway for a thousand years suggests that it may be very old, and the tonal and melodic characteristics of many of the old herding songs confirm that they are among the oldest parts of Norway's folk-music tradition.

Lullabies that belong to a living folk-music tradition can still be found in some parts of Norway. Most consist of very simple melodies, typically of limited range and often constructed from a small number of motivic formulas used for improvisation. Example 18*a* is representative of this type. The arrows in 18*a* indicate notes that are to be sung slightly higher (↑) or lower (↓) than notated.

Not all lullabies are so simple, however. Some are quite complex, with a broader range and more varied use of motives. Example 18*b* is a lullaby from Gudbrandsdal. It is obviously derived from example 18*c*, an "Alleluia" melody from the St. Olaf music (see chapter 3).

Here there appears to be a connection between a Gregorian melody and a lullaby. This is an example of how easily "foreign" material enters into lullabies. Catharinus Elling has given an account that demonstrates the phenomenon:

Example 18. Two lullabies (a and b), the latter of which is evidently derived from an old melody (c) that is part of the "St. Olaf" music.

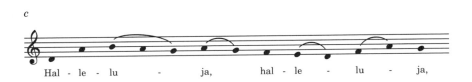

When I have asked about such things, more often than not I have gotten the answer that they didn't really have any lullabies: they just sang whatever occurred to them, i.e., whatever songs they happened to know; so it must have been some strange cradle songs that those little screamers heard now and then. (*Norwegian Folk Music*, p. 58)

Some of the texts appear to be addressed to the singer or perhaps to other listeners rather than to the child who is supposed to be going to sleep. Many lullabies, however, have texts that are appropriate to the situation: simple nursery rhymes or meaningless combinations of words and syllables.

Stev (defined on p. *7a*) are typically grouped according to the subject matter of their texts: wisdom *stev*, love *stev*, nature *stev*, and so on. Several thousand of these little poems are extant, but all are sung to a relatively small number of melodies. As a matter of fact, only about forty melodies are known today as traditional *stev* melodies. *Stev* have demonstrated considerable durability. In some parts of Norway, especially in Setesdal and Telemark, one still finds a flourishing *stev* tradition. The old practice of *stevjast*—a party game in which the participants compete with one another in the improvisation of *stev*—has, however, died out. Magnus Brostrup Landstad's description of this practice as he observed it in Telemark in the middle of the nineteenth century tells what it was like:

> To *stevjast* has been and to some extent still is a common practice at parties. When the food has been cleared from the table, two or three large ale bowls, each holding as much as four gallons or more, are brought in and set on the table that stands near the wall of the living room. The guests, especially the old ones, sit around this table while the young folks dance, the women at one end of the room and the men at the other. The ale bowls are painted in many colors and bear inscriptions as well, and in each of them is floating a carved duck that has been fashioned into a kind of dipper. The server now dishes up the strong, foaming ale into little painted wooden bowls, about the size of a large cup, called "einskjelskoppar." Each person is to empty one of these. This is called "drinking einskjells" ("einskjells" means individually, one for one), and while this is going on the drinking *stev* begin. Each participant makes his contribution to the general merriment, and the women at the lower end of the table are often dragged into the *stev* competition as they reply to the *stev* thrown their way by the men. It is usually the old *stev* that are used in this situation; they are generally considered more noble than the new ones, which often refer in a clever but malicious way to well-known people and circumstances. Because of these characteristics, the latter are disdainfully called *rennestev* ["running *stev*"], a designation that suggests both the ease with which they are created and the unceasing way in which this poetry, that has its source in the people themselves, daily gushes forth. One can, in this connection, apply the old saying, "fluvius manat, manetque aeternum," or as it is said in the well-known *stev*:

O say, this verse is without an ending,
For 'tis a river this verse is sending;
And say, this verse by itself is made,
It just came floating upon a wave.
(*Norwegian Folk Ballads* I, p. 366)

This colorful account presents an example of *stev* in the form of an antiphonal song. In such cases the *stev* were sometimes improvised on the spot, but more often they were well-known *stev* selected because they fit the occasion. Small changes of various kinds were often introduced into the *stev* in order to adapt them to the immediate circumstances. There are a few examples in which several *stev* constitute an interrelated group—a *stev* series—but most *stev* are independent entities.

Landstad, in the above account, mentioned two types of *stev*: old *stev* and new *stev*. They differ from one another in both age and form (rhyming pattern). Both have four lines. In old *stev* the second and fourth lines rhyme with one another. In new *stev* the lines of each couplet rhyme with one another. In both types, the rhyme depends on identity of vowel sound (assonance). In old *stev* the first and third lines typically have four stressed syllables, while the second and fourth lines have three. In new *stev* each line has four stressed syllables. The number of unstressed syllables can, however, vary in both types of *stev*, and the melodies are varied accordingly to accommodate the number of syllables in the text.

The exact age of each of these two types of *stev* is uncertain. The old *stev* is closely related to the folk ballad and can be traced back to the thirteenth century, where one finds examples of *stev* in the sagas. The new *stev*, with its two similar halves, is simpler and thus may in fact be more "primitive" in form. Such a conclusion corresponds well with the characteristics of new *stev* melodies, which contain an abundance of archaic elements. The forty or so known melodies exhibit great variation: the range of each varies from a fourth to a twelfth. The manner in which they are sung also varies considerably, with great differences not only from one singer to another but even from one *stev* melody to another as performed by the same singer. The performance is often strongly marked by rubato, but insofar as the meter is clear one can observe that each half line (two stressed syllables) gets one shorter and one longer beat.

Though the date of origin of the new *stev* is highly uncertain, it is clear that it virtually supplanted the old *stev* during the nineteenth century. For the past hundred years or so the new *stev* have figured more prominently in the living folk-music tradition. Example 19 is a new *stev* from Setesdal as transcribed in modern times. The arrows indicate notes that are to be sung slightly higher (↑) or lower (↓) than notated.

Example 19. A "new stev" from Setesdal.

Folk ballads constitute perhaps the least homogeneous group of the several types of Norwegian folk music enumerated above. It includes songs originating as far back as the thirteenth century, as well as newer songs that may be no more than a hundred years old. In general, however, when we speak of "folk ballads" we mean songs that have their roots in the Middle Ages, and that have survived in oral tradition through the centuries until they were finally written down during the nineteenth and twentieth centuries.

Folk ballads appeared in Norway during the thirteenth and fourteenth centuries. They appeared at the same time as the folk-ballad dance ("chain dance"), which quickly became popular. It was first taken up as something fashionable among the rich and noble, but soon made its way to the common people as well. That the folk ballad was introduced into Norway from the outside implies, of course, that many of the ballads are translations of foreign texts. That is not unusual, for the subjects of many folk ballads are common to many countries. With respect to the melodies, however, there has been less borrowing from other countries. Often the same folk ballad is sung to different melodies in various regions of the country.

Folk ballads are usually classified further according to the content of the text: sacred ballads, heroic ballads, troll ballads, historical ballads, knight ballads, or humorous ballads. There are no strictly musical differences among these groups despite the great contrasts in the character of various texts. Variations in age are sometimes reflected in the melodies, however: the older melodies use scales and melodic turns different from those in the newer ones. The systematic study of these differences has only begun, however, and for the present we are obliged to depend to a large extent on conjecture and informed guesswork when we try to determine the age of a given melody.

The old folk ballads exhibit two dissimilar structures, one consisting of four lines and the other of two. The four-line stanza has the same structure and rhyming pattern as the old *stev* (see above, p. 79). In addition to these four lines, however, the folk ballad usually has a refrain or, as it is also called, an "end-*stev*." The two-line form is a rhyming couplet. Often there are four stressed syllables in each line, but sometimes just three. The refrain of the two-line version is usually divided in two. The first part comes between the first and second lines of each stanza and is called the "in-*stev*" or "between-refrain." The second part comes after the second line and is called the "end-*stev*" or "after-refrain." There are also examples of two-line stanzas in which the two lines are sung consecutively and the entire refrain comes at the end. The content of the refrain often has some connection with that of the ballad, but there are cases in which it stands by itself. The usual reason for this is that the refrain has been imported from some lyrical introductory stanzas that were often sung before the ballad, with its narrative content, has begun.

The old folk ballads were already in the process of being forgotten by the middle of the nineteenth century when efforts were first made to get them transcribed. For that reason, many of them have been preserved only in fragments. This is unfortunately the case with the "Dream Ballad," the most distinctive of all of Norway's medieval folk ballads. It is Norway's most important "sacred ballad," i.e., religious ballad dating from the pre-Reformation period. It tells the story of Olav Aasteson, who is supposed to have slept from Christmas Eve until Epiphany and to have had visions of both heaven and hell. Regarded as the finest extant example of medieval Norwegian poetry, it has literary parallels in many "vision" poems dating from the thirteenth century, but it is developed in a unique way. The "Dream Ballad" as we know it today is the result of the restoration efforts of Moltke Moe, and the origin of the piece has been a matter of considerable dispute. Nonetheless, the parts that have been preserved give us some idea of the poem's original structure. In a series of powerful pictures we are shown the souls' fate after death, the Day of Judgment—and, in a brief glimpse, the eternal blessedness. The religious background of the "Dream Ballad" is Catholic Christendom somewhat modified by popular folk belief and intermingled with a number of elements from old Norse mythology.

All of the stanzas of the "Dream Ballad" consist of four lines followed by an "end-*stev*." In order to counteract the monotony that would otherwise result in so long a poem, however, and also to give emphasis to the images in the text, four different refrains are used in the various parts. The first part, which introduces the narrator, Olav Aasteson, has the refrain: "And it was Olav Aasteson, / He who so long had been sleeping." In the second part, where Olav tells of his long journeys, the refrain is: "The moon is shining / And the roads are so wide and long." The third part tells of the great strife on the Day of Judgment, and here the refrain is: "In the Hall of Tribulation / The judgment shall be rendered." The fourth part tells of the reward for good deeds, and the refrain is: "The tongue is speaking / And truth replying on Judgment Day." The last stanza rounds off the account and harks back to the beginning:

> Old and young men together,
> They listen with keen attention;
> Yes, it was Olav Aasteson,
> Now he has told of his vision.
> And it was Olav Aasteson,
> He who so long had been sleeping.

We know of five melodies, each with several variations, that have been used with these stanzas. The four melodies that are usually associated with the "Dream Ballad" are given in a normalized form in example 20. (Actually, these constitute only three melodies, since the last is a variant of the first.)

a

Example 20. Melodies associated with the "Dream Ballad."

b

c

18. So kom eg meg at vot - no dei, der i san - ne brun - no blå, men Gud skaut det i hu - gjen min: eg ven - de meg der - i - frå. Fyr må - nen skin' og ve-gjin-ne fal - la vi - e.

d

21. Eg var meg i au - rom hei-mi i man - ge næt-tar og trå; det veit Gud i him - me - rik, hos-si mang' ei nau eg såg. I brokk sva - lin der skal do - men stan - de.

When old *stev* are sung, variants of one or another of the "Dream Ballad" melodies often are used. This is possible because the four-line folk ballad has the same metrical form as the old *stev* when the refrain is omitted. This is also why there has been a certain intermingling of stanzas from the "Dream Ballad," from other four-line folk ballads, and from old *stev*. A number of stanzas from the "Dream Ballad" have survived as *stev*, and in the few cases in which large sections of the ballad have been preserved in the tradition, the authentic "Dream Ballad" stanzas are usually intermingled with some old *stev*. This melodic (and metrical) relationship between old *stev* and the "Dream Ballad" obviously confirms the antiquity of both.

It is difficult to state with confidence how old the "Dream Ballad" melodies—in the form that we know them—really are. Their motivic richness and wide range give evidence of a highly developed melodic style. The tonal characteristics are indeed archaic and do not exclude an origin as far back as the Middle Ages. A living tradition is capable of preserving such material virtually unaltered through many generations.

A stanza from "Horpa" (also called "The Two Sisters") is given below as an example of the two-line folk ballad (example 21). It is one of Norway's best-known troll ballads; parts of it are found in various places throughout the southern part of the country. The text is sung to several different melodies, the one given here being from Vest-Agder. (The text means: "Sister speaketh to sister thus: By the sand, we will go down to the Sjoar River, the billow carries so fair a woman from land.") As is usually the case, the refrain is divided in two: "ved sande" is the "in-*stev*" and "baara berre so vent eit viv ivi lande" is the "end-*stev*."

Example 21. A stanza from the folk ballad "The Two Sisters."

Many newer songs of various ages are often described as folk ballads as well. Examples of such songs are Edvard Storm's *Songs of the Valley People*, which were written near the end of the eighteenth century. They quickly became very popular and soon entered the folk-song tradition. This collection includes such well-known songs as "The Lonely Sunday Evening" and "Elland and the Fairy Maiden," and it is not known whether Storm wrote his verses for preexistent melodies or the melodies were written for his verses. The same is the case with the well-known song "Astri, My Astri," the words of which were written by Hans Hanson (1777–1837). The melody to which these words are most often sung is very similar to F. C. Lemming's song "The Happy One," and it is not known whether Lemming's song is older than the folk song or vice versa. In any case, it has a somewhat "modern" sound. All these newer melodies are in the standard major or minor keys, whereas the older melodies generally make use of various modes.

"Religious folk songs" is the designation usually given to melodies with Protestant texts (in contrast to the "sacred ballads," which have Catholic texts). Religious folk songs differ in two ways from all other kinds of folk music. First, the authors of the texts are usually identifiable; indeed, the text is often based on well-known hymns. Second, the melodies are often a modification of old, familiar melodies, such as old chorales. In the folk-music tradition, however, these melodies have been changed in varying degrees, sometimes to such an extent that they are almost unrecognizable.

An example of significant alteration of this kind is found in the melody for "We Now Implore the Holy Ghost" as L. M. Lindeman heard it in Valdres in 1848 (example 22). This example may be compared with the

Example 22. "We Now Implore the Holy Ghost" as heard by Lindeman in Valdres in 1848.

melody in its old form (see example 4, p. 33). It is not at all obvious that this is the same melody, but behind the many melismas one can discern the original contours. It is characteristic of such songs that the phrase endings are the same, i.e., that the cadences have been preserved. There is also a certain correspondence between the first notes of each phrase, but it falls short of complete regularity.

Another and later case in which less alteration has occurred is given in example 23*a*. It is the melody "Come, All Ye Creatures God Hath Made" as sung in Gudbrandsdalen some years ago. The melody first came to Norway by way of Erik Pontoppidan's hymnal, and in Niels Schiörring's chorale book (see p. 63) it has the form shown in example 23*b*.

a

Example 23. Two versions of the melody "Come, All Ye Creatures God Hath Made."

Opp all den ting som Gud har gjort, hans her - lig - het at pri - se. Det

min - ste han har skapt er stort og kan hans makt be - vi - se.

b

Though the alteration in this case is less radical, one can recognize many of the same characteristics: long notes broken up into several shorter ones, concluding notes in each phrase normally unchanged (not in the first and third phrases this time, however), and a liberal use of slurs and embellishments. In addition, there are some rhythmic peculiarities that are difficult to indicate in our system of notation: the rhythm is irregular, with beats of unequal length. This, however, is characteristic of much Norwegian folk music and will be discussed more fully later.

In some cases one cannot point to an "original melody" for a given religious folk song. This can happen for a number of reasons. In some cases perhaps the original melody has been forgotten. It is known, for example, that the renowned pastor and poet Petter Dass (1647–1707) often wrote his hymn texts to preexistent melodies. It is not always easy to determine which melody he had in mind, however, and it may be that many of them have survived only in a modified form. It is also likely that there are some cases in which original melodies have been written for preexistent hymn texts. No "model" has been found, for example, for the well-known religious folk song "The Great White Host." It has a fairly "modern" sound, and

An ordinary lur. *(Norsk Folkemuseum)*

cannot be old. The same is true of many of Norway's most popular religious folk songs.

INSTRUMENTS

The instruments that were in use in the Norwegian folk-music tradition until the time when the systematic collection of folk music began are as follows: a) *lur*; b) billy goat's horn (*bukkehorn*); c) willow flute (*seljefløyte*); d) "fairy flute" or wooden flute (*tussefløyte*); e) jew's harp; f) *langeleik*; g) Hardanger fiddle; and h) conventional violin, sometimes called "flat fiddle" (*flatfele*). In addition to these a three-cornered harp was also used with folk music; several exemplars can be seen in various museums in Norway (see p. 13), and we know that in some places they were used until after 1800. The tradition has died out, however, so we do not know exactly how this harp music sounded.

Also worthy of mention are the hand organ (hurdy-gurdy) and the keyed harp. Both played fairly important roles in the folk music of the other Scandinavian countries, notably Sweden, but in Norway they appear to have been rarely used. In fact, there is no concrete evidence that they were ever a part of the Norwegian folk-music tradition, although a few examples of keyed harps found in Norwegian museums suggest that the instrument has not been totally unknown. There also was a time, especially during the 1800s, when the clarinet was used as a folk-music instrument. It first came to Norway as an instrument used in military bands, and in this way became known in many communities. It never played an important role in the Norwegian folk-music tradition, however.

The *lur* is a typical herding instrument of medieval (see p. 11) or perhaps even earlier origin. It is made out of two hollowed pieces of wood that are fitted together and secured with birch bark or some other material. The result is a rather narrow pipe, usually about a meter or more in length (occasionally nearly two meters). The thinner end is formed into a small mouthpiece against which the lips are pressed, and it is blown like a brass instrument—a trumpet, for example. The range of an ordinary *lur* is from the second to the sixth or eighth partial tone. It usually is not capable of producing the fundamental tone because of the narrowness of the pipe, but some of the longer *lur*s can produce sounds up to the eleventh or twelfth partial tone. A *lur* having a fundamental tone of F (middle C = c^1) would be capable of producing the series of pitches shown in example 24.

Example 24. Pitches that can be sounded on a lur *having a fundamental tone of F.*

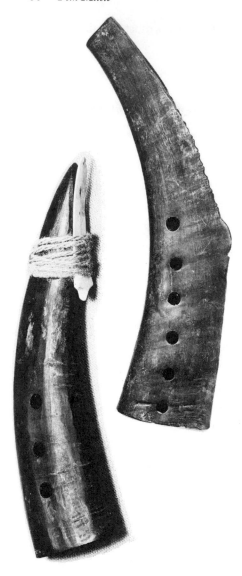

Billy goat's horns. Note that one has a flat piece of wood attached to the end to create a "clarinet mouthpiece." The other is played like a brass instrument. (Norsk Folkemuseum)

The billy goat's horn (or ox's horn) is another herding instrument. There are two main types. One type is blown like a brass instrument, with the lips pressed against a small mouthpiece that has been carved out of the end of the horn. The other type is cut diagonally at the end, and a thin piece of wood, usually juniper, is then attached. The result is a mouthpiece similar to that of a clarinet. A billy goat's horn without finger holes can produce just one pitch, as the instrument is too short to make use of overtones. The more developed billy goat's horn, however, typically has three or four finger holes, and may have as many as eight. Through the use of finger holes and the "stopping" technique (like that used by French horn players today) it is possible on a good billy goat's horn to produce quite remarkable melodies. It requires, however, a highly developed playing technique. The billy goat's horn can also be traced to the Middle Ages (see p. 11) and earlier and is known in many cultures throughout the world.

Willow flutes are made from the bark of a willow tree. They can be made only in the spring, when the sap rises up so the bark can be removed undamaged from the branch. Moreover, since a willow flute lasts for only a week or two (and even then it must be dipped in water from time to time), these instruments can at most be used during about two months of the year. Nonetheless, willow flutes were used in many parts of the country and appear to have played quite an important role in Norwegian folk music.

Willow flutes are from forty to eighty centimeters long. They are held like a transverse flute, being sealed at the left end (from the perspective of the performer). The tone is produced by blowing across an aperture near this closed end. The willow flute has no finger holes, but it can be played as either an open or closed pipe (the latter when the open end of the flute is covered with a finger). Because the pipe is relatively narrow it can easily be blown in such a way as to produce the higher partial tones. When played open, the willow flute is typically capable of producing sounds from the third to the seventh or eighth partial tones. When played closed, it sounds only the odd-numbered partial tones. The partial tones that are ordinarily played in the "closed" mode are those from the seventh to the thirteenth. A willow flute with the fundamental tone C^1, therefore, would be capable of producing the pitches shown in example 25.

Example 25. Pitches that can be sounded on a willow flute having a fundamental tone of C^1.

Wooden flute from Vaagaa made ca. 1910. It is quite similar to a European recorder. (Norsk Folkemuseum)

When the partial tones for open and closed flute are arranged in sequence, the result is a series of pitches that has a certain similarity to a major scale. It differs from the latter, however, by virtue of having a lowered leading tone (b-flat[1] in C major), a raised fourth (a pitch that lies between f[2] and f-sharp[2] in C major), and a slightly lowered submediant (a pitch slightly below a[2] in C major). This scale is a consequence of the juxtaposition of two series of partial tones and is generally called the "natural" scale. (Acoustic measurements have shown that in practice the notes of the willow flute vary somewhat from the "natural" scale.) The notes above the thirteenth partial tone are rarely used (a[3] in the above example), but it is technically possible to produce sounds up to the octave (c[4] in the example) and even higher. It seems likely that the willow flute also has a long tradition in Norwegian folk music, but we have no definite evidence of its use in ancient times.

"Fairy flute" is one of many names given to a type of wooden flute that in most respects is constructed in the same way as an ordinary recorder. The number of finger holes can vary somewhat, but the later examples of this instrument typically have seven finger holes in addition to a thumb hole. It seems to have played a rather modest role in the Norwegian folk-music tradition, but evidently was known in many parts of the country. Its age as a folk-music instrument has been a matter of some dispute, but apparently it can be traced back to the medieval bone flute (see pp. 14–15).

The jew's harp has also been a familiar instrument throughout much of Norway. It consists of a bent metal frame with a steel ribbon that oscillates between the "arms" of the frame. The frame is held against the player's teeth in such a way that the steel ribbon can swing freely between the teeth in the upper and lower jaws. The steel ribbon, which is set in motion by plucking it with one's finger, produces just one note that sounds continuously as an unvarying "pedal point," but with one's mouth as a resonator it is possible to strengthen individual partial tones to create melodies. The pitch is changed by varying the size of the oral cavity; it is relatively easy to produce

Jew's harp with storage case. (Norsk Folke-museum)

sounds as high as the sixteenth partial tone and above. The intervals from the eighth to the sixteenth partial tones yield the "natural" scale. The jew's harp has been used throughout much of Europe and Asia. In Europe it has certainly been known at least since the mid-Middle Ages. Exactly when it began to be used as a folk-music instrument in Norway is not known.

The *langeleik* is probably the oldest stringed instrument to have survived to the present day in the folk-music tradition of Norway. At one time it was in use throughout much of the country, but in recent years it has been played primarily in the Valdres region.

The *langeleik* could be described as a cross between a zither and a dulcimer. It has a hollow, oblong resonator made of wood over which are stretched seven or eight (rarely more) strings. Often three of these strings are short, the others long. The string nearest the player is the melody string, and under it lie small frets of wood or metal. The other strings provide an accompaniment in the form of a constant single chord (drones).

The *langeleik* is plucked with a plectrum. Some of the strings (including the melody string) are tuned to the same note (the tonic), the others usually in such a way as to form a major triad or open fifths (see example 26*a*). It

a

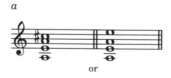

or

Example 26. Tuning of the langeleik: a *shows the tuning of the drone strings,* b *the intervals on the melody string.*

b

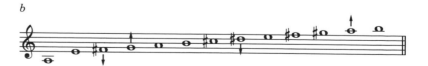

Langeleik *from Jevnaker dated 1709.*
(Norsk Folkemuseum)

is evident from the placement of the frets on many of the older *langeleiks* that the scale that was played on them was quite different from our diatonic scales. In 1848, L. M. Lindeman reported the series of pitches shown in example 26*b* as the typical *langeleik* scale. Later research has shown, however, that the scale varied somewhat from one instrument to another.

The date of origin of the *langeleik* is uncertain. The earliest mention of this instrument in Norway occurs in connection with a report concerning a legal action against Bishop Anders Arrebo, where it is stated that a *langeleik* was used in a wedding at Hemna in South Tröndelag in 1619. The reference, moreover, was such as to suggest that it was thought of as a common instrument. There is no evidence, however, that the *langeleik* was known in Norway as early as the Middle Ages.

The Hardanger fiddle is Norway's most important folk-music instrument at the present time. In recent years it has shown some tendency to expand its domain at the expense of the conventional violin, but what might be called the "original" Hardanger-fiddle territory includes Telemark, Numedal, Hallingdal, Valdres, and the west coast area from Hardanger to Sunnfjord. In Setesdal the Hardanger fiddle came into use in the late 1800s, in Nordfjord and in parts of Möre and Romsdal rather recently.

The main feature of the Hardanger fiddle that distinguishes it from the conventional violin is the presence of four (occasionally five) supplementary strings that go through an opening in the bridge and under the fingerboard. These are not touched while the instrument is being played, but vibrate sympathetically. The bridge is a little lower than that of the conventional violin, also a little flatter to facilitate the playing of double stops. The older type of Hardanger fiddle is somewhat smaller than the conventional violin. Nowadays the Hardanger fiddle is usually tuned slightly above concert pitch. Normally the A string is tuned from a minor second to a minor third

above a^1. Modern Hardanger fiddles are a little larger than the old ones, and the shape of the body is more like that of the conventional violin. Inlays of mother-of-pearl and bone on the fingerboard as well as decorations on the instrument's body give the Hardanger fiddle a distinctive appearance but have little or no acoustic significance.

The Hardanger fiddle is tuned in a variety of ways (see example 27). "Normal" tuning is a, d^1, a^1, e^2—the same as for the conventional violin except that the lowest string is tuned a major second higher. The sympathetic strings are then tuned d^1, e^1, f-sharp^1, a^1, and the Norwegian dance tunes (*slaatter*) that are played to this tuning are normally in the key of D major.

Conventional violin tuning—g, d^1, a^1, e^2—is also used on the Hardanger fiddle. It is called the "lowered bass" tuning, and the sympathetic strings are then tuned d^1, e^1, g^1, a^1. This tuning is typically used to play *slaatter* in the key of G major. Another fairly common tuning is called "troll" tuning: a, e^1, a^1, c-sharp^2 in the stopped strings and c-sharp^1, e^1, f-sharp^1, a^1 in the sympathetic strings. Another variation of "troll" tuning has a, e^1, a^1, e^2 in the stopped strings. "Troll" tuning is generally used to play tunes in the key of A major. There are some indications that "troll" tuning used to be common. The similarity between this tuning and that of the *langeleik* is striking.

Yet another tuning, which is used in the playing of a few *slaatter*, has the lowest string tuned to f and the sympathetic strings to d^1, e^1, f^1, a^1. This tuning is called "Gorrolaus" ("very loose"). All together we know of more than twenty different tunings for the Hardanger fiddle; skilled fiddlers commonly employed a dozen or more of these.

The fact that the Hardanger fiddle is tuned in so many different ways creates problems when we try to transcribe Hardanger-fiddle music in ordinary notation. The music is usually written as it would be played with conventional violin tuning—for example, an open bass string is always written as g even though in "normal" Hardanger-fiddle tuning it would sound as a. Only if the Hardanger fiddle were tuned with a "lowered bass" (i.e., like the conventional violin) would the music sound as it is written. With any other tuning, one or more of the strings would behave like "transposing instruments." Example 28 contains two *slaatter* excerpts showing the dif-

Hardanger fiddle made by Erik Johansen Helland in 1850. It belonged to Norway's most famous Hardanger-fiddle player, Torgeir Audunsson ("Myllarguten"). (Norsk Folkemuseum)

Example 27. Alternative ways of tuning the Hardanger fiddle.

Example 28. Differences between notation and actual sound of the Hardanger fiddle, depending on its tuning.

ference between the notation and the sound that is actually produced. In the first example the Hardanger fiddle has "normal" tuning, in the second "troll" tuning.

The Hardanger fiddle in its oldest form may date from the 1600s. The oldest such fiddle in existence is thought to be the so-called Jaastad fiddle. It is signed "Ole Jonsen Jaastad 1651," but there is some question about the accuracy of this dating. The oldest Hardanger fiddles whose age is not a matter of dispute all date from the period after 1750. These have varying numbers of sympathetic strings, but the number stabilized at four during the 1800s.

The oldest literary reference that may possibly allude to a Hardanger fiddle is in Christen Jenssön's *Norwegian Dictionary*, a collection of words in the Sunnfjord dialect published in 1646. The passage reads: "A farmer fiddle is called 'Haar-Gie'." Whether "Haar-Gie" refers to a Hardanger fiddle is doubtful, however, since it seems unlikely that the instrument was known in Sunnfjord at so early a date. It is more likely that "Haar-Gie" refers to a fiddle with strings made from the hair of a horse's mane or tail (*haar* = hair).

A source that may provide information about the Hardanger fiddle—or, more correctly, about Hardanger-fiddle music—was published by Johann Mattheson in 1740 under the title (here given in translation from the original German) *The Netherworldly Outdoor Concert in Norway*. The document

Title page of Johann Mattheson's The Netherworldly Outdoor Concert in Norway, *1740.*

contains two accounts of "netherworldly music" in Norway. The more important of these, a report from town musician Heinrich Meyer to Mattheson, is as follows:

In the year 1695, after I had been an apprentice for about three months, it happened that before Christmas we were rehearsing the music that was to be played during the holidays. As usually happened on Saturdays, a farmer came with milk and butter to my teacher, Paul Kröplin, in Bergen. While the farmer was waiting for the money for his goods, he stood and listened intently to our rehearsal. Then my teacher said laughingly to him, "Today you aren't going to get any payment for your butter and milk, for you have heard enough music to pay you amply." "Ha," said the farmer, "I hear this sort of thing played much better every Christmas Eve on the mountain a short distance from my farm." They all laughed at the farmer—my teacher, the cantor, and the organist, all of whom were present at the rehearsal—and said to him that what he heard must really have been something different. "Yes," he said, "and if you gentlemen come up this evening (it was Christmas Eve) you will soon be convinced that what I am saying is true." When the farmer had left, and the rehearsal was concluded, the three men were sitting there in amazement and talking together about what the fellow had said, wondering how such a thing could be possible. They finally agreed that they would go and see for themselves, and they did. When it was about midnight the farmer came and said that it was now time, if we wanted to come to the mountain. I had to go along and bring a bottle of brandy, for it was very cold. After we had sat on the mountain for a quarter of an hour or so the cantor, the organist, and my teacher the town musician grew impatient and asked the farmer how long they had to sit there, but he told them that they had to be patient a little longer.

Soon thereafter we began to hear music. First a chord was struck, then a note was sounded to tune the instruments. Then came the prelude on an organ, and immediately afterward we heard regular music with voices, cornets, trombones, violins, and other instruments, but we couldn't see anything. After we had listened to this for a long time the organist became so angry about these invisible musicians and underworld virtuosos that he cried out, "Listen! If you are of God, show yourselves, but if you are of the devil, be quiet!" Suddenly it was quiet. The organist collapsed as if he had been struck and began to foam at the nose and mouth. In this condition we carried him into the farmer's home, laid him down, and covered him well; the next morning he revived and came to his senses. We all then hastened back to Bergen, arriving in a short time; for the place where we had heard this strange concert was only one Norwegian mile [about eleven kilometers] from the city, near the Birkeland Church.

What I have written here is completely true, and the melody (which appears on the title page) I have heard with my own ears in a mountain near the city of Bergen in Norway, and above all others have preserved in memory. This is verified by my own signature.

Heinrich Meyer

The extent to which Meyer is being truthful, and the size of the ensemble the farmer may have assembled to make fools of the city musicians, cannot be determined with certainty. One possible explanation, however, is that the entire "concert" was performed by a Hardanger-fiddle player, and that the charged atmosphere (midnight, out-of-doors, secluded), with the help of the brandy, set their imaginations in motion. If that is the case, the Hardanger fiddle must have been known as far away from Hardanger as Bergen at the end of the 1600s.

The most interesting part of the account is the melody to which Meyer refers (see example 29). Meyer gives just the melody line, but its structure (two-measure segments with variations of the opening two-measure motive) shows quite clearly that it is a *halling* of the same type that will be discussed later in connection with Norwegian instrumental folk music. This, by the way, is the earliest instance on record of a Norwegian folk melody being transcribed, and it shows that as early as 1695 the *slaatt* music had several of the distinctive features that are most characteristic of Hardanger-fiddle music.

Example 29. The "netherworldly" melody that Heinrich Meyer reported hearing in Norway in 1695.

The Hardanger fiddle probably came into use in Telemark at the beginning of the eighteenth century, and it assumed an important role in the folk

Lur *player. Watercolor by J.F.L. Dreier,
ca. 1812. (Norsk Folkemuseum)*

music of that region. Telemark and Hardanger have long been important centers for both the making and the playing of Hardanger fiddles.

The ordinary violin, or "flat fiddle" as it is often called, is employed in folk
music throughout those sections of the country where the Hardanger fiddle
is not a part of the tradition. It appears to have come into use during the
seventeenth and eighteenth centuries. In some districts there is an old flat-
fiddle tradition that shares many features (with respect to both tuning and
manner of playing) with the Hardanger-fiddle tradition.

INSTRUMENTAL MUSIC

The music played on the instruments described above is rich and varied. It
includes, in addition to *slaatter*, a large amount of other material, including
seter melodies (see p. 74).

The most important *seter* instruments were the *lur* and the billy goat's
horn, but the wooden flute ("fairy flute") and the willow flute were also used
in that setting. The *lur* was much used as a signaling instrument because its
penetrating sound carries for a considerable distance. It was also useful for
scaring away wild animals. The natural limits of melodies for the *lur* are
prescribed by the relatively small number of notes that the instrument is
capable of producing. A typical *lur* melody is limited to the notes of a major
triad, often with the fifth as the lowest note. Here is an example:

Example 30. A typical lur *melody.*

The billy goat's horn, like the *lur*, could be used to sound signals of
various kinds, but with the help of finger holes it could also be used to play
melodies. Some kinds of signal melodies, such as *lalings*, could be either
sung or played. Example 31 is a billy goat's horn melody—a *gukko*—from

Example 31. A gukko *from Österdalen.*

Langeleik *player. (Norsk Folkemuseum)*

Österdalen. A *gukko* is a signal melody similar to a vocal *huving* (see above, p. 75).

The wooden flute with its softer tone was understandably less well suited for sending signals over long distances. If some shepherds nonetheless played them, it was rather to help them pass the time when the weather was nice and the animals were grazing peacefully and required no attention. The wooden flute and the willow flute are capable of playing *slaatter* as well as other tunes, so the repertoire could be quite large. The musicianship of the shepherds was considerable: they had plenty of time to practice!

Slaatter and various other melodies were played on the jew's harp, although *slaatter* are especially associated with the Hardanger fiddle and the conventional violin. In earlier days the *langeleik* was also used to play *slaatt-*

er; it is, perhaps, the oldest type of instrument still in existence used to play such music. Very little remains of the *langeleik* tradition, however.

Vocal renditions of *slaatter* also have a place in the tradition. The *slaatt-estev* and the *slaatt* motives were used in herding and other types of songs. It was also common in the folk-music tradition to accompany dancing with singing. If no fiddler was present, the *slaatter* were sung instead. The words of the appropriate *stev* (see above, p. 74) were then used or, alternatively, the tune was simply hummed or sung without words.

In more recent times, *slaatter* have been primarily associated with the Hardanger fiddle and the conventional violin, and this has had an effect on the music itself. There are important differences between the *slaatter* for Hardanger fiddle and those for conventional violin as well as between the *slaatter* from one district of Norway and those from another. The latter differences are owing in part to the fact that the corresponding dances are performed differently in the various districts.

There are two principal types of *slaatter*, those in triple and those in duple time. Both types have been given different names in different parts of the country. The triple-time type is called a *springar* in all parts of the country where the Hardanger fiddle is in general use. In Gudbrandsdalen it is called a *springleik*; in Österdalen, Tröndelag, and Möre and Romsdal it is called a *pols*.

Despite sharing a basic triple rhythm, however, there are important rhythmic dissimilarities among these dances. The western Norway *springar*, for example, has three beats of equal length and no accent on the first beat, while those of many other districts employ a kind of stylized rubato in which the tempo is constantly varied within single measures, thus resulting in beats of unequal length. A *springar* from Telemark has a long first beat and a short third beat, one from Valdres a short first beat and a long second beat, and so on. These differences obviously are closely related to differences in the movements of the dancers in the several districts.

There are two subtypes of *slaatter* in duple time. One divides each beat into two (or four) parts and is written in 2/4 time, the other divides each beat into three parts and is written in 6/8 time. Both subtypes are represented under the usual *slaatt* names. The most common names for *slaatter* in duple time are *gangar* and *halling*. The *slaatt* tradition includes a large number of *gangars*; this name is used throughout the eastern part of the area in which the Hardanger fiddle is in common use. The *halling* is, or at least used to be, known throughout much of Norway—including both the areas where the Hardanger fiddle was in general use and those where the ordinary fiddle was used—but there are nonetheless fewer *hallings* than *gangars* in the tradition. Musically, there is no clear distinction between the two, but in the districts where both names are used (Telemark, for example) the *hallings* as a rule have a slightly faster tempo than the *gangars*. In the Hardanger-fiddle area of western Norway the duple-time *slaatt* is commonly called a *rull* or *Vosserull*.

Another *slaatt* name occurring in the folk-music tradition is the *brure-marsj* ("bridal march"), of which there are many. They, naturally enough, arc in duple time, and were typically played as the bridal couple walked to or from the church. In duple-time dance tunes the two beats were normally of fairly equal length, but syncopation and phrase contraction (by means of bowing and other devices) often create nonetheless a complicated rhythmic pattern. The Telemark *slaatter*, whether in duple or triple time, are particularly rich in embellishments of this kind.

The folk music for conventional violin also includes a number of newer types of music—waltzes, Rhinelanders, and quadrilles, for example. Many of these melodies have a more modern sound, but in some cases the new dances have been transformed by their association with the older dance forms and in the process have acquired the character of the old folk-music tradition. The best examples of this phenomenon are found in the *slaatt* music of Österdalen and Gudbrandsdalen.

Example 32 is a Hardanger-fiddle *slaatt*, a *gangar* called "The Bay from Förnes." (The symbol / in measures 2, 4, 45, 47, and 49 signifies that the note that follows is to be played a quarter tone higher than notated.) Associated with this tune is a legend that can be traced back to the period after the Black Death plague had ravaged the land. The legend exists in several forms, of which the following one from Rauland, a district in Telemark, is representative:

At Mösstrond one after another died during the Great Plague. They had to haul the corpses home to Raulands church. At Förnes they had a brown horse that was as smart as a human being. If they put a corpse on his back and snowshoes on his feet, he made his way homeward on his own and brought the corpse home to Rauland. There they unloaded the corpse and turned the horse around, and on his own he then went back up to Mösstrond. In this way he made many trips in the winter. But on his last trip he lost one of his snowshoes when he was at the highest point. Then he neighed so loud that he could be heard all the way to Rauland, and people came looking for him. They found him lying in a snowdrift, dead. But they got both the horse and the corpse home to the church. The corpse was buried in the graveyard, and the bay was buried nearby in a little hollow that to this day is called "Horse Hollow." (From Rikard Berge, "Förnesbrunen" ["The Bay from Förnes"], *Norsk Folkekultur*, 1935)

Example 32. "The Bay from Förnes."

It is possible that this *slaatt* is older than the Hardanger fiddle and that it was originally played on some other instrument, such as the *langeleik*. One of the oldest examples we have of the *slaatt* for Hardanger fiddle uses "troll" tuning (see above, p. 92), but most use "normal" tuning as in the example on pages 100–101. Like most Hardanger-fiddle *slaatter*, this one is constructed from two-measure motives that are repeated several times with variations. Through the use of this variation technique, Hardanger-fiddle *slaatter* are built up into large pieces even though the thematic foundation generally consists of no more than three or four different two-measure motives. The *slaatt* in example 32 is based on four or five different motives, and their variations divide the piece into different sections. The example also shows the liberal use of double stops. The "two-voice" characteristic of many *slaatter* is rooted in a special alternating drone technique, in which any of the four open strings can be used as a pedal point while the melody is played on one of the adjacent stopped strings (see measures 1 and 2, for example). Conventional double stops are also used to some extent to further enrich the sound (as in measures 41–42, for example). The older Hardanger-fiddle *slaatter* were much simpler in format than this; many are constructed out of just two or three motives. The development toward larger and more complex forms has occurred over a long period of time, and many fiddlers have played a role in this development. Among those who have contributed most, however, are the nineteenth-century fiddler Torgeir Audunsson (Telemark) and two from the twentieth century: Halldor Meland (Hardanger) and Torkjell Haugerud (Telemark).

The flat-fiddle *slaatter* generally exhibit a different construction. The basic units are frequently 4 + 4 measures, so melodies are typically developed within an eight-measure span. Each *slaatt* typically consists of two, or occasionally three, eight-measure units. These are repeated, but the variation technique employed in the Hardanger-fiddle *slaatter* plays a much smaller role here and double stops are rarely used.

Example 33 is a *springleik* from Lom in Gudbrandsdalen. It consists of two eight-measure units that are repeated.

Example 33. A springleik from Gudbrandsdalen.

There are flat-fiddle traditions with a more archaic stamp in which double stops are used with some frequency. These traditions also use some of the alternate tunings shown in example 27. It is possible that these features are derived from a tradition that served as a common starting point for both the Hardanger-fiddle and the flat-fiddle music of later times.

INTERVALS IN NORWEGIAN FOLK MUSIC

Many intervals in Norwegian folk music sound unusual to one who is not familiar with the tradition. When compared with the music that most are accustomed to, which is based on the diatonic major and minor scales, this music often contains intervals that are quite different. There has been considerable discussion about their exact measurement and why they are used in folk music. These issues have not been resolved, but some basic principles have emerged.

Three folk-music instruments—the *lur*, the willow flute, and the jew's harp—produce the "natural" scale (though both the *lur* and the willow flute diverge slightly from this scale). On the other folk-music instruments, where either the maker of the instrument or the performer determines the intervals, there is great variation in the intervals and scales that may be used. The same is true of vocal music. What is most clear in all of this is a tonal framework that, depending on the range of the melody, may comprise a fourth, a fifth, or a combination of both for a full octave. Within this framework the half step is rarely used. The "building blocks" of the music seem to consist, rather, of whole steps and approximate three-quarter steps.

BEARERS OF THE TRADITION

It is characteristic of all folk art that the content of the tradition is regarded as the common possession of all who stand within that tradition, and that the creators of the individual works of art are as a rule anonymous. Nonetheless, individuals can have great significance both for the development of the tradition and for its continuation. There can also be no doubt that some works of art within the tradition must have been created by outstanding artists. In other cases, individuals have served as the ones who brought together several different strands of the folk tradition. They have carried the tradition further, sometimes in a modified form, and in so doing have played an important role in the development of the tradition.

We know the names of some of these "bearers of the tradition" in Norway. In the area of vocal folk music, Anders Eivindson Vang (1795–1877), a schoolteacher in Valdres, should be mentioned. He knew a large number of folk melodies, especially religious folk songs, and it was from him that L. M. Lindeman got the eighty-six melodies based on tunes in Thomas Kingo's hymnal, later known as "Kingo tunes."

Olea Cröger (1801–55), the daughter of a clergyman, was both a tradition bearer and a collector of tunes, most of which she transcribed using a system of numbers. Because she grew up in Telemark in close contact with the folk-music tradition, she became interested at an early age in both folk music and folk poetry, and as a music instructor at Kviteseid teacher's college from 1832 onward she had a good opportunity to become acquainted with much of the Telemark tradition. She worked with both M. B. Landstad and L. M. Lindeman. The music for Landstad's *Folk Ballads* of 1853 (see below) is based to a large extent on her work as a collector, though it was Lindeman who was responsible for the publication.

The most famous tradition bearers, however, were instrumentalists, especially Hardanger-fiddle players, and the most eminent of these was Torgeir Audunsson (1801–72). He was affectionately known to his countrymen as "Myllarguten" ("the miller boy") and was something of a celebrity throughout much of Norway during his lifetime, thanks in part to Ole Bull, who arranged concerts at which both of them appeared. Myllarguten also gave his own concerts in a number of places in southern Norway, and in 1862 in Copenhagen. Undoubtedly one of the best performers of all time on the Hardanger fiddle, he was renowned for his skill in improvisation, taking a simple *slaatt* and developing it into a larger and more complex form. He was the person chiefly responsible for the development of the Hardanger-fiddle *slaatter* that occurred in the mid-1800s.

Myllarguten was not alone, however, and his significance consists not only in what he himself did but also in the influence he had on other im-

portant fiddlers of the day. The most important of these were Haavard Giböen in Telemark (1809–73) and Per Bolko in Hardanger (1795–1876). Two who made their mark in the latter half of the nineteenth century were Ola Mosafinn from Voss (1828–1912) and Knut Dahle from Telemark (1834–1921). It was from Dahle that Johan Halvorsen (in 1901) transcribed the *slaatter* that became the basis for Grieg's *Norwegian Peasant Dances*, Op. 72.

The attempt to transfer Hardanger-fiddle music to the concert hall created an offshoot from the authentic folk-music tradition. Myllarguten, who was the first to give such concerts, held quite firmly to the old tradition, but some of those who came after him modified their *slaatt* playing to adapt it to the new situation. The best-known performers in this group were Sjur Helgeland from Voss (1858–1924) and Lars Fykerud from Telemark (1860–1902). They wrote *slaatt*-like program music ("*slaatter* for listeners") with an obvious eye to what they thought the public wanted to hear. Titles such as "The Three Dairy Maids on Vikafjell" and "Sunday on the Seter" are typical of this genre.

The flat-fiddle players have not attracted as much attention as the foremost Hardanger-fiddle players. Nonetheless, some of them had great importance in advancing the tradition. The best known of these was Loms-Jakup (1821–76), a gifted performer who left his mark on the music of Gudbrandsdalen.

THE COLLECTION AND PRESERVATION OF NORWEGIAN FOLK MUSIC
The systematic collection of Norwegian folk music got seriously under way in the 1840s. Prior to that time, only a few melodies had been published. The earliest example we have of a Norwegian folk melody appearing in print is the "netherworldly" *halling* (see above, p. 93) printed by Johan Mattheson in 1740. The next example is found in a French treatise by J. B. de La Borde, *An Essay on Ancient and Modern Music* (1780). The treatise contains twenty-one Norwegian folk melodies, all of which were obtained from Johann Ernst Hartmann—the person who had given La Borde the old Icelandic melodies (see p. 15). During the period 1812–14 there appeared a large Danish collection of folk melodies, *Selected Danish Songs from the Middle Ages*, edited by Rasmus Nyerup and Knud Lyhne Rahbek. The publication also included a number of Norwegian melodies. It is sometimes difficult to determine which melodies are Norwegian and which Danish, but at least thirty of them are of Norwegian origin.

The first important collection of folk melodies to appear in a Norwegian publication appeared in 1840 in Jörgen Moe's *Collection of Songs, Folk Ballads, and Folk Poems in Norwegian Peasant Dialects*. L. M. Lindeman contributed fifteen melodies to the collection. The following year Lindeman published the first of his own collections, *Norwegian Mountain Melodies*, consisting of sixty-eight melodies arranged for piano. At this time Lindeman had not yet initiated a systematic gathering of folk music. He presumably had learned of many of these melodies in the course of casual contact with those who knew them—on trips to the countryside, for example, or through students from the rural areas whom he had met in Oslo. There is also reason to believe, however, that he had gotten some of them from his father, O. A. Lindeman, who at an earlier time may have transcribed some of the folk melodies that he had happened to hear.

During the years 1842–45 another large Danish collection appeared: A. P. Berggreen's *Folk Songs and Melodies*, a three-volume work. It contained piano arrangements of folk music from several countries, including fifty-nine Norwegian melodies. It is interesting to note that Ole Bull also played a role, albeit a modest one, in the collection of folk music: he contributed five melodies, arranged for piano, to Chr. Tönsberg's book, *Norwegian National Costumes* (1851). In 1853 an important collection by M. B. Landstad appeared, *Norwegian Folk Ballads*, which included 114 melodies contributed by L. M. Lindeman. They were printed without harmonization, and included an important contribution by Olea Cröger. It was also in 1853 that Lindeman began to issue what was to become the great standard collection of Norwegian folk melodies: *Older and Newer Norwegian Mountain Melodies*. The publication of this multi-volume work continued until 1867, by which time it contained 592 melodies. In 1907 a supplementary volume containing forty-four additional melodies arranged for piano was published by his son, Peter Lindeman. In addition, L. M. Lindeman published several smaller collections of folk songs in choral arrangements for various combinations of voices. Some of these will be discussed later (see p. 153).

A few later collections are worthy of mention. In 1861 Berggreen published a new and greatly expanded edition of his collection. Each country included in the collection was now given its own volume, the Norwegian volume containing a total of 175 melodies. The first important collection of Hardanger-fiddle music was published by Carl Schart in 1865: *Seven Norwegian Slaatter for Hardanger Fiddle*, transcribed as played by Myllarguten. Another collection did not appear until 1905, when Johan Halvorsen published the seventeen *slaatter* that became the basis for Grieg's *Norwegian Peasant Dances*.

After Lindeman, a number of individuals participated in collecting Norwegian folk music. Catharinus Elling (1885–1942) and Ole Mörk Sandvik (1875–1976) made especially important contributions in this area. Among the many collections that have been published, two are of fairly recent date. One is the standard seven-volume collection of Hardanger-fiddle music, *Norwegian Folk Music. Series I: The Hardanger-fiddle Slaatter*, published from 1958 to 1981. The other is *Norwegian Religious Folk Songs*, published in two volumes (1960, 1964) by O. M. Sandvik. These collections cover two important areas of Norwegian folk music, but in other areas much work remains to be done.

In recent years new technology has assisted in the collection of folk music. The tape recorder has been of especially great importance for folk-music research. Both the Norwegian State Radio and the Norwegian Folk Music Collection now have large libraries of folk tunes recorded on tape.

Sandsærdig Beretning 36

om den store Ildebrand i Drammen,
hvorved 350 Huse nedbrændte og over
5000 Mennesker bleve husvilde.

Cover of a skillingsvise *that purports to be a "truthful account of the great conflagration in Drammen in which 350 houses burned down and over 5000 people were left homeless."*

POPULAR SONGS (SKILLINGSVISER)

Lars Roverud, a nineteenth-century musician and music teacher, published in 1815 a short essay entitled *A Look at the Condition of Music in Norway* in which he reported the following:

> There are many good voices, especially female voices, among the common people, but nearly all of their songs are of inferior quality. The texts of most of their songs are mainly written by schoolmasters (especially the kind whose whole sense of worth has to do with black buttons and buttonholes) and quite simple people, as a consequence of which they are rather mediocre. Most of those that I have heard were:
>
> 1. Love songs—plaintive jeremiads over the unfaithfulness of a boy or girl in relation to his or her lover . . . presented in a disgusting manner.
> 2. Preaching—for example, the worthlessness of good deeds with respect to salvation, if only one can receive God's grace in the last hour, that one shall despise this world, etc.—everything according to the taste of Hans Nielsen Hauge [the leading representative of Pietism in Norway] and his followers.
> 3. Occasional songs—such as: at the execution of a delinquent; about the mountain avalanche; about the great flood, etc.—all of one and the same character in both melody and text.

The type of song that Roverud discusses with so little respect probably includes some traditional folk ballads, but at least the third category in the list shows that at that time there existed a type of song that is not usually considered a part of the folk tradition. These "occasional songs" belong to another genre, namely *skillingsviser* ("penny songs"; also called "street songs"). *Skillingsviser* (singular form = *skillingsvise*) are song texts that were published in individual pamphlets. They were called *skillingsviser* because they were most often sold for a *skilling*, a coin of little value. There is evidence that in other European countries this type of song is almost as old as the art of printing, some being published as early as the sixteenth century. They achieved general popularity in Scandinavia only in the latter half of the eighteenth century. In Norway it was not until the nineteenth century that there were enough print shops to handle the local production.

Among the older *skillingsviser* are a number of texts that are derived from the folk-song tradition. Various religious folk-song texts also were printed as *skillingsviser*. Many of the religious texts of Petter Dass, for example, were published as *skillingsviser* in the eighteenth and nineteenth centuries.

Although a clear distinction cannot be drawn between *skillingsviser* and traditional folk ballads, there are important differences. While folk ballads as a rule are of anonymous origin, and are formed in and by the tradition, *skillingsviser* are in most cases songs that have been written by one person who frequently is identified on the publication. *Skillingsviser*, unlike folk ballads, are often connected with local circumstances and events. This is of course especially true of "news" *skillingsviser* based on current local events.

Skillingsviser rarely included a melody. Frequently one was simply referred to a familiar melody to which the new words could be sung. Sometimes the sellers of the pamphlets tried to teach a new melody, appropriate to the *skillingsvise* they were selling, to the buyers of their product. The fact that *skillingsviser* were not firmly tied to certain melodies resulted in local adaptations that had a much greater impact on the melodies than on the texts.

There probably was some connection between the folk-music tradition and the *skillingsvise* melodies, but because the great wave of *skillingsviser* in Norway occurred only in the nineteenth century it is evident that these melodies generally have a much more modern stamp than the traditional folk ballads.

It is not easy, however, to determine exactly what melodies were used for many of the *skillingsviser*. When the collecting of Norwegian folk music was begun in the nineteenth century, *skillingsviser* were not included. They were evidently considered uninteresting and of less value. Only in recent years has there been a serious effort to track them down.

In the older *skillingsviser* (those published before 1800) most of the texts are religious. During the nineteenth century these were supplanted by love songs and "news" songs. The oldest known example of the latter concerns a huge snow avalanche in Sunnmöre in 1679, in which the buildings on twenty farms were destroyed. The text was written by a clergyman in the area and was printed in Copenhagen in 1681. The genre can be traced forward thereafter to a large number of songs about the sinking of the Titanic in 1912.

Near the end of the nineteenth century the *skillingsvise* tradition acquired a new offshoot: the railroaders' songs. The task of building railroads throughout the country required enormous manpower, and the work crews moved from place to place bringing their songs with them. Much of this manpower came from Sweden, providing one reason why the Norwegian song tradition in its latest phase is closely related to that of Sweden.

Skillingsviser decreased in importance during the first decades of the twentieth century. The mass media dominated the communication of news, and songbooks replaced the old song pamphlets. Nonetheless, *skillingsviser* constitute an important part of the background for the rebirth of the ballad that is evident again today.

SAMI FOLK MUSIC

The traditional folk music of the Sami people is the *joik*. Only one instrument—the *runebomme*, a kind of drum—has played an important role in their music. It was used by medicine men during religious ceremonies to establish contact with the invisible powers, to cure illness, and to foretell the future. The *joik* was also used on such occasions, and this "heathen" use was the principal cause of its being prohibited by law and threat of punishment after the Christianization of the Sami people was aggressively pursued at the beginning of the eighteenth century. The perception of the *joik* as something evil eventually established itself so deeply in the Sami consciousness that even today it is disliked by many Sami people. The *joik* has survived, however, especially the secular examples of it, and the chief problem now is not whether it is going to die out but to what extent it will be changed by the influence of the modern society that surrounds it.

In its traditional form the *joik* is one of the most archaic vocal artifacts to have survived on European soil. It shares many of its basic features with similar products of other sub-polar peoples, from the inhabitants of Siberia to the Native Americans and Eskimos of North America.

The word *joik* is a transitive verb as well as a noun: a Sami "joiks" his neighbor, his sweetheart, the wolf, the northern lights, and so on. The *joik* is a means of communicating with everything that is important in the life and circumstances of the Sami people. A *joik* is rarely associated with a coherent, descriptive text. There are catch words, hints—just enough to give the listeners who know the *joik* the appropriate associations. Otherwise it consists of singable nonsense syllables, "la" or "lo" for example. With that kind of text it is important that the *joik* be able to convey its meaning by purely musical means, such as melody, rhythm, and manner of performance. This musical meaning is not of universal character: it can be fully understood only by those who stand within the tradition. It appears, however, that Sami people in certain areas (perhaps not all) use wide intervals and a broad melodic range to indicate something large, bold, or energetic. The rhythm is also sometimes varied in accordance with the content of the *joik*— for example, to depict a reindeer at rest or in motion. By the same token the voice can take on a more frenzied sound when it is a pursuing wolf that is being "joiked."

It has often been said that most *joik* melodies are pentatonic. The Kautokeino tradition, however, appears to make extensive use of much more open melodic structures than are usual in pentatonic melodies, often employing intervals of a third, a fourth, a fifth, an octave, and even more. The frequent use of unusual rhythms and meters is also characteristic of the *joik*, as is evident in example 34.

Example 34. A typical joik.

The structure of a *joik* is simple, the basic material often consisting of just four short phrases. The absence of a concluding cadence, however, shows that the melody can and should be repeated as long as one wishes. A phrase-by-phrase analysis of the *joik* shows that the most common patterns are ABAC and ABCB.

7

A Period of Cultural Growth
(ca. 1800–ca. 1840)

The first forty years of the nineteenth century constituted an eventful period for Norway both politically and economically. The years immediately following the turn of the century were beneficial to the national economy and to Norwegian merchants in particular. In 1807, however, Denmark-Norway was drawn into the war between England and France—on the side of the French—with disastrous results for Norway. Aside from Denmark, England was Norway's most important trading partner. The war destroyed any possibility of trade with England, and a British blockade made commerce with Denmark extremely difficult. Crop failures in 1807 and 1808 compounded the problem; the consequent famine caused many to die of hunger. Henrik Ibsen wrote memorably of this in his great epic poem, *Terje Vigen*:

> So time went on and the war began—
> Eighteen-o-nine was the year;
> People still talk of the suffering then,
> Of the hunger, the illness, the fear.
> The British closed off every port in the land,
> Saying, "Test our blockade if you dare!"
> The rich had no meat, the poor had no bread,
> Parents went without food that their young might be fed;
> Death and misery were everywhere.

The war against England, which many Norwegians viewed as a tragic mistake, and the resulting famine gave impetus to the latent desire for independence among Norwegian leaders. In 1813 there was yet another crisis and widespread famine, and for a brief period thereafter, from February to November, 1814, Norway was an independent kingdom with Danish

Crown Prince Christian Frederik as king. The constitution of the kingdom of Norway (modeled after the U.S. Constitution and at that time one of the most liberal in Europe) was formally adopted on May 17, which is celebrated as Norway's most significant national holiday.

Meanwhile, however, Norway's political fate for the remainder of the nineteenth century was being determined by others. At the peace conference in Kiel (Germany) on January 14, 1814, it had already been decided that Norway should be ceded by Denmark to Sweden. Thus not only Sweden but all of the major European powers stood opposed to Norway as a separate nation at this time, and the country was powerless to maintain its independence. The Norwegian negotiators of the settlement with Sweden were very skillful, however, and managed to preserve the main points of the new constitution in the context of the Swedish-Norwegian union. In November 1814 the Swedish monarch, Karl Johan, was declared king of Norway by vote of the Norwegian parliament.

Norway's position within the Swedish-Norwegian union was the subject of a fairly continuous tug-of-war until the final dissolution of the union in 1905, and the debate over this issue throughout most of the nineteenth century greatly strengthened the national consciousness of the Norwegian people. Indeed, it appears that during the nineteenth and twentieth centuries national feelings have played a larger role in Norway than in many other European countries. The insistent demand for a distinctively Norwegian art that emerged during the mid-1800s should be understood against this background.

During the first three decades after 1814, however, the opportunities for cultural expression were severely limited. The talent and strength of the new nation were largely consumed by the task of stabilizing the new political arrangements and by the serious economic crises that then plagued all of Europe. Cultural contributions were, for the time being, necessarily relegated to second place.

In the main, therefore, Norwegian cultural life during the early nineteenth century was primarily a leisure-time activity for members of the upper class. One indication of this is the fact that the music societies continued to function throughout most of this period in much the same way as they had before the turn of the century. Comic opera continued to play a central role for at least the first two or three decades of the century. In general, there were few new musical impulses. From a cultural point of view, Norway remained united with Denmark long after the political breach of 1814. Scattered traces of an independent Norwegian culture can indeed be found, but it was not until the middle of the century that these came together to create a genuine cultural breakthrough.

In the history of continental European music, the period marks the transition from Viennese Classicism to Romanticism. Norway's music life was too underdeveloped to fully reflect the transition, but there are indications that it was affected to some extent by the changes taking place. The influence of Viennese Classicism was clearly evident, for example, in the music of Waldemar Thrane, Norway's foremost composer of the time, and there is some evidence of the influence of Romanticism as well. The strongest influence on Norwegian music, however, was still the legacy of the eighteenth century: early Classicism and the comic opera. It was not until after 1840 that Romanticism began to play a dominant role in Norwegian music.

On the whole, this period in Norwegian music history may be viewed as a kind of midpoint, a time of anticipation. It is filled with the residue of what had gone before together with a few hints of renewal as harbingers of what was to come, but only in rare instances was it able to create compositions of enduring value. It was a time of preparation, a period of growth presaging the rich development and flowering of the latter half of the century.

MUSIC LIFE IN OSLO

In 1814, Oslo (then called Christiania) was suddenly elevated to the status of national capital without being completely qualified to assume the tasks involved. It was a fairly small city: in 1820 its population was about 15,000. To be sure, in 1811 it had acquired a new university, but that too was of modest size. Other cultural institutions in the city at that time consisted of a drama society, established in 1799, and a related music society (the Music Lyceum), established in 1810. The position of town musician continued as before; it was not abolished until the last incumbent, Peder Thuesen, died in 1841. The position no longer was of much importance, however, although the town musician at the turn of the century, Frederik Christian Groth, was an accomplished musician who had considerable influence on the city's music life in the early 1800s. He was the conductor of the Dramatic Society orchestra from 1799, and he probably served in the same capacity with the Lyceum orchestra during its first years.

The Lyceum was the center of Oslo's music life for twenty-eight years; during this time it underwent many changes, including periods of prosperity and periods of decline. It was created, according to its founding document, "for the advancement of music and in order to support needy and generally capable artists." The organizers were men who were well known in the music life of the city, some of whom will be discussed in more detail later. The Lyceum held its first public concert on October 7, 1810. Included on the program were an overture by Peter Winter, a flute concerto by Antoine Benoit Tranquille Bergiguier, and a funeral cantata by Hans Hagerup Falbe.

Hôtel du Nord in Christiania (Oslo). The Music Lyceum gave concerts here during the years 1828–38. (Oslo Bymuseum)

The original governing statutes of the Lyceum are no longer extant, but a small volume containing those of 1813 has been preserved. The introduction to this volume includes the following statement:

> The Music Lyceum is established in order that local devotees of music, by working together, might find an opportunity to develop their talent and, in so doing, improve the public appreciation and taste for art. Since the lack of funds should not hinder any on whom nature has bestowed talent from availing themselves of this organization, its expenses should be defrayed by public concerts; thus its members should pay as dues only what each might freely wish to contribute. Its revenues shall be used to defray the costs of the association's rehearsals and to create a fund for the purchase of music and instruments and, if possible, to pay or provide support for capable musicians. Its purpose is to entertain and to be useful.

It is worth noting that the Lyceum here presents itself as an egalitarian organization whose raison d'être is purely musical. Membership in the association was not to be contingent on economic resources or social standing. Moreover, the statutes explicitly stated that social activity was not even a secondary consideration. The association was to hold both public and private concerts, and the rules dealing with the attendance of members at both rehearsals and concerts were very strict.

Little is known of the Lyceum's development during its first years. Lars Roverud, a member, was rather critical in a document written in 1815:

> [The Lyceum] now concerns itself almost exclusively with giving comic operas for a paying public . . . Sad to say, one misses the spirit and feeling that should permeate this entire organization. It has a fairly adequate number of instrumentalists and female singers, but one cannot help noting the serious lack of male voices.

It appears from the Lyceum's statutes that the leadership was divided between two individuals: the instructor (*instruktör*) and the leader (*anförer*). "The instructor serves as the conductor and the leader as the concertmaster," according to the statutes. The division of duties between the two is not entirely clear, however. The customary practice at that time was for the orchestra to be conducted by a leader who usually also played first violin. Presumably the primary task of the instructor was to rehearse the vocal parts, and possibly to conduct performances of vocal music with orchestra. It appears from later statutes of the Lyceum that the leader's position gradually assumed priority.

The Lyceum's first leader seems to have been town musician F. C. Groth, but Waldemar Thrane assumed the position soon thereafter. Thrane was, in any case, the leader as early as 1815, and after returning in 1818 from his studies in Paris he served continuously in that capacity until illness forced his retirement in the autumn of 1828. Thereafter Ole Bull was leader for a short time, and he was succeeded in 1830 by a German musician, August Schrumpf, who held the post until the organization was disbanded in December, 1838.

It is far more difficult to ascertain who served as the Lyceum's instructors. Apparently the incumbents came and went much more frequently than did the leaders. H. H. Falbe probably served as the first instructor, at least on occasion. He was an extremely busy man, however, and others must have assisted him. Both Lars Möller Ibsen and the Swedish musician Otto Wetterstrand served as paid instructors, and perhaps also Lars Roverud.

The programs of the Lyceum consisted largely of popular comic operas, some by lesser-known French and some by Danish composers. Usually they were presented in cooperation with the Dramatic Society. The concert programs also included overtures and opera extracts from the works of Spon-

Home of the Christiania Theater from 1837 to 1899. (Oslo Bymuseum)

tini, Cherubini, and later Rossini. Representing the Germans were primarily Ludwig Spohr and Joseph Mayseder (violin virtuoso and composer), and occasionally Carl Maria von Weber. The Viennese Classicists were represented by several symphonies and oratorio arias of Haydn as well as a few overtures and an occasional opera extract by Mozart. Two symphonies of Beethoven were presented, but the record does not state which.

An important part of the work of the Lyceum was to support other artists giving concerts in the city. A number of musicians, both Norwegian and foreign, gave concerts "with the kind assistance of the Music Society."

It is generally agreed that the Lyceum enjoyed its best years from 1819 to 1828, while under the leadership of Waldemar Thrane. During this period it played an important role in the city's music life. Thereafter the fortunes of the society steadily declined until its dissolution.

Meanwhile the city had established a permanent theater. The Swedish actor and theater director Johan Peter Strömberg (1772–1834) had made an abortive attempt to start a theater in Oslo as early as 1810. Although he obtained official permission to open a public theater in the city, nothing came of the idea at that time. He renewed his permit in 1827, however, and

the Strömberg Theater gave its first performance on January 30, 1827. It soon became evident that Strömberg was not the right person to lead the undertaking, and after a year and a half he was obliged to give up the directorship. The theater was then taken over by a committee consisting of some of the city's most prominent men, and the Danish actor Jens Lange Böcher was engaged to provide the necessary leadership.

Even during Strömberg's brief tenure the theater had a resident orchestra, and it continued after the reorganization in the autumn of 1828. Waldemar Thrane was its leader from the beginning, but early in 1828 he quit because of a disagreement with Strömberg. That autumn, following the reorganization, he resumed the post but had to resign before the reopening of the theater because of illness. When the new Christiania Public Theater gave its premiere production on October 23, 1828, it was the young Ole Bull who served as substitute leader of the orchestra.

Bull left the city in 1829 and was briefly succeeded as leader by the violinist Jacob Töstie, who served until August Schrumpf was appointed to the position in the spring of 1830. The theater soon added comic operas and even serious operas to its repertoire, and a vocal instructor was engaged whose duties included rehearsing the chorus and giving the actors the necessary training in singing. It appears that as early as 1828 Otto Wetterstrand was appointed as vocal instructor. He was succeeded in 1829 by L. M. Ibsen, who held the position until the Danish musician Poul Diderich Muth-Rasmussen was installed in 1837. Both Schrumpf and Muth-Rasmussen were replaced by Friedrich August Reissiger in 1840.

The theater undertook fairly demanding productions during this period. The repertoire included Étienne Nicolas Méhul's *Joseph and His Brothers*, Daniel François Auber's *Fra Diavolo*, François Adrien Boieldieu's *The White Lady*, and Mozart's *The Abduction from the Seraglio* and *Don Giovanni*.

Amateur musicians continued to play a large role. By all accounts the foremost of these was the cabinet minister Hans Hagerup Falbe (1772–1830). Falbe was born in Copenhagen. His father was of German extraction and his mother was Norwegian. He matriculated at the university in 1787, where he studied law, and was subsequently appointed to a position in the Danish government. During the period 1792–95 he took an extended trip abroad. Upon returning to Copenhagen he held several high positions, and in 1809 was sent to Norway with the title of councillor of state. In 1814, when Norway won its independence from Denmark, Falbe chose to remain in Norway. He became a Norwegian citizen, and in 1822 became cabinet minister.

All that is known about Falbe's music training is that he learned to play the keyboard at an early age. In Copenhagen he participated in the activities of the music association as a member of the Royal Music Academy, which included in its membership some of the city's foremost professional musicians, such as Friedrich Kunzen and Claus Schall. It is quite possible that Falbe received instruction from one or more of these. By 1809, when he came to Norway, he had already produced several compositions and was well known in music circles in Copenhagen. As early as 1795 or so a number of his songs and cantatas were performed in the Royal Music Academy, and around the turn of the century several of his dances were published. In 1800 he wrote his most popular work, a humorous orchestral tone poem entitled *The Night*. It is really a set of dances with such titles as "The Night's Peacefulness," "The Watchman's Cry," and "The Conflagration." He also wrote several larger works during his Copenhagen period including a cantata, *The Lord's Prayer* (1807), and a comic opera, *The Anglomaniac* (1808), both of which were performed and evidently well received there.

Upon arriving in Oslo, Falbe immediately became the center of local music activities. As early as December, 1809, he composed a prologue (see below) entitled *The Hope for Peace or the Triplet Sisters of the North*, and he was among the founders of the Lyceum in 1810. Most of his compositions after he came to Norway were cantatas and other occasional pieces. Fourteen cantatas and seven prologues have been preserved. The terms "cantata" and "prologue" here denote the same type of composition: a work of several movements for choir, soloists, and orchestra. Some works have been lost, including such larger pieces as a *Theme and Variations for Bassoon and Orchestra* that was performed in 1813, and a comic opera entitled *The Privy Councillor*, with text by Henrik Anker Bjerregaard, that was performed in 1829. Three songs from the latter were printed and have been preserved.

Falbe also wrote a number of large instrumental works. A symphony and a complete string quartet have been preserved as well as fragments of two other string quartets. They are not dated but probably were written after his arrival in Oslo. The Lyceum needed such works, and the only compositions by local composers on their concert programs were those of Falbe and Thrane.

Falbe's larger works reveal both his strength and his weakness as a composer. A general characteristic is their lack of organic structure. The symphony, which comprises four movements, is a good example. The first movement consists of a slow, Haydn-like introduction followed by an Allegro in somewhat abbreviated sonata form. In the introduction several fine motives are strung together without any relationship between them. The ensuing Allegro is rather freely treated, with the inclusion of new melodic material both in the development and in the sharply abbreviated recapitulation. In short, a symphonic use of motivic material is lacking, giving the movement a dilettantish cast despite the fact that in other respects it shows the composer to be an experienced musician. Harmonically the movement is quite simple, yet solid and rather impressive; it makes effective use, for example, of secondary dominants. The orchestration, which borders on that of early Romanticism, is good and represents the most modern feature of his style. He called for an orchestra of the same size as that required for Haydn's and Mozart's late symphonies, but he assigned a more important role to the wind instruments than was customary at the time.

Thus Falbe's larger instrumental works generally show that his structural point of departure was not primarily the style of the Viennese Classicists, but rather the overtures of contemporary comic opera, where one often finds the loose formal construction that characterizes, for example, the first movement of his symphony.

Among the few surviving songs from Falbe's comic operas is a Romance from *The Privy Councillor* (see example 35). The designation "romance" signifies a piece of melodious music, usually lyrical and somewhat sentimental

Example 35. H.H. Falbe, "Romance" from the comic opera The Privy Council- lor.

in character, of the kind often encountered in the vocal and instrumental compositions of Viennese Classicism and early Romanticism. The term is also used in connection with both serious and comic opera and occurs in several of Falbe's cantatas and prologues.

The Romance given in example 35 demonstrates Falbe's ability as a melodist. The music is fluid and pleasant to the ear; it has a kind of Mozartian elegance and grace, even though it is considerably simpler and more superficial than analogous works by Mozart. As is typical in comic opera, rests sometimes occur in the middle of a melodic phrase, often within words (see the vocal part in measure 20). Otherwise the song moves easily and naturally.

Falbe's most successful compositions were his many dances. A total of eighty-eight have been preserved, some in print and some in manuscript. In these small forms structural weaknesses are less conspicuous, and his fresh melodic talent comes to the fore. The dances were very popular during his lifetime and were played frequently well into the nineteenth century.

Lars Möller Ibsen (1786–1846) must also be considered an amateur musician. The son of an actor, he was born in Copenhagen. He was groomed to follow in his father's footsteps, and it is thought that he came to Oslo in the summer of 1810 in the hope of getting work at Strömberg's Theater. As noted earlier, however, Strömberg's plan to open a theater at this time was not successful. Ibsen came in contact with Falbe and Paul Thrane, however, both of whom were attracted to the young would-be actor when they discovered that he had musical talent and a good singing voice.

Initially Ibsen served as a tutor for Thrane's children. Then, with Thrane's help, he set up a small business. At first he and Waldemar Thrane operated it together, but when the latter left to pursue other interests Ibsen took it over. He was hardly an enthusiastic merchant, but he persevered for many years, selling everything from sugar and flour to books and music items. For a time he was also a music publisher with his own lithographic equipment. Among his publications was *Norske Lyra*, one of the first music periodicals in Norway. He also printed a number of his own compositions as well as some by Falbe and others. In 1840, however, he went bankrupt and was forced to give up his business. In his later years he held a minor position in a bank.

Ibsen was deeply involved in the music life of the city. In 1823 and 1824 he gave two recitals, on each occasion including some of his own compositions. He also served as a choir director and was an active member of the Lyceum and the Dramatic Society, where he appeared both in speaking roles and as a singer in comic operas. His most important contributions, however, were as a voice teacher. In 1821 he founded an Institute of Singing, and it appears to have had a favorable reception in the years that followed. From 1825 onward he was a voice teacher at the cathedral school. For a time he was employed as instructor at the Lyceum, and in 1829 he became vocal instructor at the Christiania Theater, a position he presumably held until 1837. Another pedagogical contribution was his translation and publication in 1822 of E. F. Eber's instruction book for voice students.

Ibsen was a well-known composer in his time. Twenty of his songs have been preserved, as well as some short dances for keyboard. He also wrote comic operas, but only two short songs are extant. A cantata with text by Simon Olaus Wolff, composed in 1823, has been lost. The authors of his song texts, in addition to Wolff, were such contemporary poets as Conrad Nicolai Schwach, Mauritz Hansen, and H. A. Bjerregaard. Among Ibsen's later songs is a setting of a text by Henrik Wergeland, "To Norway's Tri-colored Flag."

As a composer, Ibsen must be characterized as a dilettante. He apparently never had any systematic training in composition, and his music vocabulary is quite elementary. His extant compositions are rather short and simple in form; the songs, for example, are uniformly strophic. The harmony rarely strays beyond the dominant of the dominant and relative keys. However, his best songs possess a naive freshness that has kept them alive. "While the North Sea Roars" and "How Splendid Is My Native Land" were for many years among Norway's best-known songs, and the former is still sung today.

As a melodist, Ibsen made frequent use of broken chords and, to a lesser extent, of sequences. Some of his melodies are marred by incongruous coloratura-like passages. This carryover from comic opera occurs less frequently in his later songs. In keeping with the general mood of the time, he wrote a considerable number of songs with a nationalistic flavor. He was, for example, among the most zealous in extolling the latest symbols of Norway's national pride, her newly acquired steamships. He was at his best in these national, folk-like songs, and in a few instances he made lasting contributions to the song literature of his adopted homeland.

One of the most original figures in the music life of this period was Lars Roverud (1776–1850). Because he refused to study theology in accordance with his father's wishes, he was disinherited. In 1794 he entered the university in Copenhagen and became a musician. From about 1807 onward he supported himself as a teacher of voice, violin, piano, and music theory.

Roverud was a fiery person with many ideas. Not all of them came to fruition, but he nonetheless left his mark on the music life of both Oslo and the country as a whole. He saw the promotion of the art of singing as his special task. He was a tireless champion of the idea that people should learn to sing for personal enjoyment. He laid less stress on the development of concert singing; that, he thought, would come later.

In 1811 Roverud opened a music printshop in conjunction with a small music store. He evidently did not print a great deal, but a few song collections and some other short pieces appeared with his imprint.

In 1815 he published a little pamphlet entitled *A Look at the Condition of Music in Norway, with a Proposal for its General Dissemination Throughout the Country Through the Founding of an Institute in Oslo*. It contains an interesting survey of the country's music life, including a rather caustic critique of Norwegian folk music (see p. 108). It also sets forth a detailed but unrealized plan for a public music school in Oslo.

In the summer of 1819 Roverud went to Leipzig to study a group method of teaching voice, and in 1828 he enjoyed a short period of study in Stockholm. Otherwise he worked tirelessly as a voice and music teacher in Oslo. He also gave concerts from time to time; it is known that at a Lenten concert he once presented Beethoven's oratorio, *Christ on the Mount of Olives.*

For a number of years Roverud offered courses in vocal and instrumental music for school teachers. In 1825 he came across a Danish monochord, which interested him greatly. With the help of professor Christopher Hansteen he made some improvements on it, and thereafter used it in his teaching. From 1835 to 1847 he received public support to conduct courses throughout the country. These courses had great importance for the teaching of singing in the elementary schools, as is evident from the fact that the monochord remained the principal instrument used for vocal instruction in the schools for many years. The courses were eloquent proof of the dedication and zeal with which Roverud sought to enrich the musical experience of the common people.

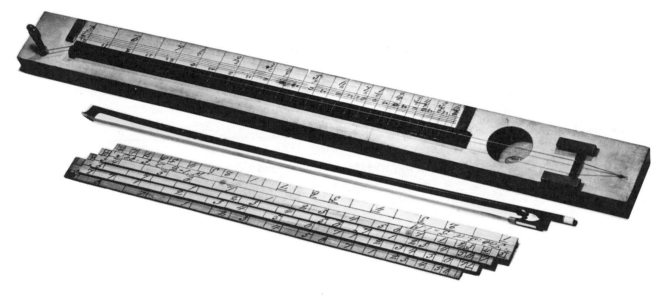

Monochord. The "lineals" pictured beside the instrument can be mounted by the fingerboard to show the fingering in the various keys. (Norsk Folkemuseum)

Hans Skramstad (1797–1839) appears to have been a talented musician who under more favorable circumstances might have developed into an important artist. As it turned out, however, he accomplished very little. Little is known of his music education or the early years of his career. He apparently studied in Oslo and Paris, and tradition has it that he spent some time in Stockholm as a piano teacher. Returning to Oslo in the spring of 1835, he announced that he was available as a teacher of piano and music theory. He evidently had few students, however, for he spent much of his time on the family farm at Toten. In 1839 he went to Bergen, where he died under somewhat mysterious circumstances.

Of the twelve works for piano that Skramstad is believed to have composed, all that remain are a waltz, a march for piano four hands, and four compositions in variation form: Opus 1, on "The Lonely Sunday Evening"; Opus 2, on "Old Man Noah"; Opus 4, on a Tyrolean melody; and Opus 6, on the melody "How Very Little More Is Wanting." Both the waltz and the march are short compositions in ternary form that present no formal or technical problems, while the variations are concert pieces that make significant technical demands on the performer.

Although some of his works have been lost, it must nonetheless be said that Skramstad was not a productive composer. His primary goal was to succeed as a piano virtuoso. In this he failed, and the disappointment evidently was more than he could bear.

WALDEMAR THRANE

Waldemar Thrane (1790–1828) was Norway's most important composer during this period. His father, Paul Thrane, a well-known businessman in Oslo, was greatly interested in music and was one of the founders of the Lyceum. He had his children learn to play various instruments and invited friends and relatives to concerts given by his own orchestra in his home.

Waldemar was the sixth child in the family. Under the early tutelage of town musician F. C. Groth he learned to play the violin. He made good progress, and at the age of seventeen became a member of the orchestra of the Dramatic Society. He attended Latin school for a time, but for some reason withdrew without graduating and became a sailor. While at sea he was the victim of a serious accident that impaired his health for the rest of his life. He was forced to give up the life of a seaman, and for some years thereafter he was in business with L. M. Ibsen.

Most of his time must have been devoted to music, however. By 1815, according to Roverud, he had already studied in Copenhagen with the violinist Claus Schall, and was then leader of the Lyceum orchestra. From 1817 to 1818 he lived in Paris, where he studied violin with François de Sales Baillot and music theory and composition with Anton Reicha and François-Antoine Habeneck. Upon his return to Oslo he became leader of the orchestras of both the Lyceum and the Dramatic Society. He also served as a music teacher and gave solo recitals in such places as Oslo, Bergen, and Trondheim. In 1819 he played in Stockholm, evidently with considerable success.

Thrane devoted himself tirelessly to strengthening Oslo's music life. He reorganized the Lyceum and formed what probably was the first important string quartet in Norway. In 1828 he resigned as leader of the orchestra of the Dramatic Society to assume leadership of the orchestra of the new Christiania Theater. Owing to declining health, this was to be his last contribution to Norway's music life.

His compositions are few in number. Only two works of importance have been preserved: a symphonic overture in D major and a comic opera entitled *The Mountain Escapade*. (His concert programs also listed a "Finale for Full Orchestra," but this and a cantata composed in 1827 are lost.) A few short, relatively unimportant piano pieces and songs have also survived.

The overture in D major, which Thrane identified as Opus 1, must have been written in Paris. The orchestral ensemble is similar to that in the later symphonies of Haydn and Mozart except that Thrane used only one flute. The instrumentation is also similar to that of the Viennese Classicists. The work consists of a rather short, slow introduction followed by an Allegro in standard sonata form. The brief development is notable for its many modulations. Themes are treated in a manner typical of the Classicists. Both principal and secondary themes are employed, at one point combined in a double canon in such a way that both themes proceed simultaneously in four voices. Although the harmonic treatment gives evidence of Thrane's thorough training in Paris, it is on the whole quite conservative. The overture is marked throughout by a fresh, albeit not especially original, thematic and orchestral handling and by sound compositional technique. Stylistically, its model is Viennese Classicism (his teacher Reicha was a friend of Beethoven), so it is evident that it was not only French music that Thrane became acquainted with during his stay in Paris.

Upon his return to Oslo, purely practical duties absorbed his time. Only in 1824 was he able to resume compositional activity. During that year he wrote the music for *The Mountain Escapade*, which had its premiere on February 9, 1825, at the Lyceum. It was an immediate success and shortly thereafter was performed in both Bergen and Trondheim. The score includes an overture, an orchestral prelude to the second act, four songs for solo voice, five pieces for various vocal ensembles, three pieces for chorus, and an extended through-composed orchestral finale to the first act with soloists and chorus. Musically, the high point of the entire work is without doubt "Aagot's Mountain Song" with its *lur* prelude followed by a *kulokk*. This lovely piece is given in its entirety in example 36. This song is completely different in character from the rest, and the influence of folk music is unmistakable. A *kulokk* is difficult to imitate in a concert-hall setting, but the melody that Thrane created has much in common with the genuine article. Note, for example, the major seventh on the word "hoah!" as Aagot calls the animals (measure 24), as well as the alternation between G and G-sharp, C and C-sharp in the ensuing melody (measures 44–57). It is also interesting to note that the so-called "Grieg formula"—a descending me-

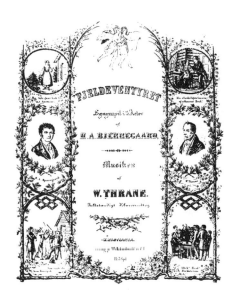

Title page of L.M. Lindeman's piano arrangements of music from Waldemar Thrane's The Mountain Escapade. *Published in 1850.*

Example 36. Waldemar Thrane, "Aagot's Mountain Song."

lodic figure consisting of a minor second followed by a major third—is anticipated here. It occurs several times throughout the *kulokk* and finally in the concluding outcry, "aa Stakkar!" ("poor thing!"). This formula also occurs several times in the song "The Sun Descends behind the Ridge," which follows the *kulokk*. A sharped fourth is also used in the melody in measures 44 (in D minor) and 49 (in A minor). The song is a little gem that has proved its durability to the present day.

There has been some doubt about whether Thrane composed these melodies himself; it has been suggested that he might rather have used preexistent folk tunes. Many years later, O. M. Sandvik transcribed a folk song in Österdalen with the same text and a closely related melody, but there is no evidence that it is older than Thrane's composition. In the absence of evidence to the contrary, one must assume that "Aagot's Mountain Song," which became extremely popular, has simply entered the folk-song repertoire and been modified by the folk-song tradition. It is obvious, of course, that Thrane could not have created these melodies apart from some knowledge of the folk-music tradition. How he became acquainted with it— whether it was secondhand through Bjerregaard, for example, who knew the Vaagaa district well, or if he had direct contact with the tradition—is difficult to determine.

The overture to *The Mountain Escapade* is strikingly different in both form and character from the overture in D major. Its episodic structure is reminiscent of the French "potpourri" opera overtures of the time. It consists of a slow introduction followed by an Allegro in a very free sonata form. The melody to "Aagot's Mountain Song" appears in the introduction, and the principal theme of the Allegro is based on a drinking song from the first act. There is an independent secondary theme that first appears in the dominant key; in the recapitulation it precedes the principal theme, this time in the tonic key. A rudimentary development consists only of the presentation of the principal theme in a few closely related keys. In general, the loose formal construction and simple structure of the overture show that Thrane simply adopted the popular comic-opera style of the period.

The prelude to the second act is a short, simple piece in ternary form (introduction + ABA). It leads directly into Marie's aria, "Lovely Morning so Fresh and Clear," which is a short piece of "mood music" depicting dawn in a Norwegian valley. The introduction is an Andante in which two horns play the leading roles. This is followed by a lengthy Allegretto melody in *halling* rhythm accompanied by sustained chords. It is quite possible that the *langeleik* was the inspiration for this movement, consisting as it does of a lively melody over a series of sustained chords.

The rest of the music is in the usual style of the comic operas of that time. It contains no especially national traits, nor was there any need for it to do so since most of the songs are sung by characters who could be considered ordinary townspeople or civil servants. Aagot is the only completely "national" figure of importance in the work. The music is spirited and uncomplicated, forming a suitable background for the somewhat undistinguished libretto. The weakest parts are the dramatic sections: the finale of the first act (depicting a fight on a mountain meadow) and the octet at the close of the second act. It cannot be denied that they are somewhat too protracted and the action, as a consequence, becomes rather static.

Notwithstanding all the criticisms that can be made, however, *The Mountain Escapade* has proven to be surprisingly durable. It is still performed from time to time, and audiences continue to be entertained by the text's naive humor and accessible music, especially the unforgettable "Aagot's Mountain Song." It is the earliest example we have of the fusion of the European music tradition and Norwegian folk music—a process that was to yield such rich results later in the century.

MUSIC LIFE ELSEWHERE IN NORWAY

Music life in other parts of the country exhibited many of the same characteristics as that of Oslo. In the larger towns, music societies were active under conditions similar to those in Oslo, with amateurs and professional musicians sharing responsibilities. Christian Blom (1782–1861), who was one of Norway's ablest amateur musicians, gave leadership to the music life in Drammen. He was born in the small township of Sem, where his father served as judge of the local district court. As a youth he was sent to Copenhagen to attend school. The intention was for him to study medicine, but for some reason his studies were interrupted and he became a seaman. For the rest of his life the sea was to be the focus of his career. First he served as captain of one of his uncle's ships, later of his own. In his old age, after he had given up being a ship's captain, he continued to be a ship owner. When not at sea he lived in Drammen, where he contributed abundantly to the city's music life.

Nothing is known of Blom's music education; we must assume that he received instruction of some sort while in Copenhagen. He may have taken lessons from his brother Fredrik, a violinist who later settled in England as a professional musician.

Christian played both violin and cello and is presumed to have had intimate knowledge of both instruments. His first work as a composer appears to date from about 1820 when he wrote the song "Sons of Norway." His extant compositions include almost forty songs, four or five chamber-music works, a symphonic overture, and two small choral pieces. We also know of three or four other compositions that have been lost.

"Sons of Norway" (sometimes called the "Crowned National Anthem") is Blom's best-known song, and therewith hangs an interesting tale. In 1820, in a competition arranged by an organization called the Society for Norway's Welfare, a private citizen offered two prizes (one for a text and the other for a "suitable and easily singable melody") for a Norwegian national song. H. A. Bjerregaard won the prize for the text and, after some revisions recommended by the jury (which included H. H. Falbe and L. M. Ibsen), Blom won the prize for the melody.

Blom later used the melody of "Sons of Norway" in his *National Overture for Orchestra*, which for many years was performed at the Christiania Theater's productions on May 17, Norway's Constitution Day. A grandly conceived piece, it concludes with four-part mixed chorus singing the entire anthem with orchestral accompaniment. Apart from the choral conclusion, the overture consists largely of independent thematic material, with only a few snatches of the melody of "Sons of Norway" appearing here and there. The piece is somewhat rhapsodic in nature and the recapitulation is quite short.

Most of Blom's larger works date from his later years. The period began in 1850 with his *Requiem*, a choral setting of a text by Theodore Thaarup. Then followed a series of chamber-music works of which a string quartet, written in 1855, presumably was the first. His third quartet dates from 1856, a string quintet from 1857, and his fourth quartet from 1858. There is also an unfinished composition for solo cello and string quartet; it is undated but is generally believed to have been the last composition he worked on before his death. If one adds to this list a string quartet that is lost, it must be granted that the total constitutes a considerable output for a composer in his seventies.

Blom's compositions are marked by their fresh melodic inventiveness. Occasionally, especially in his earlier works, the harmony is a little tentative. In the compositions dating from his last period, however, the harmony is secure and more colorful than one would expect from an amateur musician. It includes such features as altered dominants of dominants and Neapolitan sixth chords. The principal weakness of his compositions lies in their formal construction, which sometimes amounts to little more than a series of melodies loosely strung together. The themes in his chamber music display a fine sense for instrumental motivic construction. Occasionally the influence of Haydn is apparent. In the third movement of his fourth string quartet he uses the folk tune "Do You Know Guro?" as the theme for a series of variations. This is apparently the first time a Norwegian folk tune was employed as a theme in a chamber-music work. Considered as a whole, Blom's compositions bear witness to a significant musical talent—but also, unfortunately, to an obvious deficiency in music training.

In Bergen the local music association served as the foundation for the music life of the city. The Harmonic Society was a legacy from the previous century. Relatively dormant at the turn of the century, it was reorganized in 1809 and in the ensuing years became very active. Toward the end of the 1830s, however, concert activities declined, and in 1843 the society was dissolved.

Among the most important musicians in Bergen at the time were Gottfried Bohr (1773–1832), who engineered the reorganization of the Harmonic Society in 1809, and the violinists Johan Henrich Poulsen (1770–1838) and Mathias Lundholm (1785–1860). Both Poulsen and Lundholm were able musicians, and both served terms as leader of the society's orchestra. Both also were teachers of Ole Bull. Lundholm was probably Bull's teacher from the autumn of 1819 until he (Lundholm) left the city in 1827. He had studied with Baillot and is thought to have played an important role in Ole Bull's development as a violinist.

In Trondheim the music life was also supported to some extent by the music societies. The Music Society, founded in 1786, appears to have become inactive after the turn of the century. In 1815, however, a new association called the Music Rehearsal Society was established. It remained active throughout the 1820s, coming to full flower around 1830. Shortly thereafter, however, its fortunes waned, and in 1835 it too disbanded.

The most important musician in Trondheim at that time was Ole Andreas Lindeman (1769–1857). Lars Roverud voiced the opinion of many of his contemporaries when he wrote in 1815:

> In Mr. Lindeman, the organist at the Church of Our Lady in Trondheim, we have an excellent pianist, teacher, and music theorist. A former student of the Danish orchestra leader Wernicke, he is justly regarded as Norway's foremost musician.

Lindeman, the son of a judge, was born in Surnadal (near Trondheim). He attended the cathedral school in Trondheim, and in 1788 went to Copenhagen with the intention of studying law. An interest in music had already manifested itself, however, and it now came to the fore. During his stay in Copenhagen he became a pupil of Israel Gottlieb Wernicke, despite the fact that Wernicke lived in Kolding, more than a hundred miles from Copenhagen. From Wernicke Lindeman received sound music training, presumably with a fairly strong emphasis on the Baroque tradition in which Wernicke himself had been trained. Lindeman was appointed organist in the Church of Our Lady in Trondheim in 1799, remaining there for the rest of his life. His work spanned a period of more than fifty years, for he remained active into old age.

Lindeman's importance for Norwegian music was great. By virtue of his thorough training he quite naturally became the central figure among Norwegian musicians, and as an able music teacher he had considerable influence on his own sons and on many others.

Perhaps his most important contribution to Norwegian music was his chorale book. He had worked on it for a long time, but it was at the request of the government's department of ecclesiastical affairs that it was completed. Authorized in 1835 "for exclusive use in the worship services of the churches in the kingdom," it was the first Norwegian chorale book and was intended to replace the Danish one in use at the time. In the preface Lindeman stated that it was his desire "so far as possible" to present the melodies "in all essential respects in accordance with their original form and character." In so doing he went a long way toward shaping the chorale reform program taking place in Norway today. Moreover, he can hardly be blamed for the fact that the sources and constraints within which he worked prevented his going further than he did. With respect to rhythm he limited himself exclusively to the isometric form of the chorale. The melodies are given in half notes, usually in $\frac{2}{2}$ time. They generally exhibit good formal structure (despite the absence of the original rhythmic variety) and the harmonizations are ably realized.

Notwithstanding its many virtues, Lindeman's chorale book never became popular in Norway because of circumstances that made many congregations unreceptive to a chorale book of this type. Many places in Norway maintained a folk tradition in which the manner of singing and the melodic materials were different from those in Lindeman's chorale book. When an attempt was made to compel such congregations to use the authorized form, either they quit singing altogether or the authorities had to yield to the local traditions. That is why, in later discussions of the poor singing in the churches of Norway, the blame was often laid on Lindeman's chorale book.

Of Lindeman's own compositions, all that remain are three songs and twenty-nine piano pieces. Most of the latter are short dances with such titles as Anglaise or Minuetto. Example 37, an Anglaise, is one of several of his piano pieces published in volume 16 of *Piano Treasures* (Paris, 1861). It is in ternary *da capo* form and both melody and harmony are simple and flowing.

Lindeman's compositions display a Rococo galant character; though most of the extant works probably date from his period of study in Copenhagen, they are nonetheless quite conservative for their time. A somewhat larger etude-like piano composition, "Solfeggio," shows nothing essentially new in his style. According to tradition Lindeman also composed a piano concerto, but it has been lost.

OLE BULL

Ole Bull (1810–80) is the great legend in the history of Norwegian music. At the height of his glory he was acclaimed by the concert-going public in both Europe and America, and the pride and admiration of ordinary Norwegians was boundless. Yet both professional musicians and music critics in Norway and elsewhere generally expressed some reservation when Ole Bull

Example 37. O. A. Lindeman, "Anglaise."

was mentioned. A legend does not have the tangible quality that can withstand closer inspection by doubting critics—and Ole Bull was a legend. His importance in the cultural life of Norway during his lifetime was enormous, but his lasting importance has been quite limited. The legend died with the man, and today when one looks at the compositions he left behind it is always with a bit of astonishment: Is *this* the music with which he conquered the hearts of music lovers of the entire civilized world?

A key to the secret of his legendary career is to be found in two melodies from his hand that today are considered national treasures, "The Shepherd Girl's Sunday" and "In Solitary Moments." These marvelous little pieces demonstrate his true genius: the ability to create and shape melodies. In moments of inspiration he spellbound his audiences with his ability to "sing" a melody on the violin, and this ability is reflected in these melodies.

Ole Bull was born in Bergen. His unusual musical abilities were evident at an early age; indeed, he began playing the violin at the age of five. He received his first instruction from town musician Niels Eriksen, but he later studied with both J. H. Poulsen (a student of G. B. Viotti) and C. M. Lundholm. He made rapid progress and appeared several times as a soloist at concerts of the Harmonic Society.

The Bull family spent its summer vacations at Valestrand, a farm north of Bergen. This proved to be extremely important for Ole, for here he came

Ole Bull and his Gasparo da Salò violin. Painting by E. J. Baumann. (Norsk Folkemuseum)

in contact with expert country fiddlers and heard indigenous Norwegian dance music (*slaatter*). Even at this early age the foundation was being laid for his love of folk music.

In 1828, in accordance with his father's wishes, Ole went to Oslo with the intention of studying theology. His academic progress had not gone as well as his musical development, however, and he failed the university entrance examination. Meanwhile, he had become involved in the music life of the city. He played in the Lyceum orchestra and in private string quartet programs, and when Waldemar Thrane became ill Bull took over as leader of both the Theater and Lyceum orchestras. With that his future was sealed, for he was on the path that was to lead him to world fame.

Bull soon realized that the environment of Oslo was too restrictive for him, that in order to progress further as a musician he had to move out into the centers of European music. He left Oslo in May, 1829, going first to Copenhagen and then to Kassel, Germany, where he had planned to study with Ludwig Spohr. The plan did not work out for some reason, and a few months later he returned to Oslo. The following two years were spent in Norway, primarily Oslo, but in the autumn of 1831 he set out again, this time bound for Paris.

There are many differing accounts of his Parisian residency, and it is difficult to separate completely fact from fiction. The most important facts of his life at this time have been established, however. Shortly after his arrival in Paris he made the acquaintance of the Moravian violinist Heinrich Wilhelm Ernst. Although four years younger than Bull, Ernst was already an outstanding performer of the Paganini school. The two often played together, and Ernst presumably became Bull's mentor during the first part of his stay in Paris. In the spring of 1833 he gave a solo recital, then left the city. He went first to Switzerland, where he met his fellow countryman Hans Skramstad, and then to Italy.

His two years in Italy, from 1833 to 1835, proved to be a time of great development for him as a violinist. His real breakthrough as a performing artist dates from a concert he gave in Bologna in 1834. By the time he returned to Paris in the spring of 1835 he was well known in Italian music circles as a violin virtuoso.

Bull spent the winter of 1835–36 in France and soon established his reputation there as well. In the spring of 1836 he went to London, where he gave a series of overwhelmingly successful concerts. In July he returned to Paris to marry Félicie Villeminot, whom he had met during his first visit to Paris. He spent the winter of 1836–37 on concert tours in England, and in the autumn of 1837 he began a tour that was to take him to Germany, Russia, and Sweden. His success was overwhelming, and when he returned to Norway in the summer of 1839 he was received as a national hero.

Bull's life thereafter consisted largely of a series of concert tours interrupted only by short periods of rest. During 1843–45 he made his first trip to America. Here too his success was enormous; indeed, Bull rarely met elsewhere such excitement and spontaneous appreciation as he experienced in the United States.

The years 1849–50 found him in Norway again, during which time he wrote his most famous work, *A Visit to the Seter.* This piece was initially entitled "The Tenth of December" and was dedicated to the Norwegian Students' Association.

It was also during this period that Bull initiated efforts to establish a Norwegian theater that would be independent of the Danish theater tradition. This theater, called the National Stage, opened in Bergen on January 2, 1850. Bull himself directed the theater and conducted the orchestra during the first season, but in autumn of that year he turned over the leadership to a board of directors and resumed his travels as a concert violinist.

The theater applied for a government subsidy, and it was a great personal disappointment to Bull when the request was denied. He then began laying plans for a Norwegian "colony" in the United States, traveling to America in 1852 to put these plans into action. He bought land in Pennsylvania and invited Norwegian immigrants to settle there. Many accepted the invitation, and a small pioneer colony was established with a capital named Oleana. Bull, however, did not have the practical skills necessary to give leadership to such an enterprise. The land he had purchased was poorly suited for cultivation, and the settlement soon failed.

Félicie died in the spring of 1862; eight years later Bull married Sarah Thorpe, the daughter of a prominent American lumberman who later became governor of the state of Wisconsin. His last years were spent mostly in America, but he returned to Norway each summer and lived at his summer home called Lysöen (Isle of Light) near Bergen. He continued giving occasional concerts until the last year of his life.

Ole Bull had a good sense for what his audiences wanted to hear. After he achieved recognition as a violinist in the 1830s he was, as a rule, successful in his concerts. Naturally, he encountered occasional opposition from music critics and professional musicians, but for the most part even they acknowledged that he was as an outstanding—indeed, in some respects unsurpassed—violin virtuoso. This certainly was the case while he was at the height of his powers in the 1840s. When he continued giving concerts consisting largely of the same works up until the 1870s, the critics understandably reminded him that he belonged to a bygone era.

Bull has often been considered a self-taught performer, but this is not entirely correct. Both Poulsen and Lundholm, with whom he studied while growing up in Bergen, were able violin teachers. The latter presumably was very knowledgeable with respect to technique. And although it is true that in Paris he did not take formal instruction, his good friend Ernst undoubtedly gave him some guidance. He apparently heard Paganini himself play only once.

Bull was not content to imitate Paganini's style, however. He developed a personal style that differed in some respects from that of the Paganini school. A special feature of his playing was his use of polyphony by means of double, triple, and quadruple stops. This was made possible by a relatively flat bridge and a specially constructed bow that was larger and heavier than most, with little tension on the hairs. Another feature was his unique ability to play a simple melody with such fervent expression that his listeners were virtually entranced. Moreover, he had superb technique in the execution of harmonics and rapid staccato passages. Even his harshest critics acknowledged his mastery in these areas.

Bull's programs consisted primarily of his own compositions, and as time went on they grew greatly in number. Only a few of these are still in existence, probably because he wrote them solely for his own use. It may be that in many cases they were only sketched out and that he gave little thought to preserving them. The most important compositions that have survived are the *Violin Concerto* in E minor (*Concerto fantastico*), *Siciliano and Tarantella*, "Polacca Guerriera," "Nocturne for Violin and Orchestra," "Adagio Religioso" (also called "A Mother's Prayer"), and *A Visit to the Seter*. Two songs for male chorus, including "In Solitary Moments" (which was originally written for violin with the title "La Mélancolie") and a few other short pieces have also been preserved. Among the larger compositions that have been lost is a violin concerto in A major written during his stay in Italy in 1833–35.

Bull's compositions were often the objects of severe criticism. It was said that their form was loose and uncertain and that they lacked cohesiveness. They were also criticized for their poor harmony, a weakness attributed to Bull's inadequate training. It is possible that he himself was aware of these deficiencies, for several times in his letters he wrote of his studies in composition and of improvements he had made in his works. He published only three of his larger compositions, however.

The works that have been preserved partially justify Bull's critics, for the formal structure of the larger ones clearly leaves something to be desired. Consider, for example, the *Violin Concerto* in E minor. The first movement starts routinely enough with a slow introduction, and in the exposition—which in some respects is handled nicely—the secondary theme section occurs in the parallel key (E major) instead of the relative key (G major). The development, on the other hand, strikes one as rhapsodic, with excessive passage work, new thematic material, and no treatment of the themes from the exposition. The principal theme is merely hinted at in the recapitulation, and this time the secondary theme appears in the relative key. All in all, the movement does not transgress the principles of Classical form more seriously than several other compositions of the Romantic era, but neither does Bull use any other means to create a unified composition. The movement simply dissolves into a series of disconnected episodes.

Similar characteristics are also evident in Bull's other larger works, although *Siciliano and Tarantella* is somewhat more successful in this respect. Here the Siciliano forms a quiet introduction to the Tarantella, which has a clear rondo form. The theme is repeated three times, with each repetition preceded by an interlude, and a steadily accelerating tempo creates a somewhat superficial but nonetheless forceful effect.

Criticism of Bull's harmony, on the other hand, has been somewhat exaggerated. Perhaps he was a less than brilliant harmonist, with fairly limited resources and an occasionally monotonous penchant for the diminished seventh chord. Nonetheless, his basic skill was quite sound, producing passages in which the harmonic movement is truly excellent.

As a performing musician Bull was most often criticized for his inability to shape the larger phrases. When it came to displaying the musical beauty of the details he was virtually without equal, but he often took liberties that interrupted the flow of the composition.

Aside from the melodies of "The Shepherd Girl's Sunday" and "In Solitary Moments," none of Bull's surviving works entered the performance repertoire once he himself ceased playing them. They were written for himself and his specialized technique, and no one else has succeeded in bringing them to life.

Throughout his life Bull was an ardent nationalist, and this manifested itself also in his music. Even as a child he became acquainted with Norwegian folk music, especially during his summers at Valestrand. In later years he often played folk melodies and used them as the basis for his improvisations.

When the illustrated book *Norwegian National Costumes* came out in 1852, it included three small Norwegian folk tunes "transcribed and set for piano by Ole Bull." The settings are extremely simple, but they contain occasional touches that reflect the influence of the Hardanger fiddle. He also used folk tunes in some of his own compositions. We know of at least three instances in which he did this: "Norway's Mountains," *A Visit to the Seter,* and "Improvisation on the Hillside." Of these, only *A Visit to the Seter* has been preserved in its entirety. It is a little rhapsody composed of folk tunes and an original melody for which Jörgen Moe later wrote the text, "The Shepherd Girl's Sunday." The melody with which the piece begins and the *halling* with which it ends were probably composed by Bull with materials derived from the folk-music tradition. Nor was he interested only in Norwegian folk tunes. The folk melodies of other countries also captured his interest, as is evident from his compositions based on Irish, Scottish, Spanish, Italian, and American melodies.

Bull's most important and enduring contribution to the cultural life of

Norway goes beyond the purely musical realm. More than anyone else, he gave Norwegian artists a sense of national self-confidence. At the height of his fame he was undoubtedly the best-known and most widely acclaimed violinist in the world. Paganini had largely ceased his concert activities when Bull became popular, and there was no one else who could challenge his position. He never failed to propagandize in behalf of his homeland, and his effectiveness as a self-appointed ambassador for Norway in the concert halls of the world was enormous.

His various practical enterprises for the promotion of Norway's cultural life were not so successful, however. Plans for a Norwegian conservatory of music, like so many similar ideas, came to naught; and Oleana ended in complete failure. His most successful practical undertaking was undoubtedly the National Stage in Bergen, though it managed to keep going for only thirteen years. Bull was unable to provide the necessary leadership or to hold it together once it began to decline. It is to his considerable credit, however, that he was able to start a purely Norwegian theater as early as 1850, when Norway was still dominated culturally by Denmark and politically by Sweden.

8

The Emergence of National Romanticism
(ca. 1840–ca. 1860)

Politically the years 1840–60 constituted a relatively peaceful time in Norway, as its partnership with Sweden was on the whole fairly amicable. A movement for a closer bond among Denmark, Norway, and Sweden gained some currency, primarily in student circles. In general, however, this idea was met with indifference, although some regarded it with a certain sympathy based on a deeply rooted fear of the great European powers, especially Russia. A united Scandinavia, it was thought, would constitute a stronger political counterbalance against the designs of the great powers than could the three countries acting individually.

The Norwegian economy advanced rapidly after the crises of the 1830s and experienced steady growth throughout most of this period. The revolutions of 1848 that engulfed most of the countries of Europe had little direct impact on Norway. Denmark did become involved, however, as uprisings occurred among the German-speaking population in the Danish duchy of Schleswig-Holstein. Denmark was actually at war with Prussia for a brief period in 1848, and was aided by both Norwegian and Swedish volunteers motivated by the spirit of Scandinavianism.

The revolutionary turmoil of 1848 was also the background for the creation of labor unions in Norway. They demanded, among other things, better schools and universal suffrage, but had little success at this time. Industrialization had hardly begun in Norway then, and Marcus Thrane—the leader of the labor movement (and a nephew of the composer Waldemar Thrane)—was strongly opposed to the use of force. Although labor disputes did lead to violence in a few communities, the Norwegian labor unions did not develop into a revolutionary movement.

The population of Norway increased considerably during the middle of the nineteenth century. This fact, combined with the prevailing social and economic circumstances, led to the emigration of large numbers of people, primarily to North America. The first ship carrying Norwegian emigrants to North America left Stavanger in 1825, but it was during the 1840s that significant numbers of Norwegians began to make the long journey across the Atlantic. The flow continued throughout the nineteenth century and on into the early twentieth century; it is estimated that by 1920 some 800,000 Norwegians had emigrated to the United States. The magnitude of this population outflow may be judged from the fact that the total population of Norway in 1800 was only about 880,000.

These immigrants contributed richly to many facets of life in the New World, not least in the area of choral music. They brought with them a well-developed love of singing, and itinerant teachers and preachers soon established "singing schools" in which the old hymns and folk tunes were sung and the fundamentals of music were taught. Choruses were formed, and during the last decade of the nineteenth century and the first three decades of the twentieth century the Norwegian Lutheran Church sponsored a series of "choral unions" in which many choirs joined together in a single massed ensemble of as many as 3,000 voices. The music was sacred, usually *a cappella*, and high musical standards prevailed.

The year 1912 saw the founding of the St. Olaf Choir by F. Melius Christiansen (1871–1955), a native of Eidsvold, Norway, who had emigrated to the United States in 1888. The choir set a new standard for *a cappella* choral singing in America and became the model for similar choirs established at many other colleges and universities. Both by example and through their many alumni, these choirs have had an enormous influence on the quality of choral singing in America.

The most intense conflicts that occurred in Norwegian society in the middle of the nineteenth century were those that stirred within its cultural life. The strong national currents rooted in the political liberation of 1814 encountered a powerful school of thought inspired primarily by German Romanticism. The result was a national Romantic cultural trend which, about the middle of the century, developed into a full-fledged manifestation of independent Norwegian culture. Because of its two principal components, this cultural development is often referred to as the "national Romantic renaissance." There was really no serious disagreement about the goal of an independent Norwegian art, but rather about the means of reaching this goal. To what extent should one build Norwegian art on the old, primarily Danish, elements that theretofore had dominated the cultural life of the country, especially that of the cities and towns? On this point opinions were divided, differences were sharp, and artists who participated in the debate inevitably came to varying conclusions. In the end, however, this turmoil itself became the genesis of an independent Norwegian art.

The national Romantic renaissance found expression in many different areas of Norway's cultural life. Relatively early it manifested itself in a renewed interest in folk culture. Magnus Brostrup Landstad, Peter Christen Asbjörnsen, and Jörgen Moe began collecting the old Norwegian folk ballads, fairy tales, and legends, and Ludvig Mathias Lindeman began collecting folk melodies. These efforts accelerated beginning in the 1840s, and the resulting body of folk material became the foundation for distinctively Norwegian works of art that were soon to follow.

The national Romantic renaissance was expressed in an almost symbolic way in March of 1849, when the newly formed art association arranged three famous "evening events" involving painters, poets, and musicians. Ole Bull played *A Visit to the Seter*. There were tableaus of Norwegian scenery and folk life painted by Adolf Tidemand and Hans Gude and readings of original poems by Johan Sebastian Welhaven, Andreas Munch, and Jörgen Moe. Most acclaimed of all was the concluding tableau, entitled "Bridal Procession in Hardanger." Gude and Tidemand had created the scenery for this, and Halfdan Kjerulf had composed music for a poem by Andreas Munch. The evening was a display of fresh art created by the young talent of Norway. The artistic value of the various elements was undoubtedly uneven, but it was evident to all that Norway's cultural independence had been convincingly demonstrated.

The quest for a distinctively Norwegian culture was not the only characteristic of this period, however. Contact with European music, especially German music, increased greatly. Romanticism had by this time won the day in Europe's leading centers of music. The "Classical" Romanticism of Schubert, Mendelssohn, and Schumann was dominant, and a more radical form of Romanticism had already found its first great exponent in Hector Berlioz. It was also in the 1840s that Wagner began to assert himself, although his style had little or no influence on Norwegian composers at that time.

The establishment of the music conservatory in Leipzig in 1843 was of great significance. Its founders included Mendelssohn and Schumann, and it quickly earned a reputation as one of Europe's premier music schools. From 1850 onward it was the school of choice for most Norwegian musicians, where they encountered a milieu that was shaped to a large extent by "Classical" Romanticism.

At the same time that many Norwegian musicians were being educated abroad, the number of foreign musicians—especially German musicians—who settled in Norway increased. Thus the music life of Norway was enriched by a number of able and dynamic artists who, both by their own contributions and by their excellent example and influence, significantly raised the musical standards of the country.

MUSIC LIFE AND ACTIVITY

The status of music in Norway in the early 1840s was not very encouraging. One evidence of this is the fact that the music societies in all of the larger cities had ceased to function. In Oslo, for example, the Lyceum was dissolved in 1838 and was not replaced until 1846, when a new organization, the Philharmonic Society, was formed. The latter was started by the Dano-Swedish cellist Georg Andreas Gehrmann (1806–76), who spent much of his time during the 1840s in Oslo. He served as leader of the society for two years, and was then succeeded for a short time by Friedrich August Reissiger. In the autumn of 1848 the German musician Carl Arnold became its conductor and maintained a strong leadership for about fifteen years. Both vocal and instrumental music were cultivated by the society. Most of the performances were private, but occasionally public concerts were given as well. The society was to a large extent an association of amateur musicians, and it was of less musical importance than the Lyceum, for example, had been in the 1820s.

On the positive side, the 1840s witnessed the emergence of the men's chorus movement. A number of singing societies came into being at this time, including three large male choruses in Oslo: the Norwegian Students' Male Chorus, the Businessmen's Chorus, and the Craftsmen's Chorus. The movement grew rapidly, as is evident from the large number of choral conventions held between 1850 and 1870. Singers gathered by the hundreds for what in essence were folk festivals. Speeches were given, poems were read by the leading bards of the day, and large crowds attended to see and hear the spectacle. For a time the movement so dominated the music life of the country that to some extent it hindered the development of other forms of amateur music.

The most important music establishment in Oslo at mid-century was the Christiania Theater. During the period 1840–50, when F. A. Reissiger was its orchestral conductor, no fewer than thirty operas were produced. Of these, twenty were first performances in Norway, and several of the operas were produced a number of times. It is likely that the musical quality of these productions was not always of the highest order, but they made an impor-

Caricature of harried theater-orchestra musicians, who at one time were expected to be able to play several instruments (albeit not simultaneously!). (From Mentz Schulerud, Norsk kunstnerliv, *Oslo, 1960)*

tant contribution to the music life of the city nonetheless. The repertoire was primarily French, with Auber's operas heading the list. Italian and German operas were also performed, however, including Mozart's *Don Giovanni* and *The Marriage of Figaro*. The theater also presented comic operas and stage plays with incidental music, hence a considerable amount of music was offered to the public.

In 1850 Reissiger was replaced by Paolo Sperati (1821–84). Sperati had come to Oslo in 1849 as conductor of a touring Italian opera company, and he was so successful that Reissiger was dismissed and the Italian installed in his place. Despite Sperati's undoubted ability as an opera conductor, it appears that the change did not prove to be advantageous so far as the quantity of operatic performances was concerned. During his sixteen-year tenure (1850–66) Sperati produced only four operas that were new to the Norwegian theater, three of which were Italian. He remained in Oslo until his death, playing an important role there as a conductor and music teacher. He also composed a number of pieces of occasional music, but nothing of importance.

Numerous public concerts were also given in Oslo at this time. Foreign musicians regularly came to the city on their concert tours, and Norwegian artists (both natives and immigrants) made their contributions as well. Orchestral concerts, however, were exceedingly rare. The Philharmonic Society, as noted earlier, gave public performances now and then, and these occasionally included a symphony, but the meager orchestral resources were really not equal to the task.

It was not until 1857 that Oslo had an opportunity to hear a fairly complete symphony orchestra for the first time. At that time Johann Gottfried Conradi and Halfdan Kjerulf initiated a series of subscription concerts for the purpose of presenting large vocal and instrumental works. The orchestra was composed of professional musicians and was led by Conradi, with Kjerulf serving as chorus master. In the beginning there was great interest in the undertaking. The first concert, given in the autumn of 1857, included a performance of Beethoven's Fifth Symphony, and it made a powerful impression. The public's interest in these concerts gradually waned, however, and after four seasons the series was discontinued. The Philharmonic Society was reorganized and continued to give public concerts from time to time.

In Bergen, too, there was for a few years during the 1840s a music association called the Philharmonic Society that gave concerts of a predominantly private character. It did not become firmly established until 1856, when it was reorganized under the name Harmonien. Ferdinand Augst Rojahn, a German musician who had come to Norway in 1840, served as music leader of the society during the late 1850s. Also important in the music life of Bergen at this time was the National Stage, a professional theater that opened on January 2, 1850, thanks in large measure to the efforts of Ole Bull (see p. 139). The theater had its own orchestra, which was conducted during the first season by Bull and in later years by Rojahn and others. The offerings included comic operas but no serious operas.

GERMAN MUSICIANS IN NORWAY

As previously mentioned, a significant number of foreign (primarily German) musicians traveled to Norway during this period, and many of them settled there. The influx began in 1840 with a complete orchestra called the Harz Music Society, a twelve-member ensemble that had been formed some ten years earlier. The group first went to Oslo on a private concert tour in the spring of 1840. That autumn, when Reissiger was appointed conductor of the orchestra at the Christiania Theater, he arranged to have the entire ensemble incorporated into the theater orchestra. In 1845 the Harz Music Society was dissolved as an independent orchestra, but most of the musicians remained in Norway. Among them was F. A. Rojahn, mentioned earlier. Another was Carl Warmuth, who opened a music and instrument business in Oslo that later was expanded to include a rental library, a music publishing house, and a concert booking agency. The firm had a significant impact on the music life of the city, especially after Warmuth's son, Carl Jr., entered the business in 1861.

Friedrich August Reissiger (1809–83) came to Norway in the summer of 1840. He was installed as conductor of the Christiania Theater orchestra, replacing August Schrumpf, who had served in that capacity since 1830 and remained as a member of the orchestra. Reissiger had been a student at the Thomaner School in Leipzig before going to Berlin in 1830 to study theology. To support himself in Berlin, however, he was obliged to give music lessons, and on the advice of Mendelssohn's teacher, K. F. Zelter, he decided to study music instead of theology. He studied composition with Siegfried Dehn and published several of his works. By the time he went to Oslo he had fifty opus numbers to his credit. In Berlin he had a good reputation as a composer and music teacher, but as a conductor he had little or no experience.

His ten years as orchestra leader at the Christiania Theater were not an easy time for him. His limited experience hampered him initially, and a certain antagonism between him and several members of the orchestra and its former conductor, August Schrumpf, added to his problems. Moreover, he became the object of sharp criticism in the local press. That he nonetheless managed to present some thirty operas, including many never before staged in Norway, was no small achievement.

Reissiger was active in other ways as well. In 1842 he formed the Choral Institute, virtually a precursor of the Philharmonic Society, in which choral works both small and large were rehearsed and performed, some with piano accompaniment, some with orchestra. Among the oratorios presented were Mendelssohn's *St. Paul*, Graun's *The Death of Jesus*, and Beethoven's *Christ on the Mount of Olives*. Despite these notable achievements, however, he never won a secure position at the theater and was ultimately replaced by Sperati. Shortly thereafter he moved to Halden, a town near Oslo, where he became an organist and leader in the music life of the community. He remained there until his death in 1883.

As previously noted, Reissiger was very productive as a composer while he was living in Berlin. He wrote primarily piano pieces, usually in the form of popular marches and dances, as well as a number of songs for one or two voices and piano. These songs were widely disseminated in Germany, and those with humorous texts appear to have been especially popular. In Norway the only composition from his Berlin period that became well known was his *Feenreigen Waltzes* for piano, Op. 18.

After his arrival in Oslo he was so busy with practical duties that little time was available for composition. Nonetheless, he produced a significant number of works during his years in Norway. The most important of these were his works for male chorus. He composed no less than sixty pieces in this genre, many of which are still sung in Norway. Among the best known of these are "A Singer's Prayer" (also published for solo voice and piano) and "Olav Trygvason." During his tenure as orchestral leader at Christiania Theater he also composed incidental music for several plays, including *The Elves* by Johan Ludvig Heiberg and *Queen Margareta* by Adam Oehlen-schläger, both dating from 1849. Reissiger also had responsibility for the music accompanying the staging of Claus Pavels Riis's *At the Seter* in 1850. The musical material consisted essentially of folk melodies, however, and he therefore called himself the arranger rather than the composer of this music. The overture, a potpourri of Norwegian folk tunes, is still played today.

Upon the death of King Karl Johan in 1844, Reissiger composed a *Requiem* that was performed in Our Savior's Church. A manuscript of this work was found many years later. *At Karmöy*, a large work for orchestra and narrator, was performed several times during Reissiger's life and became quite well known. Unfortunately, both this and a cantata written for a memorial ceremony for Oehlenschläger in 1850 have been lost. Reissiger was organist at the Roman Catholic church in Oslo, and tradition has it that he wrote six masses, but this has not been confirmed. His only large chamber-music work has been preserved, however. It is a string quintet built on Norwegian melodies (Op. 59), first performed in 1862. It is in four movements and makes use of Christian Blom's "Sons of Norway," Ole Bull's "The Shepherd Girl's Sunday," and several Norwegian folk melodies. The form is somewhat rhapsodic, but as a whole the quintet is ably crafted and is thus a good example of robust national Romanticism in artistic garb.

Since so many of Reissiger's compositions are lost it is difficult to give a summary judgment of him as a composer. Those works that survive show him to have been a well-trained musician. The smaller works, especially, are melodious and display good form, but occasionally the music sounds somewhat facile and impersonal. His harmony is generally conservative, never going beyond what was considered permissible in early Romanticism. Genuine chromatic harmony was not his strength: his works are discreetly spiced with chromaticism, but for the most part only as passing tones. Within his chosen limits, however, Reissiger produced some admirable works that have proven their vitality through the years and are a credit to their creator both as a musician and as a noble human being.

Another able German musician, Carl Arnold (1794–1873), came to Oslo in 1848. Arnold's father died when he was a boy of twelve, but he had already displayed an aptitude for music and others saw to it that he received a thorough music education. He was an accomplished pianist and had completed a number of extensive concert tours before coming to Norway. He had also earned some respect as a composer. His opera *Irene* had been performed in Berlin in 1832, albeit without much success. Other early works include a number of piano pieces—fantasias, sonatas, and variations—as well as songs and chamber music. Notable among the works for piano is a rondo on the Norwegian folk tune "The Lonely Sunday Evening," presumably written sometime during the 1820s.

Upon his arrival in Oslo in 1848, Arnold was appointed leader of the Philharmonic Society. He also soon became a highly regarded music teacher; among his pupils were both Halfdan Kjerulf and Johan Svendsen. In 1857 he became organist at the newly built Trinity Church, and he remained in this position until his death in 1873.

Arnold was less active as a composer during his years in Oslo than he had been previously. His compositions during this period consist of some occasional music—a cantata for the fiftieth anniversary of the university in 1861, for example—a few songs for male chorus, and several piano and organ pieces.

Only a small part of Arnold's creative output is available today, but the compositions that remain fully justify the great respect accorded "old Arnold" by his students and colleagues. Though not markedly original, his music is of consistently high quality. His harmonic style is fairly chromatic, with altered chords and abrupt modulations, and shows the influence of German Romanticism. His handling of form in the larger works also reveals a Romantic stamp. The fantasia in C minor for piano, for example, employs the Romantic single-movement sonata form with an adagio interlude within the development section. A *Sonata* in B-flat major for piano four-hands, which may have been written after he came to Oslo, has three movements of which the first is in sonata form and the last in rondo. The recapitulation in the first movement is greatly abbreviated, and many liberties are taken throughout relative to the canons of standard sonata form.

Arnold's thematic material shows less evidence of the influence of Romanticism than do his harmony and formal structure. It rarely transgresses the standards of Viennese Classicism, with the result that his music has a more reserved and conservative character than one might expect. His later works point to an even more conservative style in which the harmonies become simpler and chromaticism plays a smaller role. A double fugue for organ (published posthumously) employs a somewhat chromatic theme, but all indications are that Bach's organ works had served as the model.

In 1850, ten years after the arrival of the Harz Music Society, another German orchestra of similar size, called the Schwarzenbacherkapell, came to Oslo. It was engaged to play at the Klingenberg amusement park in the summer of 1850, and the following summer it toured the country, playing in such cities as Bergen and Trondheim. The musicians thus made contacts in various places, and many of them took positions and settled there permanently. Among those who contributed significantly to Norway's music life was Carl Rabe, who became concertmaster at the National Stage in Bergen, and who later founded a music store that bears his name.

LUDVIG M. LINDEMAN

In several respects L. M. Lindeman occupies a unique position among the Norwegian composers of his day. He stands outside the German Romantic and Leipzig conservatory traditions with which most of his contemporaries were identified. Indeed, as a composer he appears to have been quite oblivious to contemporary musical developments on the continent; both in his education and in his artistic stance he was a product of the German Bach tradition. All of his music training came from his father, Ole Andreas Lindeman, who, through I. G. Wernicke and J. P. Kirnberger (see p. 70), was a direct musical descendant of J. S. Bach. The younger Lindeman appears to have regarded it as a kind of filial duty to preserve this tradition. One can observe that the Bach tradition was evident in other musicians of the Romantic period as well: Mendelssohn, for example, had studied with Zelter, who also was a pupil of Kirnberger. But Mendelssohn, notwithstanding his enthusiasm for Bach, was after all a true son of Romanticism. In contrast, Lindeman's admiration and love for Bach's music marked his entire career, including his compositions, to such an extent as to set him quite apart from the Romanticism of his day. One could almost say that he was a late Baroque musician who happened to live in the nineteenth century. The only truly Romantic element in Lindeman's outlook was his love of folk music. In 1862 he wrote: "The love of Norwegian folk music is a heritage from my forefathers, and folk melodies have been ringing in my ears ever since I was in the cradle."

Ludvig Mathias Lindeman (1812–87) was born in Trondheim and received a thorough training in music from his father. He made such rapid progress that even as a twelve-year-old he served as substitute organist for Sunday worship services. In 1833, after completing Latin school and taking private instruction in preparation for university study, he went to Oslo with the intention of studying theology. The day after his arrival, however, he substituted for his brother, Jacob Andreas, as organist at Our Savior's Church, and music soon came to occupy most of his time. From 1834 to 1840 he played cello in the theater orchestra, and in the late 1830s he also became a singing teacher in several of the city's schools. In 1839, when Jacob Andreas left his position at Our Savior's Church, Ludvig became the

L.M. Lindeman. (Universitetsbiblioteket i Oslo)

organist and gave up his theological studies for good. He served as organist at Our Savior's for the rest of his life.

Except for numerous trips to various parts of eastern Norway to collect folk tunes, Lindeman traveled little. It was a rare opportunity, therefore, when he was included in a group of European organists who were invited to London to assist in the dedication of the new organ at Royal Albert Hall. He gave a total of eight successful concerts in which, among other things, he improvised on Norwegian folk tunes.

Lindeman was also active as a teacher. In 1883, in cooperation with his son Peter, he established a school for organists in Oslo which later became the music conservatory.

Lindeman had an enduring influence in several areas of Norwegian music. His pioneering work in the collection of folk tunes was of great importance. In his position as an organist, and especially through his chorale book, he exerted a decisive influence on the development of Norwegian hymnody which has continued to the present day. His compositions established a style that influenced Norwegian sacred music well into the twentieth century.

Lindeman's acquaintance with Norwegian folk music during his childhood and youth must have been largely through secondary sources. His first publication in this area consisted of fifteen folk melodies that he contributed as a supplement to Jörgen Moe's folk-ballad collection in 1840. He probably got some of these from his father's collection, some from students from various parts of the country whom he met in Oslo, some from singers and fiddlers whom he happened to meet, and so on. The folk melodies in *Norwegian Mountain Melodies Harmonized and Arranged*, a collection he published in 1841, probably came from similar sources. In 1848, however, he received a grant to support the collection and preservation of folk melodies, and thereafter he made more rapid progress in his work. The most important result of his first trip was a collection of eighty-six "Kingo Melodies" first published in its entirety by O. M. Sandvik in 1941.

Lindeman later undertook a number of similar collecting expeditions, and during the years 1850 to 1885 several folk-tune collections appeared. Among them were *Norwegian Folk Ballads Set for Four Male Voices* (1850) and the melody appendix to M. B. Landstad's *Norwegian Folk Ballads* (1853). The year 1853 also saw the publication of the first volume of his huge collection (eventually comprising 636 melodies) that appeared under the title *Older and Newer Norwegian Mountain Melodies, Collected and Arranged for Piano*. Additional volumes were issued from time to time until 1867, and the last volume was published posthumously in 1907. Example

38 is number 327 from this collection, a hauntingly beautiful hymn tune from Valdres entitled "Jesus Christ our Lord Is Risen." It is one of the "Kingo Melodies" collected on Lindeman's first journey in search of just such examples of hidden treasure. Lindeman's setting is fittingly simple and displays a fine sense for the melody's harmonic possibilities.

Example 38. L.M. Lindeman's piano setting of the hymn "Jesus Christ our Lord Is Risen."

Later collections include *Fifty Norwegian Mountain Melodies Arranged for Male Voices* (1862), *Thirty Norwegian Heroic Ballads for Three Like Voices* (1863), and *Norwegian Heroic Ballads Arranged for Mixed Voices* (1885). In the arduous task of collecting these folk melodies, Lindeman received the willing help of many outstanding singers of folk tunes—people who were themselves repositories of various portions of the folk-music tradition and placed their knowledge at his disposal.

All of Lindeman's published collections were designed for practical use, and the various tonal and rhythmic difficulties in the notation of the melodies were resolved in practical ways, with unavoidable compromises with respect to accuracy. In his handwritten transcriptions, on the other hand, he took great care to record the rhythmic and tonal peculiarities of the melodies. The remarkable precision of his notation is such that his manuscripts are of enduring ethnomusicological interest.

As a church musician Lindeman became involved in one of the bitterest controversies in the history of Norwegian music—the so-called "hymn controversy." In church-music circles at this time there was much dissatisfaction with O. A. Lindeman's chorale book, which had been authorized "for exclusive use in the worship services of the churches in the kingdom." Everyone agreed on the need for reform, but there was disagreement about the direction it should take. The controversy continued with varying degrees of vehemence from 1858 to 1877 and ranged from polemical articles in the press to official reports by the Ministry of Ecclesiastical Affairs.

The leaders of the proponents of reform were Johan Didrik Behrens and, after 1874, Otto Winter-Hjelm. Lindeman was the leader of what might be called the "conservative" faction. The reformists sought a return to the rhythmic forms of the Reformation era because they believed that in this way congregational hymn singing would be improved. Lindeman held that those rhythmic forms were sung primarily by trained choirs and did not lend themselves to congregational singing. As an alternative solution to lethargic hymn singing he pointed to his practical experiences at Our Savior's Church, where he had achieved improvement by using faster tempos with the isometric chorales and with occasional dotted notes to underline their inherent rhythms.

The controversy was launched by Behrens in 1858 in a book entitled *On the Lutheran Hymn and its Reintroduction in the Norwegian Church*. In 1859 a book was published under the auspices of the Ministry of Ecclesiastical Affairs with the imposing title *Martin Luther's Spiritual Songs . . . by M. B. Landstad. The Original Melodies Previously Associated with These Texts Rhythmically Presented in Four-Part Harmonizations with Accompanying Commentary by Ludv. M. Lindeman*. In 1870 Lindeman was asked by the ministry to revise the chorale book for Landstad's hymnal (which had been authorized in 1869). He was the only person who could possibly have been asked to undertake this task. As early as 1840 he had published a supplement to Wilhelm Andreas Wexel's *Christian Hymns* to which he had contributed ten melodies of his own, including the well-known "Built on a Rock the Church Shall Stand." Later he had written many new hymn tunes, some to texts by the great Danish churchman, educator, and poet N. F. S. Grundtvig (1783–1872). Since he was also the organist of the principal church in the largest city in the country, it was only natural that the ministry turned to him.

Lindeman accepted the assignment, and his proposal for a new chorale book was published in 1871. In 1876 a committee was appointed by the ministry to evaluate the proposal. Its report, submitted in the spring of 1877, contained a number of strong objections to Lindeman's proposal. Despite these objections, however, the new chorale book was published virtually unchanged and was authorized in December of 1877 "for use in divine worship in the churches of the kingdom."

Meanwhile, in 1876 Otto Winter-Hjelm had published his *Thirty-seven Older Hymn Melodies, Rhythmically and Harmonically Restored*. In 1879, as a kind of finale to the controversy that had raged for some twenty years, Winter-Hjelm wrote a series of articles that appeared in *Morgenbladet*, one of Oslo's principal newspapers.

With the official authorization of the chorale book, however, Lindeman's view had prevailed. Thus it mattered little that a new "reformist" chorale book was published by the organist Erik Hoff (1832–94) in 1878. Entitled *Melody Book for All Authorized Hymnals*, it contained 265 tunes of which about sixty were composed by Hoff himself. Hoff had not taken an active part in the hymn controversy but tended toward Winter-Hjelm's view. His *Melody Book* included a number of the old chorales in their original rhythmic forms, but he always gave the isometric form as an alternative. His book was never authorized, however, and was rarely used. It was not until the publication in 1926 of the *Chorale Book for the Norwegian Church* that quite a few chorale melodies in their rhythmic form appeared once again in Norwegian church hymnals.

Example 39 shows three settings of the same chorale melody: *a* is O. A. Lindeman's version, *b* is L. M. Lindeman's, and *c* is Otto Winter-Hjelm's.

A comparison between *b* and *c* in example 39 gives a good picture of the two positions in the hymn controversy. In *b* the isometric form of the melody is the starting point, but an attempt is made to enliven the rhythm by dotting the most heavily stressed syllables. In *c* the melody is restored to a form in use at the time of the Reformation. One difficulty with the latter solution is that there are often several rhythmic forms of the same tune, with the result that one must choose between the "older and better" and the simpler, more usable forms. A comparison with example 5*b* on p. 34 shows that Winter-Hjelm's form of the melody is very similar to the Nürnberg version of 1534.

Example 39. Three contrasting settings of the chorale "Come Now to Me God's Son Doth Say."

Despite the rich treasure of religious folk tunes that Lindeman collected, he included none of them in his chorale book. It was his opinion that neither these nor the newer ballad-like melodies (used in the Danish church to some extent) belonged in church hymnody. He did, however, include a number of his own melodies.

Lindeman contributed to the church music of Norway in other ways as well. From 1849 until his death he taught liturgical singing in the theological seminary at the University of Oslo, and in 1870 he published a *Norwegian Service Book*.

He also published several song books in connection with his efforts to improve singing in the schools. Among the best known of these are *Melodies for a Small Songbook for the Home . . . Harmonized for Two Like Voices . . . for Use in Schools and Societies* and *Melodies for the Songs in the Reader for Folk Schools and Homes . . . for Schools and Choral Societies*. Both appeared in several editions during the 1860s and 1870s. He also wrote many new melodies for these collections, several of which, such as " 'Twixt the Mountains and Hills," have become very popular in Norway. Also worthy of mention is *Melodies for Brorson's Swan Song* which, although prepared for publication in 1864, was first published in its entirety for the Lindeman jubilee of 1912.

Lindeman composed a number of other works as well. His earliest extant composition, entitled *Two Waltzes*, was published by Winther around 1835. Both waltzes are in the salon style of the period and show little evidence of Lindeman's authorship. Of greater interest is his *Seventeen Variations on the Chorale "Who Knows How Near His End May Be."* This composition exists in manuscript form and is dated 1836. Here Lindeman exercised his contrapuntal skills in various canonic forms, concluding with a five-part fugue. A series of variations for piano four-hands on the folk tune "Old Man Noah" is dated January 1, 1839. It was probably at about this time that he wrote three fugues on B-A-C-H (published posthumously). He also tried his hand as a theater composer, contributing the music for four melodramas produced from the performance of Henrik Wergeland's play *The Campbells* in January, 1838. These, unfortunately, have not been preserved.

A large number of Lindeman's compositions were lost in a fire in his apartment in 1859, including a piano sonata and several organ fantasias and string quartets. His extant compositions for organ include *Thirty-six Fugal Preludes*, *Fifty-four Short Preludes*, and a set of variations on the chorale "If Thou But Suffer God to Guide Thee." We also have an "Octave Etude" and several smaller pieces for piano, as well as a cantata (written for the dedication of a church) for soloists, choir, and organ. All of these have been published. Unpublished works in manuscript form include several occasional cantatas for soloists, choir, and orchestra (including one for the university's memorial service for King Carl XV in 1872, and one for the crowning of King Oscar II in 1873) and some smaller pieces for organ.

Nearly all of Lindeman's compositions reflect his admiration for the Bach tradition. The three fugues on B-A-C-H stand at the center of his compositional output, both as a symbol of his respect for the German master and as paradigmatic examples of his use of Baroque formal principles. One can nonetheless discern traces of Romanticism in his harmony and in the slightly homophonic cast of the music.

He came closest to the Baroque style in the organ variations on "If Thou But Suffer God to Guide Thee." Here we can see his skill in both double counterpoint and canon, and in several small interludes (marked "stretto") he even managed to vertically distribute the four phrases of the chorale melody so that they appear more or less simultaneously in the various voices. All together there are eleven such "stretto" passages with various solutions to this contrapuntal problem. Example 40 shows the second of these solutions, with the variation that follows. Note that the first phrase of the chorale is assigned to the alto, the second to the bass, and the third (not counting the repetition) to the tenor—all sounding simultaneously from the beginning. The last phrase appears in the soprano in the last three measures of the passage. Here, too, it obviously was Bach who served as the model: a similar distribution of the various phrases of the chorale appears at the close of his set of five canonic variations for organ on "Vom Himmel hoch" (BWV 769). In the variation of example 40, the chorale melody appears in half notes in the soprano, while the two contrapuntal voices form a canon at the octave with one beat between the entrances.

Example 40. L.M. Lindeman, Organ variation on the chorale "If Thou But Suffer God to Guide Thee."

In the organ preludes, Lindeman employed various forms of double counterpoint with great artistic freedom. His cantatas employ both homophonic and polyphonic techniques, with choral sections ranging from simple settings to fully developed fugues.

There is an impressive breadth to the scope of Lindeman's contributions to Norwegian music life. As a collector of folk music, a church musician, and a music teacher he was influential in several different areas. Now that his life work can be viewed in historical perspective, it seems clear that his most enduring achievements are his published collections of Norwegian folk melodies and his original hymn tunes. His *Older and Newer Norwegian Mountain Melodies* remains to this day the principal published source for anyone interested in Norway's folk tunes. And many of his hymns have sung themselves into the hearts of the people both in Norway and elsewhere, among them "Built on a Rock the Church Shall Stand," "Easter Morrow Stills Our Sorrow," and "Jesus, Priceless Treasure."

HALFDAN KJERULF

Artistically, Kjerulf stands in sharp contrast to Lindeman, for he was entirely comfortable with a musical idiom very close to that of German Romanticism. He had, indeed, studied at the Leipzig conservatory, but his affinity for Romanticism was deeper than that: it was an expression of his very being and his approach to life and art. But Kjerulf was also a *national* Romanticist. He shared Lindeman's interest in folk music and, as he acknowledged, was indebted to Lindeman in some respects. He was intimately familiar with Norwegian folk music both by direct contact and through Lindeman's collections, and it had an important influence on his musical style.

Halfdan Kjerulf was born in Oslo on September 17, 1815. His father, Peder Kjerulf, had emigrated to Norway from Denmark at the beginning of the 1800s. Halfdan received his first instruction in music from Lars Roverud and Otto Wetterstrand, both of whom were active as music teachers in the city at that time. He learned to play the piano, and he probably learned some elementary music theory from Roverud. Like his father, who held a high position in the Ministry of Finance, he planned to become a civil servant and began the study of law. His legal studies were interrupted by serious illness in 1839, however, and he never returned to them.

Even in his youth Kjerulf had done some composing. A few short piano pieces from these early years, primarily dances in the popular style of the period, have been preserved. They show nothing of his distinctive character as a composer, but they demonstrate his lively interest in music despite his lack at that time of formal training.

In the summer of 1840 he took a pleasure trip to Paris. This excursion proved to be of great importance to him, for in Paris he encountered a thriving music life with outstanding concert performances of both the Viennese Classicists and the early Romantic composers. He also heard the music of Berlioz, who at that time was a controversial figure in French music.

The winter and spring of 1840–41 were a difficult time for Kjerulf and his family. In December, shortly after his return from Paris, a sister died. The following February his father passed away, and three months later a brother also died. Upon the death of his father, Halfdan, as the oldest of the children, was obliged to assist in supporting the family. To do so he took a position as foreign editor of *Den Constitutionelle*, one of the two leading newspapers in Oslo at that time.

He did not, however, forsake his interest in music; indeed, in the autumn of 1841 he published his first volume of compositions, consisting of six songs. He later regretted its publication because he judged it to be dilettantish and immature. Nonetheless it is of great interest, not least because it contains an early version of "Water Sprite," his setting of a text by Johan S. Welhaven. The song was later revised, with many changes in the accompaniment, but the melody remained largely as it was in 1841. Kjerulf could not have known much about Norwegian folk music at this time, but this melody shows that even then he had a fine feeling for the distinctive sound of authentic Norwegian music.

Throughout the 1840s Kjerulf studied composition on his own. He was dissatisfied with his theoretical knowledge, but he had no one to whom he could turn for guidance. It was a great encouragement for him when in 1845 he was invited to become the conductor of the newly formed Norwegian Students' Male Chorus. His work with this group allowed him to develop a good knowledge of the possibilities of the medium and inspired him to write two of his best-known compositions for male chorus: "Sunshine" and "The Bridal Procession." In 1845 he began giving piano lessons; the following year he left his position as a journalist and thereafter earned his living as a music teacher.

When Carl Arnold came to Oslo in 1848, Kjerulf immediately began studying harmony with him. Arnold also helped him procure a stipend that enabled him to study abroad in 1849–51. He went first to Copenhagen, where he studied with Niels W. Gade, then in 1850 to the Leipzig conservatory, where one of his teachers was Ernst Friedrich Richter. Here, at the age of 35, he finally acquired a solid conservatory education.

After returning to Oslo in the summer of 1851, Kjerulf resumed his work as a music teacher. He was fortunate to have a number of gifted pupils who later were to play important roles in Norwegian music, including both Agathe Backer Gröndahl and Erika Nissen. Kjerulf lived quietly and unobtrusively in Oslo and did not become deeply involved in public music life. He had resigned as conductor of the Norwegian Students' Male Chorus when he went to Copenhagen in 1849, and thereafter his only direct association with a performing group was with a private male vocal quartet. One important contribution to Olso's music life, however, was the previously mentioned series of subscription concerts, which he initiated in collaboration with Johan Gottfried Conradi. The project eventually had to be abandoned for lack of support, unfortunately, and nothing of the kind occurred again until the 1860s when Winter-Hjelm and Grieg offered a similar series of concerts.

It was only toward the end of his life that Kjerulf began to receive some recognition for his compositions. In 1863 he was awarded the *Litteris et artibus* medal, and in 1865 he was made a member of the Royal Swedish Academy of Music. Kjerulf was a victim of serious illness during his later years. He died on August 11, 1868.

Most of Kjerulf's compositions were written after his studies in Leipzig. He restricted himself mainly to the smaller forms, rarely attempting cyclic works. There is some indication that he composed two movements of a piano sonata, but both are lost. We do have from his hand the music for a comic opera, *Midshipmen in Port*, to a text by Henrik Wergeland. There are also two works for mixed chorus: "Serenade by the Seashore," Op. 8, and "The Troubadour," Op. 17b. The great body of Kjerulf's output, however, consists of approximately 130 songs and forty pieces for male chorus. He also wrote over thirty piano pieces, but unfortunately they are seldom played today.

Kjerulf's compositions strongly reflect his admiration for German Romanticism. His musical style shows the influence of Schumann; in his piano music Chopin may also have been one of his models. Nonetheless, many of his works have a distinctly Norwegian sound that clearly shows the influence of the folk music of his native land. In some works this sound is quite direct, suggesting a conscious use of folk-music elements. In other cases the source of this distinctive character is less obvious and appears to reflect a more subconscious use of musical elements that simply "felt" authentically Norwegian to the composer.

As noted earlier, Kjerulf was familiar with Norwegian folk music not only through the published collections of Lindeman and Berggreen but also from direct contact with the living tradition. It is known, for example, that in the summer of 1849 he took a vacation trip with the painter Hans Gude and others, and that their route took them to Hallingdal, Hardanger, and Sogn. The influence of the *slaatter* and folk ballads Kjerulf heard on the trip is evident in an interesting little piano piece he wrote that same autumn, entitled "Something That Yet Is Nothing" with the subtitle "Echo from a Mountain Journey." It is a short mood piece in the middle of which appears a *halling*, Kjerulf's first attempt to imitate Norwegian *slaatter* on the piano. The design is simple: a melody played over a sustained tonic and fifth. If this was indeed derived from folk music, it must have been the sound of the *langeleik* that Kjerulf had in mind. He later advanced to a considerably more refined folk-music style, but this first attempt is evidence both of the impression this meeting with folk music had on him and of his spontaneous desire to reproduce it within an artistic framework.

The fact that Kjerulf's music derived its inspiration from two quite different sources—German Romanticism and Norwegian folk music—resulted in two equally different strands in his production which he himself referred to as, respectively, "general European" and "Norwegian." These two strands can be traced throughout the entire body of his works but are most clearly evident in the songs and piano pieces. The influence of German Romanticism is apparent in such songs as "Last Night the Nightingale Woke Me" (Op. 3, No. 2), "By the Moon's Silver Light" (Op. 20, No. 2), and "You Will Come" (Op. 17, No. 3). The same may be said of the piano pieces "Lullaby" (Op. 4, No. 3), "Berceuse" (Op. 12, No. 2), and many others. As clear examples of "Norwegian" compositions we may point to the songs "Ingrid's Song" (Op. 6, No. 4) and "Enticing Sounds" (Op. 3, No. 6). Two of his better-known piano pieces that belong in this category are "Humoresque" and "Caprice," Nos. 1 and 4, respectively, of Opus 12.

One "Norwegian" composition that is not very well known may serve as an example of the type. It is a short piano piece called "Peasant Dance," given in its entirety in example 41. This piece, which was composed in 1856 but never published during Kjerulf's lifetime, appears in a manuscript that also contains the three pieces comprising Opus 4. It provides a good illustration of the daring use of dissonance in Kjerulf's "Norwegian" works. The tendency is evident in the very first chord, which consists of a major second and a major seventh (reduced to the closest prime intervals above the bass). It is the liberal use of pedal points that creates such dissonances, both here

Example 41. Halfdan Kjerulf, "Peasant Dance."

and later in the composition. This is also one of the few pieces in which Kjerulf makes use of the structure so typical of Hardanger-fiddle music: independent two-measure motives that are repeated many times in somewhat varied forms. It is quite clear in this case that the Hardanger-fiddle *slaatter* were the source of his inspiration, with respect to both the use of dissonance and the overall structure. No doubt it was precisely this bold use of dissonance that the editor found objectionable, as a result of which the piece was not included when Opus 4 was published.

A good example of Kjerulf's "general European" style is the song "Evening Forest Longings," written in 1850 while he was in Leipzig (see example 42). The brief text by the German poet Carl Mayer is typical of the nature mysticism of early Romanticism:

O precious flowers, glowing in the light of eventide,
Your leaves, next evening's golden rays, are poor and pale beside!
What tongue, what song can man employ
To tell of forest's evening joy?

Example 42. Halfdan Kjerulf, "Evening Forest Longings."

Kjerulf shaped the song quite independently of the four-line AABB construction of the text. With the help of a piano postlude he created an ABA′ form, although A′ is abbreviated relative to A. The A section is built on the first line of the text: the piano interlude and the repetition of the last part of the first line of the text echo the preceding three-measure phrase. The B section includes the rest of the text and is significantly longer than A. Both the formal construction and the melody line display a fine alternation between the voice part and the piano accompaniment. Harmonically the piece is marked by a large number of secondary dominants. The principal key is A-flat major, but except for the coda authentic cadences occur in this key in just three places: measures 4–5, 18–20, and 22–23. There are secondary cadences to the subdominant chord of the relative minor key (B-flat minor, measures 2–3 and elsewhere), to the dominant chord of the relative minor key (C major, measure 7), and to the relative minor key (F minor, measure 8). Note also the use of the subdominant minor chord (D-flat minor to diminished) in measure 3, and the fine effect achieved by the use of parallel passing tones in sixths in measure 4 and measures 13–14.

Also worth noting is the use of F in the piano postlude as a dissonant appoggiatura at the beginning of measure 26. It is used within the voice-leading context of the lowest treble voice (A-flat, G, F, G, A-flat) and in this case does not seem especially surprising; in later works, however, Kjerulf employed considerably harsher dissonances resulting from a similar linear technique. On the whole, this song with its mellow sounds and mildly somber mood is a good example of one side of Kjerulf's art. Other songs are quite different, however. His folk-like Björnstjerne Björnson songs are well known in Norway; they vary from the cheerful and lively "Ingrid's Song" and "Venevil" to the more elegiac "Synnöve's Song" and "Evening Mood." But he also wrote other, more obscure songs reflecting dark and gloomy moods—as, for example, the three songs for bass voice published posthumously as Opus 18. Here we find the intensely emotional "Bereavement" (text by Johan Runeberg), "The Hermit" (text by Joseph von Eichendorff) with its mood of calm resignation, and the dramatic "The Ship" (text by Charles Mackey in a translation by K. Vollheim).

Kjerulf's songs are generally simple in form; nearly half are strophic, and most of the others are modified strophic. Even those that are through-composed are almost modified strophic. In the songs with a distinctly Norwegian stamp, Kjerulf nearly always used a simple strophic form as a natural imitation of the folk ballad. In some of the piano pieces he employed more complex forms—as, for example, in "Sketch IV" (Op. 7, No. 4), which exhibits some aspects of sonata form. The majority of his compositions for piano can be classified as ternary, however. Nonetheless, his piano works do not sound stereotyped because, within the basic ternary form, he gave each composition a distinctive cast. Kjerulf also composed a number of duets that are similar in form and style to the songs for solo voice and piano.

The influence of folk music is less evident in Kjerulf's compositions for male chorus. Except for a few touches in "The Bridal Procession" they belong largely to his "general European" category, but they nonetheless include some of his finest compositions. As noted earlier, he first achieved mastery of this medium because, as conductor of the Norwegian Students' Male Chorus, he had developed a thorough knowledge of the possibilities and limits of such ensembles. Of his compositions written before 1850, virtually the only ones that were not reworked later are "Sunshine" and "The Bridal Procession."

After returning from his study abroad, Kjerulf organized a private male quartet that enabled him to test his vocal compositions and arrangements. In addition to about forty original compositions for male chorus, he produced over fifty arrangements—some of his own works, others of folk ballads, and still others of the songs of various other composers. His best-known compositions for male chorus from his later period include "Norway's Mountains," "Jubilate," and "Life's Voyage," with texts by Henrik Wergeland, Thomas Moore, and Ambrosius Stub, respectively. His works for male voices place significant demands on the performers, but for a good ensemble the rewards justify the effort.

Kjerulf's love of Norwegian folk music also found expression in a series of piano arrangements of folk tunes. These were published in two collections: *Twenty-five Selected Norwegian Folk Dances* and *Norwegian Folk Ballads Arranged for Piano*. The latter collection contains forty-two melodies. In a preface to the dance collection he wrote: "As I release this attempt to create easy settings for piano of a few Norwegian folk dances, I am obliged to add that the melodies are derived primarily from the collections of Lindeman and Berggreen, and that Lindeman's excellent collections especially have, with good reason, influenced my handling of the material."

Kjerulf's arrangements are completely independent of his predecessors, however. They are the most important works of their kind prior to those of Grieg, who undoubtedly was influenced by them. Kjerulf's handling of the dances, especially, displays many interesting features, including frequent use of various types of pedal point with resulting dissonances that at times become quite harsh. "Bridal Dance" (No. 12 in the collection) points forward in many ways to Grieg's *Norwegian Peasant Dances*, Op. 72. Kjerulf extended the piece by inserting an interlude, "Impromptu," built on motives taken from the *slaatt*, and in the main section one finds both harsh dissonances resulting from voice leading and the use of the dominant of the dominant with lowered fifth that was later to become so characteristic of Grieg.

Kjerulf's arrangements of *slaatter* reveal his surprisingly thorough knowledge of Hardanger-fiddle music—enough to lead one to ask what contact he may actually have had with this tradition. Some light is shed on the subject by a brief passage in the preface to the collection. Kjerulf wrote: "Numbers 4 and 7 are derived from a transcription for Hardanger fiddle by Hovar Giböen . . . It should also be noted that the Hardanger fiddle's peculiar tuning (the 4 strings tuned to a, d^1, a^1, and e^2) has influenced both the transcription and the arrangement." It is possible that the violinist Christian Suchow called these *slaatter* to Kjerulf's attention, for he had spent some time with Giböen both to transcribe *slaatter* and to learn how to play the

Hardanger fiddle. In 1859 Suchow gave concerts in Oslo that included a group of *slaatter* played on the Hardanger fiddle. Kjerulf may also have had other direct contacts with the Hardanger-fiddle tradition about which we have no information. It is interesting, in any case, that in the preface to his arrangements of *slaatter* Kjerulf acknowledged the significance of the Hardanger fiddle to his work.

Kjerulf rightly holds a central position in the history of Norwegian music. His work is an essential part of the foundation upon which Grieg and his generation built. Important as his influence was to Grieg and his contemporaries, however, this was not his greatest contribution. His compositions are important in their own right—indeed, they include some of the most valuable works in Norway's musical heritage. His best songs are works of outstanding quality and will always have a secure place in Norway's repertoire. Because of the decline of the male-chorus tradition, however, his compositions in that genre are rarely sung today. On the other hand, several of his piano pieces, especially his arrangements for piano of Norwegian folk tunes, are of considerable interest and deserve wider recognition.

As a composer, Kjerulf has often been regarded primarily as a forerunner of Grieg. He was that too, and it is interesting to observe that in many places in his compositions he anticipated precisely those elements in Grieg's style that were most forward-looking and creative. Now, more than a century after his death, Kjerulf's intrinsic value as a composer in his own right can be seen more clearly than before. His works belong to an earlier period in Romanticism than Grieg's, but that does not diminish their artistic worth. In his generation Kjerulf remains a towering figure in Nordic music.

KJERULF'S CONTEMPORARIES

Male choruses played an important role in Norway's music life during the second half of the nineteenth century, and the man whose name is most intimately connected with this movement was Johan Didrik Behrens (1820–96). He studied violin in Bergen, the city of his birth, but his interest in singing was awakened at an early age. Although he went to Oslo in 1841 to study theology, vocal music soon began to occupy most of his time. In 1846 he became singing instructor in the city's Latin school, whereupon he forsook his theological studies. He spent the rest of his life as a singing teacher and choral conductor. Aside from various concert tours with his choir, he remained in Oslo until his death in 1890.

Behrens had a decisive influence on all three of the large male choruses founded in Oslo during the 1840s. He served as the first conductor of the Businessmen's Chorus upon its formation in 1847. In 1848 he also became conductor of the Craftsmen's Chorus, which had been reorganized in that year. Owing to the pressure of other responsibilities, however, he was forced to relinquish this post after six years. Behrens had earlier joined with Hartvig Lassen and Johan Hals in the establishment of the Norwegian Students' Male Chorus. Kjerulf was the first conductor of that group, but in 1849, when Kjerulf left for Copenhagen, Behrens succeeded him. Thus from 1849 to 1854 Behrens was conductor of all three of these important singing groups. His influence eventually extended even further, however, for through his contributions to the large song festivals during the latter part of the century he had an impact on male-chorus singing in virtually every part of the country.

Behrens's most enduring accomplishment is his collections of songs for male chorus, which were published sporadically over a period of many years. The most important of these is a series entitled *Collection of Part Songs for Male Voices*, issued from 1845 to 1869, containing five hundred pieces. It includes works by most of the Norwegian composers of the period, many of them compositions written expressly for the series. There are also arrangements of folk songs and a large selection of foreign music, both original compositions and arrangements. Behrens himself wrote several of the texts in the collections, translated others, and harmonized or arranged a number of the pieces.

In 1858, as previously mentioned, he published a book on Lutheran hymnody that provoked the so-called hymn controversy (see p. 155). In 1875 he founded the Johanites, a chorus consisting of older student singers, which he continued to conduct until shortly before his death. In 1878 he and the Norwegian Students' Male Chorus participated in the world exhibition in Paris and were highly praised for their performances.

Behrens was not very prolific as a composer. The only original works of which we have any knowledge are eight melodies that he wrote for the *Melody Book for Norwegian Song Books*, a collection published in 1876 primarily for use in the schools. They include melodies for "The Old Mother" and "Knowledge Shall Lead Us" (both texts by A. O. Vinje) and "Solveig's Song" (by Henrik Ibsen). None of them has become established in Norway's song repertoire, however.

Johan Gottfried Conradi (1820–96), another pioneer in the male-chorus movement in Norway, actually was involved in this area before Behrens, for as early as 1843 he had formed a male chorus for students and artisans. In 1845 he founded two more groups: the Businessmen's Chorus and the Craftsmen's Chorus. None of these groups lasted very long in its original form, but the latter two were reorganized by Behrens in 1847 and 1848, respectively. As early as 1850 Conradi also organized the first song festival in which several choruses participated. Behrens's personal qualities, how-

Johan Gottfried Conradi. (Universitetsbiblioteket i Oslo)

ever, made him the natural leader of the male chorus movement, and Conradi gradually moved on to other areas of endeavor.

The son of a druggist, Conradi studied pharmacy and, for a short time, medicine, but he eventually abandoned both to concentrate on music. It is believed that he was largely self-taught, and certainly his early compositions demonstrate his initial lack of formal training. From 1843 to 1848, while he was active as a conductor in Oslo, he also tried his hand at composing, among other things, some stage music. The period 1848–53 found him traveling around eastern Norway establishing choral and orchestral societies. From 1853 to 1855 he was music director of the newly opened Norwegian Theater in Oslo. In 1855 he received a stipend that enabled him to go abroad to study music; he spent two years in formal study, primarily at the Leipzig conservatory. Upon returning to Oslo, he collaborated with Kjerulf for two years in the subscription concert series discussed earlier (see p. 148). From 1857 to 1862 he also conducted the Craftsmen's Chorus, and in 1860 he became conductor of the Laborers' Chorus.

Conradi's earliest known compositions are a short song, "To Stella As She Slept" (1841), and two volumes of dances for piano published in 1843. All of this music is in the "salon" style of the time and makes no claim to being anything more. In 1844 he wrote music for the musical comedy *The Yellow Gloves* (text by J. F. Bayard), which was performed at the Christiania Theater. It exists in manuscript and includes both original works and arrangements of pieces taken from the musical comedies of other composers.

Several of Conradi's compositions have been lost. Among them are an occasional cantata with text by Henrik Wergeland, which was performed at Our Savior's Church; "War Song," a setting for male chorus of a text by J. Theodor Rördam; and the music for *The Coast Guardsmen*, the play offered by the Norwegian Theater at its inauguration in 1852 (text by H. A. Bjerregaard).

Among his later extant works are *Four Quartets for Male Voices* (Op. 6) and several songs for solo voice and piano with texts by Johan S. Welhaven (Opuses 8 and 9). These works, which probably were written around 1850, show that Conradi had gained considerable experience since his earlier compositions, but the craftsmanship remains exceedingly elementary. The same is true of several pieces for male chorus published in 1854, including *Four Songs for Four Male Voices*, Op. 10.

In 1855 Conradi resumed his activities as a composer for the theater. In April of that year Andreas Munch's *An Evening on Giske* was performed in Olso, followed in May by Christian Monsen's *The Gudbrandsdalers*. For the former Conradi wrote the concluding song, and for the latter a total of nine numbers, all of which have been preserved. The music for *The Gudbrands-*

dalers, which was published in a piano version in autumn, 1855, must be considered one of his most important works. It consists of two large pieces for chorus (the introduction and the conclusion), two marches, a short melodrama, a programmatic piece ("Battle Music"), and three songs for solo voice. This music, too, is harmonically and melodically very simple, but it reflects considerable imagination. Some of it is quite melodious and undoubtedly was successful on the stage. In two of the songs, "Scotland's Praise" and "Norway's Praise," he was obviously trying to create melodies characteristic of each country.

It appears that Conradi composed very little after concluding his studies in Leipzig. Indeed, the only known work dating from his post-Leipzig period is a piece for male chorus entitled "Sunset." First published in 1845, it was revised and reissued in 1858. The revised version of this little piece displays a much surer technique than his other works and has deservedly become quite popular.

Conradi was also active as a writer on musical topics. His most important contribution in this area was *A Brief Historical Overview of the Development and Present Status of Music in Norway*, published in 1878. It was the first written history of Norwegian music and it remains an important source of information about the status of music in Norway in the nineteenth century.

Another composer of this period whose importance is exceeded only by that of Kjerulf and Lindeman was Martin Andreas Udbye (1820–89). Because his parents were members of the working class, his only opportunity for an education was in the public school in Trondheim, his native city. He was a gifted child, however, and thus was able to enrich his education independently. In 1836, when he was only sixteen years of age, he became a tutor, and two years later a teacher in that same public school. He continued in the latter capacity until 1885, when he withdrew from all of his public positions.

Udbye's chief interest, however, was music. He had learned to play violin and cello at an early age, and in addition to his school work he studied music theory on his own. In 1844 he became organist at the Hospital Church in Trondheim. In 1851–52 he received private financial support that enabled him to go to Leipzig, where he studied composition with Moritz Hauptmann and organ with Carl Ferdinand Becker. In 1858–59, through a grant from the government and the Trondheim Academy of Science, he was able to pursue further study abroad and visit a number of European cities. In 1869 he was appointed organist at the Church of Our Lady in Trondheim.

Udbye managed to publish only his smaller compositions, and most of these, unfortunately, date from early in his life. Two published volumes of songs, probably written before 1860, are of minor importance. His short organ pieces, of which a few were published, also deserve little attention. His chamber music, on the other hand, is of greater interest, especially his three string quartets. All were written in the years 1852–55, and rank among his chief works. The first quartet was written when he was in Leipzig, the others after his return to Norway. The first two were issued by a German publisher, and the third remains in manuscript. Although they generally observe the rules of Classical form, they exhibit Udbye's independence in the handling of this form and his sound training in music theory.

The most important of Udbye's smaller works are his compositions for *a cappella* chorus, some for male, some for mixed voices. While they have been overshadowed by other Norwegian choral works, the best of them, such as "The Storm on Its Tempestuous Path" (Op. 15, No. 2, for male voices) and "By a Water Lily" (Op. 28, No. 10, for mixed chorus), deserve to be performed.

Udbye was not at his best in these smaller forms, however. A rather striking evaluation of him was given in early 1858 in a critique carried in the Danish periodical *Tidsskrift for Musik*: "Even the objections that we have felt obliged to express often suggest a striving on the part of this composer toward the larger forms; thus, although the characteristics to which we have objected may not be appropriate here, they nonetheless bode well for the future." This "striving toward the larger forms" gradually found expression in Udbye's compositional output: of his forty-six opus numbers, sixteen are for orchestra and various vocal combinations, two are large works for chorus, soloists, and piano (or organ), and three are purely orchestral works.

Udbye's most productive period as a composer was from the mid-1850s to 1873. Thereafter he wrote only one work of any importance: "Tröndelagers' Farewell," written for a Trondheim song festival in 1883. (Tröndelag is the name of the region in which Trondheim is located.) The first work in which he used an orchestra was *The Horsemen of Aasgaard* (Op. 11), written in 1855. This was a setting for unison male chorus, solo voice, and orchestra of a poem by Johan S. Welhaven. The lengthy text is set in a single unified movement, but within the whole there are some strophic sections. Even in this early composition one can discern Udbye's inclination toward the dramatic, both in his choice of a text and in the musical expression. It is worthy of note that one section is written in 5/4 meter, a radical feature at that time.

Udbye wrote a total of seven works for the theater including incidental music for stage plays, musical comedies, comic operas, and one serious opera. Only three of these were ever performed, including *Homesickness* (1864) and *The Nobleman and the Rose of Fluberg* (1870). Udbye's serious opera, *The Peace-making Woman* (the first serious opera written in Norway) has never been performed. It was written in the winter of 1857–58, with a libretto by Udbye's friend and fellow teacher, Carl Müller of Trondheim. The action takes place in Norway during the unsettled period of the civil war of the late Middle Ages. The principal characters are the three kings Inge, Magnus, and Erik, and King Inge's daughter, Margrete. Udbye here retained the old practice of dividing the opera into distinct numbers, a total of fifteen in two acts. The practice of treating larger sections (or entire acts) as a unified whole, which was so characteristic of German opera at that time—and which Udbye had attempted in *The Horsemen of Aasgaard*—was not employed in his larger works until later.

The weakness of the opera, as with several of his earlier works, is especially evident in a certain stiffness that characterizes the lyrical sections. Udbye had difficulty freeing himself from his models, and the music sounds rather dry. The libretto, too, was somewhat lacking in imagination. Nonetheless, the opera was accepted for performance at the Christiania Theater and was virtually ready for its premiere when a devastating fire in 1877 put an end to any further operatic performances there. The opera was never again scheduled for production, and Udbye thus never heard a complete performance of the work. Individual selections were performed several times, however, and the overture was published in an arrangement for piano four-hands.

Udbye's last large works were *The Lost Son* (Op. 44, 1872) and *Icelanders in Norway* (Op. 45, 1873). The former is a setting for baritone (or bass) solo and orchestra of Egil Skallagrimsson's saga, translated by Peter A. Munch. The latter is a setting for male chorus, mixed chorus, soloists, and orchestra of a text by J. Brun. It consists of three sections entitled "On the Fjord," "In the Hall," and "In the Church," but the music joins them together into a single, unified whole.

In these two later works Udbye was apparently able to conquer several of the weaknesses that were evident in his earlier compositions. Perhaps the librettos were also more suitable for his purposes. The melodies are more supple, often finding expression in lines that are quite expressive. *The Lost Son*, especially, contains some lovely melodic passages. The text for *Icelanders in Norway* is not of the best quality, but its dramatic content and vivid colors no doubt appealed to the composer. Here too the melodic material was carefully worked out, and the large choral sections—as is usually the case in Udbye's compositions—come off with good effect.

Like most of the Norwegian composers of this time, Udbye was interested in folk music. He left a manuscript of an orchestral suite built on Norwegian folk tunes, and he used folk melodies in several of his compositions, such as his marches for military band. Folk tunes do not seem to have played a prominent role in his works, however. They do not appear to have significantly influenced his musical vocabulary, though occasionally one can discern features drawn from folk music—as, for example, in the duets of *Norwegian Farm Life*, Op. 10.

Udbye never secured a position that enabled him to devote himself entirely to music. He was obliged to work as a school teacher throughout his life in order to support his family, and he had additional responsibilities as both an organist and singing teacher. The limiting circumstances under which he worked must share some of the blame for the loneliness and bitterness of his later years. His last composition, no longer extant, is said to have been appropriately entitled "Lonely Warriors."

Udbye's contemporary and fellow townsman, Thomas Dyke Acland Tellefsen (1823–74), chose to leave the difficult circumstances of his native land in favor of the better conditions on the continent. After going to Paris in 1842 to study piano, he returned to Norway only for brief visits. In Paris he achieved considerable celebrity, especially after Chopin's death. As a composer he must be ranked near the other composer-virtuosos of his day. He often played his own compositions and, although they have not endured in the piano repertoire, they were well received at the time. Both as a pianist and as a composer he was strongly influenced by Chopin.

Tellefsen was born in Trondheim, where his father, Johan Christian Tellefsen, was organist at the famous Nidaros cathedral. Music was assiduously cultivated in the Tellefsen home, and Thomas's rich musical gifts were nourished at an early age. In his childhood his musical interest was primarily in singing; it was not until he was thirteen or fourteen years old that he became interested in the piano. His pianistic talents developed rapidly, however, and at eighteen he made his debut in a solo recital in Trondheim. In 1842, with the help of loans and gifts from friends in Trondheim, he went to Paris. There he studied with the Norwegian-born pianist Charlotte Thygesen, a pupil of Friedrich Kalkbrenner. From time to time during the period 1844 to 1847 he was also a pupil of Chopin.

Paris became Tellefsen's permanent home, his residency there interrupted only by concert and vacation trips to Norway and other European countries. He was a great success in his first Parisian concert appearance in April, 1851, and thereafter he was considered one of the elite virtuoso pianists in the city. He often appeared in concerts in Paris and elsewhere until about 1860, less frequently thereafter. Little by little illness and other difficulties hindered his work.

Like Chopin, Tellefsen wrote primarily for the piano. His compositions include two piano concertos, a piano sonata, a number of individual piano pieces of varying length, some chamber music with piano, and an orchestral overture. The overture, his only composition that does not require a piano, was written in 1853 and displays a competent but not especially original handling of the orchestra. In the two piano concertos, the orchestra, apart from some brief *tutti* sections, is used primarily to accompany the solo instrument.

Tellefsen's piano compositions approach those of Chopin in quality, but they are somewhat more conservative. They are technically sound with respect to both harmony and melody. The harmony is primarily diatonic, but there are occasional chromatic passages. Abrupt modulations and sudden changes of key add color to these works and demonstrate that Tellefsen was intimately familiar with some of the harmonic devices of Romanticism.

His chamber music includes two sonatas for violin and piano, a sonata for cello and piano, a trio for violin, cello, and piano, and a sonata for two pianos. These appear to owe less to the influence of Chopin than do his other compositions. The harmony is more moderate than in most of his works. It is pleasant and well-constructed music, but it has a somewhat impersonal sound.

Tellefsen also made some use of elements derived from Norwegian folk music in his compositions. In the last movement of his first piano concerto, for example, he used a bridal march taken from Lindeman's *Older and Newer Norwegian Mountain Melodies*. In general, however, the Norwegian element is evident in the use of individual features characteristic of the folk music rather than direct use of authentic folk melodies. Tellefsen gave distinctively Norwegian names to some of his piano pieces in order to indicate their character, such as "Dance of the Fairy Girl" (Op. 9), "Bridal Dance" (Op. 26), and "The Valhalla Festival" (Op. 40). Other compositions incorporating Norwegian characteristics include some of the mazurkas and parts of the violin sonatas (Op. 19 and Op. 37). Those characteristics especially suggestive of a folk-music origin are certain melodic turns (violin figurations), the use of pedal points (often double pedal points in the form of an open fifth), and occasional powerfully stressed dissonances.

The most successful of Tellefsen's compositions are some of the mazurkas, especially those with distinctively Norwegian features. These display original ideas and fine harmonic and rhythmic details. Among his larger works the *Toccata* (Op. 22) stands out as one of the best. It is in sonata form and is quite original in its ideas and execution. The principal weakness of Tellefsen's compositions is that he never managed to free himself from his mentor's style. Chopin's brilliant compositions defied imitation by all who followed him, even those who were both clever and talented.

To summarize the main features of Norway's music life during these two decades we must call to mind once again the two components of the national

Romantic school. One of these, it will be recalled, was the powerful influence of European, especially German, music. This influence reached Norway partly by way of the many German musicians who came there to live and work, partly through the Norwegian musicians who went abroad to study, and it raised the standard of Norway's musical achievements to a level fairly comparable to that on the continent. The other component was the strong national influence mediated partly through direct contact with Norwegian folk music, partly via the general "national Romantic ethos" which, to a greater or lesser degree, captivated everyone—including the musicians—at that time.

The union of these two forces created the impetus for the powerful development of Norwegian music that ensued during the latter half of the nineteenth century. From the tension between these two components came much of the power that drove Grieg and his contemporaries onward to the summit of Norway's music history. Halfdan Kjerulf was the most important of those composers who participated in the emergence of national Romanticism in Norway, and it was he who also played an essential role beyond the boundaries of his native land.

9

The Golden Age
(ca. 1860–ca. 1890)

The history of Norway in the latter half of the nineteenth century is filled with important political events. The struggle with Sweden for Norwegian independence became acute toward the end of the century. The controversy nearly led to war between the two countries but ended with the negotiated dissolution of the Swedish-Norwegian union in 1905. Before that, in the 1870s and 1880s, the so-called parliamentarist controversy was the principal issue occupying the minds of the people. It took the form of a demand that the government ministers should be allowed to attend meetings of the Norwegian parliament (the Storting). The intention, however, was to make the government responsible to the Storting, thus reducing the power of the king. The Storting acceded to this demand, leading in 1884 to the impeachment of the government.

Not surprisingly, these tumultuous events had a profound effect on various aspects of Norwegian life. The economy of the nation prospered, but the gradual triumph of industrialism created new problems in both the social and the political realms. Many of Norway's leading artists took an active part in the public debate of these issues.

In literature and music this period was one of rich flowering. More than at any time before or since, Norway's writers and composers played an important role in the cultural life of Europe. The writers stood at the pinnacle of international fame, but among composers Edvard Grieg was an important European figure in the last part of the century. And Grieg was not alone: other Norwegian composers, notably Johan Svendsen, also played a role beyond the borders of their native land.

Music on the continent during the 1870s and 1880s was marked by the clash between the Classically oriented Romanticism of which Johannes Brahms was the leading exponent and the more radical "new German" faction whose chief representatives were Wagner and Liszt. Most Norwegian composers continued to receive their education at the Leipzig conservatory, where Classically oriented Romanticism held sway. Some were educated in Berlin, but they had little exposure to the more radical trends there. Johan Selmer was the only important Norwegian composer of this period to study in Paris, and his encounter with the program music of Berlioz was decisive for him.

Obviously no musician at this time could remain wholly untouched by the figure of Wagner. All had to take a position relative to him, and several of Norway's composers were influenced by him, especially Svendsen. Despite his admiration for Wagner, however, the Classical tradition was so strong in Svendsen that he was far from becoming an imitator of his great contemporary. Selmer was the first Norwegian composer to join the radical wing, but it was Berlioz, not Wagner, who had the greatest influence on his artistic development.

During this period music activities in Norway evolved in both breadth and quality. The most important development was the establishment of the Music Society in Oslo in 1871, primarily through the initiative of Grieg. When he came to the Norwegian capital in the autumn of 1866, the Philharmonic Society was still in existence; indeed, in the spring of 1867 it gave three concerts under his direction. That autumn, however, the Philharmonic Society was dissolved. In the years immediately following Grieg gave his own subscription concerts, though not without difficulties and dissension, and the need for a permanent music society to sponsor such concerts became urgent.

In the autumn of 1871, therefore, the Music Society was founded. Backers of the undertaking, in addition to Grieg, included L. M. Lindeman and Karl Hals, head of the Hals Brothers piano manufacturing firm. Grieg was the sole conductor during the society's first season. After Svendsen's return to Oslo in 1872, the two of them shared the duties and concert life quickly advanced to new heights. In 1874 both Grieg and Svendsen received government stipends. That autumn Grieg left Oslo and returned to Bergen, the city of his birth.

Except for a concert in the spring of 1877 conducted by Grieg, Svendsen was sole conductor of the Music Society orchestra for the next three years. In the autumn of that year he went abroad, and during his absence the concerts were conducted by the young Ole Olsen. Returning to Oslo in 1880, Svendsen resumed the leadership of the Music Society orchestra until 1883, when he was appointed conductor of the Royal Theater orchestra in Copenhagen. From 1883 to 1886 Johan Selmer was conductor of the Music Society orchestra. He was succeeded by Iver Holter, who held the position until the turn of the century. Throughout its existence, the Music Society gave Oslo a permanent organization offering regular orchestral concerts,

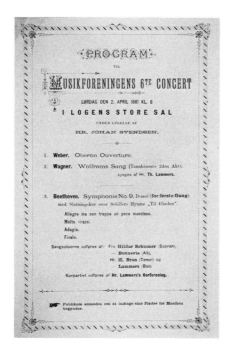

Program from a concert by the Music Society on April 2, 1881, including the Norwegian premiere of Beethoven's Ninth Symphony. Note that the choral part is sung by the Lammers Choir, which had been established just two years previously. (Universitetsbiblioteket i Oslo)

and it laid the foundation on which the modern Oslo Philharmonic Orchestra was built.

Opera productions still occurred only irregularly. As previously mentioned, many operas were produced by the Christiania Theater. The conductor of the theater orchestra from 1866 to 1894 was Johan Hennum; the years 1873–77, when Ludvig Josephson (a Swede) was theater director, were an especially rich period for Norwegian opera. After a devastating fire at the theater in 1877, however, there was a period of many years when opera performances in Oslo were very rare. There were a few performances during the 1880s, but on the whole opera was a kind of stepchild in Norway's music life until the establishment of the Norwegian Opera Company in 1959. That so few Norwegian composers have accomplished anything in the field of opera is undoubtedly owing in part to the weakness of the opera tradition in Norway and, as a consequence, the limited opportunity to get such works performed.

The male-chorus movement continued to flourish throughout most of the 1800s. Indeed, male choruses were much more advanced than mixed choruses, which were considerably less stable organizations at this time. The Music Society was able to put together a respectable mixed chorus for its concerts from time to time, but it was in each case an ad hoc ensemble, not a continuing organization. In 1878 Olaus Andreas Gröndahl founded a mixed chorus, and in 1879 Thorvald Lammers founded another, thus giving Oslo two permanent mixed choruses capable of performing some of the more demanding literature. During the 1880s and later they performed many of the most important oratorios from the late Baroque and Romantic periods and premiered the few compositions in this genre produced by Norwegian composers. The Lammers chorus, renamed the Cecilia Society in 1902, has continued this tradition to the present day.

A number of Norwegian performers earned reputations abroad during this period as well. Agathe Backer-Gröndahl, Edmund Neupert, and Thorvald Lammers were composers as well as performers and will be discussed later. Erika Lie Nissen was another performer of international standing; indeed, her contribution in this realm was perhaps even greater than that of Backer-Gröndahl and Neupert. She was active for many years as a concert pianist in Oslo, and she made several concert tours abroad. Her first teacher was her older sister, Ida Lie, who was also a pianist. She then studied with Kjerulf and later went to Berlin, where she attended Theodore Kullak's piano academy.

OTTO WINTER-HJELM AND RIKARD NORDRAAK

The generation of Norwegian composers who began their careers in the 1860s did not face an easy task. National Romanticism was still the watchword, and they were accordingly expected to compose "Norwegian" music. Moreover, they themselves wanted to do just that, but *how* it was to be accomplished was not clear to them. Their training was based for the most part on German Romanticism, and an authentic Norwegian tradition had yet to be created. With his songs Kjerulf had provided a foundation on which others could build, and there is no doubt that they were important for both Rikard Nordraak and the young Edvard Grieg. Kjerulf's piano music was relatively unknown, however, since most of it was not printed until after 1860. As far as symphonic music is concerned, there was no Norwegian tradition of any consequence that the young composers could use. It is no wonder then that Grieg, for example, had to grope around for some time before he was able to develop an independent and distinctively Norwegian style. The youthful Nordraak was somewhat ahead of Grieg in this. Both in *Six Songs* (Op. 1), dating from 1863, and in "Kaare's Song" of the same year, one finds a personal, independent tone.

The first Romantic composer who tried to write distinctively Norwegian music in symphonic form, however, was neither Grieg nor Nordraak. It was Otto Winter-Hjelm (1837–1931), whose second symphony (1863) was an attempt to integrate Norwegian musical material within a Romantic symphonic context. He went so far as to use a folk tune as one of his themes in the last movement. That this effort did not prove to be of greater importance is owing to the fact that this material was too thin to carry the weight of an entire symphony.

Otto Winter-Hjelm was a native of Oslo. He began his music education with Halfdan Kjerulf and Herman Neupert and in 1857 went to Leipzig to study at the conservatory. He was able to stay for just one year, but in 1861 he received a public grant to enable him to undertake further study. This time he went to Berlin, where he remained for two years, studying piano with Theodor Kullak and composition with Richard Würst.

Otto Winter-Hjelm. (Universitetsbiblioteket i Oslo)

Returning to Oslo in 1863, he immediately became engaged in various music activities. He became conductor of the Philharmonic Society and saw to it that public concerts were given more frequently than had previously been the case. He also tried to establish a music school. Beginning alone in 1864, he worked at it for two years. Then in 1866, when Grieg came to the city, the two young men collaborated in the creation of a music academy that unfortunately lasted for just one year. Winter-Hjelm continued as a private teacher, and in this role made many contributions. In 1874 he became organist at Trinity Church, a position he retained for forty-seven years. From 1887 to 1913 he was also a respected and feared critic for *Aftenposten*, one of Oslo's principal newspapers. And from 1890 to 1897 he was singing instructor at the Oslo cathedral school.

Winter-Hjelm authored several textbooks that were published during his lifetime. While his textbook in elementary music is somewhat labored in its presentation, his books on organ playing and piano playing reflect his sound practical experience as a teacher. The collection of exercises for singers was less effective. His greatest contribution to church music was made in connection with the hymn controversy discussed earlier (see p. 155). He also composed some chorale melodies, two of which appeared in the Norwegian chorale book of 1926.

Most of Winter-Hjelm's larger compositions date from the 1860s. While studying in Berlin he wrote two orchestral works that he saw fit to destroy, and then *Symphony No. 1* in B-flat major, which was premiered in Oslo in 1862. In 1862 he also completed the *String Quartet* in D major, and his *Symphony No. 2* in B minor followed in 1863. The *String Quartet* in D minor probably dates from about the same time, but thereafter his production slowed. Most of the larger works composed later are cantatas. The most important of these are one written for the university's Luther festival in 1883 and another, *The Light* (with text by Björnstjerne Björnson), written in 1897 for performance at the university. The latter ranks with the two symphonies among his principal works. His smaller works include about fifty songs for mixed chorus, male chorus, or solo voice, and piano, some piano pieces, and two volumes of organ preludes.

The background for Winter-Hjelm's compositions was Viennese Classicism and early Romanticism. He was an ardent admirer of Mendelssohn and Schumann but a firm opponent of Wagner and the whole radical direction in the music of his day. His handling of form is largely modeled on that of Classicism, but Romantic tendencies appear in occasional details. In the last movement of the first symphony, for example, he introduced new thematic material in the development, and in the second symphony the inner movements are linked together. His harmony has a somewhat more Romantic cast. Dissonant chords abound, even sequences of dissonant chords, and his frequent use of altered chords suggests that he was not so unaffected by Wagner as his protestations would lead one to think. Also suggestive of Romanticism is the heavy and rather dense instrumentation of his orchestral works.

As previously noted, Winter-Hjelm's second symphony is interesting because of his use of a Norwegian folk tune ("Do You Know Guro?") as a theme in the last movement. The whole symphony, for that matter, has a pronounced national Romantic flavor. The first movement bears the subtitle "Viking Life" and the second "Mountain Life." Nearly all of the themes in the symphony exhibit a folk-tune influence, especially in their rhythms. This symphony was the first orchestral composition to use Norwegian folk music, both directly and indirectly. (F. A. Reissiger and Christian Blom had used Norwegian folk tunes in their chamber music.) Nonetheless, it appears that Winter-Hjelm's symphony did not have any direct successors. Although composed several years before Svendsen wrote his first symphony, it was not performed until 1916, hence it is unlikely that Svendsen knew of it.

If Winter-Hjelm made his contribution to Norwegian music by means of practical activity carried on throughout a long and productive life, Rikard Nordraak was his direct opposite: he made no practical contribution worth mentioning to Norway's music life, and he died at twenty-three. As a composer, however, he holds an important place at the beginning of the "golden age" of Norwegian music.

Nordraak was born in Oslo in 1842. His mother, Fredrikke Carine Tang, was of Danish extraction. His father, Georg Marcus Nordraach, was an uncle of Björnstjerne Björnson, the famous late-nineteenth-century Norwegian poet, novelist, and orator. Thus Nordraak and Björnson were cousins, but they were bound by personal friendship and shared ideals as well as family ties.

Nordraak's musical gifts became evident when he was a child. His first training was with Herman Neupert (Edmund Neupert's father), and he soon began to write short pieces for the piano. It was planned, however, that he would pursue a career in business, so when he was fifteen he was sent to business school in Copenhagen. Nonetheless his musical interests prevailed, and instead of studying business he studied music with a well-known Danish singer and composer, Carl Ludvig Gerlach. In March, 1859, he took the final step toward a career in music, traveling to Berlin for advanced study. There he studied piano with Theodor Kullak and composition with Friedrich Kiel, but after just six months he had to return home.

Nordraak remained in Oslo for two years, studying both piano and composition with a German-born teacher, Rudolph Magnus, who was a church organist in the city. His first published compositions, *Four Dances* for piano, came out during the winter of 1859–60. Later, however, he chose to exclude these early compositions from his catalogue of works. It was a wise decision, for they show little of his distinctive genius as a composer. He also joined the New Norwegian Society in this period and became acquainted with Ole Bull and L. M. Lindeman. Ole Bull, especially, had a major impact on his attitude toward Norwegian folk music.

In the autumn of 1861 he returned to Berlin and resumed his studies with Theodor Kullak and Friedrich Kiel. This time he stayed for almost two years, returning to Oslo in the summer of 1863.

His "real" Opus 1, *Six Songs* with texts by Björnstjerne Björnson, Magdalene Thoresen, and Johannes Ewald, was published in 1863. He

Rikard Nordraak, Edvard Grieg, and Emil Hornemann in Copenhagen in 1865. (Gyldendal Norsk Forlag)

spent the winter of 1863–64 in Oslo, during which time he wrote "Yes, We Love This Land"—the song that was to become the Norwegian national anthem. Sung publicly for the first time on May 17, 1864, it was published in a version for male chorus shortly thereafter and quickly became popular throughout Norway.

In the summer of 1864 Nordraak went to Copenhagen, where he remained until the next spring. These few months were to be the most active and productive period of his short life. He joined Grieg and the Danish composers Emil Horneman and Gottfred Matthison-Hansen in the creation of a music society, called Euterpe, "for the sake of Scandinavia and in the Scandinavian spirit." His "Kaare's Song" was performed with great success at one of the Euterpe concerts. In the course of the winter of 1864–65 he

wrote the music for Björnson's play *Mary Stuart of Scotland*, and he published his Opus 2, *Five Norwegian Poems*, consisting of songs with texts by Björnstjerne Björnson and Jonas Lie. This was to be the last of his compositions that would be published during his lifetime.

Nordraak again returned to Berlin in May, 1865, to continue his education, but he was stricken with tuberculosis in October and died the following March. He was buried in Berlin, where in 1906 a monument was erected over his grave. In 1925 his coffin was brought to Oslo and interred in the cemetery of Our Savior's Church.

Nordraak did not live long enough to produce much music. About forty compositions, mostly smaller works, have been preserved. They consist of fourteen songs, six pieces for male chorus, incidental music for Björnson's plays *Sigurd Slembe* and *Mary Stuart of Scotland*, and a few piano compositions.

Ten of his fourteen songs are settings of texts by Björnson. All are in simple strophic form, and the piano generally serves a purely supporting function. Most of his songs have a short piano postlude that is characteristic of his style. "Ingerid Sletten" (Op. 1, No. 2) is a good example of his song style (see example 43). Both the melody and the harmony of this song are simple, but its artistic refinement makes it very effective. The melody consists entirely of triadic elements and diatonic scale passages. The harmony is restricted to the basic chords within the tonic minor and relative major keys, but these are used with exquisite taste and artistic economy. The dominant chord of the tonic key, for example, appears only once in each stanza, and that in the closing cadence. This song also has a piano postlude in which a discreet imitation of a *gangar* dance rhythm appears in the inner voice, while the tonal stasis in the upper and lower voices suggests the sound of the *langeleik* or perhaps the Hardanger fiddle.

Example 43. Rikard Nordraak, "Ingerid Sletten," Op. 1, No. 2.

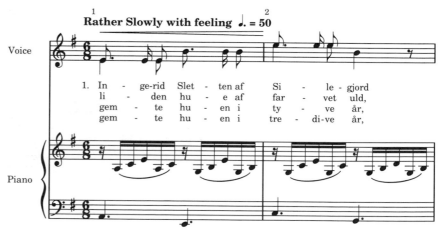

hav - de hver-ken sølv el - ler guld; men en
hav - de hver-ken stas el - ler før; men
måt - te ik - ke sli - de den ud! Så
måt - te ik - ke skæm - me den ud! Så

li - den hu - e af far - vet uld, som hun
fat - tigt min - ne om far og mor der
bæ - rer jeg den så glad som brud, når
bæ - rer jeg den så glad som brud, når

hav - de fåt ud - af mor. 2. En står.
skin - ned langt mer' end guld. 3. Hun
jeg for al - te - ret går. 4. Hun
jeg for vor Her - re

Of his songs for male chorus the first that must be mentioned is, of course, "Yes, We Love This Land," which soon after its composition (but after Nordraak's death) was declared Norway's national anthem. Others, too, have won a permanent place in the male-chorus repertoire. "There Is a Land" has come to be regarded as almost a folk song, and "Olav Trygvason"—like F. A. Reissiger's setting of the same text—is one of the most popular works for male chorus in Norway. The latter, Nordraak's only vocal composition that is not in simple strophic form, includes some variation in the fourth and fifth stanzas.

His incidental music for *Sigurd Slembe* consists of just one piece, "Kaare's Song," for baritone solo, male chorus, and orchestra. It made a very strong impression when it was first performed. Björnson later said of it: "It seemed to me to be the most powerful work that had been composed in Norway to that time." Both the text and Nordraak's setting have gradually paled, however, and it would be difficult today to describe so minor a work in such extravagant terms. His music for *Mary Stuart of Scotland*, on the other hand, seems much stronger. Nordraak wrote incidental music for the entire drama, consisting of "Purpose," two marches, "Hunting Song," "Taylor's Song," and some smaller pieces. This music displays Nordraak's uncomplicated style applied with fine artistic balance. "Purpose" has rightly become very popular, and "Taylor's Song" is perhaps Nordraak's finest and most gripping composition. It is deeply felt and, from an artistic point of view, well crafted.

Nordraak's largest composition is a piano piece, "Scherzo Capriccio," which is identified on the manuscript as Opus 3. It also was given the subtitle "The Mountain Brook," but this is thought to have been added by Grieg, who arranged for its publication after Nordraak's death. In form it is a kind of rondo: ABA′ CDC′ AA′ and coda. The tonic key is E major, but the middle section (CDC′) is in the subdominant key and its parallel minor (A major and A minor). The several sections are clearly delineated, and the overall effect is somewhat episodic. The strength of the piece lies in its numerous borrowings from Norwegian folk music, which here sound spontaneous and fresh: it is liberally spiced with *slaatt* rhythms, and it contains many strong dissonances presumably derived from Hardanger-fiddle music. Thematically it appears to be less dependent on folk music, though a few small melodic figurations probably were derived from the *slaatter*.

Other piano compositions by Nordraak include the simple and charming "Troubadour's Waltz" and "Valse Caprice." The latter was also used in the incidental music for *Mary Stuart of Scotland*.

Because Nordraak died so young, it is not surprising that among the few compositions he left behind are some that bear witness to a composer who had not yet fully hit his stride. His best works nonetheless display an astonishing maturity and disclose a well-defined musical personality. Of Grieg's contemporaries, Nordraak is the only one whose style was completely independent of his influence. This is owing partly to the fact that he matured earlier than Grieg, partly to the fact that he developed in a completely different direction. It is, of course, impossible to say how he might have continued had he lived longer. Despite his short life and limited production, however, he made an estimable contribution to Norwegian music, and with his ardent patriotism and profound love for folk music he became a source of inspiration for many of the composers of his day—not least for the greatest of them all, Edvard Grieg.

EDVARD GRIEG

Grieg's importance to Norwegian music cannot be overemphasized. It is true that both nationally and internationally he is the most important composer that Norway has produced, but that alone is not enough to explain his enormous influence in the history of Norwegian music. Part of the secret of his central position has to do with the time in which he worked. He was the culmination of a national Romantic movement that had its roots far back in the eighteenth century. His life work was the fulfillment of dreams and hopes that had been harbored by the bearers of Norwegian culture and the lovers of Norwegian music for nearly a hundred years. The idea of art, and especially of music, as an expression of that which was distinctively Norwegian reached its climax in the latter half of the nineteenth century—and Grieg was the man of the hour, the one whose genius enabled him to grasp these historical aspirations and give them an adequate artistic expression.

After Grieg's time, ideas about national distinctiveness and international fellowship changed, and the era of national Romanticism was irretrievably past. Part of the weakness of the generation of composers that came after Grieg appears to be that they did not fully understand this important fact. Impressed as they were by Grieg's compelling artistic personality and distinctive musical language, they became entangled in a national Romanticism that had already run its course. Grieg, of course, cannot be blamed for this. Indeed, he became himself a precursor of what was to come, for his last compositions point forward toward some of the new stylistic trends that emerged only after his death. The strange thing is that these elements of Grieg's later style largely escaped his immediate successors in Norway.

Grieg was born in Bergen in 1843. Both of his parents were quite musical and active in the music life of the city. His mother, Gesine, was a trained pianist who appeared in a number of concerts in Bergen. She was also Edvard's first music teacher. His father, Alexander Grieg, a businessman, was deeply interested in music and sufficiently accomplished as a pianist to join his wife in playing simple arrangements for piano four-hands. Edvard began taking piano lessons at the age of six and made his first attempts at composition when he was quite young. Ole Bull, a friend as well as a relative of Grieg's mother, heard some of these youthful compositions and, convinced that the boy had unusual talent, persuaded Edvard's parents to send him to study at the Leipzig conservatory.

Edvard arrived in Leipzig in 1858 at the tender age of fifteen. He remained there for four years, interrupted only by a serious illness that required him to spend the summer of 1860 at home to regain his strength. That autumn he returned to Leipzig, and in 1862 he graduated from the conservatory. He did not feel that his music education was complete, however, and after spending a winter in Bergen he went to Copenhagen to continue his studies. In Copenhagen he became acquainted with Niels W. Gade and became involved in the rich music life of that city. It proved to be a period of rapid maturation for him as a composer. Aside from various trips, including one to Rome in the winter of 1865–66, he remained in Copenhagen until the autumn of 1866. As previously mentioned, in Copenhagen he was one of the founders of the Euterpe music society (see p. 187).

Grieg's compositions from these early years trace his development from student to mature artist. The works from his Leipzig period are competent, but they show little of his individuality as a composer. Some of these compositions were published as *Four Piano Pieces*, Op. 1, and some as *Four Songs*, Op. 2, but they are rarely performed today. The same is true of the compositions dating from the first part of his stay in Copenhagen, among them a symphony in C minor (without an opus number) written in 1863–64. Only in *Melodies of the Heart* (Op. 5), four songs written toward the close of 1864 with texts by Hans Christian Andersen, do we detect for the first time a more personal style. The third of the set, "I Love But Thee," became his best-known song internationally.

Grieg's distinctive style found brilliant expression in his next work, *Humoresques*, Op. 6. Written in 1865, these four short pieces for piano show an almost astonishing development toward a personal style clearly influenced by Norwegian folk music. This rapid development has often been attributed to Grieg's association with Nordraak at this time. The two men became acquainted in Copenhagen and spent a great deal of time together. Nordraak's influence on the development of Grieg's style cannot have been very great, however. His characteristic idiom was in all important respects completely different from Grieg's, and Grieg developed his own style quite independently of Nordraak's music. There is no doubt, however, that the friendship between the two men was of great importance to both of them.

Several important works followed the *Humoresques*, including the *Piano Sonata* in E minor, Op. 7, and the *Violin Sonata No. 1* in F major, Op. 8. Composed during the summer of 1865, these two works demonstrate that

Grieg had also mastered the sonata form in a way that reflected his personal style. The violin sonata, especially, has maintained a place in the concert repertoire.

Grieg moved to Oslo from Copenhagen in the autumn of 1866. The following summer he married his cousin, Nina Hagerup, who was a singer. In Oslo he worked as a conductor and music teacher; as time permitted, especially during his summer vacations, he composed. His contributions to the city's music life, including his pivotal role in the founding of the Music Society, were discussed earlier (see p. 182). In 1874 both Grieg and Svendsen received government stipends, whereupon Grieg left Oslo to give his full attention to composing.

Many of the works written during Grieg's Oslo period were settings of texts by his great contemporary, Björnstjerne Björnson. In addition to several songs—among them the famous "The First Meeting" (Op. 21, No. 1)—he wrote *Before a Southern Convent*, Op. 20, *Bergliot*, Op. 42, and incidental music for *Sigurd Jorsalfar*, Op. 22 (later published as an orchestral suite, Opus 56). The opera fragment *Olav Trygvason* (Op. 50) was also written at this time. Many works not associated with Björnson texts were written during this period as well, including several of his most important instrumental compositions: *Pictures from Folk Life*, Op. 19, for piano; *Twenty-five Norwegian Folk Songs and Dances*, Op. 17; *Violin Sonata No. 2 in G major*, Op. 13, written in the summer of 1867; and the *Piano Concerto in A minor*, Op. 16, written in Denmark during the summer of 1868. The piano concerto is the work that perhaps did the most to establish Grieg's reputation as a composer. Its melodic charm and sonority are such that it has won a permanent place on concert programs the world over.

Grieg's place of residence changed frequently during the years following his departure from Oslo in the summer of 1874. He went first to Bergen, where he lived during most of the period from 1874 to 1876, and was in Oslo again from 1876 to 1877. He then spent the winter of 1877–78 in Lofthus, an idyllic spot in the Hardanger fjord region of western Norway. Grieg became very fond of this place, and in the years that followed often returned there during the summer months. For that reason these years in Grieg's life have been called his "Lofthus period." He also began to spend a good deal of time on concert tours, a practice that he was to continue until the end of his life. From 1880 to 1883 he again lived in Bergen, where he served as conductor of Harmonien (precursor of the Bergen Philharmonic Orchestra) from 1880 to 1882. This was the last salaried position he was to hold.

Grieg's productivity as a composer during this time did not match the rich and rapid output of his earlier years. Indeed, there were long periods when he composed virtually nothing of importance. Some of the works he

Caricature by Gerhard Munthe and Andreas Bloch of Edvard Grieg as "The Mountain Thrall." The text of the Norwegian folk ballad by this name, which formed the basis of Grieg's Opus 32, includes these words: "Fish may swim through flowing water, and warbling birds may fly; all of them—all have their own true love, but I—all alone am I." (Gyldendal Norsk Forlag)

did produce during this period, however, exhibit a profundity and expressivity far beyond anything he had achieved in the charming and fresh products of his youth.

His first composition after his departure from Oslo was begun in the summer of 1874, forming a bridge between the two periods. It was the incidental music for Ibsen's *Peer Gynt*, Op. 23, which occupied him from 1874 until the autumn of 1875. Although it is clear that he proceeded at a much more cumbersome pace than he had on most of his earlier compositions, the result was a body of music that retains all the melodic charm and freshness of his youthful works. The two orchestral suites that Grieg later arranged from this music (Opus 46 and Opus 55) are among his best-known compositions.

The winter of 1875–76 was a difficult time for Grieg. The death of both of his parents in the autumn of 1875 and other serious personal problems left him depressed and unmotivated for serious work. It proved nonetheless to be a rich period, for it was at this time that he wrote his most important composition for piano—the *Ballade* in G minor, Op. 24—and several of his best songs, including the *Six Songs* to texts by Henrik Ibsen, Op. 25.

His next productive period as a composer was during his stay at Lofthus in 1877–78. One of his most important works, the *String Quartet No. 1* in G minor, Op. 27, dates from this time, as does also *The Mountain Thrall*, Op. 32, for baritone solo, string orchestra, and two horns. Also written at

Troldhaugen—Edvard Grieg's home on the outskirts of Bergen. (Glydendal Norsk Forlag)

this time was *Album for Male Voices*, Op. 30, consisting of arrangements for solo voices and male chorus of twelve pieces from L. M. Lindeman's collection of Norwegian folk tunes.

The years 1878–80 were a hiatus in Grieg's creative life. It came to an end in the summer of 1880, when he wrote most of the A. O. Vinje songs of Opus 33. This collection contains several of Grieg's best-known songs, including "Last Spring," "The Wounded Heart," and "At Rondane." Other works followed, including *Norwegian Dances*, Op. 35, for piano four-hands, written in the summer of 1881; the *Cello Sonata* in A minor, Op. 36, from the winter of 1882–83; and in 1884 the *Holberg Suite*, Op. 40.

In 1885 the Griegs moved into Troldhaugen, their newly built villa located about six miles south of Bergen, destined to be their home for the rest of their days. This event also marks the beginning of a new period for Grieg as a composer. It did not greatly alter his way of living, however, for he

continued to take many concert tours, and during the summer months he often went to the mountains. In the ensuing years his health, which had been seriously impaired during his Leipzig years, began to decline, and the last ten to fifteen years of his life were marked by steadily worsening illness. The damp climate in Bergen was not good for him either, forcing him to spend the last two winters of his life in Oslo. Despite his poor health, however, he continued to perform as a concert pianist and conductor until his death in Bergen in September, 1907.

Grieg's productivity as a composer diminished steadily in his later years, but a few of the works written then are excellent. Most of his *Lyric Pieces* for piano, for example, were written after 1885, though the earliest of them may date as far back as 1864. During the years 1867–99 he published ten opus numbers, each under the title *Lyric Pieces*, as well as several collections with other titles that can almost be classified in the same group. Of the *Lyric Pieces*, only Opuses 12 and 38 were published before 1885. The next in the series, Opus 43, was written in the summer of 1886, and thereafter the collections followed one another at ever-shorter intervals. Many of these little mood pieces are indisputable gems and are often performed.

That Grieg wrote so many short pieces during these years may be due in part to his declining health, as a consequence of which he lacked the strength to create larger works. He did manage to write one large work, however: the *Violin Sonata No. 3* in C minor, Op. 45, composed during the winter of 1886–87. It was to be his final chamber-music work, and it is one of his best. A string quartet in F major was started in 1891 but was never completed. The first two movements were published posthumously in 1908, and some fragments of what might have become the other two movements were also found after his death. A number of songs also date from this time; most significant of these is *The Mountain Maid*, a cycle of songs with texts by the contemporary Norwegian writer Arne Garborg, composed in the summer of 1895 and published as Opus 67. Also worthy of mention are *Five Songs* with texts by Vilhelm Krag, Op. 60, and two collections of songs with texts by Otto Benzon (Opuses 69 and 70).

The most important of Grieg's final works are his arrangements of Norwegian folk tunes. While it is true that his *Symphonic Dances* for orchestra, Op. 64, is not considered one of his best works, even here he used some of Norway's finest folk tunes. His last three collections based on folk tunes, however, include some of his best work: *Nineteen Norwegian Folk Songs* for piano, Op. 66; *Norwegian Peasant Dances*, Op. 72, also for piano; and lastly *Four Psalms*, Op. 74, consisting of arrangements for mixed chorus *a cappella* with baritone solo of four old Norwegian hymn tunes. It is in these last opuses, especially, that Grieg's style displays its most progressive features.

Edvard and Nina Grieg in a famous painting by Peter Severin Kröyer, 1898. (Gyldendal Norsk Forlag)

Songs constitute an important part of Grieg's production as a composer. He wrote songs throughout his career, about 180 in all. In 1900 he wrote of this in a letter to the American musicologist Henry Finck: "I don't think I have any greater talent for writing songs than for writing other kinds of music. Why, then, have songs played such a prominent role in my music? Quite simply because I, like other mortals, once in my life (to quote Goethe) was brilliant. And my brilliance was: love. I loved a young woman with a marvelous voice and an equally marvelous gift as an interpreter. This woman became my wife and has been my life companion to the present day. She has been, I must say, the only true interpreter of my songs."

Although one should not conclude from this that Nina Grieg was the inspiration for all of her husband's songs, there is no doubt that she was of great importance for his work in this genre. We know that she was the

immediate inspiration for the four songs in *Melodies of the Heart*, Op. 5. It is also quite certain that the knowledge of the production and potential of the human voice that is so clearly reflected in Grieg's songs can in large measure be attributed to her. It may be, however, that Grieg's unique talent drew him especially toward the writing of songs. The ability to give musical expression to non-musical impressions—i.e., to create or reflect a specific mood by simple melodic and harmonic means—was central to his compositional talent, and it is displayed at its best in this medium. The suggestive, almost mesmerizing power of his best songs is such that they must be ranked among the finest specimens in Europe's Romantic art-song tradition. Obviously, his aptitude for creating vocally idiomatic melodies also played a role; indeed, in some of his early songs this creative melodic gift was expressed so powerfully that the songs were well received despite their weak texts.

Most of Grieg's songs are either strophic or modified strophic in form; only rarely does one find a song that is through-composed. Nearly all of the songs with *nynorsk* ("new Norwegian") texts—i.e., those with texts by A. O. Vinje and Arne Garborg—are strophic. Indeed, the strophic form is essential to their character: it is the form of the folk song recreated in an artistic setting. Grieg's originality, in any case, does not consist in his handling of form. His uniqueness is expressed to a far greater extent in the melodic line and the harmonic dress in which it is clothed. Also characteristic, especially in the longer songs, is a motivic transformation that corresponds to the content of the text.

"The Wounded Heart," Op. 33, No. 3 (text by A. O. Vinje) provides a good example of the concentrated expressive power that occurs in Grieg's songs (see example 44). The form is strophic, with modifications only as necessary to accommodate irregularities in the text. The text tells of a person

Example 44. Edvard Grieg, "The Wounded Heart," Op. 33, No. 3.

who has conquered the pain and sorrow in his or her life as well as the painful memories of defeat. With these victories has come the ability to create new life values: "From scars bright blooms come to flourish." In the music this victory is reflected in the change from minor to major (C-sharp minor to C- sharp major = D-flat major). Also, the dissonance created by the F-double-sharp in the melody against the G-sharp in the accompaniment in measure 2 eloquently expresses the pain of which the text speaks, while the triumphant repetition of the last line in each stanza mirrors the hard-won victory.

The entire melody is based on just two short motives. The melodic repetition of the first phrase in the third phrase of the text is characteristic of Grieg: aside from the anacrusis, the melody is identical except that it is transposed up a fourth. Elsewhere there are other similarities between the two melodic lines. This technique, which occurs quite often in Grieg's music, has been called "melodic rhyme." In the concluding phrase the melody breaks forth in glorious, triumphant sound. It is hard to imagine a better musical interpretation of the words "From scars bright blooms come to flourish."

The rather complicated and fairly strong chromatic harmony is characteristic of Grieg's middle period. The use of chromatic appoggiaturas in measures 2, 3, 6, and 7, the deceptive resolution in measure 4, the somewhat irregular use of the Neapolitan sixth chord in measure 8, and, not least, the use of the altered dominant of the dominant in the transition to the major key in measures 9–10—all of these are characteristic features of Grieg's harmony. The simplified notation of the altered dominant of the dominant chord in measure 9 complicates the analysis of the chord progression in this section. The chord a–c-sharp^1–e^1–g^1 in measure 9 is introduced as a dominant seventh chord in D major. It is reinterpreted enharmonically, however, as b-double-flat–d-flat^1–f-flat^1–g^1, i.e., the altered dominant of the dominant in D-flat major (with root omitted). The subsequent progression to the six-four chord in measure 10 is normal. Grieg often made highly effective use of the altered dominant of the dominant chords with their possibilities for enharmonic reinterpretation.

The songs span a broad expressive range—from the deep inward pain of "The Wounded Heart" and other Vinje songs to the unbridled humor of, for example, "Midsummer Eve," Op. 60, No. 5 (text by Vilhelm Krag). Impressions of nature frequently constitute an essential part of their emotional background—as, for example, in the Vinje songs "At Rondane," Op. 33, No. 9 and "Last Spring," Op. 33, No. 2, or "At the Brook" from *The Mountain Maid*, Op. 67, No. 8 (text by Arne Garborg).

The Mountain Maid, Grieg's only song cycle, is perhaps his most important song opus. It exhibits a remarkable breadth of expression, from the uninhibited joviality of "Kidlings' Dance" (No. 6) to the pain of "Hurtful Day" (No. 7). Most of Grieg's songs exhibit a fine balance between the voice and the piano, with the voice perhaps dominating slightly. There is often a short piano prelude and interlude, and motives from the voice part are often imitated in the accompaniment, but the piano rarely dominates. A good example of such an exception is "Summer Night," Op. 70, No. 3 (text by Otto Benzon), one of his later, more declamatory songs where the almost Impressionistic sounds of the piano are the most important element and the singer does little more than recite the text.

Most of Grieg's dramatic music was produced early in his career. It consists of three works: incidental music for *Sigurd Jorsalfar*, Op. 22; *Peer Gynt*, Op. 23; and an unfinished opera, *Olav Trygvason*, Op. 50. (*Olav Trygvason* was written before *Peer Gynt* but was not published until 1888, hence the higher opus number.) The melodrama *Bergliot*, Op. 42, composed in 1871, might also be considered dramatic music. Of these, the *Peer Gynt* music is by far Grieg's best-known work in the genre. It is played all over the world primarily in the form of two orchestral suites, Opuses 46 and 55. The suites, however, contain only a portion of the *Peer Gynt* music, and the sequence of pieces in each one is completely different from their order in the play. They reveal the eerie beauty of the *Peer Gynt* music, but they convey no idea of the power of this music to enhance the dramatic action.

Although it is true that Grieg's genius as a composer was first and foremost that of a lyricist, Opus 23 shows that he could also write dramatic music of great power. The music for the scene with the three herd girls (No. 5), "In the Hall of the Mountain King" (No. 8), and other parts of this music reveal aspects of Grieg's talent that are rarely evident elsewhere. Even in Opus 23, however, Grieg is at his best in the lyrical sections: "Solveig's Song" (No. 19), "Solveig's Cradle Song" (No. 26), and "Morning Mood" (No. 13), for example, are dear to the hearts of all music lovers.

The opera fragment *Olav Trygvason* consists of just three scenes. Grieg and Björnstjerne Björnson, the librettist, had intended to create an entire opera together, but an unfortunate disagreement arose between them and the work was never completed.

Grieg wrote relatively few works in sonata form. His opus list includes only seven such compositions: the *Piano Sonata* in E minor, Op. 7; three violin sonatas (Opuses 8, 13, and 45); the *Piano Concerto* in A minor, Op. 16; the *String Quartet No. 1* in G minor, Op. 27; and the *Cello Sonata* in A minor, Op. 36. In addition to these there is the *Symphony* in C minor, dating from 1863–64, which Grieg did not want to count among his works, and the unfinished *String Quartet No. 2* in F major, written in 1891. The concert overture "In Autumn," Op. 11, also is in sonata form, but it consists of a single movement.

Grieg did not find it easy to work within the confines of this Classical form. This was true of most of the Romantic composers, but perhaps it was especially difficult for so markedly lyrical a composer as Grieg. His themes, often short and ill-suited to further development, did not lend themselves to a symphonic context. In the works of his youth, however, it appears that he more or less subconsciously employed the early Romantic formal principles with which he was familiar from the compositions of such masters as Schubert and Schumann. He filled these forms with a flood of melodic invention and imaginative sonorities, composing works that have fully proven their durability despite the fact that the individual movements are sometimes lacking in coherence. The episodic character of his writing in the larger forms is especially noticeable in the outer movements, where the structural requirements of sonata form are greatest.

The *Piano Sonata* in E minor, Op. 7, is not altogether typical of Grieg's writing in the larger forms, in that it retains some signs of the conservatory student's respect for the established norms of the genre. The first two violin sonatas (Opuses 8 and 13), however, as well as the *Piano Concerto*, Op. 16, show how Grieg's fervid imagination overcame all formal difficulties with a steady flow of new melodic, tonal, and rhythmic ideas. The first movement of the *Piano Concerto*, for example, contains no less than seven distinct themes in addition to the introductory motive—the so-called "Grieg formula," a descending melodic line consisting of a minor second plus a major third. Some of the themes are related, to be sure, but there are nonetheless quite a few semiautonomous sections in the movement. The melodic and harmonic charm conquers all difficulties, however. The concerto has won a place as one of Grieg's most popular works and, indeed, as one of the most frequently performed concertos from the Romantic period.

Nine years were to pass after the completion of the *Piano Concerto* before Grieg attempted another composition in sonata form. This was the *String Quartet* in G minor, Op. 27, and it is entirely different in character from his youthful compositions in sonata form. He could no longer use the same structural solutions that he had employed a decade earlier, and it is clear that he was now aware of the difficulties. In an 1878 letter to his Danish friend Gottfred Matthison-Hansen, he wrote:

> I have just completed a string quartet, which, however, I have not yet
> heard. It is in G minor and is not designed to win the approval of the

masses. It strives for breadth, flight, and above all sonority for the instruments for which it was written. I needed to do this as a study. Now I am going to begin another piece of chamber music. I think it is in this way that I am going to find myself again. You have no idea what difficulty I have with the forms; but that too is a result of the fact that I was stagnating—and this, in turn, resulted in part from [devoting myself to] numerous commissioned works (*Peer Gynt, Sigurd Jorsalfar*, and other unpleasantries), in part from catering too much to popular tastes. To those things I intend to say "Farewell, shadows," if that is possible.

Grieg pointed here to two of the most important features of the string quartet, for in both sonority and form it broke new ground in ways that were to leave their mark on European music thereafter. It is probable that this quartet was one of the most important models for Claude Debussy's string quartet ten years later, and it is likely that it influenced other chamber-music works at the end of the century as well.

The quartet has several interesting features, one of which is the extensive and sophisticated use of chromatically altered chords. There are also several examples of parallel dissonant chords and places where Grieg employed large "blocks of sound." The latter are long sustained chords, both consonant and dissonant, whose relation to the prevailing tonality gradually becomes ambiguous. The use of parallel dissonant chords and "blocks of sound" later became especially important for Impressionism.

With respect to form, it is the strong motivic coherence—not only within the four individual movements but also among them—that gives the quartet its distinctive character. The theme that permeates the entire quartet was taken from a song that Grieg had written just a year earlier for the Ibsen text "Fiddlers" (Op. 25, No. 1). It appears in minor as the introduction, in major as the conclusion, and with small alterations as the secondary theme in the first movement and an introduction to the last movement. It also supplies motivic material for numerous other themes in all four movements. There is a similar motivic relationship between the principal theme of the first movement and several themes in the others. This obviously conscious effort to create thematic-motivic unity throughout the quartet resulted in an unusually well integrated composition. Together with the expressive and sometimes dramatic idiom, this unity makes the quartet one of Grieg's most captivating efforts. It certainly must be considered one of the principal works in the entire corpus of Norwegian chamber music.

After the quartet Grieg wrote two sonatas: the *Cello Sonata* in A minor, Op. 36, and the *Violin Sonata No. 3* in C minor, Op. 45. Neither possesses the quartet's concentrated thematic unity throughout the several movements, but the latter is nonetheless a very important work. The thematic concentration in the first movement is remarkable, and structurally it is perhaps the freest and most independent of Grieg's cyclic works.

Although in the string quartet Grieg indeed mastered the problems inherent in writing for the larger forms, this mastery did not lead to an outpouring of sonatas. Each time he tried to create a larger work he faced the structural challenge anew. This is clearly evident in his compositions for piano, which do not include a single sonata after the youthful *Piano Sonata* in E minor, Op. 7. In the few larger works for piano written later in his career he sometimes used the variation form (*Ballade*, Op. 24; *Old Norwegian Melody with Variations*, Op. 51), and on one notable occasion the Baroque suite form (*Holberg Suite*, Op. 40).

The *Ballade* in G minor is Grieg's most important work for piano solo. Written two years before the string quartet, and closely related to it in mood and personal background, it consists of a set of variations on the Norwegian folk tune "The Northland Peasantry." This tune appears in Lindeman's *Older and Newer Norwegian Mountain Melodies* (No. 337), though Grieg altered it slightly for his purposes.

Grieg's handling of the variation form in the *Ballade* earned it a central position among Romanticism's works in this genre. The theme is presented first in an unusually rich harmonization, and is followed by a series of variations in which the character varies from one to the next while the formal structure of the theme is retained. In the last part of the work, however, Grieg ventured into the realm of free variations. Here it is no longer the entire theme that is varied, but rather its component motives become the basis for a freely constructed section that nonetheless retains its relationship to the whole. While the first nine variations are more individual and illuminate the theme from various sides, variations 10–14 constitute two great dynamic waves. Variations 10 and 11 merge directly into variation 12, where the theme is stated in major (without repetitions), and variations 13 and 14 end with a unique climax that is suddenly interrupted by a single, deep bass note. This dramatic interruption sounds like a fateful necessity, after which the concluding repetition of the first part of the theme in its original form has the character of a deeply tragic return to the point of departure.

The *Ballade* sounds like an unresolved, vain struggle that ends at the same point from which it began. It is a work in dark colors, but it possesses a glowing intensity. It appears to bear witness to deeply personal and tragic events in the composer's life, as indeed it did. There is some information that would seem to indicate that Grieg himself regarded the *Ballade* as a work having more personal meaning for him than most. Iver Holter described an episode in Leipzig when Grieg played the *Ballade* for him shortly after its completion. "The impression was unforgettable," Holter wrote later. "Grieg put his very soul into the performance, and when he was finished he was not only so drained physically that he was bathed in sweat, but he was so agitated, so moved, that for a long time he could not say a word." Grieg himself never played the *Ballade* publicly.

Grieg's other large work in variation form—*Old Norwegian Melody with Variations*, Op. 51, for two pianos—is also based on a Norwegian folk tune, "Sigurd and the Troll Bride" (No. 22 in Lindeman's collection). Despite its outward similarity in many ways to the *Ballade*, this is considered one of Grieg's weaker compositions. He also orchestrated it, but it has not won much of a following in either form. The *Holberg Suite*, on the other hand, has been much more successful. Here Grieg abandoned all problems of form and adopted the ready-made pattern of an earlier period, writing a group of stylized dances for piano modeled after those of the late Baroque. This work was also arranged for string orchestra, and it is widely played in both versions.

Grieg also made use of time-honored forms in numerous small works for piano written over a period of many years: the *Humoresqes*, Op. 6; *Pictures from Folk Life*, Op. 19; and the ten sets of *Lyric Pieces*. Often this was some form of the ABA pattern, and even more frequently it became an expanded version of the pattern (ABABA) with various modifications. The continuing popularity of these pieces, both in Norway and elsewhere, is proof that Grieg, within the confines of these simple forms, succeeded in creating a wealth of differing mood images. Some of them are unquestionably among the finest compositions in the genre by any composer. Such pieces as "To Spring," "Solitary Traveler," and "Wedding Day at Troldhaugen" are favorites among pianists everywhere.

Grieg's arrangements of Norwegian folk tunes hold a special place among his works for piano. The three most important collections are *Twenty-five Norwegian Folk Songs and Dances*, Op. 17; *Nineteen Norwegian Folk Songs*, Op. 66; and *Norwegian Peasant Dances*, Op. 72, based on Johan Halvorsen's transcriptions of traditional *slaatter* as played on the Hardanger fiddle by Knut Dahle (see p. 105). Other works having a folk-music background are *Norwegian Dances* for piano four-hands, Op. 35; *Symphonic Dances* for orchestra, Op. 64; *Album for Male Voices*, Op. 30; and Grieg's last work, the *Four Psalms* for mixed chorus, Op. 74.

These folk-tune arrangements are especially interesting harmonically. Opuses 17, 66, and 72 provide a cross section of his harmonic style and its development over a period of more than three decades. Consider, for example, the harmony he supplied for the folk song "It Is the Greatest Foolishness" (example 45). Here we note the frequent use of altered chords (as in measures 6 and 7), bold dissonances created by the voice leading (as in measure 11), and the juxtaposition of chords in ways not permitted within

Example 45. Edvard Grieg, "It is the Greatest Foolishness," Op. 66, No. 2.

the canons of traditional harmonic movement (as in measures 14–15). Although Grieg used the technique of chromatic alteration relatively early, and even frequently in Opus 17, the departures from functional harmony and the free use of dissonances tend to pepper his later works. The bold dissonances in Opus 17 occur primarily as a result of the use of pedal point, while the freer, linearly based use of dissonance is more fully developed in his latest works, especially in *Norwegian Peasant Dances*, Op. 72. These remarkable works introduce some totally new elements into our perspective of Grieg's harmonic style and point to such later developments as the dissonant harmonies employed by Béla Bartók from about 1910. Grieg adapted these same harmonic features to a work for mixed chorus in *Four Psalms*, Op. 74.

We should also say a word about Grieg's other vocal compositions. Two relatively early works—*Before a Southern Convent*, Op. 20, and *Land Sighting*, Op. 31—have achieved considerable popularity, the former primarily in Norway and the latter internationally. Both are settings of texts by Björnstjerne Björnson. An important and unique work in Grieg's production is *The Mountain Thrall*, Op. 32, for baritone solo, string orchestra, and two horns. The text is taken from Norwegian folk poetry, but the music is entirely Grieg's. The strange sense of loneliness and nature mysticism that characterizes this folk poem and, indeed, Norwegian folk poetry in general, is brilliantly reflected in the music.

Grieg's works form the nucleus of Norway's music repertoire in several genres. It is unfortunate that he failed to write a complete opera, all the more lamentable because this was apparently due to a misunderstanding between Grieg and Björnson. Nor was it Grieg who wrote the first viable Norwegian symphony (this task fell to Johan Svendsen); indeed, his symphony, which has only been available for performance since 1981, has not yet won a place in the concert repertoire. In most other areas, however—songs, compositions for piano, chamber music, dramatic music, smaller choral works, and so on—Grieg's compositions occupy a central place in the national repertoire.

Looking at Grieg's oeuvre as a whole, one cannot help but note a strange contrast between the abundant productivity of his youth and the relatively small output of his middle and later years. Apparently it became more and more difficult for him to compose, as if his struggle with musical form and the ideal for which he strove became increasingly severe. In his later years, waning health and strength also took their toll on his creative work. Yet, whether owing to or despite these difficulties, his most personal and most deeply felt compositions are to be found among the larger works of his later years—the *Ballade*, the *String Quartet* in G minor, the third violin sonata, and the marvelous song cycle *The Mountain Maid*, Op. 67. In these works,

Edvard Grieg ca. 1900. (Troldhaugen)

which are the rich fruit of intense personal and artistic struggles in Grieg's life, one glimpses the very soul of this man who, though small of stature, was a giant among the composers of his generation.

JOHAN SVENDSEN

The symphonist among Norway's national Romantic composers was Johan Svendsen (1840–1911). With his various symphonic works he laid the foundation for a Norwegian repertoire in this genre, thereby supplementing

Grieg precisely where he was least productive. One might say that the orchestra was Svendsen's instrument: it was the one he knew best, the one for which most of his compositions were written. The few non-orchestral works he produced are generally of less importance.

Svendsen was born in Oslo. After an early manifestation of his musical talents, he began to study with his father, a military musician. Soon he too began to play clarinet and flute in the military band. His principal instrument, however, was the violin, and for a time he was a violinist in the orchestra of the Norwegian Theater in Oslo. Even as a child he did some composing, writing a number of dances and marches in the popular style of the period. A few of them, such as the waltz cycle *At the Seter*, were published and have been played frequently.

In the subscription concerts arranged by Kjerulf and Conradi in 1857–59, Svendsen played first violin in the orchestra. This was his initial exposure to symphonic music. It was a momentous experience for him, and it proved to be decisive for his entire musical future. Beethoven's symphonies, especially, made a tremendous impression on him.

Svendsen was also a pupil of Carl Arnold, a teacher for whom he had high regard throughout his life. It appears that Arnold concentrated on Svendsen's training as a violinist, giving less attention to the study of harmony and composition. The talented young musician realized, however, that he had to go abroad for further study. Although he lacked the necessary financial resources, he nonetheless went to Germany in the summer of 1862. After trying unsuccessfully to support himself with occasional jobs as a violinist, he came in contact with the Swedish-Norwegian consul in Lübeck, who secured a stipend for him from King Carl XV. Thus Svendsen was able to fulfill his dream of acquiring a thorough music education at the Leipzig conservatory.

Although it was his intention to prepare himself as a violinist, he had not given up his attempts at composition. During his stay in Lübeck he had written a "Caprice" for orchestra with violin *obbligato*, and he sent this to the conservatory prior to matriculating there. The result was that when he arrived he was placed in a class for advanced students. At his own request, however, he enrolled at the beginning level in several subjects so as not to leave gaps in his training.

After he had been at the conservatory for some time he developed a nerve disorder in his left hand, which prevented him from continuing his training as a violinist. He was obliged, therefore, to shift his primary attention to the study of composition—a change that he probably welcomed.

Svendsen's period of study in Leipzig extended from December 1863 to the spring of 1867, during which time he developed very rapidly. He com-

Johan Svendsen, Edvard Grieg, and Edmund Neupert. (Gyldendal Norsk Forlag)

pleted his *String Quartet* in A minor, Op. 1, in the summer of 1865, and in the following two years he composed several additional works: *Two Songs for Male Chorus*, Op. 2; *Octet* in A major for strings, Op. 3; *Symphony No. 1* in D major, Op. 4; and *String Quintet* in C major, Op. 5. This was an impressive list for a twenty-six-year-old conservatory student, and the musical maturity and technical quality they display is truly astonishing. His compositions won him considerable recognition and praise, including an honorary prize awarded him in 1866 by the conservatory.

Svendsen returned to Oslo in August, 1867, and gave two concerts. Among the works presented was his *Symphony No. 1*, concerning which Grieg wrote a highly enthusiastic review in *Aftenbladet*. The concerts were not similarly successful with the general public, however, and Svendsen left the city in the autumn of that same year. He spent the winter in Leipzig and left for Paris the following spring. His stay in Paris on this occasion, which lasted until the summer of 1870, appears to have been a difficult time for him. He supported himself by playing in the orchestra at the Odéon Theater, and spent some time studying the older music on file in the Paris conservatory library. On one occasion he played a violin solo in connection with a production of François Coppée's play *Le passant*. He composed very little during this time, however. The *Violin Concerto* in A major, Op. 6, was begun in Paris but was completed in Leipzig during the summer of 1870.

In 1871 Svendsen married an American woman, Sarah Levett. That autumn he returned with his bride to Leipzig, where during the following winter he served as concertmaster of Euterpe, a music society whose programs typically were in a somewhat more modern vein than the famous Gewandhaus concerts. In the summer of 1872 he was present at the laying of the cornerstone of the Wagner theater in Bayreuth. He became personally acquainted with Wagner and used his time there for a thorough study of the master's music.

The stay in Germany proved once again to be a productive period for Svendsen as a composer. In the autumn of 1870, immediately after completing the violin concerto, he wrote his *Cello Concerto* in D major, Op. 7. The following year he wrote the "Symphonic Introduction to *Sigurd Slembe*," Op. 8, and in the summer of 1872 the sprightly *Carnival in Paris*, Op. 9.

Svendsen returned to Oslo in the autumn of 1872 and immediately began to play a prominent role in the music life of the city. He became co-conductor (with Grieg) of the Music Society orchestra, and in 1874 (after Grieg's departure from the city) sole conductor. In addition, he was one of the leaders of the newly founded Quartet Society, and he served as a music teacher in the community.

Music flourished in Oslo during this period, and it proved to be a rewarding time for Svendsen as well. In 1874 both he and Grieg were given government stipends. He also composed several of his most important works during these years: *Zorahayda*, Op. 11; *Festival Polonaise*, Op. 12; *Norwegian Artists' Carnival*, Op. 14; *Symphony No. 2* in B-flat major, Op. 15; *Romeo and Juliet*, Op. 18; and the first three *Norwegian Rhapsodies*, Opp. 17, 19, and 21.

From 1877 to 1880 Svendsen took a leave of absence from his position with the Music Society and spent the entire period abroad. During the winter of 1877–78 he was in Italy, where he completed his *Norwegian Rhapsody No. 4*, Op. 22. He then went to England, and in the autumn of 1878 to Paris. Once again, the visit to Paris did not prove to be a productive period for him. He did try his hand for the first time as a song composer, however; the result was two volumes of songs, Opuses 23 and 24, and some songs without opus numbers (including "The Violet").

In the autumn of 1880 Svendsen resumed his work with the Music Society, remaining until his final departure from Oslo in 1883. It was during this period that he composed his best-known work, the "Romance" in G major for violin and orchestra, Op. 26. He also wrote two occasional cantatas and a few other pieces of minor importance.

In the summer of 1883 Svendsen was appointed conductor of the Royal Theater orchestra in Copenhagen. The acceptance of this post required him to forfeit his Norwegian government artist's grant, but it was reinstated upon his retirement, owing to deteriorating health, in 1908. Because he was largely occupied with the many practical duties of an orchestra conductor, there was little time for composing. He wrote a few occasional works, including two cantatas and a ballet entitled *Spring Is Coming*. Two other compositions dating from the Copenhagen years are better known: *Andante Funèbre* and *Prelude*.

Svendsen was influential during his tenure in Copenhagen. Among his many admirers was Carl Nielsen, later to become Denmark's most renowned composer.

Svendsen's works from his student days show him to have been a remarkably mature composer even at that time. Indeed, the "Caprice" written in Lübeck before he began his studies in Leipzig reveals a considerable knowledge of compositional form and orchestration, although the structure is not convincingly cohesive. Svendsen himself wrote of this early work in a letter: "As you presumably know, I composed the 'Caprice' when I was living in Lübeck, and as a result the piece has no definite form since at that time I had not studied the theory of form." He added: "It is high time that composers come to understand that one cannot always cling to the old forms when one wants to present new ideas."

Nonetheless, the "old forms" were precisely what Svendsen employed in his early works: all of the compositions from his first Leipzig period are constructed largely according to standard Classical forms. Fidelity to the Classical models did not prevent him from infusing them with his own individuality as a composer, however. The most important of these compositions were the *Octet* in A major for strings and the first symphony, in both of which the sonata form predominates. The slow third movement of the octet is somewhat more free, in that new thematic material is introduced in the first part of the development. Likewise, the third movement of the symphony (Allegretto scherzando) is an imaginative experiment in form: it is a kind of free rondo using a thematic-transformation technique that appears again in several of his later works. The slow middle movement of the *String Quintet* in C major consists of a theme and variations modeled on the Viennese Classicists.

The violin and cello concertos, both written shortly after the completion of his studies in Leipzig, are more lyrical in character than most of Svendsen's other compositions. In the violin concerto the conventional three-movement structure is still intact, but in the cello concerto the pattern is abandoned altogether: the work consists of one long movement in sonata form with a slow section inserted between the development and the recapitulation.

Svendsen became even more experimental in succeeding works. Although the "Symphonic Introduction to *Sigurd Slembe*" can be analyzed as a movement in sonata form, it takes many liberties within that form. Svendsen had plans to write incidental music for Björnson's entire play, but this is the only music of which we have any knowledge. Because it makes no explicit reference to events in the play it is not program music *per se*, still it is quite possible that programmatic considerations played a role in its composition. Svendsen's next work, *Carnival in Paris*, borders on program music by painting a lively picture of carnival gaiety in that cosmopolitan city.

With *Zorahayda*, however, Svendsen stepped completely and unabashedly into the realm of program music. The literary association is derived from Washington Irving's book *The Legend of the Rose of Alhambra*, and the score is prefaced with a listing of the six divisions of the composition. The form is determined by the programmatic content, but the piece is brought to a satisfying musical conclusion by a recapitulation that is not prescribed by the literary material. In this work Svendsen fully exploited the thematic-transformation technique that he had tested in the Scherzo of the first symphony. *Zorahayda* is the only piece of pure program music that Svendsen ever wrote. Of his later works, the orchestral fantasy *Romeo and Juliet* might be considered such, but the lack of any explicit reference to Shakespeare's play makes it difficult to confirm its programmatic content.

Svendsen's second symphony, his most important work written in Oslo, represents in many ways a return to the principles of Classical form. It consists of the standard four movements and in general is similar in form to his first symphony. The last movement of each, for example, has a slow introduction, and in both symphonies the themes used in the scherzo movements are related to Norwegian folk music. In the second symphony the influence of folk music extends even to the structure of the scherzo movement. The continual repetition of the *halling*-like principal theme combined with the various contrapuntal voices was obviously inspired by the Hardanger-fiddle *slaatter* of rural Norway. The thematic-transformation technique plays a lesser role here, however, only appearing occasionally in the slow second movement. As a whole, this symphony represents Svendsen at the height of his creative power. His brilliant orchestration and solid structural framework were already evident in the first symphony, but in the second symphony his rich natural gifts matured. In its wealth of ideas and depth of expression it is perhaps his finest and most personal work.

As we have seen, Svendsen occasionally invented his own themes reflecting the influence of Norwegian folk music. Although this was not a prominent element in his style, it does give a specifically Norwegian stamp to some of his works. Of greater importance is his use of genuine folk tunes in several of his compositions. The first occasion was in 1874 in *Norwegian Artists' Carnival*, where he used both a Norwegian bridal march and an Italian folk tune. The juxtaposition of these two themes had, in this case, a kind of programmatic significance: the theme of the carnival was the fusion of Norwegian festive traditions with Italian life and customs.

A Norwegian folk song played a much more prominent role in another work dating from the same year. Entitled "Last Year I Was Tending the Goats on the Hillside" (from the folk song) and scored for string orchestra, it consists of a theme (the melody of the folk song), four variations, and a coda. This composition and the slow movement of the *String Quintet* are the only extended examples of Svendsen's use of a theme with variations, though the technique appears briefly at other times (for example, in the slow movement of the second symphony).

The best known of Svendsen's compositions built on Norwegian folk tunes are his four *Norwegian Rhapsodies*. Their various melodies were taken for the most part from Lindeman's *Older and Newer Norwegian Mountain Melodies*. With original introductions, conclusions, and bridge passages built on characteristic motives from the folk tunes, Svendsen illuminated them and welded them together into unified and finished pieces. His brilliant orchestration further ensured that the *Norwegian Rhapsodies* would be some of his most colorful and charming works.

As an example of his fine sense for the unique character of folk tunes, we give here a brief excerpt from *Norwegian Rhapsody No. 2* (example 46). It is his first harmonization of "Sigurd and the Troll Bride," orchestrated for

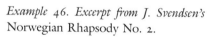

Example 46. Excerpt from J. Svendsen's Norwegian Rhapsody No. 2.

strings alone. Note how sensitively the harmony reflects the melody's vac-
illation between the major and minor third.

The form varies from one *Rhapsody* to the next, but all are soundly constructed. *Rhapsody No. 2*, for example, is divided into four sections marked,
respectively, Allegro, Andante, Scherzo, and Allegro. The two allegro sections are built on the fairy's song from "Elland and the Fairy Maiden" (No.
71 in Lindeman's collection), used in its original and in an augmented form,
respectively. In the second Allegro it appears in the introductory section in
C-sharp major and in the concluding section in A major, the principal key
of the *Rhapsody*. Thus, in terms of sonata form, the augmented version of
this theme functions as a secondary theme in the exposition, and in the
recapitulation it is transposed to the tonic. As a whole, then, the piece may
be said to be a kind of single-movement sonata with an exposition and a
recapitulation, but with an andante and a scherzo instead of a development.
So construed, the *Rhapsody* is somewhat similar in form to the Romantic
single-movement symphony.

Among Svendsen's later works the "Romance" in G major for violin and
orchestra, written in Oslo in 1881, must be emphasized. Its exquisite melodic charm and musical strength are combined with an accessible, simple
form and clear structure. The piece has enjoyed an enormous popularity in
Scandinavia for many years and deserves to be better known elsewhere. Its
singular beauty is evident from the very beginning, as can be seen in example
47.

Svendsen's vocal compositions are the least important part of his output.
Of his songs, only "The Violet" and "Venetian Serenade" are ever sung
today. The former is a fine piece, but it shows nothing essentially new of the
composer's artistic personality. His only compositions for male chorus are
the two songs in Opus 2: "To Sweden" and "Evening Voices." Both are
products of his student period and were dedicated to his royal patron, Carl
XV, who had written the poems. His only large vocal works were his occasional cantatas; they all reflect their origin and are never performed today,
though they contain passages of great power.

As a composer Svendsen stands in the middle of the Romantic period—indeed, one is tempted to say that he stands between the moderate and the radical wings in the music of late Romanticism. His attitude toward form as a compositional problem appears to have been that of a Classicist. The most important elements in his handling of form have Classical roots, though in some of his works he became more experimental. The Classical tradition is also reflected in his mastery of counterpoint: imitations, independent contrapuntal lines, and combinations of several themes were employed with discriminating artistic sense both in his symphonies and in some of his smaller compositions.

The Romantic element is more prominent in his harmony, and it is here that one finds his more radical tendencies. As a conservatory student he learned traditional harmony, but even in his early works he frequently employed chromaticism. After becoming acquainted with Wagner he made a thorough study of his music, and this had a profound influence on his harmonic style. Although he never became an imitator of Wagner—the Classical tradition was too deeply rooted in him for that to occur—his music abounds with chromatic lines, especially descending chromatic movement in the inner voices. The harmonic foundation is as a rule clearly functional, however.

Example 47, the first forty-four measures of the "Romance" in G major,

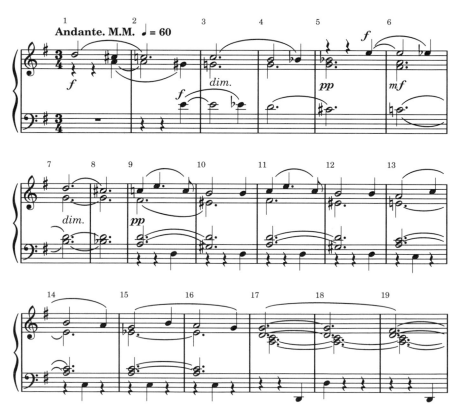

Example 47. Excerpt from J. Svendsen, "Romance" for violin and orchestra, Op. 26 (reduction for violin and piano).

provides a good illustration of Svendsen's use of chromaticism. In the first few measures there are descending chromatic lines in all voices, but from measure 11 the chromaticism continues only in the alto voice.

Despite this rich chromaticism, the harmonic progression is consistently functional. It is interesting to note the two different resolutions of the same diminished seventh chord in measures 10 and 12. In measure 10 the chord is interpreted as a dominant chord in F-sharp minor: it is followed by a deceptive cadence (to a D-major chord but with a minor seventh and major ninth) in measure 11. In measure 12 this chord is interpreted as a dominant in A minor (E-sharp = F) and resolved in measure 13 to an A-minor triad. This is then reinterpreted as a subdominant chord in the tonic G major. In the accompaniment to the principal melody of the "Romance" (starting in measure 21) the harmony is simpler and largely diatonic, with a liberal use of pedal point.

Now and then in Svendsen's works one finds instances of genuine chromatic harmony, i.e., passages in which the harmonic progression is no longer functional but simply the result of the chromatic lines. Such instances are rare in Svendsen's music, however. In general, his use of colorful harmonic progressions and sometimes abrupt modulations best reflects his position at the center of high Romanticism.

Svendsen's orchestral works generally call for an ensemble similar to that required by Beethoven's later orchestral works. Only in a few compositions—for example, *Carnival in Paris* and *Sigurd Slembe*—did he expand it somewhat. His writing for strings often appears to have been especially painstaking; not infrequently he divided them into more than the customary five groups. Some passages calling for as many as ten or even twelve string parts are required. When he wrote for full orchestra he made effective use of the distinctive characteristics of the various instruments, thus achieving a broad range of sonorities.

Svendsen was a masterful, gifted orchestral leader with a thorough knowledge of the ensemble. At the height of his career he was among the foremost conductors in Europe. As leader of the Music Society orchestra in the 1870s and 1880s he contributed immensely to the music life of Oslo, achieving with the resources at his disposal a surprisingly fine quality of orchestral performance. His renditions of the Beethoven symphonies, for example, were considered by contemporary music critics to be outstanding moments in Norway's music life. It is primarily as a composer, however, that Svendsen made his most important and lasting cultural contribution.

Catharinus Elling (see p. 257ff.) once observed that most of Svendsen's compositions are in a major key—which, it may be noted, is somewhat unusual for a Norwegian composer. His preference for major keys may appear to be a rather superficial characteristic, but it says much about him as a composer. A spirit of vitality and gaiety hovers over most of his works. One must go beyond externals to truly understand his music, however. In his best compositions he united a colorful tonal language with a genuine and fervent artistic expression, creating music that speaks as eloquently to people today as it did when it was created—when a century was nearing its end, and Romanticism was in full flower.

IN GRIEG'S SHADOW

It cannot be denied that the shadow of Grieg tended to obscure the achievements of other contemporary Norwegian composers. There were, in fact, quite a few of them. Norway's music milieu had broadened considerably by the late nineteenth century and had produced several composers who, though not on a level with Grieg, were important talents in their own right. They wrote a substantial amount of good music that was often played at the time, but that has rarely been performed since. It has been difficult for this music to compete with Grieg's legacy.

Edmund Neupert (1842–88) has already been mentioned as one of Norway's most outstanding pianists. His father, Herman Neupert, an immigrant from Schleswig, operated a music store and gave piano lessons in Oslo. It was from him that Edmund received his earliest music training. Even in his youth Edmund was an excellent pianist. At fifteen he went to Berlin, where he studied piano with Theodor Kullak and composition with Friedrich Kiel. His progress was such that in 1866 he was employed as a teacher in Kullak's music academy.

Neupert debuted as a pianist with great success in 1864, and after giving a concert in Copenhagen in 1868 he was, at the urging of Niels W. Gade, appointed to a position at the conservatory there. He remained in Copenhagen for twelve years and earned an excellent reputation as both a teacher and performer of the piano. Grieg's piano concerto is dedicated to him, and he was the soloist when the concerto received its world premiere in Copenhagen in April, 1869.

In 1880 Neupert accepted an offer of a professorship at the music conservatory in Moscow, but despite his success there he remained for only a short while. He returned to Oslo in 1881 and established a piano school for students at all levels, but it attracted so few clients that he had to give up the enterprise. Nor, apparently, was he very well received as a concert pianist: the public preferred the two outstanding pianists already living in the city, Agathe Backer Gröndahl and Erika Nissen. Disappointed and bitter, he left in 1882 for a concert tour of the United States, where he was enthusiastically received. A year later he accepted an offer to become a professor at the newly established music conservatory in New York. There he became a popular piano teacher, but he was forced to curtail concert appearances because of declining health.

Neupert left a large number of compositions—all, so far as we know, for piano, and all written before he left for North America. His opus list includes sixty numbers, about half of which are extant. The main body of his works consists of over one hundred piano etudes. Most of the remaining works are short, though he also wrote a few larger works as well as some folk-tune arrangements. The larger compositions include *Before the Battle* (subtitled "A Nordic Tone Poem"), Op. 24, and *Norwegian Ballad*, Op. 58. His best-known composition is an etude entitled "Resignation," the first of *Eight Studies*, Op. 26. Björnstjerne Björnson later wrote a text for it ("Sing Me Home"), and it became very popular.

Neupert's music clearly is the product of an able pianist and pedagogue. The etudes make excellent teaching material and have often been used for this purpose. All of his works reflect an intimate knowledge of the piano's resources, and many of them contain passages demanding great technical ability. Most are fairly short and simple in form. An important exception is *Norwegian Ballad*, Op. 58, which consists of a series of variations on two themes. Opus 14, which is lost, evidently was also a work in variation form.

The harmonic style of late Romanticism is reflected in the copious use of chromaticism, abrupt modulations to distant keys, and the frequent interjection of notes foreign to the prevailing harmony. Norwegian folk music does not appear to have had any appreciable influence on his style, and his folk-music arrangements are of little importance.

Except for "Resignation," Neupert's compositions are largely forgotten. His influence in Norwegian music history did not last beyond his own lifetime. As a concert pianist and teacher, however, he was internationally famous and was considered worthy of comparison with Liszt and Rubinstein. It is most unfortunate that his homeland did not find a place for him and the contributions he was prepared to make.

Agathe Backer Gröndahl. (Photo Collection, Universitetsbiblioteket i Oslo)

Agathe Backer Gröndahl (1847–1907) was also both a pianist and a composer. Her compositions consist largely of piano pieces and songs, of which the latter are generally the more highly regarded. Indeed, of Grieg's Norwegian contemporaries, she is the composer whose songs have best withstood the test of time.

She was born in Holmestrand (near Oslo). Her musical talent manifested itself when she was a child, and she began writing small pieces while still quite young. When she was ten years old her family moved to Oslo, where her first teachers were Otto Winter-Hjelm and Halfdan Kjerulf. She later received training in music theory from L. M. Lindeman. On the advice of Kjerulf she was sent to Berlin in 1865 to study at Theodor Kullak's music academy. After her performing debut in Oslo in 1868 she again went abroad for further training, studying with Hans von Bülow in Florence, Franz Liszt in Weimar, and others. She returned to Oslo in 1871, but was frequently away on concert tours. In 1875 she married Olaus Andreas Gröndahl.

Backer Gröndahl was an important performer in Norway for many years. She gave concerts throughout the country and was a frequent participant in chamber-music evenings in her native city. She also made numerous concert tours to the other Scandinavian countries as well as to Germany and England. Undoubtedly one of the most talented pianists Norway has produced, she received constant critical acclaim for her thoroughly musical, transparent style as a soloist and her ability to blend into the ensemble when she participated in chamber-music performances.

Excepting the two orchestral works written while she was a student in Berlin which are without opus designation, and a few pieces for mixed chorus, her opus list contains seventy numbers. She wrote approximately 190 songs and 120 pieces for piano, as well as arrangements of more than fifty folk tunes—some for voice and piano and some for piano alone.

The songs were written at various times throughout her career, and although the list includes settings of many German and a few Swedish poems, the largest number, as one would expect, have Norwegian or Danish texts. Musically, they range from simple ballads to dramatic, declamatory songs. Most are in a modified strophic form, though in a few instances she employed a purely strophic or through-composed form. The piano accompaniment is largely supportive; only rarely does it assume an independent role. Nonetheless, the piano parts are often quite complex and place substantial demands on the performer. Occasionally there are accompanimental passages that may be considered to have some "pictorial" significance.

"The East Wind" (Op. 56, No. 2) is representative of the style of her simpler songs (see example 48). It is from the song cycle *Ahasverus,* with

Example 48. Agathe Backer Gröndahl, "The East Wind," from the song cycle Ahasverus, Op. 56, No. 2.

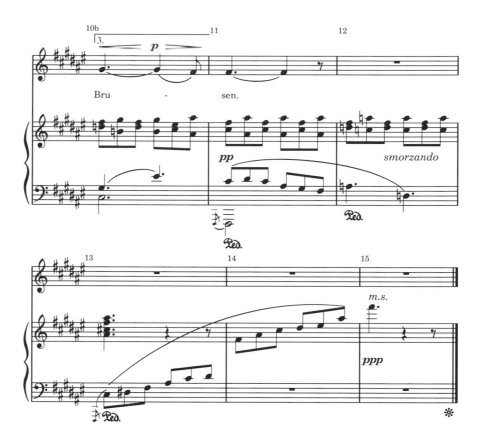

Bru - sen.

texts by Bernhard Severin Ingemann. Ahasverus is the eternal Jew who, according to legend, wanders without rest from country to country because he had refused rest to Jesus Christ on the path to Golgotha. In this song he sings of his longing for the Promised Land. Both the exotic motive of the song and the text's basic mood of unsatisfied longing are typical Romantic characteristics. The setting faithfully reflects the naiveté of the text.

The song is harmonically and melodically simple and virtually strophic. The only divergence from strophic form occurs in the concluding phrase: the first two stanzas end on a dominant chord, whereas the third stanza finally resolves to the tonic. The melody is largely diatonic; it is well suited for and undemanding of the voice. The only chromatic movement is a passing tone in measure 4. The piano has a brief introduction and postlude but is otherwise merely accompanimental. A rather sophisticated harmonic device is the use in the postlude of the altered dominant of the dominant (d–f-sharp–a–c, which should really be construed as b-sharp–d–f-sharp–

a), which leads directly to a tonic triad rather than to the usual dominant. This colorful chord progression is the only harmonic feature of the song revealing its origin as a product of the Romantic period.

Also worthy of mention is the song cycle *The Child's Spring Day*, Op. 42, with texts by Andreas Jynge. Backer Grondahl's most popular song, "Toward Evening," is from this cycle. "By the Inlet" (Op. 16, No. 2, text by Johan S. Welhaven) and "Still But a Ray of Sunshine" (text by Somerset/Lunde)—her last composition—are also among her finest songs.

Her piano works include nineteen concert etudes and two suites. Her best-known compositions for piano are the suite *In the Blue Mountain*, Op. 44, and a number of smaller pieces such as "Serenade" (Op. 15, No. 1), "Ballad" (Op. 36, No. 5), and "Summer Song" (Op. 45, No. 3). Her compositions for piano clearly reflect their origin as the creations of an able pianist with a thorough knowledge of the expressive range of the instrument. Many of them, especially her earlier compositions, require considerable technical skill of the performer. All of the etudes are technically demanding; several are unusually effective and are among her finest compositions. In later works there is a tendency toward greater simplicity.

Like her songs, her compositions for piano are generally simple in form; most consist of three sections, some of two, and a few are in simple rondo form. The structure is never very complex, though in her later compositions there are indications of greater freedom with respect to the requirements of form. A few pieces, such as the first movement of *In the Blue Mountain*, use the form of a fantasia. It is possible that programmatic elements are present in this case.

Viewed as a whole, Agathe Backer Gröndahl's compositions are in the mold of moderate German Romanticism. Her most important models seem to have been Mendelssohn and Schumann and their successors. No doubt she was also influenced by Grieg, though evidently by the more moderate elements of his style. She does not seem to have been influenced at all by the often radical harmony of his folk-tune arrangements, and in her own arrangements she added nothing original. They are, in any case, the least important of her efforts. Her strength as a composer lies in the melodic charm and fine sense of sound that pervade her works. These qualities in her best songs and piano compositions give them an enduring freshness and vivacity that we can still enjoy today.

Agathe Backer Gröndahl's husband, Olaus Andreas Gröndahl (1847–1923), was active and influential in Norway as a choral conductor and voice teacher. He had originally planned to become a clergyman, and he went so far as to begin theological study at the university. He was very musical, however, and his fine singing voice enabled him to become a member of the

Norwegian Students' Male Chorus as well as the group led by J. D. Behrens. He took instruction in music theory and piano, and in 1868 demonstrated his ability as a composer in a work for baritone solo and male chorus entitled "Young Magnus" (text by Björnson). At this point, on the advice of Behrens, he decided to devote himself entirely to the study of music.

Gröndahl studied at the Leipzig conservatory from 1870 to 1873. Voice, however, captured his interest more and more, and in 1873 he went to Cologne for a year of study with the eminent Swedish voice teacher Oskar Lindhult. In 1874 he returned to Oslo and taught voice in several schools, but his greatest contribution was as a choral conductor. In 1878 he started his own mixed chorus (the Gröndahl Choir) and conducted several of the large oratorios. From 1889 to 1913 he was conductor of the Norwegian Students' Male Chorus; among its activities under his guidance was a tour to the United States in 1905.

Gröndahl was not productive as a composer. During his studies in Leipzig he wrote *Before a Southern Convent* (text by Björnson), a large work for soprano and alto solos, women's chorus, and orchestra. He also wrote a cantata for the dedication of the Freemasons' Lodge in 1894, and a few pieces for male chorus. His compositions, though few in number, give an impression of sound training and severe self-criticism.

Johan Selmer (1844–1910) has already been characterized as the most wholehearted representative of radical Romanticism in Norway. A native of Oslo, he received his early instruction in piano and music theory from J. G. Conradi. He had originally planned to become a lawyer, but his legal studies were interrupted after just one year because of a serious chronic illness. His doctors recommended sea travel as a possible way to control or cure the illness, and during the ensuing years he visited most of the seaports of Europe as well as several in North America and Asia. The constant travel without any opportunity to do productive work finally became unbearable for him, however, and in 1869 he went to Paris to fulfill his dream of becoming a musician. There he became a student of Ambroise Thomas and Alexis Chauvet. He also heard for the first time the music of Berlioz, an event that proved to be decisive for his musical future.

Selmer's period of study in Paris was interrupted by the political unrest of 1871. He had been connected in some way with the Paris Commune, and after its defeat Selmer fled the city and returned to Oslo. That autumn he enrolled at the Leipzig conservatory. Among his teachers was Ernst Friedrich Richter, and he also profited greatly from his friendship with Svendsen, who was in Leipzig at the time. A worsening of his illness in 1872 again interrupted his studies, and he went to Italy to recover. After six months in Italy he returned to Germany but did not resume regular music studies.

Johan Selmer. (Universitetsbiblioteket i Oslo)

Indeed, his formal studies were largely concluded, and there is reason to believe that this irregular and spasmodic education, partly owing to his illness, accounts for a certain unevenness in his body of work.

He gave a concert of his own compositions in Oslo in 1871, and similar concerts were given in 1874, 1876, and 1879, all with considerable success. In 1879, when he was given a government stipend—the first composer since Grieg and Svendsen to be so honored—it was a recognition of the strong position he had won with his music. He was correctly perceived as the leader of the most radical wing among Norwegian musicians of his day. He was also influential as conductor of the Music Society orchestra during the years 1883–86. Thereafter he held no permanent position; he traveled a good deal, spending much of his time in southern European countries in the hope that the climate would improve his health. His health steadily deteriorated in his later years, however, and during the last decade of his life he was able to complete only a few minor works.

Selmer's compositions comprise sixty-one opus numbers. His principal works are for large orchestra, some with chorus and/or soloists. He also wrote 110 songs with piano accompaniment, a number of duets, some piano pieces, and several choral works.

His earliest orchestral work was "Scène funèbre," Op. 4, written in Paris in 1870 and reflecting his impression of the Franco-German war. It was to have been performed at a concert in Paris in the spring of 1871 while the Communards held the city. Selmer heard the work in rehearsal but the public performance did not occur because the city was stormed by the Versailles troops. Its public premiere was given at Selmer's own concert in Oslo that fall. "La Captive," Op. 6 (text by Victor Hugo), for alto solo and orchestra, was started during Selmer's stay in Paris and completed during his studies in Leipzig. He also became acquainted with Wagner's music while in Leipzig, and its influence is evident in his compositions dating from the 1870s. These include, in addition to the works already mentioned, "The Spirit of Scandinavia," Op. 5 (1872), for male chorus and orchestra; "The Turks Approach Athens," Op. 7 (1876), for baritone solo, male chorus, and orchestra; the lost "Alastor," Op. 8 (1874), a symphonic tone poem based on Percy Bysshe Shelley's poem of the same name; and "Nordic Festival Parade," Op.11 (1876), a symphonic march.

Selmer's style became more clearly defined in his later works. Among the most important of these are "Carnival in Flanders," Op. 32 (1890), and "Between the Mountains," Op. 35 (1892), both for orchestra; *Der Selbstmörder und die Pilger*, Op. 27 (1888), for alto and baritone solos, mixed chorus, and orchestra; and lastly his true magnum opus: *Prometheus*, Op. 50, an orchestral composition written in 1897–98.

Selmer was first and foremost a composer of program music. This fact is evident not only in the explicitly programmatic compositions but in others as well. Only three of his compositions—"Alastor," "Carnival in Flanders," and *Prometheus*—constitute program music in the true sense of the word, but everything he wrote was programmatic in that each work attempts to portray in minute detail the immediate situation or impression from which it arose. This is most evident in his songs, where the content of the text is sometimes reflected with almost painful accuracy in the music.

Example 49, "Mir träufeln bittre Thränen von den Wangen," is the last of his settings of three Petrarch sonnets. Written in 1904, these songs are among his last compositions. The structure of the sonnet—with the rhyming pattern ABBA ABBA ABC ABC—lends itself to musical treatment in an AABB form, but Selmer chose instead the through-composed form. It is generally evident that his strong desire to reflect the text in the music was the reason for this choice. There is a hint of a recapitulation in measure 33 (Tempo I), but what follows is so different that for all practical purposes the recapitulation lasts for just that one measure. The instrumental prelude is repeated before the second part and at the very end of the piece. These two repetitions are identical but they differ from the prelude in the concluding

Example 49. Johan Selmer, "Mir Traufeln Bittre Thränen von den Wangen," Op. 57, No. 3.

chords. Both melodically and harmonically, the shape of the music follows
the content of the text. The song is given a degree of coherence by the
recurrence of certain common motives and rhythmic patterns.

Harmonically it contains a plethora of colorful progressions, some of
which are in conflict with the principles of traditional harmony. It starts in
the brief piano introduction. The progression from the dominant seventh
chord in A-flat major to a major seventh chord with D as the root in measure
2 can be interpreted as a bridge from the altered dominant of the dominant

to the dominant chord in G major (D-flat = C-sharp). The continuation to the E-minor triad then becomes a normal deceptive cadence in G major. Even though these chord progressions can be interpreted according to the principles of standard harmonic movement, the rapid change of keys (from A-flat major to G major) makes it difficult to "hear" the progressions in a way consistent with this analysis. The progression from the E-minor chord in measure 2 to the A-flat major second-inversion chord in measure 3 is even more difficult to interpret in terms of standard harmonic principles. If the E minor chord is interpreted as F-flat minor, it becomes evident that the progression really is from tonic to mediant—but without a single note in common. A triad built on the mediant of F-flat major, the parallel key of F-flat minor, is an A-flat minor chord. In such progressions, harmonic relationships are audible only as "blotches of color" and one's sense of tonality is considerably weakened.

As the song continues it is clear that the composer took great care to mirror the text. Look, for example, at the move to A major in measure 11 (to the words "durch die allein"). Although it is really a Neapolitan sixth chord (a B-double-flat major chord) in A-flat major, it is used here in a simple chromatic progression to a tonic second-inversion chord in A-flat major. This is another case in which all sense of functional harmony simply disappears; it is similar in many ways to the language of Impressionism. Another example of a simple and effective technique used to heighten the expressivity of the text is the move to A-flat minor in measure 26 (at the words "Doch bald zu Eis erstarren die Gedanken").

Selmer's late songs show his mature style as a Romantic composer and reveal both his strengths and his weaknesses. His greatest strength undoubtedly was his intense desire for expression in his music. To this end he was willing to sacrifice everything—to abandon conventional musical principles, sometimes to such a degree that what he wrote virtually defies comprehension. One does not always approve of certain of his compositions, but one is never indifferent to them. His constant experimentation with nonfunctional chord progressions might be considered a weakness in the context of a harmonic fabric that in general depends on functional relationships. In his best songs, however, he managed to unite these disparate elements in such a way as to achieve a satisfying result.

Selmer's most important work, *Prometheus*, drew its inspiration from several sources: the Greek myth about the hero who stole fire from the gods and gave it to humankind, Shelley's poem "Prometheus Unbound," and a series of etchings on the same subject by the German artist Max Klinger. The composition's descriptive text, which was written by Selmer himself, depicts humanity's joy over the gift of fire, Zeus's anger, the cruel punishment that Prometheus had to endure, and the jubilation over his ultimate deliverance. The composition is divided into two movements. The first movement is in a modified ternary form with an altered recapitulation, but the form of the second is determined entirely by the programmatic content of the text.

One would have to say that the problem of form is evident in much of Selmer's music. His desire to give his compositions a fixed form conflicted with his even stronger desire for musical characterization and detailed description. It cannot be denied that when such conflicts occurred the latter desire usually prevailed. Selmer himself once wrote: "In the service of poetry I am reckless; there I throw rules and tradition overboard." He was not always able to get away with this recklessness unscathed, however. Many of his compositions, including both larger works and songs, suffer from a loose and episodic structure.

Selmer's harmony is completely motivated by his attempt to create musical characterizations; he used chords for expressive purposes that have little to do with their tonal relationships. His harmony has been compared to that of Wagner, who did indeed have some influence on Selmer's style. The alleged similarity to Wagner's harmony, however, is not as great as it might initially appear to be. Selmer's harmony is characterized by rough-edged juxtapositions of tonally distant chords, in contrast to Wagner's tension-filled, chromatic voice leading.

Selmer also occasionally used Norwegian folk melodies in his compositions. "Between the Mountains" is one such example. Folk music was of only marginal importance in his music vocabulary, however.

His orchestration is generally sophisticated, but first and foremost it is experimental and representational. He did not hesitate to employ unusual instruments—such as the *schellenbaum* (a percussion instrument of Turkish origin that makes a jangling noise) in "The Turks Approach Athens," or a kettle lid in "Carnival in Flanders," where he depicted a group of street urchins in a trio for kettle lid, piccolo, and bassoon.

No Norwegian composer has been more victimized by changes in the public's musical taste than Selmer. He played an important role in Norwegian music during the last decades of the nineteenth century. His compositions were often performed in Norway as well as on the continent, sometimes with Selmer himself as guest conductor. His songs were frequently sung, especially by Thorvald Lammers, who was an ardent admirer of Selmer's best works in this genre. His contemporaries regarded him as virtually on the same level as Grieg and Svendsen. He was the third "big name" in late nineteenth-century Norwegian music—highly regarded by many, often controversial, but never ignored. As late as 1921 Gerhard Schjelderup wrote concerning the second movement of *Prometheus*: "Here Selmer without question raises himself above any of his Scandinavian contemporaries."

In sharp contrast to Schjelderup's appraisal is the complete apathy toward Selmer's works since the interest in program music began to decline in the 1920s. Nonetheless, tastes and interests will undoubtedly continue to change, and the day may come when this branch of Romantic music will once again be appreciated. Whether Selmer's music will then prove to have sufficient musical power and durability to earn a permanent place in Norway's repertoire remains to be seen.

At present, very few of Selmer's works are ever performed. Of his songs still sung in Norway, the best known are "The Sheath Knife" (text by Christian Winther) and two of his pieces for male chorus—"Norway, Norway" (text by Björnson) and "Ulabrand," the poetic account of a ship's pilot by that name (text by Rosenkrantz Johnsen). These small compositions, however, do not begin to give a comprehensive picture of his music or of his individuality as a creative artist.

Another distinctive figure during this period was Johannes Haarklou (1847–1925), the son of a farmer and teacher in the Sunnfjord region of western Norway. Intending to follow in his father's footsteps, Johannes attended the teachers' college at Balestrand and then the Stord Seminary. His education was completed in 1868, and it appeared that he was well on his way toward a career as a teacher. Young Haarklou had a secret longing to become a musician, however. He had grown up with folk music, hearing *slaatter* played at home, and even as a child he had been very interested in the violin. At the teachers' college he was especially interested in music education despite the meager offerings in the subject. At Stord he got an opportunity to rehearse and direct the school chorus, which gave him his first experience as a conductor.

Haarklou's desire for further training in music was strong, and when he learned that the city of Drammen had just acquired an able organist by the name of Christian Cappelen he devised a plan to accomplish this: he obtained a teaching position in the area and became a pupil of Cappelen, who taught him the rudiments of both harmony and organ playing. In 1872 he continued his music studies with L. M. Lindeman in Oslo, where he also used every opportunity to hear what the city had to offer in the way of concerts. In 1873 he received a small inheritance from his parents that enabled him to enroll at the Leipzig conservatory.

His funds were sufficient for just two years of study at Leipzig, and a small stipend allowed him to return briefly in 1876, but his music training was still far from complete. In 1877, after a performance in Bergen of his first orchestral work, "Festival March," private funds were collected for a stipend that allowed him to go to Berlin for one year to continue his education. He enrolled at the music academy there in the summer of 1877, and for the first time became a serious student of composition. Later he wrote: "Not until I went to Berlin did I learn what composition truly is all about." The teacher who was most influential on his development at this time was Friedrich Kiel.

While in Berlin Haarklou also received solid training for what was to be his principal vocation later in life: that of an organist. In 1878, at the age of thirty-one, Haarklou finally completed his studies in Berlin and returned to Norway. He went first to Bergen, where among other things he gave a concert with the assistance of Ole Bull. He stayed in Bergen for a year, but in the summer of 1880, after a brief stay in Berlin, he settled in Oslo, which was to be his home for the rest of his life. He first served as organist for the Sagene congregation and in 1883 became organist at Old Aker Church. He was also active as a music critic from 1882 to 1921.

Deserving of special mention were his efforts to provide reasonably priced popular orchestral concerts for the less affluent people in the community. In the 1880s, with support from the Oslo Labor Union—and later with governmental support—he organized a series of concerts that were very well attended. He did more than conduct these concerts; he also arranged some of the pieces and wrote out the instrumental parts, learning in the process many things about the orchestra that further enriched him as a composer. Economically, however, the undertaking was unsuccessful because the ticket prices were so low, and he was obliged to pay most of the shortfall out of his own pocket. After three years, when governmental support ceased, he was forced to terminate the series. In 1890, after organizing a series of similar concerts in Bergen with public support, he turned his attention to other tasks.

Haarklou continued to give organ concerts throughout his life, however. He traveled throughout Norway, performing in virtually every church that had an organ. Once again ticket prices were low, and attendance was not always good, so the concerts also were financially unsuccessful. Nonetheless, Haarklou continued indefatigably with these concerts until his last years. Occasionally he took a singer with him on these trips. In 1887 he was married to Inga Marie Knoph, who had studied voice, and thereafter she often accompanied him on his concert tours. Through such efforts he undoubtedly did much to broaden interest in serious music among his countrymen.

Haarklou had a wide range of interests and was an enthusiastic writer, both as a music critic and as an active participant in debates in the daily press on the issues of the day. It was he, for example, who set in motion the work on some medieval music manuscripts that were found in the national archive. Dr. Georg Reiss undertook this research and uncovered the first information about the so-called "St. Olaf music" originating in medieval Norway (see p. 17ff.).

Haarklou was often a controversial figure and only in his later years received just recognition for his work. In 1910 he received a government stipend and in 1911 was made a Knight First Class of the Order of St. Olaf—the highest individual honor conferred in Norway.

Despite his various interests and duties, Haarklou was first and foremost a composer. His works comprise 120 opus numbers and include compositions in many different genres. The vast majority are large compositions for various combinations of voices and instruments. His oratorio, *Creation and Mankind* (text by Henrik Wergeland), which premiered in 1890, was the first by a Norwegian composer. He also wrote three serious operas—*The Vikings in Miklegard*, *The Tale of Mari*, and *Tyrfing* (a mythological sword)— and two comic operas. His larger choral works include the *Reformation Cantata*, written for the Luther jubilee in 1883. A smaller piece for mixed chorus and organ, "Hymn" (also known as "This Is the Day"), is often sung in Norway. His works for male chorus include three songs with texts by Per Sivle: "Tord Foleson," "Varde," and "Fenrir." Among his larger instrumental compositions are four symphonies, a violin concerto, a piano concerto, incidental music for Björnstjerne Björnson's play *Sigurd's Homecoming* (which also contains some songs), and—one of his most frequently played works—the orchestral suite *In Westminster Abbey*.

Some of Haarklou's best compositions were written for organ. Especially worthy of mention are two organ symphonies and a piece called "Fantasi Triomphale." His only chamber music consists of a violin sonata. He wrote a number of piano pieces and about fifty songs, but in general they are among his least important compositions. A few of the songs are very good, however—especially those with texts by Knut Hamsun, including "With Red Roses" and "What Whispers in the Night."

That such a small number of Haarklou's works have become popular is undoubtedly owing in part to the fact that his idiom is rather heavy: he tended to write "thick" music, with many dissonances resulting from contrapuntal voice leading that yields to nothing despite the harsh sounds that may occur. This, together with an often unconvincing harmonic foundation, results in music that is ponderous and sometimes lacking in charm. Since his symphonic compositions tend to be exceedingly long works, the demands on the listener's powers of concentration are great.

A number of experimental features are evident in Haarklou's style, some of which point to the stylistic developments of the twentieth century. In one section of *Creation and Mankind*, for example, he made consistent use of a whole-tone scale. However, this portion of the oratorio was written in about 1910, well after Debussy had made use of the same device. Nonetheless, there were few such radical tendencies in Norwegian music at that time. Another characteristic of his style, probably stemming from his interest in the whole-tone scale, was his frequent use of augmented triads. And his bold, linear handling of dissonances occasionally, though perhaps coincidentally, anticipates the use of dissonance by the Neoclassicists.

With respect to form Haarklou was conservative. He built primarily on Classical models and occasionally even turned to such Baroque models as the fugue. He opposed the contemporary trend toward program music, though he was influenced to some extent by Wagner's style. In some of his operas, for example, he made discreet use of the leitmotif technique.

Haarklou's later works exhibit a trend toward greater clarity and simplicity of both form and harmony. This is evident, for example, in his last opera, *Tyrfing* (completed in 1912), his *Symphony No. 4* in E-flat major (completed in 1922), and his *Organ Symphony No. 2* (from ca. 1923). The last of these compositions is one of Haarklou's best works. He presumably was following the example of the great French organ composer Charles M. Widor in using the designation "symphony" for organ compositions that exploited the instrument's capacity to simulate the varied sonorities of an orchestra. The first movement is in sonata form, the second in ternary, and the third is a broadly conceived fugue.

Haarklou's organ works are performed more frequently than most of his other compositions, though some of his choral pieces are still heard in Norway from time to time. His larger works are almost never performed, however. Two of his serious operas and both comic operas enjoyed considerable success during his lifetime, as did the first three symphonies.

Throughout his life Haarklou maintained his ties with Haukedal, the valley where he was born, returning to visit nearly every summer. Both as an artist and as a person he apparently was influenced by the rugged terrain of western Norway. Haarklou's music is powerful and impressive, but also somewhat abrupt and unpolished. It is not easily accessible, but it is solid.

As a composer, Ole Olsen (1850–1927) was very different from both Haarklou and Selmer. His music is generally euphonious and charming—much more accessible than Haarklou's, for example, but also less original. He never freed himself from the influence of his predecessors; nonetheless, in his best compositions he too made a genuine and lasting contribution to Norway's music repertoire.

Olsen was a native of Finnmark, the northernmost region of Norway, and throughout his life he retained an affection for this barren land beyond the Arctic Circle. Bereft of his mother when he was quite young, as a child he received good music training from his father, Iver Olsen, an accomplished amateur musician and organist in the local church. Young Ole substituted for his father there as early as the age of seven. Iver Olsen was also a clever craftsman of rhymed verse, and his son likewise became a deft versifier. The most important result of the latter's poetic endeavors was that he supplied the librettos for his operas.

Although Ole accumulated practical musical experience at a very early age, his formal training began in 1865: he had been sent to Trondheim to become an apprentice to a craftsman, but at the same time he studied piano, organ, and harmony from the Lindeman brothers Fredrik and Just. After two years he abandoned his plans to become a craftsman in order to concentrate on the organ. Just Lindeman, who was the organist in the Trondheim cathedral, became his primary mentor and Olsen soon began to substitute for him from time to time. The German-born architect H. E. Schirmer, who was then supervising the restoration of the cathedral, happened to hear him play one day and was impressed. As a result, Schirmer, who was interested in music and was also an old friend of Heinrich K. Schleinitz, director of the Leipzig conservatory, made arrangements for the young man to go to Leipzig.

Olsen attended the conservatory from 1870 to 1874, during which time he received instruction in composition from Oskar Paul. While still a student he composed his *Symphony* in G major (the orchestration was completed in 1875) and began working on his first opera, *Stig Hvide*, which relates the story of a Danish noblewoman.

In the autumn of 1874 Olsen became a music teacher in Oslo, and except for a few trips abroad—especially during the years 1881–83—this was to be his home for the rest of his life. In 1879 he married Marie Hals, daughter of the renowned piano manufacturer Karl Hals. During Svendsen's absence from Oslo in 1877–80 Olsen filled in as conductor of the Music Society orchestra. In 1884 he became conductor of a military band, and from 1899 to 1920 he was a music supervisor in the public schools.

Olsen's output as a composer was extensive and diversified, not least because he had the ability to work easily and rapidly. He wrote a large number of occasional pieces that, as one might expect, are of varying quality. His chief works, on the other hand, are carefully crafted throughout. His instrumental music, in addition to the symphony written in Leipzig, includes *The Horsemen of Aasgaard* (a symphonic poem), *Elfin Dance*, a concerto for French horn and orchestra, and the often-played *Petite Suite* for piano and string orchestra. He also wrote a few small piano pieces.

Artist's drawing of Brödrene Hals' concert hall, which was opened in 1880. (Ny illustrert Tidende, November 28, 1880)

Olsen provided incidental music for the play *Erik XIV* (by Josef von Weilen), which was performed in Vienna in 1882, and for the fairy-tale comedy *Svein the Intrepid* (text by Nordahl Rolfsen), which has proved to be his most successful work. This latter was exceptionally well received when it was performed in 1890, and some of its melodies, especially "Sunset Song," have become very popular.

Olsen wrote a few, primarily occasional, cantatas, several of which enjoyed considerable success when they were performed. Examples of such works are *Griffenfeldt* (for male chorus and orchestra), the Freemason cantata *Brotherhood*, and *Ludvig Holberg* (1884). Similar in type is the oratorio *Nidaros* (the ancient name for Trondheim), which was performed in connection with the celebration of Trondheim's nine-hundred-year jubilee in 1897. He wrote several smaller works for male chorus; some of them, such as "Banner Guard" and "In the Jotunheimen Mountains," have been widely sung in Norway. As conductor of a military band he also tried to develop a repertoire of Norwegian military marches. He arranged a number of Norwegian folk tunes (some of which he had transcribed from original sources himself) for a Janissary band and published a large collection of Norwegian marches.

Olsen's musical style is characterized by a rather cautious but sometimes quite sophisticated use of the techniques typical of late Romanticism. He was a sincere admirer of Grieg and Svendsen and he learned a great deal from both. His music was less influenced by folk music than Grieg's, and he was by no means as original as Grieg or as elegant a harmonist as Svendsen. There is relatively little chromaticism in either his melodic lines or his harmony. When it does appear, it is usually in the form of passing tones or embellishments. Occasionally, however, he employed colorful chromatic chord progressions. His best works are infused with a freshness and a melodic and harmonic charm that have ensured their continuing popularity. These characteristics are especially evident in the lovely "Sunset Song" from *Svein the Intrepid*, but the rest of the music for this sprightly comedy is also full of lively ideas and fresh melodies.

The symphonic poem *The Horsemen of Aasgaard* displays fairly daring orchestration and chord progressions for its time. Based on Johan S. Welhaven's poem by the same name, it must be regarded as pure program music. It was performed quite often during the composer's lifetime but is rarely played today.

Olsen's most important compositions are his operas. The operas of Wagner had made a profound impression on him when he was a student in Germany, and thereafter he regarded the writing of dramatic music as his principal calling. The influence of Wagner's dramatic ideas is evident in his occasional use of the leitmotif technique, and the Wagnerian influence probably also accounts for the rather thick orchestral sound for which he has sometimes been criticized. Wagner's influence is less evident in his harmony. Of his four operas, only *Lajla* (1893; text based in part on a novel of the same title by Claus Riis) has ever been staged. Excerpts from *Stig Hvide* (1876; with textual material taken from Bernhard S. Ingemann's novel *Erik Menved's Childhood*) and *Stallo* (1902; based on an old Sami folk tale) have been performed in concert versions. His last dramatic work, *The Mountain Islands* (completed after 1910), has never been performed in its entirety. Moreover, the uneven quality of Olsen's librettos makes it quite unlikely that any of his operas will be staged in the future.

As a composer, Iver Holter (1850–1941) was much like Ole Olsen in that his music is pleasant and attractive but lacks a strong personal stamp. However, his output was far more limited than Olsen's, perhaps because he was so constantly occupied with other duties. He made his mark primarily as a conductor, teacher, and organizer.

Holter was born in Gausdal, where his father was a clergyman. He showed musical talent at an early age and presumably received encouragement from his mother, who was an able amateur pianist. She died when Iver was only seven years old, however. When the elder Holter was transferred to Gjerpen, Iver began to take violin lessons from Fridrich W. Rojahn, organist in the nearby town of Skien. In 1869 he went to Oslo to study medicine, and he soon became active there as a professional violinist. He played in Grieg's "subscription concert" orchestra and later in the Music Society orchestra under the direction of both Grieg and Svendsen. The latter also gave him lessons in music theory.

His interest in music eventually became dominant, and in 1876 he terminated his medical studies and went to Leipzig to study composition. His teachers included Salomon Jadassohn, Ernst Friedrich Richter, and Carl Reinecke. Among the works he composed at this time was the first movement of his *Symphony* in F major, which was performed in Leipzig and well received. In 1879 he went to Berlin to continue his studies, returning to Oslo in 1881. In the spring of 1882, with the assistance of Edmund Neupert, he gave a concert consisting of his own compositions. That autumn he succeeded Grieg as conductor of Harmonien (precursor of the Bergen Philharmonic Orchestra). Except for a second period of study in Leipzig during the winter of 1884–85 he remained in Bergen until 1886. A highlight of this stay in Leipzig was a performance of his *Symphony* in F major (which had been completed in 1881).

In 1886 Holter succeeded Selmer as conductor of the Music Society orchestra in Oslo, and it was in this position that he made his most significant contribution to the music of Norway. During his tenure, which lasted until 1911, he organized the permanent symphony orchestra (known today as the Oslo Philharmonic) that was to become so vital to the music life of the city. Holter inherited an orchestra that was merely a miscellaneous group of musicians assembled for concerts from time to time; by 1911 he had built an orchestra with a solid nucleus of permanent, salaried musicians. As its conductor, he was keenly aware of the new currents in European music and performed many works by such composers as Wagner, Brahms, Saint-Saëns, Carl Nielsen, and Jean Sibelius—some of whom had never before gained a hearing in Norway. He was also a strong champion of Norwegian music, premiering a number of works by contemporary Norwegian composers.

Holter was a choral director as well, conducting the Craftsmen's Chorus from 1890 to 1905 and the Businessmen's Chorus from 1905 to 1918. His most important achievement in this area, however, was the creation in 1897 of the Holter Choral Society, which performed many large works during the ensuing years.

As a teacher Holter had an influence on several Norwegian composers of the next generation, including Sigurd Lie and Eyvind Alnaes. He also served as editor of the periodical *Nordisk Musik Revue* from 1900 to 1906.

Holter's compositions are not numerous; perhaps he himself felt that his strongest skills lay in other areas. In addition to the *Symphony* in F major (Op. 3), his works include *Midsummer Eve*, subtitled "Idyll for String Orchestra" (Op. 4); *String Quartet No. 1* in E-flat major (Op. 1); *String Quartet No. 2* in G major (Op. 18); incidental music for Goethe's play, *Götz von Berlichingen*, also issued as an orchestral suite (Op. 10); "Romance for Violin" (Op. 12); and the *Violin Concerto* in A minor (Op. 22). His vocal works, in addition to some songs and smaller choral pieces, include a comic opera, *Donna Julia* (never performed), and six large cantatas. Among the latter are *To the Fatherland* (Op. 14) and *St. Olaf's Cantata* (Op. 25), written for the St. Olaf jubilee in 1930.

Holter's music is the product of a skillful musician. In form and harmony he was generally dependent on Classical models; in his larger works the prototypes are the works of the Viennese Classicists. The *Violin Concerto*, for example, consists of three movements of which the first and last are in sonata form and the slow middle movement is in ternary form. His harmony was little influenced by the chromaticism of late Romanticism. Holter generally preferred unaltered chords in standard tonal relationships. Modulations were achieved primarily through mediant progressions and changes of mode (major-minor) that sometimes border on non-functional relationships. In his later works, such as the *St. Olaf's Cantata*, one can discern a tendency toward a somewhat freer and more daring handling of dissonance.

In general, however, it must be said that despite his zeal at the turn of the century to perform what was then considered modern music, Holter's own compositional style owed little to modern tendencies. Consider, for example, the chorale for male chorus from his Opus 15 *Cantata for the Seventh Great Song Festival*, written in 1896 (example 50). His preference for unadorned triads is especially clear in a religious piece such as this. The form (AA'BA'') is carefully balanced, with the brief interlude in imitative style (B) serving as a nice contrast.

Holter's compositions have been performed only rarely in recent years; once their novelty wore off they seem to have been quickly forgotten. The suite from *Götz von Berlichingen* has been played most often, followed by the *Violin Concerto*. The compositions most likely to be revived at some time are the "Romance for Violin" and the *String Quartet No. 2*. Although they are not of first-rank importance, they are fine, solid works by a competent composer and deserve to be performed.

Example 50. Iver Holter, "Chorale" from Cantata for the Seventh Great Song Festival, *Op. 15.*

Per Lasson (1859–83) really belongs to the next generation of composers, but his untimely death at the age of twenty-four places his creative output contemporaneous with that of the previous generation. A native of Oslo, Lasson received piano instruction in his youth from an uncle, Bredo Lasson. Later, while studying law, he took lessons in harmony from Svendsen. For the most part, however, he was self-taught. He contracted tuberculosis in 1881, and thereafter spent much of his time at German health spas.

As one would expect, his compositions are not numerous. They include nine piano pieces, fifteen songs, a "Festival March" for the 1882 presentation ceremony into the university Student Society's "Order of the Pig," and an overture entitled "Young Blood." His best-known composition is "Crescendo," a salon piece for piano that is widely enjoyed both in Norway and elsewhere. Another composition for piano worthy of mention is "Une Demande," which is a fine little mood piece.

The few compositions that Lasson managed to complete indicate that he was a gifted composer, with a fresh musicality and a fine melodic talent. It is unfortunate that his life was cut short long before he was able to reach full stylistic maturation.

CHURCH MUSIC

The most important development in the area of church music during this period was the resolution of the hymn controversy (see above, pp. 155–56). After the official authorization of L. M. Lindeman's chorale book in 1877 there were no important developments in Norwegian church music until the publication of a new chorale book in 1926.

Lindeman's heir as the leading church musician in Norway was Christian Cappelen (1845–1916). He regarded the extension of Lindeman's work—or, more correctly, its preservation—as his most important task. His service book of 1890 is built entirely on Lindeman's of 1870, and he desired nothing more than to keep Norwegian church music on the path marked out by his predecessor. As a composer, however, Cappelen was much more Romantic in his orientation than Lindeman.

Cappelen was born in Drammen. He received some music training during his youth and in 1860 was sent to Leipzig to attend the conservatory. He remained there for three years, studying with such teachers as Ignaz Moscheles, Ernst Friedrich Richter, and Moritz Hauptmann. Following his studies in Leipzig he spent five years in Oslo as a music teacher, moving to Drammen in 1868 to become organist at the Strömsö Church. In 1875 he received a public grant that enabled him to undertake further study in Leipzig and Dresden. Upon returning to Drammen in 1882 he became organist in the Bragernes Church. He remained in this position until 1887, when he succeeded Lindeman as organist at Our Savior's Church in Oslo.

During the nearly twenty years that he worked in Drammen, Cappelen was the city's leading musician. His fame as an organist spread rapidly, not least because of his numerous public concerts. He gave such concerts in many churches throughout Norway, first alone and later with two renowned singers, baritone Thorvald Lammers and soprano Gina Oselio. He was the logical choice to succeed Lindeman upon his death in 1877 as choral director and organist at Our Savior's Church. This was the most important church-music position in Norway, and Cappelen remained there for the rest of his life. He was renowned for his organ playing, especially his free improvisations, an area in which he was unusually skilled. From 1890 onward he was also a teacher of hymnology and liturgics at the theological seminary of the University of Oslo.

As a composer Cappelen was influenced chiefly by the somewhat conservative type of Romanticism to which he was exposed in Leipzig. The composer whom he most desired to emulate was Mendelssohn, but he also admired the work of Schumann and Chopin. These influences are evident in his songs and piano pieces as well as his religious compositions.

Cappelen's opus list includes thirty-one numbers. His best-known composition is a melody that first appeared in a cantata written for the silver jubilee of the Deaconess Home in Oslo in 1894. It was used for the hymn "My Lot Became a Blessing" in the chorale book of 1926. He also wrote the *Cantata for the Dedication of a Church* and *A Worship Cantata for the Hundredth Anniversary of the Constitution on May 17, 1914*. None of his four cantatas has been preserved in its entirety.

Other compositions worthy of mention include a "Romance" for cello and piano (Op. 31), and "Prayer" (Op. 20), a sacred aria for soprano with piano accompaniment. Cappelen also wrote some songs and two volumes of piano pieces. Central to his output, however, were his organ works. They include an improvisation on "The Great White Host," a chorale prelude on "Praise to the Lord," *Twelve Postludes* (Op. 28), and "Legende." The organ works are melodious and pleasant to the ear and are often played in Norway today.

His improvisation on "The Great White Host" is the only work in which he employed a Norwegian folk tune, and folk music does not appear to have affected his musical style in any way. Moreover, it cannot be said that he achieved a particularly distinctive style as a composer, but his compositions are ably, if somewhat conservatively, crafted.

10

Late Romanticism
(ca. 1890–ca. 1920)

The controversy over the Swedish-Norwegian union intensified at about the turn of the century, and in 1905 the union was finally dissolved. As part of the process by which this was achieved, two plebiscites were held: one dealt with the question whether the union should be dissolved, the other with the selection of Prince Carl of Denmark as king of Norway. The dissolution of the union was adopted by an overwhelming majority, with only 184 dissenting votes. The plebiscite on the choice of the king also yielded a large majority for Prince Carl, who was crowned King Haakon VII.

Understandably, these events aroused considerable attention among the Norwegian people, but they had little direct significance for Norwegian cultural life. The union with Sweden had not resulted in any dependence on Swedish culture; in this respect the relationship was quite different from that with Denmark, which had dominated Norway culturally as well as politically for nearly four centuries before 1814. The political separation from Sweden in 1905, therefore, had relatively little influence on the work of Norway's artists.

Norway was neutral during World War I (1914–18) and thus was not officially involved in the hostilities. The Norwegian merchant marine fleet suffered heavy losses, however, and there was a shortage of many commodities in the land. On the other hand, the country earned huge profits through shipping, thus creating the appearance of wealth in the years immediately following the war. The economic crisis of the early 1920s soon demonstrated, however, that this wealth existed only on paper. It also had consequences for the nation's music life. The Opéra Comique (see p. 249) was started in 1918 on the basis of pledges of large gifts from private donors; but it soon became evident that these pledges were not going to be paid, and in 1921 the enterprise was forced to close.

These events—the dissolution of the union with Sweden, World War I, and the economic crisis of the 1920s—constitute the background for the cultural period to which we now turn. Awareness of these events hardly prepares one for what happened in Norwegian music, however, for after the outpouring of creativity by Norwegian composers during the "golden age" of Norwegian music (ca. 1860–90), the period that followed strikes one as something of a regression. There was certainly no lack of numbers: during the years flanking the turn of the century Norway had many composers, many conductors, many performers—but none worthy to wear the mantle of Svendsen or Grieg. Norway's golden age continued in the fields of visual art and literature: it was during this very period that Edvard Munch and Knut Hamsun created the works that were to place them among the world's elite in their respective fields. For music, however, the glory days seemed to be over.

In both literature and art the period beginning in about 1890 is usually characterized as "Neoromanticism." The reason is to be found in the strong currents of realism and naturalism that manifested themselves during the 1880s, thus marking a distinctly new direction in those fields. In music, however, the situation was somewhat different, for the realism and naturalism of the 1880s had little influence on Norwegian composers. Thus the new generation that emerged about 1890 constituted a natural continuation of the Romanticism of Svendsen and Grieg, and the period is usually called late Romanticism.

The same situation prevailed in music on the continent. There too this period is usually termed late Romanticism, inasmuch as most European composers at the turn of the century continued on the path of Romanticism and carried to its culmination the tradition that they had inherited from the preceding generation. The contrast between what we may call the "Classical" and the "radical" lines became somewhat blurred on the continent, however. In such composers as Gustav Mahler, Richard Strauss, and Max Reger one finds features of both trends. The truly new development during this period was Impressionism, the leading representative of which was Claude Debussy. Although Impressionism retained many characteristics of Romanticism, its break with functional harmony marked out a direction in which further development was possible. It was the most important precursor of the modernism that found expression in the works of Stravinsky and Bartók from around 1910 onward.

Neither Impressionism nor the stylistic changes on the continent that occurred around 1910 had much influence on the Norwegian composers of this generation, however. This is somewhat surprising, for Grieg in many ways anticipated both groups. He was quite aware that in the last phase of his development he had left his countrymen behind. After he had premiered his *Norwegian Peasant Dances* for piano in 1906 he wrote in his diary: "What hurt me was that the *Norwegian Peasant Dances* didn't strike home as they should have. I played them with all the affection and magic that I could muster. But where my evolution as a composer has led me, I don't have my own people with me, and that is hard to bear. Here they are forever expecting me to write in the style of my early works, which time and again are praised at the expense of my recent ones."

No doubt there are many reasons why most of Norway's composers at this time continued to build on Grieg's style of the 1860s and 1870s, especially on the non-Impressionistic features of that style. One reason, perhaps, is that most Norwegian composers continued to go to Germany (Leipzig or Berlin) for their training. Unlike the Norwegian painters of the period, they did not go to Paris, where Impressionism was rapidly emerging in music as well as in the visual arts. It must also be remembered that Grieg's earlier works were primarily the ones that had achieved such great international success. Thus the younger Norwegian composers tended to regard them as the great ideal. A third reason was that Christian Sinding, the leading Norwegian composer of that generation, had already developed his personal style before Debussy was able to produce the profile of Impressionism. Moreover, once Sinding had established his reputation as a composer his musical language did not change significantly. Consequently, he tended to be a conservative influence on his contemporaries.

In any event, Impressionism did not seriously assert itself in Norway until after 1910, almost simultaneously with the even more modern trends that had developed in continental music by that time. These developments will be discussed in the next chapter.

The division of Romanticism into a moderate and a radical wing can be traced among Norwegian composers after the turn of the century as well. Selmer's principal successors as composers of program music were Hjalmar Borgström and (though he was influenced more by Wagner than by Selmer) the opera composer Gerhard Schjelderup. Most of the others—Catharinus Elling, Johan Halvorsen, and Eyvind Alnaes, for example—adhered to the moderate tradition. Sinding, as we shall see shortly, was in most respects a member of the latter group as well.

OPERAS AND CONCERTS

One looks in vain for new music organizations of any kind during this period. In Oslo, the Music Society continued its activities as in the past, with Karl Nissen (1879–1920) succeeding Iver Holter as conductor in 1913. Nissen served in this capacity until 1918, though a number of guest conductors were also used during this period. He was a distinguished pianist, but he lacked orchestral experience when he began his duties. He developed rapidly as a conductor, however, and presented many excellent programs of works from the classical repertoire. After Nissen's departure the concerts of the Music Society were conducted—for what proved to be its last year—by Ignaz Neumark and Georg Schnéevoigt.

In 1919 the Music Society disbanded. A salary conflict at the National Theater left the society without an orchestra, since the society orchestra was dependent on cooperation with the theater orchestra. In order to give the city a permanent symphony orchestra, the Philharmonic Society was established in 1919 and began its activities that autumn with no less than three conductors: Schnéevoigt, Neumark, and Johan Halvorsen. Although the new organization experienced severe economic problems, it managed to overcome the difficulties and in time developed into a much more stable orchestra than the city had previously had.

The Harmonic Society in Bergen underwent a similar reorganization and also emerged as an independent orchestra in 1919. Harald Heide (1876–1965) served as its conductor until 1947, raising the orchestra to new levels of excellence.

Opera continued to be engaged in a fairly hopeless struggle for survival with spoken drama. During its last years, the Christiania Theater (which closed in 1899) averaged one opera production annually, with the principal roles being filled by guest artists. Johan Hennum was the conductor until 1894, and from 1894 to 1899 the position was filled by Per Winge. Prior to the opening of the new National Theater in 1899, an effort was made to include a permanent place for opera in this edifice that was intended from the beginning to be the foremost theater in Norway. The effort was unsuccessful, notwithstanding the strong support of the theater's director, Björn Björnson. However, operas were staged somewhat more frequently than before. An average of two opera premieres were given each year from 1899 to 1919, and under the able leadership of Johan Halvorsen the musical quality of these productions was excellent. The orchestra consisted of forty-three permanent members and was fairly adequate to satisfy the demands of most operas.

In 1918 the opera situation in Oslo was significantly, if temporarily, improved. The Opéra Comique presented its opening production that autumn, and for three years thereafter the city had a resident opera company consisting primarily of Norwegian singers. The conductors were Leif Halvorsen and an Italian, Piero Coppola, while the opera director was a Hungarian, Benno Singer. Twenty-six different operas were presented during these years, and the artistic quality is said to have been very high. None-

Artist's conception of a scene from the Camille Saint-Saëns opera Samson and Delilah, *with which the Opéra Comique opened on November 30, 1918. (*Dagbladet, *December 1, 1918)*

Opera Comique.
Samson og Dalila.

theless, after three years it proved financially impossible to continue the operation. The Opéra Comique's final performance was given on September 1, 1921, and Norway was not to have a resident opera company again until 1959.

A number of distinguished performing musicians lived in Norway at this time. Such artists as Gina Oselio (1858–1937) and Ellen Gulbranson (1863–1947) were opera singers of international stature. The most important singers of the next generation, Kaja Eide Norena (1884–1968) and Kirsten Flagstad (1895–1962), also began their careers during this period. Flagstad, for example, performed with the Opéra Comique. The foremost Norwegian pianist of this generation was Martin Knutzen (1863–1909), who remained unchallenged in that position after his stunning debut in 1889. He was also a distinguished piano pedagogue. Unfortunately, his career was cut short by poor health. He played his last concert in 1906.

Two large national music festivals were held in Norway during this period—one in Bergen in 1898, with Grieg as artistic director, the other in Oslo in 1914. The objective in both cases was to give a comprehensive overview of Norwegian music through a series of concerts, and both appear to have been unusually successful.

Thorvald Lammers (1841–1922) received his first instruction in music from his talented mother, but with no intention that he become a professional musician. He studied law and worked in that field for several years. In 1870, however, he decided to become a singer. He first studied with Fritz Arleberg in Stockholm, then with Francesco Lamperti and others in Milan, where he made his debut in 1873. In 1874 he was engaged by the Christiania Theater as a bass soloist, but after the theater was destroyed by fire in 1877 he embarked on further studies abroad. He went to London, Berlin, and Leipzig, studying primarily sacred music.

In 1879 Lammers settled in Oslo and became active during the following years as a singer and voice teacher. He presented many concerts in Oslo and elsewhere in Norway, often including new Norwegian compositions on his programs. Many songs of Grieg, Selmer, Sinding, and others were premiered by Lammers. In his later years he did much to familiarize his countrymen with Norwegian folk music as well. His wife, Mally Lammers, was also a singer, and for several years beginning in 1896 they traveled around the country giving "folk-music evenings." The "Dream Ballad" (see p. 81ff.) was among the pieces often included in their programs of unaccompanied songs.

The mixed chorus started by Lammers in 1879 was renamed the Cecilia Society in 1902, and it continues to exist under that name today. Lammers directed this chorus until 1910, presenting such large sacred works as Cherubini's *Requiem* in C minor (in 1880), Mendelssohn's oratorio *St. Paul* (1882), and Bach's *St. John Passion* (1894).

Lammers's compositions include songs for solo voice and piano, some short choral pieces, and several large choral works. His best-known songs are "The Silver" (Henrik Ibsen) and "For the Wounded" (Björnstjerne Björnson). His song collection, *A Dozen Stevs* (twelve songs for solo voice and piano with *stev* texts) has also maintained a place in the song repertoire. His larger choral compositions include *On Akershus* (Ibsen), *Caesaris* (Henrik Wergeland), and an oratorio *Peace* (Björnson). The oratorio was premiered shortly before his death in 1922.

As a composer Lammers reflected the style of the past. He possessed a considerable melodic gift, however, and created several fine songs that have not been forgotten over the years. His harmony is that of early Romanticism, even though his compositions came into being toward the end of the late Romantic period.

CHRISTIAN SINDING

Christian Sinding (1856–1941) is often regarded as Grieg's heir. With respect to compositional style, however, this view is incorrect. Although one certainly can find traces of Grieg's earlier style in Sinding's music, the principal influence was German Romanticism. That most of Sinding's music later was left in neglect may be owing in large measure to the general reaction against Romanticism but also, perhaps, to the fact that during his lifetime he was somewhat overrated. The Grieg legacy could only be passed on to another Norwegian composer of similar international stature, and Sinding was expected to fill this role even though he probably was not equal to the task. Nonetheless, in his best works he displayed fine compositional skill.

Sinding was born into an artistically gifted family in Kongsberg, a small city near Oslo. His brother Otto was a painter, his brother Stephan a sculptor, and Christian's musical talent was recognized at an early age. He first planned to become a professional violinist, taking violin lessons from Gudbrand Böhn and instruction in music theory from L. M. Lindeman while still a schoolboy. In 1874 he went to the Leipzig conservatory, where his teachers included Henry Schradieck in violin, and Carl Reinecke and Salomon Jadassohn in theory and composition.

He soon realized that his greater talent lay in composition, and he began to emphasize this aspect of his education. Except for a few brief interruptions he remained in Leipzig for about four years. His studies did not lead to immediate success as a composer, however. He later repudiated a number of his early works and in some cases destroyed the manuscripts. Among the latter were a violin sonata and a piano sonata.

Sinding's first successful work was his *Piano Quintet* in E minor (Op. 5), which was premiered in 1885. This was followed by his *Variations* in E-flat minor for two pianos (Op. 2), which was premiered in 1886, the *Piano*

Christian Sinding. (Universitetsbiblioteket i Oslo)

Concerto in D-flat major (Op. 6), which appeared in 1889, and his *Symphony No. 1* in D minor (Op. 21), a work in progress for many years before it was premiered in 1890. He thereafter revised the symphony once more, and it reached its final form in 1892. These works won for Sinding a central role in the music life of Norway, and they were played frequently on the continent as well. He reached full artistic maturity, therefore, in the latter half of the 1880s after a lengthy period of development. Thereafter he became a highly productive composer, eventually completing 132 works.

From 1880 onward Sinding received grants on a fairly regular basis from the Norwegian government. These grants, in addition to his income from C. F. Peters of Leipzig, the editorial firm that published his works, gave him some degree of financial stability. In 1910 he was awarded an annual government stipend, and in 1924 he was given Henrik Wergeland's home, Grotten, as an honorary residence. In 1921 he also received a special cash award from the government. That year he became professor of composition at the Eastman School of Music in Rochester, New York, but he remained in this position for just a few months. Sinding spent almost forty years in long periods of residence in Germany and was closely tied to German music and German cultural circles in general. This undoubtedly explains in large part why, at the age of eighty-four (1940), he allowed himself to be exploited by the Nazis in the political propaganda that attended the German occupation of Norway.

Orchestral compositions comprise a significant part of Sinding's output. The most important works in this category are his four symphonies: the first in D minor; the second in D major, Op. 83 (1904); the third in F major, Op. 121 (1920); and the fourth, which bears the subtitle "Winter and Spring; Rhapsody for Large Orchestra" and was premiered in 1936 on the occasion of Sinding's eightieth birthday. Also worthy of mention are the "Rondo infinito," Op. 42 (1897); the *Piano Concerto* in D-flat major, Op. 6 (1889); three violin concertos—in A major, Op. 45 (1898), D major, Op. 60 (1901), and A minor, Op. 119 (1917); and an orchestral suite, *Episodes chevaleresques*, Op. 35 (1899), originally written for piano.

The most important of the above works are those written before about 1900. His first symphony, which brought him to the attention of the music world, contains many of the characteristic features of his general style. The music is bold and fresh, though occasionally both the harmony and the orchestration are somewhat ponderous. The form, as in most of his larger works, is strictly Classical, with four movements in the standard order. The first and second movements, Allegro moderato and Andante, are in sonata form. The third movement, Vivace, is a rondo, and the fourth is again in sonata form. These movements are held together by common thematic material, a technique Sinding often used in his larger works. The harmony is marked by frequent and sometimes abrupt modulations, but it generally has a clear functional basis and the chord progressions are fairly conservative compared with other European music of the time.

Of Sinding's other large-scale works, the piano concerto and the first violin concerto are also exceedingly important. The "Rondo infinito" has also maintained a strong place in the repertoire. It was written originally "in modo d'una sonata" as a setting for voice and piano of Holger Drachmann's poem "Autumn." Sinding later explained why he transformed it into an orchestral piece: "There were no singers to perform it, so I finally revised the finale as a rondo for orchestra." This work, too, exhibits a bold, almost brutal, strength of expression. It is, as the title suggests, a rondo, but it is held together by an ostinato-like rhythm that is sustained throughout nearly the entire piece.

Sinding's most important chamber-music composition is the piano quintet. It was this work that brought him international recognition and fame, but it also encountered some opposition. Several conservative critics disapproved of this bold new manner of expression, and some also criticized certain liberties taken in the voice leading in this Classical medium. Although it contains some daring passages, the quintet is built on familiar models and does not go significantly beyond the stylistic features of Romanticism. Nonetheless, the expressive strength and immediacy throughout all four movements show Sinding at his best, and the work is justly considered the centerpiece of his output. Other chamber-music compositions worthy of mention are *Violin Sonata* ("In the Old Style"), Op. 99; *String Quartet* in A minor, Op. 70; a "Serenade" for two violins and piano, Op. 92; and five romances for violin and piano.

Sinding wrote some 250 songs for voice and piano and ranks with Grieg and Kjerulf as a leading Norwegian composer of art songs. He set Norwegian, Danish, and German texts ranging in emotional tone from unrestrained merriment to bitter despair. These pieces vary in form from large modified strophic and through-composed songs to simple strophic, balladic melodies. His two *Anemone* cycles, Op. 28 and Op. 75 (with texts by Ivar Aasen), contain primarily songs that are simple in character, but they are also some of his finest and most deeply felt compositions of this type. "Sylvelin," Op. 55, No. 1 (text by Vetle Vislie), another fine song that has earned a secure place in the international vocal repertoire, is particularly lyrical and introspective.

Another of his best songs, but one that displays an entirely different character, is "A Bird Cried Out," Op. 18, No. 5. The text, which Grieg had previously set (Op. 60, No. 4), is by Vilhelm Krag:

A bird cried out on the endless sea, wild and lonely;
Forlornly sounding its mournful cry,
Wearily flapping, on, on it did fly,
Winging toward dim horizons, over the sea.

Sinding gave this somber text a dark but colorful garb in an unusually fine blending of words and music (example 51). Even within the confines of this concise form one finds examples of Sinding's rich chords and expressive power. Note, for example, the bold use of the subdominant ninth chords at

Example 51. Christian Sinding, "A Bird Cried Out," Op. 18, No. 5.

sei-led på sor - te vin-ger bort-o-ver hav.

the beginning and again at the end of the piece. The ninths function as appoggiaturas leading to the octave, but the result is a rather sharp dissonance. The chord on the second beat of measure 9 sounds more incidental than functional: the octaves G/g and b-flat/b-flat¹ are best interpreted as passing tones between the tonic chord in the root position (first beat in measure 9) and the tonic chord in first inversion (first beat in measure 10). Measure 7 also is harmonically interesting, for after the progression from a C major triad to an A-flat major triad (from the dominant to the mediant in F minor) it proceeds to the same subdominant chord that was used in measure 1 (except this time the third, d-flat, is delayed one beat). The climax of the song in measure 11 ("Winging toward dim horizons") is carefully anticipated melodically and harmonically, with close attention to the text. The harmonic basis for the increase in tension is simple: a transition from the subdominant to the dominant of the dominant with root omitted (= a diminished seventh chord) on the second and third beats of measure 10. Thus the poignant text is simply yet intuitively illuminated.

Sinding's compositions for piano are generally less distinguished than many of his other works. Except for "Rustle of Spring," which is by far the most popular composition of his entire oeuvre, his piano pieces are seldom played. His most important composition in this category is *Variations* in E-flat minor for two pianos, Op. 2. Other larger works for piano include *Fifteen Caprices*, Op. 44; *Sonata* in B minor, Op. 91; and *Variations* in B-flat minor ("Fatum"), Op. 94.

The most important of his larger vocal compositions is the cantata *To Molde*, Op. 16 (text by Björnstjerne Björnson). He wrote several other cantatas, however, including a *Jubilee Cantata*, 1914, which is also significant. His only opera, *The Sacred Mountain*, was staged in Dessau (Germany) in

1914 and played in concert form in Oslo in 1931, but it has since disappeared from the repertoire.

Sinding's compositional style changed little through the years. The musical language of German Romanticism that he adopted in about 1890 remained his preferred idiom, virtually unchanged, for the rest of his life. Despite a few radical features, his style is generally conservative—harmonically rich, with numerous and sometimes abrupt modulations and a fairly extensive use of chromatic chord progressions, but with no tendency to blur the sense of tonality. His harmony was influenced more by Liszt than by Wagner. In matters of form he followed the moderate wing of Romanticism. The most radical characteristic of his style is the use of the same motivic material in several movements of his larger works, but by his day this device was no longer new.

Sinding's independence and originality are most evident in his musical expressiveness. An aggressive freshness and virile strength are evident in many of his principal works. His music occasionally sounds somewhat bombastic, but his most successful compositions are imbued with a spirit of joyous music making. Sinding possessed an excellent melodic gift and a fine sense for the symphonic handling of thematic material. His earlier works were the most inspired and have proven to be quite durable. When he continued to compose in the same style well into the present century, the resulting works sounded outdated because he was unable to preserve the fixed musical language of his youth in a living, inspired form. The best of his earlier compositions do live on, however, and deservedly so.

SINDING'S CONTEMPORARIES

Most of Sinding's contemporaries in Norway, as we have said, belonged to the moderate wing of Romanticism. The oldest member of this group was Catharinus Elling (1858–1942). Elling studied at the Leipzig conservatory in 1877–78 and also earned a degree in philology at the University of Oslo in 1883. In 1886, on the recommendation of Grieg and others, he received a grant that enabled him to go to Berlin to continue his studies in music. He remained there for ten years, and they proved to be his richest period as a composer. Upon returning to Norway in 1896 he became a teacher at the Oslo music conservatory. He was also a church organist, a collector of Norwegian folk tunes, a music critic, a publisher, and the author of several articles and books on subjects ranging from folk music to music history.

Elling's orchestral compositions include a *Symphony* in A major (1890), *Theme with Variations* (1897), and a *Violin Concerto* in D minor (pub. 1918). He also wrote some chamber music, including two string quartets, a piano quartet, and a violin sonata. Among his larger vocal works are an opera *The*

Cossacks (1890–94), an oratorio *The Prodigal Son* (1895–96), and two choral works: "King Inge and Gregorius Dagsön" (for male chorus and orchestra) and "Sing Praise to Life's Eternal Spring" (for mixed chorus). He also wrote incidental music for Shakespeare's *Twelfth Night* and Ibsen's *Emperor and Galilean*, about two hundred songs, several smaller choral pieces for various combinations of voices, and some short pieces for piano solo and for violin and piano. This extensive output was a significant contribution to Norwegian music at the turn of the century. His compositions were well received and he was highly regarded as a writer on music and as a teacher. His students included Fartein Valen and David Monrad Johansen, both of whom later became important figures themselves in the history of Norwegian music.

As a composer Elling was quite conservative. In his handling of form, for example, he followed the models of Viennese Classicism. Both his *Violin Concerto* in D minor and his *String Quartet* in D major consist of the standard four movements in the usual sequence. The first movements of both are in sonata form, the inner movements in ternary form. The last movement of the quartet is also in sonata form. The last movement of the *Violin Concerto* is a rondo, which is also consistent with Classical models. Elling was somewhat more independent of the Classical influence in his handling of tonality. This is evident in his preference for the subdominant modulations characteristic of early Romanticism. The principal tonality of the first movement of the *Violin Concerto*, for example, is D minor, but in the exposition the secondary theme appears in the key of B-flat major (the subdominant of the relative major). In the recapitulation it occurs in the expected D major. Elling's themes also are typically Classical in character. The melodic line is nearly always diatonic and consists of two- and four-measure phrases.

As a composer of songs Elling generally employed small and simple forms. The melodic lines flow gracefully and naturally and are virtually devoid of chromaticism. Although the piano accompaniment occasionally "sets the scene" for what is transpiring in the text, it generally plays only a supportive role. The overall effect of the settings, with their relatively simple harmony and smooth melodic lines, is often one of aloofness and restraint—an impression that does not really fit the impassioned texts that Elling often chose for his songs. Though he wrote two hundred of them, virtually the only song heard today is "The Sparrow."

His larger vocal works show him to have been an able choral composer. The chorus plays an important role in both *The Prodigal Son* and *The Cossacks*. The latter is a grandly conceived tragic opera in four acts. The libretto by Edvard Hagerup Bull is based on Nikolai Gogol's short story "Taras Bulba," and its colorful cast of characters makes significant staging demands.

Musically, the opera as a whole creates a pleasing impression. The choral sections are excellent, there are many good parts for the soloists, and the orchestration is interesting and imaginative. Some of the scenes tend to be a bit lengthy, and the text is not always convincing; nonetheless, *The Cossacks* remains perhaps the most important work Elling produced.

As a composer, then, Elling combined solid skill with a conservative stance. Compared with the prevailing style of the period, his music exhibits a certain detached serenity that probably was not intended. One source of this impression is the simplicity of Elling's harmony, which always remains comfortably within well-established paths. He occasionally used rather sudden modulations to distant tonalities, but his harmonic resources never ventured beyond those of early Romanticism. His melodic lines are characterized by simple, diatonic intervals and recurring, often symmetric, patterns.

Elling composed relatively little after the turn of the century, when his work with Norwegian folk music began to dominate both his interest and his time. From 1898 to 1918 he regularly spent his summers collecting folk tunes in various parts of the country. His travels took him to Setesdal, Sunnfjord, Gudbrandsdalen, Valdres, and Telemark, where he eventually gathered some fourteen hundred melodies. He published several collections drawn from this material: religious folk tunes, *stev* tunes, and folk ballads set for voice and piano; religious folk songs set for mixed chorus; and a number of folk melodies arranged for piano solo and for violin and piano. His collections of religious folk tunes became especially popular, and several of the melodies were included in the 1926 chorale book for the Church of Norway.

Elling also wrote several scholarly works about Norwegian folk music. The most important of these were *Our Heroic Ballads* (1904), *Our Dance Tunes* (1915), *Norwegian Folk Music* (1922), and *Our Religious Folk Tunes* (1927). He approached folk music as a well-trained musician and evaluated the tunes on the basis of his artistic criteria. It seemed more important to him to render a melody in what he regarded as an artistically good form than to reproduce it precisely as he found it in the folk tradition. This was an unfortunate point of departure that had negative consequences both for his published collections and even more for his scholarly writings. Despite these defects, however, Elling's work as a folk-music researcher has been of great value, for it provides valuable information about the folk music of Norway.

Per Winge (1858–1935) was another Norwegian composer firmly anchored in the moderate wing of Romanticism. He is often regarded as heir to the Kjerulf tradition in Norway's music history. Like Kjerulf, he is important chiefly as a composer of songs; his music also exhibits something of the same clarity and elegance that are so characteristic of the works of Norway's first master of the art song.

Winge studied law for several years before he began the study of music with Neupert, Winter-Hjelm, and Svendsen. He continued his music studies in Leipzig (1883–84) and Berlin (1884–86). Upon completing his studies, he became conductor of the Bergen Harmonic Society orchestra. He held this position until 1888, when he left to become organist at the Bragernes Church in Drammen. He substituted for Iver Holter as conductor of the Music Society orchestra in Oslo in 1893–94. In 1894 he succeeded Johan Hennum as orchestral conductor at the Christiania Theater, and from 1899 to 1902 he held the same position at the Central Theater. In 1908 he became organist at the Grönland Church, remaining in that position until 1927. From 1912 to 1928 he was director of the Norwegian Students' Women's Chorus and for two years (1916–18) director of the Norwegian Students' Male Chorus. He was also a music teacher in his later years, serving on the faculty of the Oslo Conservatory from 1895 onward.

Winge's output as a composer was not great. It consists mainly of works in two quite dissimilar genres: songs and incidental music for dramatic productions. The latter includes music for a number of plays of various kinds: *1001 Nights* (Holger Drachmann), *Life Is a Game* (Vilhelm Krag), *King Aaron* (Thomas Krag), and above all the popular children's play *The King's Heart* (Barbra Ring). He also wrote an operetta entitled *333*, which was performed in 1899. His songs number about sixty. Other compositions include a *Piano Trio* in F major, four duets for two violins and piano, a "Sonatina" for violin and piano, some small piano pieces, songs for women's chorus and male chorus, and a *Constitution Day Cantata* for baritone solo, mixed chorus, and organ.

His most important instrumental compositions are the *Piano Trio* and the "Sonatina." The trio has four movements, the sonatina three. In both cases the outer movements are in sonata form in accordance with Classical principles, though Winge took a few liberties in the last movement of the sonatina. That he is a representative of late Romanticism is more evident in his themes and still more in his harmony. He often used the altered chords typical of Romanticism in quite sophisticated progressions. The dominant of the dominant with a lowered fifth appears frequently in various relationships, and he had a special affection for augmented triads—a characteristic that to some extent points forward toward Impressionism. Much of his dramatic music, including the songs, is considerably more popular in character and overall design. This is a result of the fact that the dramatic works for which the music was written were generally quite light in character, and the music reflects this lightness.

Winge's most important compositions are his songs, some of which were clearly written with painstaking care both melodically and harmonically.

The majority are either modified strophic or through-composed in form, but his *Children's Songs* are simpler in character and, accordingly, strophic. This collection includes his two best-known compositions, "Lullaby for Little Boy" and "I'm Singing for My Little Friend." In these short songs Winge united simple, singable melodies with skillful and appropriate harmony for a thoroughly charming result.

The compositions and arrangements for women's chorus also show Winge's solid talent and thorough training. They constitute a fine contribution to women's choral literature. As director of the Norwegian Students' Women's Chorus, Winge also did much to improve the national standard of performance in this area.

Johan Halvorsen (1864–1935) was prominent in Norway's music life during the first quarter of the twentieth century. Born in Drammen, he began playing the violin at the age of nine, and his musical talent quickly became apparent. Christian Jehnigen, director of the local National Guard Music Corps, noticed the budding young musician and recruited him to play the piccolo and the flute. Jehnigen also gave him violin lessons. Desiring greater musical opportunities than those available to him in Drammen, however, Halvorsen went to Oslo. In 1881 he was accepted by Paolo Sperati as a cadet in the Second Brigade Music Corps and he also obtained a position in the Möllergaten Theater orchestra. In 1883 he went to Stockholm to begin a formal course of study in music. He received a full scholarship at the music academy there, where his teachers included Johan Lindberg in violin and Conrad Nordqvist in harmony. During his years at the academy he was also concertmaster of the Royal Dramatic Theater orchestra. In 1885 he became concertmaster of the Bergen Harmonic Society orchestra. After just one year in this position, however, he went to Leipzig for further violin study with Adolph Brodsky and there became concertmaster of the conservatory orchestra.

Halvorsen left Leipzig in 1887 and began an unsettled period of fairly constant travel. He spent a year in Aberdeen, Scotland, and in 1890 went to Helsinki, Finland, where he remained for three years as a teacher at the conservatory and a frequent concert soloist. Several times during this period he visited St. Petersburg (now Leningrad), where he appeared as a soloist and studied violin with Leopold Auer. In 1893 he set out on further travels, but that autumn he went to Bergen as conductor of both the orchestra at the National Stage and the Bergen Harmonic Society orchestra. Therewith he began the array of activities that eventually took him to Oslo in 1899 and was to be his for the rest of his life: theater conductor, symphony conductor, and composer.

As conductor of the National Theater orchestra he succeeded in getting

*Johan Halvorsen. Painting by Henrik
Lund. (Universitetsbiblioteket i Oslo)*

a number of operas performed, including premieres of several works by
Norwegian composers. The theater orchestra, which consisted of about
forty-five musicians, also gave symphony concerts from time to time. In
1919, however, a financial crisis required the National Theater to greatly
reduce its orchestra. This led to the creation of the Philharmonic Society,
which acquired most of the musicians who had been dismissed from the
theater orchestra. Halvorsen served as conductor of the new orchestra for its
first season, but thereafter was only a guest conductor. Meanwhile, at the
National Theater he was left with a small orchestra of fifteen that played only
the music required for the various theater productions. In 1930 Halvorsen

resigned from the National Theater position and the orchestra was disbanded.

At the height of his career, Halvorsen was Norway's most distinguished orchestral leader since Johan Svendsen. Indeed, he was Svendsen's musical heir in a number of ways: he too was a violinist, had as a conductor acquired an intimate knowledge of orchestral resources, and as a composer had followed in the same tradition.

While still in Bergen he had demonstrated his talents as a composer with incidental music for the Indian play *Vasantasena* and the popular march "Entrance of the Boyars," which soon became an international success. After becoming conductor of the National Theater orchestra in Oslo in 1899 he continued to be a highly productive composer of stage music, writing the incidental music for a total of about thirty plays. Among the better known of these are *Gurre* (Holger Drachmann, 1900), *Tordenskjold* (Jacob Bull, 1901), *The King* (Björnstjerne Björnson, 1902), *Queen Tamara* (Knut Hamsun, 1904), *The Water Sprite* (Sigurd Eldegard, 1905), *Mascarade* (Ludvig Holberg, 1922), and *The Journey to the Christmas Star* (Sverre Brandt, 1924). Halvorsen arranged some of this music into suites for concert use; examples are the *Suite Ancienne* (from the Holberg play *The Lying-in Room*), *The Water Sprite*, *Norwegian Fairy Tale Pictures* (from *Peik and the Troll Chieftain*), *Vasantasena*, and others.

Halvorsen also wrote a number of pieces unrelated to the theater. His best-known composition is "Entrance of the Boyars," but several others have also become quite popular, such as his "Passacaglia on a Theme of Handel" for violin and viola, "Veslemöy's Song" for violin and orchestra, and *Bergensiana*—a set of variations for orchestra on the popular Bergen melody "I Took Up My Newly Tuned Zither."

His larger works involving the orchestra were written during the later years of his life. His first large instrumental composition was a violin concerto that was performed in 1909, but he was not satisfied with it and later destroyed it. His three symphonies, however, have been preserved. The first, in C minor, was premiered in 1923. The second, in D minor, followed in 1924, but it was revised and given the title "Fatum" for a performance in 1928. The *Symphony No. 3* in C major was premiered in 1929. He also composed two *Norwegian Rhapsodies* for orchestra, one in 1921, the other in 1922.

Halvorsen's symphonies follow the Classical tradition as well as the example of Johan Svendsen. Both of the first two symphonies have four movements in the standard forms and order. The second can hardly be called program music despite the subtitle "Fatum" added later, which merely indicates the composer's attitude toward his material. The only suggestions of a struggle with fate occur in the first movement and parts of the last. There certainly is nothing gloomy about this symphony. The concluding section in D major sounds triumphant, and both inner movements are bright and graceful. The third movement sounds a bit like a Norwegian *springar*. The structure follows the formal principles of Classicism throughout, but the influence of late Romanticism is evident in the breadth of the overall plan and the rather dense texture of the orchestration. The form of the second symphony is in some ways reminiscent of Tchaikovsky.

The third symphony, consisting of three movements instead of four, displays greater structural and harmonic freedom from Classical models. For example, the eight-measure melody in C major with which the first movement begins—a melody that later will become the secondary theme of the movement—is immediately transposed note for note to F-sharp major in measures 9–16. Such a deliberate juxtaposition in the first sixteen measures of the symphony of two diametrically opposed tonalities on the circle of fifths strikes one as an attempt at tonal liberation. However, Halvorsen was in no way using a dodecaphonic approach. Despite an abundance of chromatic lines and rapid shifts of tonality, the music is always clearly tonal. Analogously, the Classical patterns remain discernible in the formal structure even though Halvorsen had taken numerous liberties with them. The overall character of the third symphony is bright and graceful, so much so that even at its first performance it was characterized as a "summer symphony." Much of it had, in fact, been composed at Halvorsen's summer home in southern Norway.

Halvorsen's role as successor to Svendsen is most evident in the *Norwegian Rhapsodies*. Here he followed Svendsen's example of refined orchestration and the imaginative, masterful use of Norwegian folk tunes taken, like those of Svendsen, from Lindeman's collections. Although Halvorsen's *Norwegian Rhapsodies* sound somewhat heavier—perhaps because of the thicker orchestration and more detailed development of the motives—they are nonetheless very effective.

An important chapter in Halvorsen's work with Norwegian folk music was his notation of the Hardanger-fiddle *slaatter* of Knut Dahle. Dahle, a Hardanger-fiddle player from Telemark, had asked Grieg to write down some of the old *slaatter* that he had learned; otherwise, he said, these tunes would die with him. Grieg approached Halvorsen, who enthusiastically agreed to the task. In November, 1901, Dahle came to Oslo and played seventeen *slaatter* for Halvorsen. His transcriptions of these tunes became the basis for Grieg's *Norwegian Peasant Dances* for piano, Op. 72 (see p. 205); and at Grieg's insistence, they were included when Opus 72 was published by Peters in 1903. Halvorsen himself also began playing the Hardanger fiddle at this time. A few years later he became the first composer to specify the use of a Hardanger fiddle when he included it in the instrumentation of his incidental music for *The Water Sprite*. Other Norwegian composers have since made similar use of this instrument.

In an overview of Halvorsen's opera omnia one is struck by how often his best works were tied to specific situations or scenes. It appears that this was a characteristic of his talent that especially equipped him to be a composer of theater music. A good illustration of this is to be found in Halvorsen's own account of how he happened to write "Entrance of the Boyars":

> At Holst's hotel, where I lived when I first came to Bergen . . . , a letter came from Grünfeld with an offer of a position as a teacher at the conservatory and first violinist in a quartet in Bucharest. Salary 7,000 francs, start immediately. I was tempted, because I had not yet signed a contract. I got hold of an encyclopedia to find out where in the world Bucharest was. There I read about Queen Carmen Sylvia, patroness of the arts, and about the descendants of the rich and aristocratic Boyars who a certain number of years ago made their entry into Bucharest. This would go over in the newspapers, I thought. And that queen! She would call me and my quartet up to the palace immediately. I had to find some way to express all these images, so I wrote a march that I called "Entrance of the Boyars." That same afternoon, just as I had finished writing the march, in walked Edvard Grieg: "Well, how goes it! I see you're already in full swing"—he saw the manuscript on the piano. He read through it quite carefully and then he said, "That's darn good!"

When we hear this charming music, the picture of the colorful parade comes alive for us. This capacity to create mental images is perhaps the strongest asset of Halvorsen's music and it may explain the curious fact that while his symphonic works are rarely played, his smaller compositions— "Entrance of the Boyars," "Veslemöy's Song," and several of the suites arranged from his incidental music—continue to hold a firm position in Norway's repertoire. "Entrance of the Boyars" is also widely played in the United States in an arrangement for band.

Sigurd Lie (1871–1904) was granted a pitifully short time in which to make his mark on the music life of Norway. Despite a promising beginning, he was able to leave only a few completed and fully mature compositions.

Lie, like Halvorsen, was born in Drammen, where his father was a teacher in the local high school. The family moved to Kristiansand when Sigurd was a small boy, however, so it was there that he grew up. Both his parents were active amateur musicians, and their home was a center of music making. Thus he had the opportunity from an early age to develop his musical bent, and he was expected to participate in amateur performances as soon as he was able to do so. The cathedral organist in Kristiansand, Ferdinand August Rojahn, gave young Lie violin lessons as well as instruction in music theory. His musical gifts and perseverance quickly manifested themselves and yielded rich results. He gave several concerts in Kristiansand during the 1880s and continued his studies with Rojahn until taking his university entrance examination in 1889.

Lie had also shown outstanding talent in mathematics, and in accordance with the wish of his parents he enrolled in the scientific curriculum at the University of Oslo. Concurrently with these studies, he took violin lessons from Gudbrand Böhn and lessons in music theory and composition from Iver Holter. After one year, he dropped out of the scientific curriculum and concentrated entirely on his music studies. He also was appointed as a violinist in the Christiania Theater orchestra at this time.

The next few years were busy ones for Lie. He worked at his studies with a perseverance that often was injurious to his health. In the spring of 1891 he went to Leipzig, where his teachers included Arno Hilf and Carl Reinecke. During this time he had the first attack of the tuberculosis that was to cause his early death. It was a relatively mild attack, however, and he was able to continue his studies. He also wrote several compositions in Leipzig: *Six Songs* (texts by Vilhelm Krag), Op. 1; *Four Piano Pieces*, Op. 2; *Four Songs* (Vilhelm Krag and Theodor Caspari), Op. 3; and a piano quintet and a string quartet. The quintet was performed but remained unpublished and later was lost. The quartet is preserved in manuscript.

Lie remained at the conservatory until the autumn of 1893, when he returned to Oslo. In the spring of 1894 he received a grant that enabled him to go to Berlin, where he studied primarily composition with Heinrich Urban. His most important works from this period are a concert piece for violin and orchestra, based on the Norwegian folk tune "Elland and the Fairy Maiden," and a *Suite* in G major for string orchestra. He also wrote a number of songs.

In the autumn of 1895 Lie went to Bergen as concertmaster of the Bergen Harmonic Society orchestra under the baton of Johan Halvorsen. In 1896 he also became conductor of the Bergen Music Society orchestra, which consisted primarily of amateur musicians. While in Bergen he composed a number of works: *Erling Skjalgson* (text by Per Sivle), a large work for baritone solo, male chorus, and orchestra; a cantata for mixed chorus and orchestra for the opening of the 1898 Bergen exhibition; several songs; and some pieces for male chorus.

Lie returned to Oslo in 1898 as conductor of the orchestra at the Central Theater for the 1898–99 season. He made plans for an opera that he hoped to write, but nothing came of them. He did, however, compose some songs, including "Snow" (text by Helge Rode), his best-known composition. *Symphonic March for Full Orchestra*, a large instrumental work, also dates from this period. His *Two Norwegian Dances* for violin and piano were published at this time, though they had been composed somewhat earlier. Justly considered his best instrumental works, they enjoy a continuing popularity in the repertoire.

Lie gave a concert of his own works in Oslo in the fall of 1899. The program included *Erling Skjalgson*, the *Symphonic March for Full Orchestra*, and two movements from his *Oriental Suite* for orchestra, as well as art songs and selections for male chorus. That autumn he was also awarded a scholarship that enabled him to return to Berlin to continue his studies. He remained abroad until 1902, albeit with many interruptions. The summers of 1900 and 1901 were spent in Bergen, where in the autumn of 1901 he gave another concert of his own compositions. The program included the first three movements (the fourth was not finished) of a *Symphony* in A minor, which he had written in Berlin, and some songs: "Wartburg," a ballad for bass-baritone solo and orchestra, and a song cycle also called *Wartburg*.

Lie returned to Oslo in the summer of 1902. He was selected to succeed Olaus A. Gröndahl as director of the Businessmen's Chorus, but his health had deteriorated to such an extent that he was forced to enter a sanatorium and thus was unable to perform the duties of the position. In January, 1903, he sent the still-unfinished symphony to his former teacher, Iver Holter, with the request that he complete it because Lie did not think he could manage it himself. Holter did as he was requested and the complete symphony was performed in February, 1903. Although it was faulted for its lack of formal clarity after this performance, the two inner movements appear to have been successful.

By early 1904 Lie's health had improved sufficiently for him to assume his duties as director of the Businessmen's Chorus. Once again he threw himself into his work, and among other things took the chorus on a summer tour to northern Norway. He also did some composing, principally songs and pieces for male chorus. The improvement in his health proved to be only temporary, however. He suffered a serious relapse that autumn, and soon thereafter succumbed.

Lie's most important compositions are his songs and his works for male chorus. He wrote some eighty songs, of which about sixty have been published. Many of them are rather complicated—especially the earlier ones, in which the influence of Wagner is evident both melodically and harmonically.

As he matured, however, his songs became simpler and lighter. About half of the songs are through-composed; the rest are fairly evenly divided between pure and modified strophic. Only "Snow" is well known, but several others are among the best songs written by a Norwegian composer. "The Ocean" and "Spring," both with texts by Idar Handagard, are particularly excellent.

Lie composed about twenty works for male chorus, including several that have often been performed. His best-known compositions in this genre are settings of texts by Theodor Caspari: "Jubilate" and *Three Peer Gynt Songs.* Those written near the end of his life can be considered representative of his most mature style.

Of Lie's instrumental compositions, the *Two Norwegian Dances* for violin and piano are most frequently played. Reminiscent of Grieg, they also clearly reflect the influence of Norwegian folk music (which occasionally is discernible in other of his compositions as well). Both dances are in ABA form. The outer sections of the first are marked by a *halling*-like rhythm, while the middle section sounds somewhat like a *springar.* In the second dance the outer sections have a *springar* rhythm and the slower middle section evokes the feeling of an elegiac folk song.

Of other larger cyclic works, both the *Symphony* in A minor and the *String Quartet* in D minor follow Classical models with respect to form, but their harmony and thematic material are more late Romantic in character and occasionally display a somewhat experimental touch. Here the influence of Wagner is evident. The symphony also has a certain similarity to Sinding's D-minor symphony, especially in the first movement.

Lie also composed music for piano, including four *Pictures of the Seasons.* All of his piano compositions are character pieces, generally competent works that add nothing essentially new to the portrait of Lie as a composer.

Sketches for Lie's unrealized opera, with a text that he himself adapted from Ibsen's great epic poem, *Terje Vigen,* have been preserved. They include drafts of an overture and a few vocal numbers, suggesting that Lie had not gotten very far with the project. He also left behind sketches of incidental music for Vilhelm Krag's fairy-tale play *The Blue Mountain* and Adam Oehlenschläger's *Aladdin.*

Although but few of his compositions bear the stamp of maturity, Sigurd Lie nonetheless earned during his short life a secure place in the history of Norwegian music. His talent and great productive capacity might have enabled him to accomplish much, but his untimely death robbed him of the opportunity to realize his considerable promise.

Eyvind Alnaes (1872–1932), although active in many areas both as a composer and a performer, also made his greatest contribution as a composer of songs. Indeed, it is not an overstatement to say that he was the foremost Norwegian composer of songs in the generation that followed Edvard Grieg.

Born in Fredrikstad, he received his basic music education at the conservatory in Oslo, where he was enrolled from 1889 to 1892. Iver Holter was among his teachers. During this period he composed the songs that were later published as Opus 1. On the recommendation of Grieg he was awarded a scholarship that enabled him to go to Leipzig to continue his training. He remained there for three years, studying composition with Carl Reinecke and piano with Adolf Ruthardt. On his return to Norway he was appointed organist in the Bragernes Church in Drammen. In 1897 he received a government stipend, which he used for study in Berlin. There he completed, among other things, his first symphony.

Alnaes earned his living as an organist. He served in the Bragernes Church until 1907 and in the Uranienborg Church in Oslo from 1907 to 1913. From 1913 to 1932 he was cantor and organist in Our Savior's Church in Oslo. He was an outstanding accompanist as well, often appearing in concerts in this capacity. He was also the director of several choruses, including the Businessmen's Chorus (1905–31) and the Holter Chorus (1920–31).

Alnaes was a member of the hymnal committee from 1922 to 1926 and had primary responsibility for the harmonizations in the chorale book of 1926. He also published volumes 2–4 of *Norway's Melodies* and wrote several textbooks. In 1932 he was made a Knight of the Order of St. Olaf.

It is rather amazing that in addition to these many responsibilities Alnaes was able to compose a considerable amount of music. His opus list totals forty-five, but there were several other works without opus numbers. In addition to some eighty-five songs, he wrote more than twenty piano pieces and two volumes of compositions for male chorus. His *Christmas Motet* for mixed chorus, soprano solo, and organ continues to be performed regularly. He also made arrangements of Norwegian folk tunes—some for piano, some for male chorus. His most important works with orchestra are *Symphony No. 1* in C minor, Op. 7 (1898), *Symphony No. 2* in D major, Op. 43 (1923), *Symphonic Variations on an Original Theme*, Op. 8, and the *Piano Concerto* in D major, Op. 27 (1913). His chamber music is limited to two suites for violin and piano and one for two violins and piano. Two occasional cantatas and a collection of short chorale preludes for organ close this extensive list.

The songs were written throughout the years from the early 1890s to about 1930. No stylistic changes of any importance appear to have occurred during this entire time. All of his songs are in a decidedly late Romantic style, with rather complex but generally functional harmony. Occasionally in the later works one can discern tendencies toward an Impressionistic use of chords and a freer handling of dissonance in the interest of tonal color. At least two-thirds of the songs are through-composed, and most of the others are in modified strophic form. Aside from the songs with texts by A. O. Vinje, Alnaes's compositions show little evidence of the influence of folk music. The Vinje songs are in a class by themselves, however, and here one distinctly senses a kinship with the folk-like songs of Kjerulf and Grieg.

"A February Morning by the Gulf" (Op. 28, No. 3) is a good example of Alnaes's songs (see example 52). The text, by Nils Collett Vogt, consists of four short stanzas.

> Under the heavens, the sky-blue heavens that seem so near,
> Behold, like a miracle, almond trees clad in white appear.
>
> For ne'er before have I seen them blooming so dazzling white,
> Their fragrance wafts through the wint'ry air in the morning light.
>
> The sunlight glistens from every branch, thoughts t'ward heaven soar
> And build a temple where thankful hearts may their God adore.
>
> Where angels hover, where longings peal forth in newborn song,
> My soul, enlightened, at last can join the adoring throng.

Alnaes's setting of this poem is through-composed, though the third stanza begins much like the first. The voice part consists of a typically idiomatic, flowing melody. The harmony is generally simple, but note the sudden modulations: from A-flat augmented (the altered dominant in D-flat major) to E major (with one note in common) in measures 12–13, and similarly back to D-flat major in measures 16–17. These tonal shifts strike one as surprising, to say the least, as is the progression from the dominant ninth chord in G-flat major to the tonic chord in A major (with D-flat = C-sharp as the common bass note) in measures 29–30. The modulation back to D-flat major in measures 33–34 is by means of an altered dominant of the dominant: the dominant seventh chord in D major (here notated with F-double-sharp instead of G) is reinterpreted as an altered dominant of the dominant in D-flat major (G–B-double-flat–D-flat–F-flat). The song is held together by motivic material that for the most part is common to all four stanzas, though it is used with a fine sensitivity for the varying requirements of the text.

Alnaes's compositions for male chorus have been sung quite frequently, but his instrumental works are rarely heard. "Hymn to the Fatherland" (Op. 4, No. 1), for piano, is played occasionally. Of his works with orchestra,

Example 52. Eyvind Alnaes, "A February Morning by the Gulf," Op. 28, No. 3.

only two have been published: the *Piano Concerto* in D major (in an arrangement for two pianos) and the *Symphonic Variations*. Despite the positive reception accorded his first symphony at its premiere in 1898, his larger symphonic works have not won a place in the repertoire. They are more conservative in character than the songs and were criticized even during the composer's lifetime for being excessively dependent on older models without containing anything essentially new. The criticism was largely justified.

The *Piano Concerto* is cast in the standard three movements. The first movement is in sonata form, though Alnaes took a few liberties with it. The last movement is a kind of stylized waltz in rondo form. The *Symphonic Variations* consist to a large extent of clever character pieces in a variation format, with a simpler harmonic structure than that of his best songs. The weakness of this work is primarily the theme itself: it is rather static and thus incapable of awakening sufficient interest. Apparently his melodic gift was not sufficient to enable him to create themes capable of symphonic development.

This is quite surprising, for in Alnaes's songs it is precisely his melodic gift that surfaces as their greatest strength. Some of his less successful songs have been criticized for a certain saccharine quality in their melodics, but he fortunately was able to avoid this in his best songs. Many of these are still often sung. They include "February Morning at the Gulf"; "Rocking Song," Op. 1, No. 4 (Vilhelm Krag); "Longings for Spring," Op. 17, No. 3 (Nils Collett Vogt); "Happiness Between Two People" and "The Ice Is Crackling in All the Crevasses," Op. 26, Nos. 1 and 2 (Viggo Stuckenberg); and "The Hundred Violins," Op. 42, No. 2 (Arnulf Överland). His best-known composition is the balladic "Last Journey" (text by Henrik Wergeland). This sailor's song, an exquisite setting of a lofty text, has done more than any other composition to make Alnaes known and appreciated as a composer both in Norway and abroad.

As stated earlier, Gerhard Schjelderup and Hjalmar Borgström were the principal representatives in Norway of the more radical wing of German Romanticism. They should not, however, be regarded as radical in the broader context of contemporary European music. It was not until after 1920 that the truly radical innovations in European music (Expressionism, Barbarism) first made some inroads in Norway, and even then only to a limited extent. If contemporary developments in continental music had any influence at all on these composers, it can at most be seen in certain Neoclassical features that appear in their later compositions. Moreover, each represented Romantic radicalism in his own way. As a composer of opera, Schjelderup was influenced primarily by Wagner. Borgström, on the other hand, was particularly involved in program music; his immediate precursors were Norway's Johan Selmer and, on the continent, Berlioz, Liszt, and early Richard Strauss.

Gerhard Schjelderup (1859–1933) was born in Kristiansand and grew up in Bergen. His family was one in which music was especially cultivated: two of his siblings also became professional musicians. As a youth he played the cello, an activity he continued to pursue after going to Oslo in 1876 to study philology. Music gradually became his main interest, and in 1878 he left for Paris, where he studied cello under Auguste Franchomme and composition with Augustin Savard and Jules Massenet. In 1882 he returned to

Norway, performing over the next few years as a cellist. He went to Paris again in 1885, remaining there until 1888. During both sojourns in Paris he composed a number of works, including his *Symphony* in C minor; *Life in the High Mountains*, a setting for chorus and orchestra of a text by Henrik Ibsen; *Prometheus*, a large work for vocal soloists, chorus, and orchestra; and a number of songs.

Schjelderup spent the winter of 1888–89 in Bergen and then departed for Germany. He remained there for many years, making short visits to Norway from time to time. In 1916 and for some years following he again made his home in Norway, serving as the first chairman of the Society of Norwegian Composers from 1917 to 1921.

The decisive turning point in Schjelderup's artistic development was his encounter with Wagner's music dramas. In 1887 he attended the premiere of the entire *Ring* cycle in Karlsruhe, and at the Bayreuth festival a year later he heard *Parsifal* and several other Wagnerian operas. These works made a tremendous impression on the sensitive young composer; thereafter he regarded the creation of music dramas, more or less in the spirit of Wagner, as his artistic mission.

His first opera was *East of the Sun and West of the Moon*, with a libretto by Kristofer Janson. While working on it he received encouragement and advice from the Wagnerian conductor Felix Mottl, and in 1890 the first act was produced at the Royal Theater in Munich. Although the opera was finished at this time, it was never performed in its entirety. Schjelderup's next work was a one-act opera, *Sunday Morning*, for which he wrote his own libretto. Premiered in Munich in 1893, it marked his public debut as a composer of operatic works.

Schjelderup composed nearly a dozen operas in all, most of which were performed in Germany. *A Norwegian Wedding* (also called *The Abduction of the Bride*) was premiered in Prague in 1900. Then followed two one-act operas, *A Hallowed Evening* and *Spring Night*, both of which were premiered at the National Theater in Oslo in 1915. *Spring Night* was later made into a full-length opera and produced under the title *Starry Nights*. He also wrote *The Storm Bird* (Schwerin, 1926), *A People in Need, Sampo and Lappelil, The Scarlet-red Flower*, *Opal* (Dresden, 1915), and *Stormy Night and Rosy Dawn*.

He wrote incidental music for several plays: Karl Gjellerup's *The Sacrificial Fire*, Otto Borngräber's *King Friedwahn*, and the second act of Henrik Ibsen's *Brand*. Ibsen's play interested him so much that he also composed a symphonic poem with the same title. Other large compositions include a symphony entitled *To Norway*, the fairy-tale ballet *The Magic Horn*, and a single-movement orchestral work, "Summer Night on the Fjord." He also wrote two string quartets, about forty songs, a few pieces for male chorus, and some smaller pieces for violin and piano and for cello and piano.

Schjelderup's outlook on music and music drama was profoundly idealistic. His debt to Wagner is obvious, but he himself thought that he differed from the German master in some ways. He once wrote in a letter as follows:

> I am continually searching for something that lies closer to us, something more intimate than Wagner's gods and heroes. I believe that only with the help of music can this intimate drama become a reality. I will try to present not just the outer surface of reality and of life, as one encounters it all over the world; I will try . . . to open people's innermost selves and reveal the rich treasure that often is hidden behind the simplest exterior, the most modest nature. My work shall be dedicated to the hidden poetry of life as it really is, to life's innumerable, unheralded heroes, to the rich and infinitely complex life of the soul. It is toward this bold ideal that my efforts are aimed, and it is as if I saw a whole new world before my eyes.

This is an ambitious program, and one cannot help but ask whether Schjelderup managed to carry it out. From the above statement we may assume that he was less interested in the dramatic action than in mood painting and portrayals of individual characters. It is characteristic of him that his leitmotifs are primarily identified with individuals, not with certain actions, objects, or ideas. His greatest talent as a composer appears to have been his ability to create expressive imagery through orchestral means, while the ability to assess dramatic potential evidently was less well developed.

Schjelderup's complex harmony in some ways reflects the Wagnerian influence. Unlike Wagner, however, he did not use chromaticism primarily to create great harmonic tensions, but his sudden modulations and unexpected harmonic twists rather were intended to create colorful effects. On the whole, Schjelderup's interest seems to have been directed more toward details than toward the larger whole. The thematic material often is clearly depictive; it does not always flow gracefully, however, and exhaustive motivic development sometimes results in works that are excessively drawn out. The orchestration is fine in many ways, but it has a tendency to a certain thickness that results in an unfortunate lack of clarity.

Few of Schjelderup's compositions are played any more. That his operas have rarely been performed in Norway is owing in part to the weak opera tradition there; in Germany, several of them were quite successful. Some of his shorter orchestral works have been played frequently in Norway—for example, "A Sunrise in the Himalayas" (from *The Sacrificial Fire*), "Summer

Night on the Fjord," and the prelude to *A Norwegian Wedding*. His symphonic poem *Brand* was exceptionally well received at its premiere in 1914 but has seldom been played since. This large work, the programmatic text of which is based on Ibsen's play, makes great demands on performers and listeners alike. Its lengthy depictions of selected scenes in the play occasionally border on monotony, but one cannot deny it a place as an important example of Norwegian program music.

Schjelderup also did significant work as a music historian, writing biographies of both Grieg and Wagner. His principal contribution in this area, however, was his work as coauthor (with O. M. Sandvik) of the two-volume *Norway's Music History*, published in 1921.

Hjalmar Borgström (1864–1925) was born in Oslo, where his father, Carl Christian Jensen, was a civil servant. Both parents encouraged music making in their home. Hjalmar received his first instruction in music from an older sister when he was very young, but he became a serious student at the age of fourteen when he learned to play the piano and violin and began composing small pieces. In accordance with the wish of his parents he also began the study of commerce, but he had no special liking for it. In 1879 he heard Johan Selmer in a concert of his own works, and this became an inspiration for him to assert his desire to become a musician. "Even then I understood that my own artistic future had to go in that direction," he wrote later.

His parents now consented to his wish to study music, and in 1880 he became a pupil of Johan Svendsen. In 1883, when Svendsen went to Copenhagen, Hjalmar continued his studies with L. M. Lindeman and Ole Olsen. During this time his "Polka-Caprice" for piano, Op. 1, and some other piano pieces and songs were published under the name of Hjalmar Jensen, but to avoid confusion with another composer by the same name he obtained permission in 1887 to use his mother's family name, Borgström. His first large composition, the choral work *Who Art Thou with the Thousand Names?* (text by B. Björnson), reflects the influence of Lindeman's polyphonic style. It was premiered in Oslo in 1889 and aroused considerable interest.

After Lindeman's death in 1887, Borgström went to Leipzig to continue his music studies. According to his own account he learned little new during this time. He heard a great deal of music, however, including many of Wagner's works, and he composed a *String Quartet* in C minor and a *Symphony* in G major. He himself was on the podium at the premiere of the latter in Oslo in 1890. At this time he was awarded a scholarship that enabled him to go to Berlin. For the next several years he lived mostly in Germany, sometimes in Berlin and sometimes in Leipzig. While in Germany he composed a number of works, including two operas. In 1903 he moved to Oslo, where he worked as a composer, writer, and music critic.

At the center of Borgström's compositions are his five symphonic poems, four of which were written in rapid succession shortly after his return to Norway in 1903. The first, "Hamlet," Op. 13, for piano and orchestra, was performed in November, 1903. "Jesus in Gethsemane," Op. 14, followed in 1904. "Johan Gabriel Borkman," a symphonic prelude to Ibsen's play by the same name, appeared in 1905 as did also "The Night of Death," which was scored for string orchestra, piano, trumpet, and percussion. The fifth of the symphonic poems—and his most important composition—was *The Thought*, Op. 26, for large orchestra, which was premiered in Oslo in 1917.

Borgström also composed a number of works without programmatic content. Larger works of this type include a *Sonata* in G major for violin and piano (Op. 19), a *Piano Concerto* in C Major (Op. 22), a *Symphony* in D minor (Op. 24), a *Violin Concerto* in G major (Op. 25), and a *Piano Quintet* in F major (Op. 31). He also wrote a large cantata for the Reformation festival of 1917 (text by Theodor Caspari), a "Romance" for violin and orchestra (Op. 12), some small piano pieces, and about thirty songs. His total production thus consists of a rich and diversified series of works.

Borgström's firm anchoring in the late Romantic style is evident from his earliest compositions. Even in the piano pieces preceding his first stay abroad one finds examples of slightly irregular rhythms, sudden modulations, and willing experimentation with dissonances, all features common to most of his works.

Borgström wrote the librettos for both of his operas. *Thora from Rimol* is set in the time of the sagas, *The Fisherman* in modern times. The latter shows the influence of Wagner in its use of the leitmotif technique and powerful exploitation of the orchestra. Neither opera has been performed, however.

Borgström's first mature works were the symphonic poems, written after his return to Norway in 1903. Here his musical vocabulary became fully developed. The harmony is late Romantic, with abrupt modulations that sometimes seem almost brutal. One can also detect some Impressionistic features. Occasionally the abundance of chromaticism, as in *The Thought*, foreshadows a breaking down of tonality, but Borgström did not pursue this path. On the contrary, the harmony in his later works seems more moderate. The form of each of the symphonic poems is determined by its programmatic content. The first four are single-movement works, whereas *The Thought* is divided into five movements with individual headings. The program of *The Thought* is highly abstract: pure thought is born in outer space, then enters earthly and materialistic bonds, and finally frees itself from these bonds and returns to the space whence it came.

As one would expect, the non-programmatic works are more reflective of the Classical tradition. The piano concerto, the violin concerto, and the piano quintet all have three movements in the standard order. The symphony has four movements, with a scherzo as the second movement and a slow third movement. The most experimental feature with respect to form is the fantasia-like first movement of the violin concerto.

The piano quintet, completed in 1919, is considered by many to be Borgström's best work. It is simpler in both form and content than his earlier compositions. The only departure from the Classical tradition is that both the principal and secondary themes from the first movement appear again in the last movement, thus emphasizing cyclic interdependence by distinctly Romantic means. The harmony is clearly functional, though there is scattered evidence throughout that the composer was rooted in late Romanticism. The instrumental scoring is skillful and the thematic material is quite strong. Against the background of Borgström's earlier production it is tempting to regard this work as an expression of Neoclassical tendencies.

Borgström's songs, often sung in the past, are rarely heard today. One reason for this is that they make great demands on both the soloist and the accompanist. Among his most important works in this genre are the five songs of Opus 21 (texts by Nils Collett Vogt). Here the accompaniment is carefully worked out in a manner that approaches Impressionistic tone painting, and the melody in some cases is boldly chromatic. The later songs, such as the *Nine Poems of Cally Monrad*, Op. 30, are much simpler.

Borgström's greatest impact upon the history of Norwegian music came from the fact that in the period immediately following the turn of the century he was, both as a composer and as a music critic, Norway's most important advocate of program music. He was highly respected as a critic, even by those who did not share his views. That his music is played so little today is owing to two things. First, like Johan Selmer he became a victim of changing tastes. Second, several of his works are marred by a certain unevenness: passages of admirable distinction are succeeded by passages that sound banal to modern ears. His best works, however, are sustained by a genuine and convincing musicality that transcends stylistic limitations.

TOWARD A NEW AGE

Two important composers, Halfdan Cleve and Arne Eggen, mark the transition from late Romanticism to the early modern period in Norwegian music. Both were active far into the twentieth century, but they were so thoroughly rooted in the music of late Romanticism that they never advanced to a new style.

Halfdan Cleve (1879–1951), who was born in Kongsberg, displayed exceptional musical gifts as a child. He received a sound introduction to music at an early age from his father, Andreas Cleve, who was an organist. His later teachers included Otto Winter-Hjelm in Oslo and the Scharwenka brothers in Berlin. In 1902 he attracted considerable attention both as a pianist and as a composer when he made his debut in Berlin, playing his first piano concerto and other compositions. He lived mostly in Germany until 1914 and then settled in Oslo, where he was a teacher at the music conservatory for many years.

Most of Cleve's compositions involve the piano. Most significant of these are his five piano concertos, the first four of which were composed while he lived in Germany. The first, in A major (Op. 3), was written in 1902; the second, in B-flat minor (Op. 6), in 1904; the third, in E-flat major (Op. 9), in 1906; and the fourth, in A minor (Op. 12), in 1910. The fifth concerto, in C-sharp minor (Op. 20), was composed after his return to Norway and was first performed in 1916. Other important works include a *Piano Sonata* (Op. 19) and a *Violin Sonata* (Op. 21). He also composed a number of shorter, often technically demanding piano pieces, as well as some orchestral pieces and songs. Among the latter are his *Flower Songs* (texts by Olaf Schou) for voice and orchestra.

Cleve's dependence on the late Romantic tradition is clearly evident in his first piano concerto. A virtuosic piano style is combined with a brilliant orchestration similar to that of Tchaikovsky and Rachmaninoff. The work is both charming and impressive in its technical mastery of a sophisticated style, but it does not sound particularly original. The third concerto, for piano and string orchestra, exhibits a more personal style. A buoyant, sometimes almost mechanical rhythm combined with a somewhat restrained use of sound give this work a more contemporary flavor. The fourth concerto is once again in a somewhat more Romantic vein.

His later cyclic works—the piano and violin sonatas—are also in the mainstream of moderate Romanticism with respect to form. Both consist of three movements. In the piano sonata he employed a technique often used by Romantic composers to create cyclic coherence: material from the first movement (the principal theme in this case) reappears in the last movement. His harmony, especially in the later works, is highly chromatic—similar to that of Max Reger. Yet despite sudden harmonic shifts to distant keys, his music is firmly anchored in functional harmony.

Cleve continued writing music until his last years, but only a few of his compositions were ever published. Norwegian national Romanticism had relatively little influence on him. Though one finds hints of folk music here and there in his works, it was not an important feature of his compositional style. He assimilated the continental Romantic style that prevailed at the turn of the century, and in all essential respects this remained his foundation for the rest of his life.

In contrast to Cleve, Arne Eggen (1881–1955) was strongly influenced by Norwegian national Romanticism and the Grieg tradition; indeed, this was probably the most important factor in the evolution of his style. Elements of national Romanticism can be found in most of his works, whereas the only evidence of the influence of contemporary continental music is a few traces of Neoclassicism. In Eggen's case, however, these two influences did not come into conflict with one another.

Eggen was born in Trondheim and first studied to become a school teacher, graduating from teacher's college in 1902. He later enrolled at the Oslo Music Conservatory, where he specialized in organ, graduating in 1905. Among his teachers there were Catharinus Elling and Peter Lindeman. In 1906–07 he studied in Leipzig, where his teachers included Stephan Krehl (composition) and Karl Straube (organ).

He became organist at the Bragernes Church in Drammen in 1908 and served there for the next sixteen years except for study tours in 1909–10 funded by a government travel grant. He moved to the Bryn and Tanum churches near Oslo in 1924 and remained there for the rest of his life. He was awarded a government stipend in 1934.

Eggen's oeuvre contains two operas: *Olaf Liljekrans* (libretto adapted from Ibsen's play of the same name) and *Cymbeline* (libretto adapted from Shakespeare's play). Both were performed in Oslo, the former in 1940 and the latter in 1948. Other vocal works include a melodrama, *Little Kersti* (text by Hulda Garborg); an oratorio, *King Olaf* (text by Olav Gullvaag); and *Mjösen*, a composition for mixed chorus and orchestra. Instrumental compositions include a symphony, "Ciaconna" for organ (also arranged for orchestra), two violin sonatas, a cello sonata, and a suite for violin and piano. He wrote a number of songs— some with piano accompaniment, some with orchestra—and several small piano pieces. He also published some arrangements of folk tunes. This impressive list of compositions accounts for his prominent position in the music life of Norway in the 1930s. The high regard in which he was held by his colleagues is evident in his election as chairman of the Society of Norwegian Composers for a number of years.

The national Romantic heritage is a strong presence in the opera *Olaf Liljekrans*, as might be expected in a work dealing with this subject. In the dance scene and several other numbers from this opera ("Björgulf the Fid-

Scene from a 1940 production of Arne Eggen's opera Olav Liljekrans. *(Nationaltheatret, Oslo)*

dler," for example), the connection with Norwegian folk music is also clear. The Grieg tradition can be observed as well in his *Violin Sonata* in A minor, which is similar in many ways to Grieg's violin sonatas. One also encounters in this sonata a characteristic feature of Eggen's larger works: the second movement is labeled "Chaconne" and is constructed over a three-measure bass ostinato. The form of the movement is ABA + Coda.

Eggen's preference for Baroque forms, especially that involving the bass ostinato technique, also manifested itself in his "Ciaconna" for organ. Perhaps his finest instrumental work, it was first performed in 1917. Many years later it was arranged for orchestra, and it was premiered in this version in 1945.

The final section of the "Ciaconna" (for organ) is reproduced in example 53. The ostinato bass melody is stated four times. The first and fourth statements are slightly embellished, and in the latter the last measure is repeated before the concluding chord. This final chord is extended over four measures, of which the first two contain an elaborate chain of suspensions and passing notes in the inner voices.

Example 53. Arne Eggen, "Ciaconna" for organ.

This example shows how Eggen sometimes achieved strongly dissonant sounds through the copious use of notes foreign to the prevailing harmony. The density of the dissonances is such that the piece might well be compared with a Neoclassical composition, but the tonal harmonic basis is indisputable.

Eggen is best known as a composer of songs, most of which adhere to a relatively simple late Romantic style. The harmonic foundation is nearly always tonal, though this is occasionally obscured by dissonant voice leading and rapid modulatory passages. His skill as a melodist shows to good advantage in the songs, several of which have become very popular. Among the best known works are "The Sparrow" (Arne Garborg), "Thus the Girl Shall Have Her Way" (A. O. Vinje), and "Solfager" (B. Risberg). Also important is his ceremonious setting of "Sing Praise to Life's Eternal Spring" (text by Björnstjerne Björnson).

Cymbeline was one of Eggen's last works, and stylistically it stands somewhat apart from most of his other efforts in its freer handling of tonality and greater use of dissonant voice leading. The tonal harmonic basis is weakened to some extent in a manner that points toward Neoclassicism, though it would be incorrect to say that it represents a completely new style for Eggen.

Cleve and Eggen represent a time of transition to a new period in the music of Norway. During the years immediately following World War I the musical trends of the twentieth century finally began to take root in Norway, notwithstanding the continued influence of strong national Romantic currents as late as the 1930s. The background of the national Romanticism of the 1930s was no longer late Romanticism, although the national Romantic music dating from this period has many points of similarity with that of the Grieg tradition. It rests on a different foundation, however, for the composers who now reached maturity were obliged to take a position regarding the radical tendencies in the music of the time.

11

Trends in the Twentieth Century
(ca. 1920–ca. 1950)

The decisive historical event during this period—for Norway as for so many other countries all over the world—was World War II and all that it involved. Norway was occupied by the Germans in April, 1940, and most of the country remained occupied until the liberation in 1945. King Haakon and the government managed to escape to England, however, where they continued the fight with the support of virtually the entire Norwegian merchant marine.

Norwegian cultural life very nearly came to a standstill during the war, partly because of the country's isolation, partly in support of the resistance movement against the German occupation and the Norwegian puppet regime of Vidkun Quisling. The only music activity of any consequence was in the form of private house concerts.

With respect to musical progress, the entire period from 1920 to 1950 was rather weak. From 1920 until the mid-1930s the economic crisis tended to restrict cultural development, and thereafter the gathering storm that led eventually to World War II cast dark shadows over all forms of cultural expression. Not until 1950 did it become possible for a new period of growth to get under way once again.

The war and the German occupation greatly strengthened the national solidarity and sentiment of the Norwegian people, as is evident not least of all in the works of art produced at this time. Actually, however, Norwegian music had displayed a fairly strong national and conservative character throughout the first half of the twentieth century, at least in comparison with continental European music. This does not mean that Norway's composers were unaware of what was happening on the continent, but many were not in sympathy with the radical tendencies of the new music and most quite consciously tried to develop a national style. Thus they could only adopt those stylistic traits considered compatible with a distinctively Norwegian idiom.

In continental music, Impressionism had by 1920 largely run its course. Subsequent development took two differing paths that first remained quite separate from one another. One was Expressionism, which by then was evolving into twelve-tone music. The leading composer in this movement was Arnold Schoenberg, and his immediate successors and protégés were Alban Berg and Anton von Webern. These three composers, who are often referred to as the Second Viennese School, for a long time stood apart from the rest of continental music.

Nearly all the other important composers until the time of World War II went another way. While Schoenberg's point of departure was primarily the late Romantic chromatic style represented by, for example, Gustav Mahler, the musical language of the other composers was more indebted to that of Impressionism. In the years around 1910 there emerged a strongly dissonant and percussive rhythmic style that is sometimes called Barbarism (from Bartók's 1911 piano piece entitled "Allegro barbaro") or Primitivism. The leading representatives of the movement, Stravinsky and Bartók, emphasized nationalistic elements in their music from this period.

Further development occurred rapidly, however, and before 1920 there was a change toward a far more settled style that was strongly rooted, not least with respect to form, in Baroque and Classical music. This style, usually called Neoclassicism, gradually influenced most of the continental composers. Not until the 1940s did twelve-tone music become more widely disseminated. It then became known especially in the form given to it by Webern, the so-called serial music, in which other musical parameters beyond pitch, such as dynamics, tonal color, and rhythm, are also arranged in series.

Around 1950 sound created by electronic means began to enter the picture. This, in conjunction with *musique concrète* and experimental attempts to extract new sounds from traditional instruments, is usually called Neoexpressionism; it constituted the radical wing in continental music through the 1960s. Aleatory music, which may include possibilities for the performers to improvise within certain prescribed limits, also emerged in Europe at this time.

In Norway the influence of Impressionism was delayed until about 1920, when it began to have quite a strong impact. In the years that followed one can also discern influences from Expressionism, especially in the compositions of Fartein Valen and Arvid Kleven. There was on the whole a greater receptivity to continental currents in the first part of the 1920s than was the case in the years preceding or following that time. Around 1925 a powerful nationalistic trend marked by a distinct preference for Nordic literature and

Norwegian folk art came to the fore, sweeping aside most of the continental influence. This remarkable movement reached its climax in the St. Olaf jubilee of 1930, observing the 900th anniversary of the death of King Olaf Haraldssön—an event that understandably called for a nationalistic mode of expression.

That such an extreme form of nationalism prevailed was evidently owing to the chance convergence of several factors. The leading Norwegian Impressionist, Alf Hurum, left the country in 1924 and thus had no significant influence on the subsequent development of Norwegian music. Arvid Kleven, the other leading representative of continental modernism in Norwegian music, died in 1929. Interest in the St. Olaf jubilee was in itself a strong nationalistic incentive. And finally, of course, Norwegian composers could justify their own nationalistic stance by pointing to the folk-music elements in the works of other contemporary European composers, such as Bartók and Stravinsky. Only two Norwegian composers remained completely unaffected by the nationalist movement: Fartein Valen, who defies classification, and Pauline Hall, who was first identified with Impressionism and later with Neoclassicism. Neither managed to make much of an impact on Norwegian music during the 1920s and 1930s.

Music was not the only Norwegian art form dominated by nationalism at this time: similar movements occurred in painting and literature. The leaders of the literary movement were such *nynorsk* poets as Olav Aukrust, Ivar Mortensson Egnund, and Hans Henrik Holm. Among painters we find parallels in the works of the so-called "Telemark Romanticists" led by Henrik Sörensen, and perhaps even more clearly in the monumental frescoes painted during the 1920s, many with themes derived from the old Nordic literature. Nationalism in these fields never became as pronounced as it did in Norwegian music, however.

Although this movement was akin in many ways to the Grieg tradition, it was not exclusively rooted in Grieg's national Romantic music. A strong interest in Norwegian folk music emerged at this time, and composers were not content to deal with this aspect of their culture exclusively through mediation by the national Romantic composers. They attempted to get as close as possible to the original sources, partly by immersing themselves in the old collections of Lindeman and Landstad, partly by studying the results of later attempts to gather folk music (for example, those of O. M. Sandvik), and partly by establishing personal contact with the living tradition.

Obviously, in the long run these composers were not totally impervious to continental developments either. Neoclassicism, in particular, had a fairly strong influence in Norway. Two great Scandinavian composers, Jean Sibelius of Finland and Carl Nielsen of Denmark, also made their mark on Norwegian composers during the first three decades of the twentieth century. Sibelius tended to strengthen the nationalistic tendency, Nielsen the Neoclassical.

This nationalistic trend, intermingled with several elements of Neoclassicism, continued to dominate Norwegian music into the 1950s. It was not until about 1960 that twelve-tone music began to have a broader influence, and soon thereafter influences began to be felt from such newer continental trends as electronic music, *musique concrète*, and aleatory music.

IMPRESSIONISM AND THE ST. OLAF JUBILEE

The earliest serious representative of Impressionism in Norway was Alf Hurum (1882–1972). By 1916, when he gave the first concert of his own works, he had studied in Berlin, Paris, and St. Petersburg (now Leningrad). His compositions from this period already display some features of Impressionism, and in his *Exotic Suite* of 1918 the Impressionist influence is conspicuous. Other works worthy of mention include the orchestral suite *Fairy Tale Land* (1920), a symphonic poem *Benedict and Aarolilja* (1923), *Nordic Suite*, two sonatas for violin and piano, and a string quartet. He left Norway in 1924 and spent most of the rest of his life in Hawaii, where he founded the Honolulu Symphony Orchestra and served as its conductor from 1924 to 1926. Thus his influence on Norwegian music was smaller than it otherwise might have been. In 1927 he completed a symphony that was performed in both Bergen and Oslo the following year. This versatile and gifted artist later worked chiefly as a painter.

The Norwegian composer who drew the most attention during the 1920s was undoubtedly Arvid Kleven (1899–1929). He studied first in Norway with Gustav Fredrik Lange and then in Paris. His debut came about in 1922 with the symphonic poem *Lotusland*, Op. 5, and he was immediately hailed as a new and promising presence in Norwegian music. He followed this with another successful symphonic poem entitled *The Forest's Sleep*, Op. 9. As he continued to develop, however, he began moving in other directions that were less well received by his contemporaries. When his *Sinfonia libera in due parti* was performed in 1927 it encountered an extremely unfriendly reception. The critics wrote of "a monstrous delirium of sounds" and "an aimless heap of fantastically ugly disharmonies." This reaction undoubtedly was owing in part to the fact that Kleven's development had taken him closer to Expressionism, but it must be remembered that the prevailing trend in Norway had already rejected continental Modernism and was moving in a more conservative and nationalistic direction. Kleven set about revising the work but did not live to complete it.

Nonetheless, he managed to compose a good deal of music during his short life. In addition to the works already mentioned he wrote *Symphonic Fantasia* for orchestra (Op. 15), a *Violin Sonata* (Op. 10), "Poema" and

"Canzonetta" for violin and piano, a cello sonata, songs with orchestral or piano accompaniment, and several piano pieces.

Kleven is usually classified as an Impressionist, and at least in his earlier works it is evident that he had learned a good deal from French Impressionism. In *Lotusland*, for example, the arabesque-like motives that frequently appear in the woodwinds, the somewhat episodic structure of the piece, the orchestration, and the harmony all have features that are reminiscent of Debussy. However, his earlier style seems more fundamentally akin to late Romanticism as represented by Sergei Rachmaninov. The luxuriant melodic cantilenas, opulent chords, and above all the tonal harmonic foundation all point in that direction. Even in as early a composition as *Lotusland* Kleven proved himself a competent orchestrator. His orchestral works sparkle with a brilliance that is rare in Norwegian music. Already from this work it is clear that his primary interest was the overall sound, and this becomes progressively more evident through his development. As a melodist, however, Kleven was inconsistent. Distinctive melodic passages alternate with others that are rather trite. As a whole, *Lotusland* must thus be regarded as a promising but uneven youthful work.

Kleven's later development as represented by the *Sinfonia libera* cannot be fully traced because much of this composition has been lost. Of the original work, only the instrumental parts for the first movement have been preserved. There is also an extant revised score (presumably from the last year of the composer's life), but it includes only the beginning of the first movement.

We can, however, follow his development through the *Violin Sonata* and *Symphonic Fantasia*. In the former he made some use of the Classical sonata form, but he took many liberties with it. Each of the four movements consists of sections of constantly changing tempos and varying character. The result is a piece that sounds somewhat episodic.

The first movement is constructed in a large ternary form, although it also borrows many features from sonata form. The second movement starts out "Largamente" but the bulk of the movement consists of a rondo marked "Allegretto grazioso." The third movement is in ABA' form, with B consisting for the most part of a repetition of the "Largamente" passage with which the second movement began. It leads without a break into the fourth movement, marked "Quasi una fantasia." This last movement is quite short and seems to summarize the entire sonata through its motivic relationship with the first three movements.

Harmonically the sonata represents what might be called "extended tonality": functional harmony is virtually abandoned, yet the music retains a feeling of diffuse tonality. The chords are essentially triadic, but Kleven's proclivity for tight, veiled sounds sometimes can be interpreted as complex chords that include notes at various compound intervals (e.g., 11ths, 13ths). Although vaguely tonal, the sonata has no single tonal center; it begins in D major and ends in C minor.

Both the *Symphonic Fantasia* and the extant portions of *Sinfonia libera* show that Kleven's later development was toward Expressionism. His themes are often chromatic, with the melodic lines moving for the most part in minor seconds. Chords based on intervals of a second begin to appear alongside the more traditional triadic chords. These, obviously, were the new sounds that so displeased the critics. Melodically, both compositions are highly intense; in form, they—like Kleven's earlier compositions—are loosely episodic. Despite the uncertain tonal base, there is no hint of Schoenberg's twelve-tone technique.

Several other Norwegian composers also showed an interest in Impressionism during the early 1920s. Bjarne Brustad (see pp. 318–20), for example, wrote an *Oriental Suite* for orchestra that was performed in 1921. It is a four-movement work in which a distinctively Impressionistic handling of sound is evident throughout; in the last movement a male chorus sings various vowel sounds (there is no text) to enhance the sonic resources of the orchestra. David Monrad Johansen (see pp. 305–11) was also influenced by Impressionism around this time, in such compositions as the *Piano Suite No. 1*, *Pictures from Nordland*, Op. 5 (1919), *Seven Songs with Texts from Old Norse Folk Poetry*, Op. 6 (1921), and *Two Portraits from the Middle Ages* for piano, Op. 8 (1923). Traces of Impressionism are also evident in the later compositions of Brustad and Monrad Johansen, though both were caught up in the aforementioned nationalist movement—indeed, Monrad Johansen became its leading figure.

Pauline Hall was perhaps the most "genuine" Impressionist among Norwegian composers. Her formative studies took place in Paris, and she was very sympathetic to French cultural life in general. This French orientation may explain why she was relatively unmoved by the nationalist movement, which had more in common with certain elements of the German music tradition. She later came under the influence of Neoclassicism, but it was her attachment to French music that made her unique among Norwegian composers of her generation.

David Monrad Johansen was the leading figure in the nationalist music movement in the middle 1920s. In 1924 he gave a lecture to the Oslo Music Teachers' Association in which he sounded the call for an explicit nationalism in music:

According to a slogan repeated to the point of monotony, art is international. Well, obviously it is international in the sense that good art can be appreciated and understood wherever there is culture. But to deny, on that basis, that art is indigenous, and that in large measure it assumes the form, color, and character of the setting in which it is created, is a big leap. Precisely because it is the most intimate expression of a people's temperament it is to a very high degree conditioned by its place of origin.

Monrad Johansen had by this time aroused considerable attention with such works as the *Seven Songs* of Opus 6 and his setting for male chorus of the "Dream Ballad," Op. 7. His leading position in the nationalist movement was further enhanced in 1925 when he was given a government stipend as a composer. The petition submitted in his behalf by Borgström, Sinding, Halvorsen, and others stated: "More than any other young Norwegian composer, David Monrad Johansen stands on our own soil in artistic temperament and musical sensitivity. At the same time, his thorough studies have made him intimately acquainted with modern [musical] techniques. With this background he has attained something new and promising, something of great value for our national music." Whether the style Monrad Johansen had developed at this point was "promising" remains somewhat doubtful; his later development, in any case, took other directions. Even if musical nationalism proved in the end to be a blind alley, however, it must be acknowledged that within its own limits it stimulated the creation of some works of considerable merit.

The St. Olaf jubilee became a kind of climax for the entire movement. A competition for the creation of a large choral work for the jubilee was announced, and several monumental compositions were entered, such as Arne Eggen's oratorio *King Olaf*. Ludvig Irgens Jensen won first prize with *The Homeward Journey*. A number of other large choral works, in addition to those written for the competition, were composed around this time. Among the most important of these were Monrad Johansen's *Voluspaa* (1926) and his cantata *Ignis ardens* (1930), Sparre Olsen's setting of the "Dream Ballad" (1937), and Klaus Egge's *Sveinung Vreim* (1938). It seems clear that the monumental style evident in these choral works has a parallel in a number of Norwegian paintings dating from the same period, such as the giant frescoes of Axel Revold, Per Krogh, and Alf Rolfsen.

During the 1930s the implicit tension within Norway's music life increased. The nationalist movement continued to flourish, sometimes expressing itself in rather bizarre ways—as, for example, Geirr Tveitt's attempt (in a treatise written in Germany) to create a special Norwegian music theory, giving names in old Norse to the modal scales. Meanwhile, influences from continental music were slowly gaining strength. Fartein Valen began to receive some recognition, partly with the help of Monrad Johansen, who modified his own style in a more Neoclassical direction. It is symptomatic of these developments that the Norwegian chapter of ISCM, the International Society for Contemporary Music, was established in the autumn of 1938. The members of the first executive board included Pauline Hall, Harald Saeverud, and Karl Andersen.

The nationalist movement was strongly reinforced after the outbreak of World War II and the subsequent German occupation of Norway from 1940 to 1945. This time, however, its content was much more realistic and solid. "At this time," Olav Gurvin wrote, "we also shook off a lot of empty slogans and obscure theories." The war years proved to be a richly productive period for most Norwegian composers, and the end of the war was followed by a series of premieres of many important works. Stylistically they represented a continuation of the nationalist line from the 1920s and 1930s, but in most cases they reflected such an awareness of contemporary continental music as to demonstrate that Norway's composers were at last emerging from the blind alley of Norwegian provincialism. The first result of this emergence was a mixed style wherein the nationalistic tradition became thoroughly intermingled with international influences, particularly those stemming from continental Neoclassicism.

COMPOSERS BETWEEN THE WORLD WARS

One evidence of the breadth of Norway's music life in the twentieth century is the sheer number of composers who have been active. Unfortunately, some must be omitted here altogether and others can be discussed only summarily.

Sverre Jordan (1889–1972) was a native of Bergen who spent most of his life there. He was trained as a pianist, first in Bergen and later in Berlin, and made his performing debut in 1911. Thereafter he took several concert tours through Norway, Denmark, and Germany, but in 1914 he settled in Bergen. He was conductor of the Harmonic Society chorus from 1922 to 1932 and as conductor of the orchestra at the National Stage from 1931 to 1957. He was also a music critic for many years. His compositions include incidental music for Björnstjerne Björnson's play *Crippled Hulda* (also arranged as an orchestral suite), the melodrama *Poems of Fever* (text by Knut Hamsun), a piano concerto (1945), and a cello concerto (1948). He also composed the orchestral works *Norvegiana*, *Folk-tune Suite*, *Holberg Silhouettes*, and several other orchestral suites. He wrote a number of choral works, including "Norway in Our Hearts" (text by Nordahl Grieg). His principal compositions, however, include about 150 songs, where his ability to write melodious and sonorous music found its most effective expression. Several of them have been frequently sung in Norway. His style is in most respects late Romantic, with a few elements derived from Norwegian folk music.

Eyvind Hesselberg (1898–1986) was trained both as a composer and as an organist. His teachers in Norway included Catharinus Elling and Eyvind Alnaes. He later studied in Berlin (1919) and Paris (1920). His studies abroad had a profound effect on him as a composer; of greatest importance was the influence of his teacher in Paris, Nadia Boulanger. Returning to Norway, he served for many years as a church organist. He was also active as a conductor and teacher.

Hesselberg was one of the few Norwegian composers other than Pauline Hall who were strongly influenced by the French style. He wrote several orchestral works, including *Scherzo notturno* (1924–26) and *Allegretto giocoso* (1926), as well as chamber music, cantatas, and other works for chorus and orchestra.

Olav Kielland (1901–85) was regarded as one of Norway's most eminent orchestral conductors, but he also did a good deal of composing. He studied at Leipzig, where his teachers included Stephan Krehl in composition and Otto Fred Lohse in conducting. Later he also took an advanced course in conducting from Felix Weingartner. He was conductor of the Oslo Philharmonic Orchestra from 1931 to 1945 and also served as its artistic director during most of that time. He thereafter became resident conductor of the Bergen Harmonic Society orchestra (Harmonien) from 1952 to 1955 and appeared as guest conductor of various orchestras throughout the world.

As a composer Kielland represented the strongly nationalistic wing of Norwegian music. His orchestral compositions include two symphonies, "Overtura tragica" (an overture to Henrik Ibsen's *Brand*), a violin concerto, "Marcia nostrale" (a single-movement orchestral piece), "Toward the Snow-covered Heights" (a song for solo voice and orchestra, text by O. Setrom), and *Concerto grosso norvegese*. He also wrote a number of choral compositions, songs, and piano pieces.

Harald Lie (1902–42) had only about ten productive years as a composer. A native of Oslo, he studied piano at the music conservatory there during his youth. He also did some composing, though he had little training in music theory. His musical interests so dominated his time, however, that he failed his university entrance examination. In 1923 he went to the United States, where he earned his living in a variety of jobs unrelated to music. Eventually he obtained a good position with a piano manufacturing company, which sent him to Leipzig to study techniques used there in building pianos. The trip to Leipzig proved to be a decisive moment in his life, for in the rich musical environment of that storied city his interest in composition was reawakened. He returned to Oslo in 1929 and shortly thereafter began to study composition with Fartein Valen. His first compositions were eventually discarded and destroyed, but in 1937 his career as a composer was officially launched with the performance of his *Symphony No. 1*. His second symphony was performed the following year and he began work on a third, but it was never completed. The Scherzo of what was to be the third symphony was performed under the title "Symphonic Dance." He also composed some songs for voice and orchestra, including "A Bat's Letter" and "The Key," and several choral pieces.

Harald Lie was a gifted composer whose few completed works showed considerable promise. Unfortunately, in 1932 he contracted tuberculosis, and a decade later it took his life. His style is late Romantic; it reflects the influence of Anton Bruckner as well as some indigenous nationalist features. His harmony is essentially functional, but a fairly bold use of dissonance conceals the underlying harmonic structure to some extent. His songs with orchestral accompaniment are some of the most important compositions of this type composed in Norway during this period.

FARTEIN VALEN

Fartein Valen (1887–1952) was without question Norway's most distinctive composer in the first half of the twentieth century. Because he consistently chose paths different from those of his contemporaries, however, he remained largely isolated throughout his career. His mature style approaches that of Schoenberg's twelve-tone music, but he appears to have developed that style quite independently of Schoenberg.

The son of missionaries to Madagascar, Valen grew up in Stavanger. He received some piano instruction during his childhood, and while attending high school he studied piano with Jeanette Mohr, a pupil of Erika Nissen. His early interest in music also stimulated him to compose, but his knowledge of music theory at that time consisted primarily of what he had been able to learn by himself.

He took his university entrance examination in 1906 and went to Oslo to study philology, as his father wished. His desire, however, was to become a composer, and his father had given him permission to study music on the side. He became a student of Catharinus Elling, studying with him for three years. After his father's death he gave up his university pursuits and concentrated solely on music. He graduated from the Oslo Music Conservatory in 1909 with a degree in organ, and that year his first composition, "Legend" for piano (Op. 1), was published.

From 1909 to 1916 Valen studied in Berlin. For the first two years he was a student at the music academy; thereafter he studied mostly on his own. During this time he composed a sonata for piano (Opus 2) and one for violin and piano (Opus 3). He worked very slowly at this time because his search for a personal style prevented him from proceeding more rapidly.

Fartein Valen at the piano. (Norsk Komponistforening)

Indeed, during the seven years immediately following his studies in Berlin he worked even more slowly, composing only two works. These were *Ave Maria* for solo voice and orchestra (Op. 4), on which he worked from 1917 to 1921, and the *Piano Trio* (Op. 5), which occupied him from 1917 to 1924. Over this period from 1916 to 1924—except for occasional visits to Oslo and a trip to Italy in 1922—Valen lived on the family farm in Valevaag, north of Haugesund. He was intensely occupied with compositional technique, and came to adopt atonality as his personal musical style.

In the autumn of 1924 Valen returned to Oslo, where he lived almost continuously until 1938. The most important interruption was a brief stay in Mallorca during the winter of 1932–33. At first he had to support himself with odd jobs and a little music teaching, but in 1927 he became supervisor of the newly established Norwegian music collection at the university library in Oslo. The salary was small but adequate for his needs. Moreover, in time he became a highly regarded theory teacher, counting among his pupils some of Norway's best-known composers. In 1935 he received a government stipend, which freed him of the necessity to earn a living. He left his position at the library in 1936 and in 1938 returned to the family farm in Valevaag, where he made his home with his sister Sigrid for the rest of his life.

After he had arrived at his own personal style in the *Piano Trio*, Valen began to compose much more rapidly. Although he continued his compositional-technical exercises until as late as 1943, and his tonal language underwent some changes through the years, by about 1925 he had developed the main features of a style that he felt was his own. He thereafter wrote several songs, including "Sakontala" and "Suleika" (texts by Goethe). The style of his early songs varies slightly from one to another. In some he retains something of the Expressionistic style that is evident in both *Ave Maria* and the *Piano Trio*. That he wrote so many songs is certainly owing in part to the fact that the texts helped him solve the problems of form. His style at this time can be most simply described as atonal. The texture is largely polyphonic with the interacting voices generally creating dissonances (minor and major seconds and sevenths). He used many augmented and diminished intervals in his melodic lines, but he did not employ the twelve-tone series as a tone row in the manner of Schoenberg.

After gaining some experience with the songs, Valen proceeded to some larger instrumental works. The first of these was his *String Quartet No. 1* (Op. 10), composed in 1928–29, followed by the *String Quartet No. 2* (Op. 13). In these the harmonic language is the dissonant polyphony described above, but the forms are derived from Viennese Classical and Baroque models: sonata form, rondo form, various song forms, and fugue. However, Valen had to replace the traditional tensions and contrasts with innovations consistent with his own harmonic style. This he did primarily through the use of such techniques as thematic inversion, retrograde motion, augmentation, and diminution. He also used rhythmic and dynamic devices to create passages of heightened tension. In both the sonata and fugue forms he retained the traditional transposition of the themes at the fifth and the fourth, but without, of course, achieving thereby the same degree of tension as in the older forms.

In 1930 Valen wrote the first of several single-movement orchestral works, entitled "Pastorale" (Op. 11). He was also occupied at this time (during and after the writing of the quartets) with a series of motets for various vocal combinations. These comprise Opuses 12, 14, 15, and 16. Some years later (in 1936–37) he wrote three more motets, Opuses 25, 26, and 27.

The traditional polyphonic motet style was admirably suited to Valen's musical language, and here he also had texts to assist in creating the form of the composition. The voice leading and pervasive dissonance in these compositions, however, make them extremely difficult to sing *a cappella*, which is undoubtedly the main reason that they are so rarely performed.

Most of Valen's single-movement orchestral works were written during the years 1932–34, several during his stay in Mallorca from the autumn of 1932 to the spring of 1933. Before that trip he completed the "Sonetto di Michelangelo" (Op. 17, No. 1), and when in Mallorca he completed "Cantico de ringraziamento" (Op. 17, No. 2), "Nenia" (Op. 18, No. 1), and "An die Hoffnung" (Op. 18, No. 2). "Epithalamion" (Op. 19) was also begun there but not finished until after his return to Norway. During 1933–34 he wrote "Le cimetière marin" (Op. 20) and "La isla de las calmas" (Op. 21). The series was concluded in 1939 with "Ode to Solitude" (Op. 35).

In these compositions Valen's dissonant polyphony is transferred to an orchestral setting. Most of these pieces require a relatively small orchestra and the instruments are used in traditional ways. The orchestration is well crafted and efficient. Orchestral *tuttis* are reserved for the high points; otherwise various sections play together, frequently with doubling of parts among the several instrumental groups. Distinctly contrasting levels of sound are rarely used. The formal construction is generally a series of large dynamic arches. Motives usually are introduced in a subdued introductory section; then, as the piece progresses, the motives are developed by such techniques as inversion, retrograde motion, augmentation, diminution, and occasionally rhythmic alteration. The climaxes are created by dynamic and rhythmic means and by increasing the density of the musical texture. After the final climax the music often subsides again to *piano* or *pianissimo*, and the most important motives are repeated. These characteristics may be observed in "Le cimetière marin" and several other pieces, but there are exceptions. "Ode to Solitude," for example, is a fugue that ends in a powerful *fortissimo*.

Valen had not used the piano as a solo instrument for over twenty years (since writing the *Piano Sonata*, Op. 2) when he resumed composing piano pieces in 1934. During the next three years he wrote *Four Piano Pieces*, (Op. 22), *Variations for Piano* (Op. 23), *Gavotte and Musette for Piano* (Op. 24), *Prelude and Fugue for Piano* (Op. 28), and *Two Preludes for Piano* (Op. 29). "Intermezzo" (Op. 36) and *Piano Sonata No. 2* (Op. 38) were composed during the years 1939–41. Several of these contain stylized dance movements (waltz, gigue, gavotte, musette) in which the stylization is carried far afield but the original characteristics of the dances are nonetheless discernible. Others contain what may be regarded as character pieces of varying length, much like the *Charakterstück* tradition of Romantic piano pieces.

Of Valen's mature piano works, only *Variations for Piano* and *Piano Sonata No. 2* are in a large format. The former is based on a theme consisting of a tone row in the style of Schoenberg, though the similarity may be pure happenstance. In general, as we have said, Valen's style was developed independently of Schoenberg. The twelve variations are loosely patterned after the figural variations of the Baroque era; the set concludes with a coda. *Piano Sonata No. 2* is Valen's most important piano composition—indeed, it is one of his principal works in any genre. Although inspired in part by Francis Thompson's "The Hound of Heaven," it is not program music. It consists of three movements marked Allegro maestoso, Andante, and Toccata (allegro molto). The form of each loosely follows a Classical pattern as follows: first movement, sonata form; second movement, ternary (a large ABA) form; third movement, rondo form. This work places great demands on the performer, but its intensely expressive mood is such that its effect is deeply moving.

Valen wrote his first symphony during the years 1937–39. In the process of composing it he encountered many difficulties, and at first he thought it would be his only symphony. In time, however, he came to complete three more symphonies as well as several other large works. During his last productive period, in fact, he concentrated on cyclic compositions. In any case, what immediately followed the first symphony were several smaller works, including his two organ compositions *Prelude and Fugue* (Op. 33) and "Pastorale" (Op. 34). Although he played the organ, he had not previously written anything for the instrument. That he did so now is owing to the fact that an able young organist, Magne Elvestrand, was studying with him at this time. Opus 33, one of Valen's finest inspirations, is dedicated to him. As an example of Valen's style we give in example 54 the Prelude of this fine composition.

The Prelude is constructed in a simple ternary form, though it does not follow the pattern exactly. It can be described as ABA' plus coda; the A section, however, is significantly longer than A', and B is built to some extent on the same motivic material as A, so the contrast between sections is not great. The principal themes and motives are identified in the reproduction below by the lower-case letters *a* to *f*. The most important thematic-motivic material is the *a* theme (the top voice in measures 1–4), the *b* theme (the top voice in measures 4–6), the *c* motive (in the pedal in measure 1), and the *d* theme (in the left hand in measures 2–5). A contrasting element

Example 54. Fartein Valen, "Prelude," *from* Prelude and Fugue for Organ, *Op. 33, No. 1.*

is provided by the simple theme marked *e* (measures 17–18), which is always played unaccompanied. This theme frames the B section (measures 18–24), which also contains the theme *f* (the top voice in measures 18–20) and parts of themes *a*, *b*, and *d* as well as motive *c*. The coda, like the B section, is introduced by theme *e* (measures 35–37) followed by theme *f* (measures 37–39), and the piece ends with motives from theme *a* and motive *c*.

In this piece Valen was working with definite chords in a more obvious way than he did in many of his other compositions. The character of theme *a* comes entirely from the stacked fourths in the chord f–sharp^1–b^1–e^2, and this type of chord plays an important role later in the piece. The distribution and handling of the themes at the beginning of A′ (measures 27 ff.) is typical of Valen's style.

The first composition of Valen's last period was his *Violin Concerto* (Op. 37), written in 1940. It is one of his most frequently played works, and perhaps also one of the most accessible. Its single movement is in sonata form, and the coda uses the chorale "Jesus Is My Hope and Consolation" as a cantus firmus. The background for the concerto and the use of the chorale was the memory of Valen's young relative, Arne Valen, who died of tuberculosis in 1936 at the age of twenty. The youth had been very close to Valen, and his death affected the composer deeply. The combination of the tonal chorale melody and the dissonant polyphony creates a remarkable effect. It is one of Valen's most moving works.

The *Violin Concerto* was followed by *Piano Sonata No. 2* and his two last songs (Opus 39). Then followed *Symphony No. 2* (Op. 40), composed in 1941–44, *Symphony No. 3* (Op. 41), *Serenade* for wind instruments (Op. 42), *Symphony No. 4* (Op. 43), and the *Piano Concerto* (Op. 44). At the time of his death Valen was working on a fifth symphony. Of the symphonies, the third is generally regarded as the most important. Like the first and second it is in four movements, and like so many of Valen's works it is closely related in form to Viennese Classical models. In the first three symphonies the first movement is in sonata form, the inner movements usually in ternary form, and the last movement usually in either rondo or sonata form. The fourth symphony differs somewhat from the others in that it has just three movements, the last of which consists of a large chaconne with twenty variations.

The "Serenade" for wind quintet was written immediately after the third symphony and is closely related to it. It is in sonata form and contains many of the characteristics typical of Valen. Written in response to a request from the Chamber Quintet, a Danish ensemble led by Erik Thomsen, it has become one of Valen's most frequently played compositions. His last completed composition, the *Piano Concerto*, also holds a prominent place in his output. It was written for the British pianist Alexandr Helmann, who had promised to perform it but unfortunately did not live to do so. The concerto is unusually compact: total playing time is only about twelve minutes. The three movements are marked Allegro moderato, Andante (larghetto), and Finale allegro (ma non troppo). The second movement leads directly into the third without a pause. The structure follows Valen's usual pattern: sonata form in the first movement, ternary in the second, and rondo in the third. In its brevity the concerto constitutes a characteristic and worthy conclusion to Valen's lifework.

Throughout most of his life Valen encountered a great deal of opposition. His compositions were rarely performed, and when they were they were usually given negative reviews by the critics. Only in his later years did he experience wider recognition and some success. Valen societies were established in both Norway and Great Britain, and they have done much to make his music known both at home and abroad. No broader interest among music lovers in general seems to have occurred, however. His art remains a rather exclusive body of music for the chosen few who regard it very highly.

DAVID MONRAD JOHANSEN

David Monrad Johansen (1888–1974), as previously stated, occupied a central position in Norway's music life in the 1920s and 1930s. He was the dominant figure in the nationalist movement, and this position eventually had tragic consequences for him personally. As an artist he soon liberated himself from the stagnation that this course might have involved, but as leader of the movement he made the fateful decision to support the pro-German puppet government that ruled Norway during World War II. From 1943 to 1945, for example, he was a member of the Quisling-appointed Cultural Congress. After the liberation he had to answer for this, and it also left him and his followers culturally isolated both during the occupation and for the first decade or so thereafter. Only in the 1960s was his art restored nationally to its natural place.

Monrad Johansen grew up in Mosjöen, a town in north-central Norway. He began taking piano lessons at the age of ten and also played various instruments in an amateur town orchestra. He went to Oslo in 1904 to continue his education but had to drop out of high school because of illness. He continued to study piano, however, first privately and from 1905 to 1909 with Per Winge at the music conservatory. His intention at that time was to become a pianist. In 1909 he became a pupil of Karl Nissen, and he

David Monrad Johansen. (Norsk Komponistforening)

gave his first concert in 1910 in Mosjöen. He also wanted a thorough schooling in music theory, and studied at various times with Per Steenberg, Catharinus Elling, and Iver Holter.

In 1915–16 he attended the music academy in Berlin, where Engelbert Humperdinck was one of his teachers. In 1916 he returned to Oslo for two years. During this time, under the influence of Alf Hurum, he studied French Impressionist music, especially that of Debussy. In 1919 he won a scholarship that enabled him to go to Paris the following spring. The experience that made the deepest impression on him there was his encounter with the ballet music of Stravinsky. He returned to Norway that autumn with a renewed interest in Norwegian folk art. He studied Landstad's collections of folk tunes and O. M. Sandvik's collection of folk music from Gudbrandsdalen, both of which sources had an influence on his compositions during the 1920s.

He left for Paris again in the summer of 1928, and once again French music life had an inspirational effect on him. He heard works by Stravinsky, Prokofiev, Honegger, and others and became especially interested in those of Honegger. Of equal importance, however, was the fact that he met Fartein Valen, who was also in Paris at this time. At Valen's suggestion he began to study atonal counterpoint. These studies, too, left their mark on his music, especially the cantata *Ignis Ardens*, which was written at the beginning of the 1930s.

Not yet satisfied with his studies in composition, Monrad Johansen sought out Hermann Grabner in Leipzig in 1933 and again in 1935, and under his guidance completed a thorough course in counterpoint. The results of these studies are evident in all of his later compositions.

Thus Monrad Johansen had an unusually comprehensive and varied education in his field, a fact that is stylistically reflected in his compositions. He began to compose early in his career and had already written quite a few pieces before his study in Berlin. Some of these early compositions were published, including his Opus 1 and 2 songs (texts by Idar Handagard and Knut Hamsun) and a piano piece, "Mill Dance." His *Violin Sonata* (Op. 3) was completed in 1913. In these works we see Monrad Johansen as a late Romantic composer obviously influenced by Grieg. The harmony is generally functional with some chromaticism, and the forms are traditional.

During his stay in Berlin he wrote a *Suite for Orchestra* (Op. 4), but his training there did not result in a rush of works. His study of French music upon his return to Oslo from Berlin in 1916 was more productive, for the compositions that followed give clear evidence of the influence of Impressionism. Examples are his piano pieces from around 1920, the song cycle *Nordland's Trumpet* (Op. 13), and the orchestral work "Pan" (Op. 22).

Another important composition that dates from the first half of the 1920s is his setting for *a cappella* male chorus of the "Dream Ballad." In it he used the folk ballad as a text but none of the folk melodies associated with it. The result is a work of considerable expressive power. At this time he also wrote some pieces for male chorus and arranged a number of Norwegian folk tunes for piano (Opuses 9 and 10).

We include here the song "At Alstahaug's Parsonage," from *Nordland's Trumpet* (see example 55). Although most of the other songs in the set are

Example 55. David Monrad Johansen, "At Alstahaug's Parsonage," Op. 13, No. 6.

se-lig i Sky Og se-es i Ha-vet saa vi - de.

more complex, the refined simplicity here gives a good picture of Monrad Johansen's style at this time.

The song is in A-flat major, although there are a few digressions such as the turn to A-flat minor in the concluding measures. At first glance the harmony appears to be naively simple, but interest is sustained by a number of subtle details. Note, for example, the effect of the e-natural[1] in the second measure: this makes the chord on beats four and five the dominant seventh of F minor (the root is omitted) rather than the straightforward dominant chord that we might have expected. This chord then leads to an F-minor triad with d-flat[2] instead of c[2], while the pedal point on a-flat binds the chords together and gives the song just a hint of Impressionistic vagueness. The brief piano postlude consists of a restatement of the last phrase of the song, this time harmonized in A-flat minor. Together with the subtle plagal ending, it sets the entire song in relief and shows that the apparent naiveté is in fact a sophisticated artistic tool used here to enhance expression. The song constitutes an ingenious recreation of the text in a deliberately anachronistic musical context.

*Fresco by Axel Revold in Universitetsbib-
lioteket, Oslo, depicting a scene from Voluspaa. (Photo by O. Vaering)*

Monrad Johansen's monumental work, *Voluspaa* (Op. 15), completed in 1926, is a setting for chorus, soloists, and orchestra of a *nynorsk* version of one of the grandest poems in old Scandinavian literature. In a series of mighty panoramas it depicts the entire world view of the old Nordic people from creation to the end of the world and its dream of a new earth to follow. Monrad Johansen followed the text exactly, underlining it by means of uncomplicated musical devices. The music is developed with great simplicity both in overall concept and in its details and well deserves the considerable popularity that it has enjoyed in Norway.

Voluspaa and *Nordland's Trumpet* show Monrad Johansen's nationalistic style in its purest form. This style has sometimes been called Norwegian Impressionism, which points in the right direction but is not an altogether precise designation. There is a certain kinship with Impressionism, but the texture of the music is somewhat more polyphonic than one commonly finds

in the works of, for example, Debussy. Passages in the Dorian, Phrygian, and Lydian modes occur frequently within a tertian tonal framework.

Although these works were artistically successful, it is clear that the style they represented had little potential for further development. Monrad Johansen himself was aware of this, and in the works that followed one can detect a certain groping for a new style. In *Sigvat Skald* (Op. 16) for voice and orchestra, for example, it is possible to discern something of the deep impression that Honegger's music had made on him during his stay in Paris. This piece is sharply dissonant at times but nonetheless has a firm tonal anchoring. His next large choral work was the cantata *Ignis Ardens* (Op. 20; text by Olav Bull), which was premiered in 1933. Here one can trace the results of the studies of twelve-tone music undertaken with the encouragement of Valen.

Not until he began his studies with Hermann Grabner did Monrad Johansen find the path upon which he could continue to develop as a composer, and it led in the direction of Neoclassicism. His style became conspicuously more polyphonic and drew closer in form to Classical models. His harmony also became more evidently tonal and somewhat less dissonant than in the time around 1930. His first composition after his studies with Grabner was *Symphonic Fantasia* for orchestra (Op. 21). This well-constructed work, which consists of three short and concise movements, bears witness to his Classical training. The first movement is built on a single theme that, as it is developed, dominates the entire movement. The second movement is in the form of a theme and variations, and the third movement is a fugue. *Symphonic Variations* for orchestra (Op. 23) continues in the same direction, as do several of his later works.

"Pan" (Op. 22), described by the composer as "symphonic music for orchestra," is unique among Monrad Johansen's compositions from this period. It was written in 1939 in honor of Knut Hamsun's eightieth birthday and was inspired by the latter's exquisite novel of the same name. With tender affection and consummate skill, Monrad Johansen created a tone picture that evokes the magical world of summer nights in northern Norway. He wrote: "[The composition] does not portray any particular events but attempts to give expression to the elemental forces that live in Hamsun's work and are crucial to its development." Thus he was at the least on the border of program music. Stylistically it may be regarded as a combination of his earlier, more Impressionistic style and the polyphonic style of *Symphonic Fantasia*. According to the composer's own words, the work is closely tied to Hamsun's novel in both general mood and thematic development, but his Classical leanings at this time are evident in the fact that it is cast in a clear sonata form with an abbreviated recapitulation. The music stands by itself, quite apart from any programmatic associations, and well deserves its place as one of the composer's most highly regarded works.

Monrad Johansen was relatively unproductive during the 1940s. After completing the *Symphonic Variations* he wrote a cello suite that was premiered in 1943, later revised, and performed again in 1968. In 1946 he wrote *Five Biblical Songs* for voice and piano (Op. 25), in which he created realistic and powerful musical settings of five short passages selected from the New Testament Gospels. A *Quartet* for piano, violin, viola, and cello was premiered in 1953, and his *Piano Concerto* (Op. 29) was premiered in 1955. His last compositions were two chamber-music works: a *Quintet* for flute, two violins, viola, and cello (Op. 35), written for the jubilee of the Society of Norwegian Composers in 1967, and a *String Quartet* (Op. 36), written for the Hindar Quartet's jubilee concert in 1969.

The flute quintet is an important work. It consists of three movements, marked Grave, Allegro scherzando, and Passacaglia. Stylistically it looks backward rather than forward, but it has an artistic quality and personal intensity that likely will enable it to endure.

Throughout his long and productive life, David Monrad Johansen demonstrated his ability to grow and develop in response to new ideas and impulses. The principal works from his later years—*Five Biblical Songs*, the *Piano Concerto*, and the two late chamber-music works—show that he retained his creative power and his capacity for artistic renewal.

PAULINE HALL

Among this generation of Norwegian composers, Pauline Hall (1890–1969) was the one most closely allied to French music. Both her musical talent and her education appear to have contributed to this affinity.

Hall was born in Hamar, a small city about fifty miles north of Oslo. Shortly after her birth her family moved to Kabelvaag, a remote village on an island off the west coast of Norway far north of the Arctic Circle. Here she lived for the first ten years of her life. Her father, a pharmacist, was an amateur musician, so her formative years were spent in a musically active milieu. She began playing the piano and learned how to read music, but she received her first formal music instruction when her family moved back to Hamar in 1900. She passed the university entrance examination in 1907 and the following year went to Oslo to study music. Although she began taking piano lessons from Johan Backer Lunde, what really interested her was composition, and from 1910 to 1912 she studied theory and composition with Catharinus Elling.

She then went to Paris to continue her music studies, and except for a brief stay in Dresden remained there until 1914. Her studies in Paris were

Pauline Hall. (Norsk Komponistforening)

of decisive importance to her as a composer. She later wrote: "My first stay abroad brought me such—I can almost say shocking—experiences as Stravinsky's *The Rite of Spring* and *Petrushka*, Debussy's *Jeux*, Ravel's *Daphnis et Chloé*, Moussorgsky's *Boris Godunov*, and above all, Debussy's *Pelléas et Mélisande*."

Her sojourn in Paris marked the end of her formal education, but by then her compositions had already been publicly performed on several occasions. In both 1910 and 1912, for example, she had given recitals consisting of her own compositions in Tromsö. Her first such program in Oslo was given in 1917; it included a "Sonatina" for violin and piano in addition to songs and piano pieces.

Hall spent the years 1926–32 in Berlin, during which time she was also a music and theater correspondent for the Oslo daily newspaper, *Dagbladet*. Thereafter and for the rest of her life she was associated with Oslo and its cultural life. She was a music critic for *Dagbladet* from 1934 to 1942 and again from 1945 to 1956. The two years prior to her transfer to Berlin (1924–26), she directed the Norwegian Concert Bureau and also appeared frequently as an accompanist at concerts. After her return to Oslo, from 1932 to 1938 she was the leader of a women's vocal quintet that performed on Norwegian State Radio and elsewhere.

She was also a member of several important music organizations. First among them was the Society of Norwegian Composers of which she was a member from its inception in 1917; she also served on its board of directors in 1920 and on several occasions thereafter. Her most important of such activities however, were as a founding member of New Music, the Norwegian chapter of the International Society for Contemporary Music (ISCM). She was chairperson of this group from its inception in 1938 until 1961. Her most demanding responsibility in this capacity occurred in 1953, when her group hosted the ISCM international music festival in Oslo. Thanks largely to her fine leadership, it proved to be a great success.

As a composer, Hall first became known as a writer of songs; her catalogue of works includes over fifty songs, most with piano accompaniment. Among her better-known compositions in this category are "O Flower in the Dew" (text by J. P. Jacobsen) and the powerful "Land of the Eagles" (text by Thorleif Auerdahl). The former was first performed at her debut concert in Oslo in 1917, the latter in 1925.

The most substantial part of her output, however, consists of orchestral works. Even in "Poème élégiaque," her first composition for orchestra, she demonstrated a surprisingly confident and sensitive handling of orchestral resources. After its premiere in 1920 it was described as "some of the most refined and remarkable music written for orchestra by a Norwegian composer." Her next orchestral endeavor, *Verlaine Suite*—probably the most important Norwegian work in this genre written during the 1920s—was completed in 1929. Both these works were inspired by the poems of the French symbolist writer Paul Verlaine.

Hall's affinity for French music is evident even in her early songs and piano pieces, for which Debussy and his immediate successors were her models. But in *Verlaine Suite* one most easily sees her affection for the French spirit and mode of expression. Nonetheless, even though her entire music vocabulary was derived from Impressionism, there is a certain independence in both concept and content. The suite has four movements, marked "Introduction," "Nocturne Parisien," "Ariettes oubliées," and "Foire." The first three present several impressions of pained, subdued moods, while the last sketches a lively portrait of jovial market life in Paris. Everything is executed competently and imaginatively.

Fertility of imagination and animated, evocative themes also characterize her next orchestral work, *Circus Portraits* (1933). Its three brief movements—"Parade," "The Animals Sleep," and "The Clowns Dance"—have an appealing sense of humor that undoubtedly has played a role in making this one of her most popular works.

In *Circus Portraits* some Neoclassical elements begin to surface. Her music hereafter gradually becomes more linear, with a more audacious use of dissonance. These features are perhaps most evident in her chamber music, such as the *Suite for Wind Quintet* (1945); the beginning of the first movement is given in example 56. It has six movements, marked "Alla marcia," "Rondeau," "Polka," "Pastorale," "Tempo di Valse," and "Epilogue." Both the lyrical and humorous sides of Hall's talents found expression in this Neoclassical work.

Hall's early experience as a music and theater correspondent in Berlin stimulated a lifelong interest in the dramatic arts, and in later years she devoted much of her attention to theater and film music. The first concrete result of this interest was a production of Bertholt Brecht and Kurt Weill's *The Threepenny Opera* at the Central Theater in 1930. She accomplished this almost single-handedly, translating the libretto, rehearsing the singers, and conducting the orchestra. She was an excellent writer who among other things provided translations for Norwegian performances of such works as Stravinsky's *The Soldier's Tale*, Mozart's *Don Giovanni*, and Honegger's *King David*. She translated books as well, including Alfred Einstein's *History of Music* and Robert Craft's *Conversations with Stravinsky*.

Her first original composition for the theater was incidental music for a Norwegian production of Eugene O'Neill's play *Desire Under the Elms*, performed at the New Theater in Oslo in 1934. By the end of her career she

Example 56. Pauline Hall, excerpt from the first movement of the Suite for Wind Quintet.

had written incidental music for more than twenty theater productions. Among her most successful efforts in this area were her music for two Shakespearean plays, *Julius Caesar* (1947) and *As You Like It* (1958), and that written for Henrik Ibsen's *The Pretenders* (1958). Hall composed music for a ballet, *The Marquise*, which was performed by the New Norwegian Ballet Ensemble in 1950. She also wrote music for film, radio, and TV. Thus dramatic music constituted a very large part of her output after 1945.

Because she regarded the writing of this music as an important and challenging task, she worked very hard on these compositions. Unfortunately, most such music is seldom performed once the final curtain falls on the production for which it was written. The orchestral suite that she arranged in 1950 from her music for *Julius Caesar* shows, however, that her compositional standards in this genre were very high. Here, as in her other works, she demonstrated her gift for apt characterization and succinct expression. One also begins to notice that her later musical style developed in the direction of a freer tonality and at times sharp dissonances. This is the case, for example, in the third movement of the *Julius Caesar* suite, in which minor seconds, major sevenths, and minor ninths occur with considerable frequency.

Hall also wrote several choral and piano works. Most of her choral compositions are short pieces; some were written for her own quintet of women's voices, some for male chorus, and some for mixed voices. Many of the piano pieces are early compositions. These works, too, are marked by her artistic sense and solid craftsmanship, but they add no essentially new features to the picture of her personality as a composer.

Among female Norwegian composers Pauline Hall's historical importance is second only to that of Agathe Backer Gröndahl. Her many contributions to Norwegian music were recognized in 1960 when she was awarded a government stipend. Her French-oriented musical language stood in sharp contrast to the nationalistic tendencies that dominated Norwegian music around 1930; one result of this was that she had to endure a considerable amount of opposition during what was perhaps her most important creative period. She gradually earned great respect, however—not least as a music critic, a role in which she rendered outstanding service. In this capacity she was at times severe, but she could also be encouraging when she found a basis for it. Her judgments were impartial and conscientious and always based on the relevant facts.

LUDVIG IRGENS JENSEN

Ludvig Irgens Jensen (1894–1969) matriculated at the University of Oslo in 1913 as a student of philology but also took piano lessons from Nils Larsen and Dagmar Walle-Hansen. Indeed, his interest in music was such that he independently pursued the study of music theory and composition as well. He is the only important Norwegian composer to date who did not study at a conservatory, but there is nothing dilettantish about his music. Somehow he managed on his own to acquire a thorough knowledge of the various branches of compositional technique.

Irgens Jensen's career as a composer began with the publication in 1920 of thirty-eight songs (Opuses 1–6). Even these early works show various aspects of his many-faceted talent. In the song cycle *In the Darkness* (Op. 1), for example, one finds the somber mood of the song from which the cycle is named, the naive and melancholy charm of "Lullaby," and so on. In *Japanese Spring* (Op. 2) the mood is brighter but equally fervent. During the years that followed he wrote several more songs, including the cycle *The City of Roses* and two volumes of *Nursery Rhymes and Fables*, which became very popular. At this time, however, he also began to work with larger instrumental forms. In 1924 he completed a sonata for piano and violin; the following year he wrote one of his principal works, *Variations and Fugue* for orchestra, which was revised in 1934 and given the title *Tema con variazioni*. *Passacaglia* for orchestra was written in 1926 and his *Piano Quintet* in 1927.

Scene from a 1947 production of Ludvig Irgens Jensen's The Homeward Journey *as an opera. (Sturlason)*

For the St. Olaf jubilee in 1930 Irgens Jensen composed a large oratorio entitled *The Homeward Journey* (text by Olav Gullvaag), winning first prize in the national competition for a jubilee cantata. It is the most nationalistic of Irgens Jensen's compositions even though stylistically it does not differ markedly from the rest of his œuvre. The music is predominantly linear, often with the parts moving in a kind of *faux bourdon* style, though some of the choral sections are more polyphonic in character. Its harmonic framework is based to a large extent on modal scales. There are many similarities between this work and the so-called "Norwegian Impressionism" of Monrad Johansen's *Voluspaa*.

The structure of the oratorio follows the text's division into three main parts: I. Advent—The King; II. Apostasy—The King in Exile—The Homeward Journey; III. Stiklestad—Postlude. The text is quite dramatic, but an attempt to stage it as an opera in 1947 was not wholly successful because of its intrinsic nature as an oratorio. Nonetheless, the grand character of the text is emphasized in the music, which is of epic proportions. *The Homeward*

Left to right: Ludvig Irgens Jensen, Christian Sinding, and Odd Grüner-Hegge.

Journey remains to this day one of the most important oratorios in the entire corpus of Norwegian music.

Another large choral work, *God and the Temple Dancer* (text by Goethe), was begun in 1921 but completed only in 1932 and premiered in 1935. Somewhat closer to the nationalistic tradition was his incidental music for Hans E. Kinck's play *The Horse Trader*; it was published later as an orchestral suite under the title *Partita sinfonica*.

A later composition worthy of mention is his *Symphony* in D minor. Written in 1943, it reflects his impressions of the German occupation during World War II. For the Oslo jubilee of 1950 he wrote "Canto d'omaggio" for chorus and orchestra. In this period he also composed a piano piece entitled "Folkvard Lommanson" (based on a folk ballad by the same name) and a number of songs for various combinations of voices. His many contributions to Norwegian music were recognized in 1946 when he was awarded a government stipend.

One generally encounters a conservative Neoclassical style in the works of Irgens Jensen. His music is often polyphonic, with a linear treatment of

dissonances. Modal influence is frequent, and his chords are almost always triadic. Often his chord progressions can be analyzed in conventional terms, but in general one can say that he is not bound by the principles of functional harmony. There is a clear preference for the form of theme and variations, which he handled with great skill. The abbreviated version of *Tema con variazioni*, for example, comprises thirteen variations (seventeen in the longer version) plus a coda in the form of a fugue. Some variations use the theme as a cantus firmus, some are character pieces that retain the essential structure of the theme, and some are free variations. With its imaginative compositional solutions and contrasts and its sound, occasionally brilliant orchestration, this piece is an example of Neoclassical music at its best.

Irgens Jensen's other large orchestral work from the 1920s, *Passacaglia*, also consists of a theme and variations, although it is not audibly divided into sections but is formed as one uninterrupted sequence. There are, however, four identifiable sections within the whole: an introductory section containing all of the thematic material; a passacaglia with twelve variations; a fugue; and finally, a coda in which the passacaglia theme returns in conjunction with the other themes used in the work. The structure of this work is quite original, and one of considerable grandeur. Irgens Jensen also used the variation technique in his symphony: its two movements are based on a common theme that appears in several variations as the symphony progresses.

Partita sinfonica is one of the few works by Irgens Jensen directly influenced by Norwegian folk music. It reflects the milieu depicted in the play for which it was first written, a Norwegian rural culture that was slowly giving way to modernity. The music contains both stylized *slaatt* rhythms and folk-like melodies. "Bols Song," which is the basis of the second movement of the suite, is a good example of the latter.

The conservative style of Irgens Jensen's music undoubtedly contributes to an occasional impression of austerity, which is further reinforced by a somewhat detached, reflective attitude on the part of the composer. Only on closer acquaintance does one come to appreciate the sterling quality of this music, and to realize that it is the product of a warm and vital creative artist.

BJARNE BRUSTAD

Bjarne Brustad (1895–1978) was one of the most important Norwegian Impressionist composers in the early 1920s. He did not continue as an Impressionist, however, but traversed virtually the entire range of styles in Norwegian music from the 1920s to the 1950s. For a time he was influenced by the nationalist trend, then by Bartók and Neoclassicism, and in his post-1960 compositions one finds elements of Neoexpressionism.

Brustad received his first training in music at the conservatory in Oslo, where Gustav Fredrik Lange was his teacher in violin and theory. He went on to study violin in Berlin with Emil Telmányi and Carl Flesch. Aside from several study trips and a brief stay in Stavanger, where he was concertmaster and orchestra conductor in 1918–19, he lived chiefly in Oslo. There he was a first violinist in the Oslo Philharmonic Orchestra from 1919 to 1922, and principal violist from 1928 to 1934. He was also a highly regarded teacher of both orchestration and composition, counting among his pupils several of Norway's most promising young composers.

Brustad always maintained close contact with music on the continent. During one study trip to Paris he became acquainted with Stravinsky and his music, and on a visit to Budapest in 1943 he met Bartók and other prominent Hungarian musicians. Both Bartók and, perhaps even more, Bartók's friend Zoltan Kodály had a significant influence on Brustad's later style. Hindemith's Neoclassical *Gebrauchsmusik* also played a role in his development as a composer.

Brustad's first important work was his *Oriental Suite* for orchestra, which was premiered in 1921. During the 1920s he also wrote, among other things, two violin concertos. Little by little he began thereafter to give greater emphasis to the rhythmic element in his music and to compress the formal structure. The first examples of this transformation are the four *Capricci* for violin and viola written in 1931. The style in these works is linear and nothing that might be regarded as superfluous is allowed to appear. The first two capriccios are melodic in character, while the last two stress the rhythmic development. The idiom, though essentially tonal, is not completely fettered by the principles of functional harmony; many passages are clearly bitonal.

In the early 1930s Brustad, like so many Norwegian composers of his generation, was strongly influenced by the nationalist movement. Even the *Capricci* exhibit features apparently derived from folk music, and such features became even more evident in his "Rhapsody" for violin and orchestra dating from 1933. The folkloristic element continued to play a fairly prominent role in his music until about 1950. His compositions during this period include some chamber music (trios, two string quartets), an opera (*Atlantis*) that has never been performed, and his first symphony (written in 1949).

Brustad's later works have a somewhat more international flavor. These include four more symphonies and a third string quartet, the latter dating from 1959.

With respect to form Brustad built primarily on the Classical tradition. His second symphony is representative of his larger works. It has three movements, the first of which is called a fanfare because of the principal theme, which is introduced by the brass instruments. This movement is in sonata form, with a free recapitulation. The second movement, entitled "Song without Words," is an elongated cantilena. The third movement is a kind of rondo—quite dissonant, at times polyphonic, but as a rule clearly tonal.

As stated earlier, the continental composers who had the greatest influence on Brustad's style were Bartók, Stravinsky, and Kodály. Serial twelve-tone music had no effect on him. It is clear, however, that in some of his later works, such as the third string quartet, he approached Neoexpressionism. This quartet has three movements with the titles "Point-line," "Sound Caprices," and "Motion." The sonority as well as his choice of motives appear to reflect the influence of post-serial music.

Brustad continued to be a productive composer even in his golden years. Among the larger works that date from his last period are the *Violin Concerto No. 4* (1961) and *Concerto for Clarinet and Strings* (1969). He wrote four more symphonies (for a total of nine) during the years 1970–73. All these compositions employ a lighter style and are more open and outgoing in character than his earlier works. He also wrote a piano suite entitled *From a Child's Life*, a sonata for violin solo, and a suite for viola solo.

Brustad's compositions demonstrate that he had an intimate knowledge of the instruments for which he wrote and that he used them capably in various combinations, whether in chamber music or the entire symphony orchestra. An exceptionally competent handling of the thematic material gives his music a witty and sophisticated stamp.

HARALD SAEVERUD

Harald Saeverud (b. 1897), a native of Bergen, attracted attention as a composer at an early age. The first movement of his *Symphony No. 1 in Two Symphonic Poems* was performed in Oslo in 1920, and he was immediately hailed as one of Norway's most promising young talents. By that time he had already completed studies at the conservatory in Bergen (1915–20). In 1920–21, with the help of a stipend from the Norwegian government, he studied at the music academy in Berlin. The second movement of his first symphony was performed there in 1921; it was later revised and published under the title "Ouverture appassionata," Op. 2b. What especially caught people's attention in the performances of his early works was their intense, deeply emotional expressivity.

Stylistically, Saeverud built largely on late Romanticism, carrying this trend further in such works as his second (Op. 4, 1922) and third (Op. 5, 1926) symphonies. In two compositions dating from around 1930—a *Pi-*

Harald Saeverud. (Photo by Marolyn Halverson)

ano Suite, Op. 6, and a *Cello Concerto*, Op. 7—this development took him very close to Expressionism.

Instead of proceeding into atonality, however, Saeverud turned in another direction. Neoclassical features are evident in his *Cinquanta variationi piccole* (Op. 8, 1931) and *Canto ostinato* (Op. 9, 1934). These works also exemplify two important features of Saeverud's later style: the use of variation and ostinato. Also in a style with a Neoclassical tinge are his incidental music for Shakespeare's *Rape of Lucretia* (1936) (also published as *Lucretia Suite*, Op. 10), *Symphony No. 4*, Op. 11 (1937), and several other works.

Toward the end of the 1930s a nationalistic element appeared in Saeverud's music. It is clearly discernible in such pieces as "Happy Chap's Frisky Steps," "Brooch Melody," and "Shepherd's Tune" from the *Seven Easy Pieces* for piano, Op. 14; it is perhaps more indirect in "Rondo amoroso," one of his most popular compositions for piano. The national dimension is also evident in the *Symphony No. 5*, subtitled "Quasi una fantasia" (Op. 16, 1941), and *Symphony No. 6*, subtitled "Sinfonia dolorosa" (Op. 19), both of which were influenced by the tragic events associated with the German occupation of Norway. The latter is one of Saeverud's most important compositions. Its single movement is shaped into a large, solidly built span leading up to a powerful, soaring conclusion. It is music that is passionately felt and deeply engaging.

Saeverud was, on the whole, extremely productive during the years of the German occupation. "I felt that my work had to become a personal hand-to-hand fight against Germany," he stated in an interview after the liberation in 1945; thus it was only natural that under these circumstances the nationalistic elements in his music were given greater emphasis. This is evident in "The Magic Dance" (Op. 20), a symphonic piece in which *slaatt* rhythms are strikingly prominent. It also has some Neoclassical features, however: the form is ternary, the outer movements are loosely patterned after the form of a theme and variations, and the middle movement is a strict passacaglia in which such sophisticated contrapuntal techniques as thematic inversion and a canon of the theme and its inversion are employed. "The Magic Dance" is a well-integrated piece in which long crescendos and ostinato rhythms create an almost ecstatic impression in keeping with the title.

The series of piano pieces begun in Opus 14 was continued in *Slaatter and Stev from Siljustöl* (Opp. 21, 22, and 24), which were written during the period 1942–44. (Siljustöl is the name of Saeverud's villa near Bergen.) This collection includes several of the composer's finest and best-known smaller works, such as "The Last Lullaby" (Op. 22, No. 3) and "Ballad of Revolt" (Op. 22, No. 5). The latter, dedicated to "the great and small fighters of the resistance movement," was also orchestrated. It has achieved great popularity in both forms in Norway and, in its piano version, abroad as well. Here again, the ostinato rhythm and the long, driving crescendo determine the musical form.

Saeverud's seventh symphony, subtitled "Hymn. Symphony in one movement with five sections" (Op. 27), was written near the end of the war.

He himself called it "a symphony of tribulation, of battle, of faith and gratitude; a father's and mother's symphony." It may be that this program represents a deliberate simplification on the part of the composer—a desire to achieve the broadest possible base for understanding. In any case, it is perhaps the most easily accessible of Saeverud's symphonic works. The most important thematic material is the hymn tune introduced in the first section (see example 57). It is a simple but excellent example of Saeverud's melodic and harmonic style. Both melodically and harmonically the movement's tonal center is B-flat major. The harmony throughout is largely triadic but the linear voice leading creates many dissonances that give the music its distinctive character. In other compositions—and indeed, in other parts of this symphony—the harmonic texture is considerably more complicated and varied. Not infrequently, for example, one finds chords consisting of

Example 57. Harald Saeverud, Hymn Tune from Symphony No. 7, Op. 27.

fourths, and occasionally there are also minor seconds used quite deliberately, not simply as a result of voice leading. Nonetheless, triadic chords predominate in most of his works and contribute much to their sonorous immediacy and charm.

In the years immediately following the war, Saeverud created another of his most important works: the incidental music for *Peer Gynt*. Theater director Hans Jacob Nilsen wanted to present Ibsen's famous play in a "de-Romanticized" form. Because Grieg's music, despite its great charm, is strongly Romantic and thus incompatible with this basic concept, Saeverud was asked to write new music. A warm admirer of Grieg's *Peer Gynt* music, he was at first reluctant to do so. He acceded to the request, however, and created dramatic music that in large measure united Nilsen's concept with the tragic dimension of Ibsen's great play. This *nynorsk* version of *Peer Gynt* was premiered at the Norwegian Theater in 1948, and since then the music has enjoyed considerable popularity in Norway both as incidental dramatic music and in its concert version as twelve orchestral pieces.

Saeverud was awarded an annual government stipend as a composer in 1955 and continued composing into his nineties. Compositions dating from recent years include film music for *Havraatunet* (Op. 33), *Six Sonatinas* for piano (Op. 30), concertos for piano (Op. 31), violin (Op. 37) and bassoon (Op. 44), and a dramatic ballet *Bluebeard's Nightmare*. His eighth symphony (subtitled "Minnesota Symphony") was written in 1958 and the ninth in 1966. Among his more recent works are the "Mozart-Motto-Sinfonietta" (Op. 50), written in 1971, *Overtura monumentale* (Op. 53) from 1977, and *Quintet No. 2* for winds from 1983.

In his later works with orchestra Saeverud reverted to a more traditional cyclic form. The *Violin Concerto*, for example, has three movements, the eighth symphony has four. Saeverud is first and foremost a symphonist, as is evident from the fact that he wrote no less than nine symphonies. It is therefore almost astonishing that in the smaller forms as well—the short piano pieces, for example—he has created such remarkable works. They are in their own way a continuation of the tradition of Romantic character pieces, but they are quite independent of the Grieg tradition.

Despite Saeverud's admiration for Grieg, of his Norwegian predecessors it is Nordraak rather than Grieg to whom he professes the nearest kinship; indeed, he has said that from his youth it is Nordraak's music that has spoken most forcefully to him. Nordraak's appreciation for clean lines and genuine simplicity correspond to similar characteristics in Saeverud's artistic personality. They share an appreciation for balanced, diatonic melodies and clear, full-bodied chords, though the distance between them in time and style naturally has resulted in vastly different idioms.

EIVIND GROVEN

No Norwegian composer has used folk-music elements in his compositions more consistently than Eivind Groven (1901–77). He grew up in an environment that was rich in the folk-music tradition and became one of the world's leading authorities on the subject.

Groven was trained to be a teacher and later studied at the music conservatories in Oslo and in Berlin. An excellent Hardanger-fiddle player, he was a consultant on folk music for the Norwegian State Radio from 1932 to 1946 and collected a number of *slaatter* and folk tunes from indigenous sources. He was also greatly interested in the willow flute, the special melodic features of which he discussed in his book *The Natural Scale* (1927).

Another of his interests concerned the problem of just intonation tuning (a non-tempered system based upon pure thirds and fifths) of keyboard instruments. One of his achievements in this area was the construction of an organ with an automatic conversion mechanism that made it possible to play polyphonic music in different keys with this tuning method. He discussed this matter in detail in two books (not available in English): *Tempered and Just Intonation Tuning* (1948) and *The Automatic Just Intonation Tuning Device* (1968). He also published a collection of Eskimo melodies from Alaska consisting of transcriptions of tape recordings made in Alaska by the explorer Helge Ingstad. Groven was awarded an annual government stipend as a composer in 1940.

His first large compositions were orchestral works, some with vocal components, which were written in the 1930s. One of the most important of these was *The Bridegroom* (1933), which was inspired by a short story about the Black Death by Ingeborg Refling Hagen. The first three movements are purely instrumental and might almost be regarded as program music. In the final fourth movement the composer added chorus and soloists to strengthen the expression with vocal passages of almost dramatic character.

Toward a Ballad, written some years earlier, also employs orchestra and chorus. It was inspired by Hans Ernst Kinck's short story *From Saga to Ballad*, which is a tale of bewitchment set in the transitional period when the old Norse religion was being supplanted by Christianity in Norway. Two orchestral works from the 1930s were similarly inspired by literature: "Renaissance" (1934) and *Historical Visions* (1937). The former was based on a short story of the same name by Hans Ernst Kinck, whose writings had considerable influence on Groven. Other orchestral works followed: *Mountain Tunes* (1938), "Wedding in the Forest" (1946), "Hjalarljod" (1950), *Symphonic Peasant Dances I* (1956), and "Faldafeykir" (1966).

Groven also wrote two symphonies and a piano concerto. *Symphony No. I* (1937) bears the motto "Across the Mountain Wilds." It begins with a melody that the Norwegian State Radio has adopted as a theme for use between programs and at other times. *Symphony No. 2*, which was first performed in 1946, is subtitled "The Midnight Hour." *Piano Concerto No. 1* was completed in 1950. Large choral works from later years include a setting of the "Dream Ballad" for chorus, soloists, and orchestra, where he employed both the original text and the old melodies.

He wrote a great many smaller compositions for various combinations of instruments and voices. Among the best of these are his songs for voice and piano and a number of short choral pieces. One unique work in this group is *Margit Hjukse*, a composition for chorus, soloists, and Hardanger fiddle based on a folk ballad of the same name. Groven used both the text and the melody of the folk ballad, as well as a Hardanger-fiddle *slaatt* from Telemark. All of this folk-music material is interwoven with original melodies to create a work of great expressive power.

In an interview in 1943 Groven said regarding his art and his artistic viewpoint: "It has been a tremendous struggle for me to undergird my distinctively Norwegian material with the correct harmonic foundation—i.e., in such a way that the melodies receive the proper coloring. It is of course the easiest thing in the world to harmonize a melody in such a way as to completely alter its intrinsic mood. For my part, I have considered it my duty to create the harmonies required by the folk music and, by the same token, by my own material." This statement is enlightening both in what it says and in what it does not say. Groven's ability as a melodist is beyond doubt; indeed, he had a gift for expressing himself melodically in a style so folk-like that his original melodies could easily be mistaken for folk tunes. Several of his works, such as *Margit Hjukse* and his setting of the "Dream Ballad," demonstrate his ability to combine folk-music material and original melodies in a stylistically unified whole.

In the areas of harmony and sonority, however, folk music provides scant resources with which to create a compositional style. Such instruments as the *langeleik* and the Hardanger fiddle do provide a few ideas, but to develop a satisfactory harmonic or polyphonic style requires much more than one can derive from the folk-music tradition—and this must come out of the composer's personal sense of "what sounds right." One would have to say that Groven succeeded in doing this. His music always displays fine artistic judgment, with a harmonic language that remains among the most discriminating to be found in Norwegian music in the twentieth century.

Folk music also is of little help with respect to the construction of larger musical forms. Most Norwegian folk melodies are relatively short and almost always consist of repeated two- or four-measure motives. Somewhat larger forms do appear in a few *slaatter*, where the music is developed by a kind of variation technique, but because of the dependence of the music on the related dance form this development is also usually based on regular two- or four-measure groups of motives. Groven solved this problem in his larger works principally by employing such traditional forms as sonata and rondo. When these are built on folk themes, however, there is a danger of monotony unless the regular patterns are somehow varied. Also, these themes normally do not lend themselves to treatment in the Classical manner.

Groven did not address these difficulties in the above-mentioned interview, but it must be admitted that he did not always succeed in overcoming them. In the smaller works, however—especially those in which he combined folk tunes and original material—his melodic skill and keen ear enabled him to create works of outstanding quality. *Margit Hjukse*, for example, is one of the finest specimens we have of a composition created by the successful fusion of folk and art music into a unified whole. One must go all the way back to Grieg to find comparable examples of Norwegian folk music convincingly employed in an artistic setting.

SPARRE OLSEN

The Grieg tradition undoubtedly has been a burden for many Norwegian composers. For all practical purposes the only one who managed to carry it forward in a constructive manner was Sparre Olsen (1903–84). Like his great predecessor, he came from an urban environment but delved deeply into Norwegian folk music and folk art. He too had an outstanding sense of harmony. Most importantly, perhaps, he had the good judgment to build on Grieg's later style as we know it in the *Norwegian Peasant Dances* (Op. 72) and *Four Psalms* (Op. 74).

Sparre Olsen's childhood and youth were spent in several different cities. He was born in Stavanger but his family moved first to Copenhagen and then settled in Oslo. He studied composition with Fartein Valen and Bjarne Brustad and violin with H. van der Vegt, concertmaster of the Oslo Philharmonic Orchestra. During the 1920s he worked as a teacher, critic, and chorus director and in 1930–31 studied at the music college in Berlin. Later he took trips to Vienna and London, studying with Percy Grainger among others. He was awarded an annual government stipend as a composer in 1946.

Sparre Olsen reached artistic maturity around 1930, just when the nationalist movement was at its peak. It influenced his entire artistic attitude and found an echo deep within his own personality. His close friendship and cooperation with several *nynorsk* poets—Olav Aukrust, Tor Jonsson, Aslaug Vaa, Inge Krokann, Tore Örjasaeter, and Jan-Magnus Bruheim—also had a profound influence on him. This accounts for the fact that a large, and perhaps the most important, part of his music consists of vocal works.

Especially noteworthy among his many songs with *nynorsk* texts are the Aukrust songs, particularly *Three Aukrust Songs* (Op. 3) and *Four Aukrust Hymns* (Op. 4). He also wrote songs to texts by Krokann, Örjasaeter, and many others. *Two Eddic Ballads* (Op. 8), for voice and orchestra, are important works. Solidly constructed throughout, they achieve great expressivity within the confines of a succinct form.

A major portion of Sparre Olsen's total output consists of choral works of various lengths. One of the larger works is his setting for mixed chorus, soprano or tenor solo, speaker, and orchestra of the "Dream Ballad" (Op. 22, 1937). Here he made use of the traditional melodies—supplemented, of course, with his own material—and developed the whole into an oratorio. Another large choral work is *Ver sanctum* (Op. 30), a setting for mixed chorus and orchestra of a text by Olav Aukrust. Also deserving of special mention is "David's Psalm 121" (Op. 19) for mixed chorus, solo, and organ.

Sparre Olsen also wrote dramatic music. His most important work in this area was incidental music for Tore Örjasaeter's play *Anne of Torp* (Op. 12), later published as an orchestral suite. He also wrote music for Nordahl Grieg's play *The Defeat* and for *The Eternal Journey*, Ragnvald Skrede's dramatization of Nikos Kazantzakis's novel *Life's Resurrection*.

Although much of Sparre Olsen's music is in one way or another associated with a text, he appears to have given more and more attention to purely instrumental music later in his career. His first orchestral work, written during his student days in Berlin, was "A Small Overture for a Small Orchestra" (Op. 7). Other instrumental works are his *Suite for Woodwind Trio* (Op. 10), *Preludio e fughetta* for orchestra (Op. 23), *Symphonic Fantasia* for orchestra (Op. 27), *The Nidaros Cathedral*, a fugue and chorale for orchestra (Op. 29), *Quintet for Wind Instruments* (Op. 35), "Music for Orchestra" (Op. 38), *Pastorale and Dance* (Op. 40), "Adagio for Strings" (Op. 41), "Serenade" for flute and strings (Op. 45), *Symphonic Fantasia No. 2* (Op. 47), and *Three Pieces for Flute and Viola* (Op. 50). He made piano arrangements of several Norwegian folk melodies—for example, *From Telemark* (Op. 31)—and also wrote a number of original pieces for piano. An example of the latter is *Leitom Suite* (Op. 33).

In characterizing Sparre Olsen's overall musical style, one naturally begins with his close connection to Norwegian folk music. His original melodies are similar in many ways to the melodies of the old folk ballads. One evidence of this similarity is the fact that he, like Groven in several of his works, placed his own melodies directly alongside folk tunes with no resulting discontinuity in style. Sparre Olsen's melodies are basically diatonic, frequently employing modal scales. Often they are constructed in accordance with certain implicit rules—i.e., simple formulas govern the development of the melodic line. Whether his fondness for open fifths and sharp dissonances came directly from Hardanger-fiddle music is perhaps less certain. It is equally possible that these elements of his style were derived from Kjerulf and Grieg, though they in turn undoubtedly got the ideas from Norwegian *slaatt* music.

The melodic line plays a central role in the overall structure of Sparre Olsen's music. Not only is it the most important vehicle for his musical expression, but at times it also determines his harmony. The influence of melody on harmony can be seen in both isorhythmic and polyphonic passages: two or more independent melodies are set against each other, often resulting in harsh dissonances. One technique that Sparre Olsen used with great frequency, especially in his choral works, is the parallel progression of chords: series consisting of parallel fifths, fourths, or triads in root position or either of their two inversions often occur in passages of varying length. Not infrequently such a series is combined with a countermelody or with another parallel series moving in the opposite direction. It is here that Sparre Olsen's style comes closest to that of Grieg's *Norwegian Peasant Dances.* In both cases, dissonance arises primarily from the clash of independently moving voices within a tonal harmonic structure.

The compositions least influenced by Norwegian folk music are his instrumental works. In such examples as "A Small Overture for a Small Orchestra" and "Serenade" for flute and strings, one finds some evidence of the influence of Neoclassicism. There are also occasional instances of freer melodic writing: in "Music for Orchestra" the themes are used in a manner suggestive of twelve-tone music, though without approaching a serial technique.

Most of Sparre Olsen's compositions are relatively short works. His strong lyrical strain and fine poetic sense caused him to favor vocal compositions; both in his songs and in his choral works his perceptive insight into the texts resulted in fine, convincing works. His strength can be felt especially in his expressive melodic lines, his discriminating creation of the musical fabric, and the genuineness born of personal experience that characterizes his interpretation of poetic texts.

KLAUS EGGE

Klaus Egge (1906–79) was another composer who was thoroughly caught up in the nationalist trend of the 1930s. That his personal style nonetheless developed in a completely different direction from that of either Groven or Sparre Olsen was owing both to the nature of his artistic gift and temper-

Klaus Egge (l.) and David Monrad Johansen. (Universitetsbiblioteket i Oslo)

ament and to his far more open attitude toward contemporary trends in European music.

Egge received his first music education at the conservatory in Oslo, where he completed his degree in organ. Later he studied piano with Nils Larsen and composition with Fartein Valen. In 1937–38 he studied with Walter Gmeindl at the music academy in Berlin. Thereafter he lived for the most part in Oslo, where he was a music critic for many years. He also served as chairman of the Society of Norwegian Composers from 1945 to 1972 and in this role did much to strengthen the national position of the profession. He was awarded an annual government stipend as a composer in 1949.

Egge's compositional activity may be divided into three periods. The first consists of his student years and extends to about 1938, when he returned to Norway from Berlin. His large works written in 1932–33 include *Sonata for Violin* (Op. 3), *Piano Sonata No. 1* (the "Dream Ballad" sonata, Op. 4), and a *String Quartet* (Op. 5). Somewhat later he wrote a chamber symphony (subsequently withdrawn), *Piano Concerto No. 1*, *Wind Quintet* (Op. 13), *Sveinung Vreim* (a large choral work), and a number of smaller vocal pieces.

Even in these early cyclic compositions Egge had developed a personal style. It is clearly evident, for example, in the "Dream Ballad" sonata, which is built on the traditional melodies of the ballad and, in the last movement, motives from the *slaatt* "Fille Vern." The sonata has four movements in the standard order, but the movements exhibit more the character of variations than of sonata form. The three folk melodies are presented in a slow introductory section. This is followed by an Allegro moderato consisting partly of variations in which the original form of the melodies is retained, partly of free variations based on individual motives taken from the melodies. The other movements consist of free variations in which the folk-music material is handled with considerable inventiveness.

Excepting the string quartet, in which an Eskimo melody is employed, Egge's other compositions from this period do not use folk tunes. Several recurring rhythmic and melodic features in these works, however, testify to the continuing influence of folk music. *Sveinung Vreim*, which Egge described as "a symphonic epic for soloists, mixed chorus, and orchestra," is a large choral work along the lines of the monumental nationalistic vocal compositions of Monrad Johansen, Irgens Jensen, and others.

A new turn in Egge's style became evident in 1939 in his three piano fantasias based on Norwegian *slaatt* rhythms: "Fantasia in Halling Rhythm," "Fantasia in Gangar Rhythm," and "Fantasia in Springar Rhythm." The use of folk-dance rhythms is evident from the titles of these pieces, but the structure and distinctive tonal foundation are largely derived from Norwegian *slaatt* music as well. The structure is consistently polyphonic. In "Fantasia in Halling Rhythm" (see example 58) the two lines are relatively independent of each other both rhythmically and melodically and at times they clash in harsh dissonances. Triadic harmony is totally abandoned; the third is more or less replaced by the fifth (or fourth) as the basic interval in the creation of the harmony.

The tonal foundation is diatonic and builds primarily on modal scales—or perhaps rather on varying tetrachords derived from modal scales. By a special technique involving the construction of tetrachords on different initial tones, Egge achieved an expanded tonality that enabled him to use all twelve tones of the scale within a diatonic style. This happens, for instance, in the "Fantasia in Halling Rhythm," the first part of which is given in example 58. It starts out in D Lydian, and the Lydian tetrachord beginning on d^2 is emphasized in measure 3. In measure 20 the same Lydian tetrachord begins on e^1, thus changing the key to E Lydian. Prior to this the key was changed to C Lydian in measure 14 by emphasizing the fifth C–G (especially in the left hand in measures 14 and 15). The impending key E Lydian is also anticipated by an A-sharp in measures 16, 17, and 19.

The harmonic foundation that appears here in crystallized form is presaged to some extent in Egge's earlier works as well. Even in the violin sonata—an early work—there are traces of this "expanded tonality," and in both the "Dream Ballad" sonata and the string quartet his fondness for chords constructed on fourths and fifths is conspicuous.

"Fantasia in Halling Rhythm" marks the beginning of Egge's second period as a composer, which roughly coincides with the years spanned by the German occupation. Among his most important compositions from this period are the *Trio for Piano, Violin, and Cello* (Op. 14), *Symphony No. 1* (Op. 17), and *Piano Concerto No. 2* (Op. 21). Also important are several vocal

Example 58. Klaus Egge, "Fantasia in Halling Rhythm."

works including "Norway, Land of Mountains" for soprano and orchestra (Op. 15), "Song of Norway" for mixed chorus and orchestra (Op. 16), "Dreams in Star-lit Snow" for soprano and orchestra (Op. 18), and his exquisite setting for mixed chorus of the folk tune "That Day Will Never Come."

This was an exceedingly important period in Egge's life as a composer. The first symphony was written in 1940–42 in memory of the Norwegian sailors who lost their lives during the war. In both the symphony and the piano trio the composer employed the Classical four-movement pattern, apart the exception that in the symphony the last two movements are combined into a rondo and fugue. The individual movements of these compositions also follow Classical models.

Piano Concerto No. 2 with string orchestra has the subtitle "Variations and fugue on a Norwegian folk tune." The tune from which all of the thematic material is derived is "Solfager and the Snake King." The first section consists of a theme with seven variations, followed by a solo cadenza in the piano that serves as a transition to the fugue. Although the entire concerto is played without a pause, an underlying four-movement structure is evident in that variations 5 and 6 form a kind of slow second movement and variation 7 has a distinctive scherzo-like character. The concluding fugue is in three sections and employs such typical polyphonic devices as inversion, augmentation, and strict counterpoint.

The folk-music tradition, so prominent in Egge's second period, became less apparent in his third. The first composition from this period was his three-movement *Symphony No.* 2 (Op. 22), written in 1947. Subtitled "Sinfonia giocosa," it is cheerier and lighter in character than most of his earlier works, containing fresh and lively rhythms in the outer movements that create an impression of gaiety. The middle movement is an expressive adagio with rich timbric variety. The second symphony was followed by other large works, most of them with orchestra. They include the *Violin Concerto No.* 1 (Op. 26), *Piano Sonata No.* 2 ("Sonata Patética," Op. 27), *Symphony No.* 3 ("Louisville Symphony," Op. 28), a cello concerto (Op. 29), and two more symphonies (Opp. 30 and 31).

Egge's later compositions represent a further development of the style that is characteristic of his second period. The structure of the music continues to be polyphonic; linear movement is the primary concern, the vertical aspect being of secondary importance. Regarding the structure of his music, Egge himself once said: "My harmony is just a direct result of the interaction of the melodic lines. My starting point is the lines, not the harmony. As a matter of fact, the tension between my contrapuntal lines is greater than that resulting from the relationships between the chords. My harmonies are merely supporting sounds." Fourths and fifths continue to be the basis of his chords, although stacked thirds (with dissonances) and seconds (tone clusters) occur more frequently than before.

Egge's compositions during this period tended toward twelve-tone music but without losing the feeling for a tonal center. In both *Symphony No.* 4 ("Sinfonia seriale sopra BACH-EGGE") and *Symphony No.* 5 ("Sinfonia dolce") the themes are derived from twelve-tone series, but Egge did not restrict himself to the dodecaphonic technique in the narrow sense. One notes in Egge's compositions a greater emphasis on motivic development, sometimes in the direction of a metamorphic technique. This phenomenon can be seen, for example, in his third symphony, a single-movement work whose form results from this technique.

Notwithstanding the differences that can be noted among the various periods of Egge's life as a composer, a powerful, strong-willed personality with a fiery temperament is evident throughout. A vigorous rhythm is often the driving force in his music, and although its structure changed through the years the starting point was always the line, the melodic movement. His mooring in Norwegian folk music is most evident in his early compositions, but one can also feel it as an undercurrent in his later works, which in other respects are more international in character.

GEIRR TVEITT

One of the most extreme representatives of the nationalist trend in the 1930s was Geirr Tveitt (1908–81). His youth and maturation coincided with the full flowering of this movement, and he remained completely absorbed in it even after most other composers realized that it was a blind alley. He went so far as to write a long treatise in which he attempted to develop a new system of music theory and method of composition based on what he thought was a distinctively Old Norse foundation. Fortunately, his compositions are considerably better than his theories, despite a certain unevenness in his abundant production.

Tveitt grew up in Kvam in the county of Hardanger. His family was keenly interested in music, and as a child he learned to play both violin and piano. A fairly rich folk-music tradition still flourished in Hardanger at that time. The vocal part of that tradition was especially robust, so Tveitt became acquainted with it at an early age.

He planned initially to become an architect, but while attending high school at Voss his interest in music became so strong that he changed his plans. In 1928 he went to Leipzig, studying with Hermann Grabner and Leopold Wenninger among others. The years 1932–35 were spent in Vienna and Paris: in Vienna he studied with Egon Wellesz, in Paris with Arthur Honegger and Hector Villa-Lobos.

Tveitt developed an interest in modal scales rather early in his career. In 1929 (during his studies in Leipzig), for example, he wrote twelve two-part inventions built on modal scales. Although his later style was in general less polyphonic, modal scales nonetheless remained the basis for virtually all of his compositions. Even with respect to his ill-fated attempt to lay a theoretical foundation for a new Nordic technique of composition, his basic thesis was that the modal scales are in reality old Scandinavian modes (to which he accordingly gave Old Norse names). Using the Lydian scale—which has a leading tone to both the tonic and the fifth—as his starting point, he developed an original theory of cadences wherein these two leading tones are resolved by parallel motion (in fifths or fourths) to the tonic and fifth. Parallel fifths are a frequent feature in Tveitt's compositions.

Tveitt lived in Oslo from 1935 to 1942. He then moved to Hardanger, but he also lived abroad for long periods of time and gave concerts in various countries. In his later years he again lived primarily in Oslo. He was awarded an annual government stipend in 1941. In the early 1960s he became associated with the Norwegian State Radio and produced a number of programs, using material from various Norwegian poets.

Tveitt was an unusually prolific composer; it is believed that he created at least three hundred works. Many have never been performed, however, and only a few have been published. His compositions include five operas, three symphonies, three ballets, six piano concertos, a violin concerto, two Hardanger-fiddle concertos, possibly as many as thirty-six piano sonatas, several short orchestral pieces, and a large number of songs. His first large work was the ballet *Baldur's Dreams*, which was based on an ancient legend about the Norse god. It calls for chorus, soloists, and a full orchestra with an expanded percussion section including, among other things, nine timpani tuned pentatonically. The same style was employed in the 1939 ballet *Birgingu* and his first opera, *Dragare-dokko*, also based on an ancient legend.

Tveitt's fifth opera, *Jeppe*, was based on Ludvig Holberg's comedy *Jeppe of the Hill*. It was premiered at the Bergen International Festival in 1966, then revised and offered again at the Bergen festival in 1968, and later performed in Oslo. Though somewhat inconsistent in quality, it reflects considerable imagination and dramatic ability. Of his symphonies only the first, subtitled "Christmas Eve," has been performed. Most of his concertos have been performed several times, however.

A Hundred Hardanger Tunes for orchestra occupies a unique position among Tveitt's compositions. While living in Hardanger from 1942 to 1945, he collected over a thousand folk tunes from which he selected one hundred to arrange in two versions, one for piano and one for orchestra. The orchestration displays admirable feeling and demonstrates an intimate knowledge of instrumental resources both individually and in ensemble. As so often in Tveitt's compositions, short and highly rhythmic motives are set against the melodies, usually as an ostinato accompaniment. Portions of suites 1 and 4 of this work are among the most colorful orchestral scores created in Norway in recent years.

Despite Tveitt's extremely conservative theories, his use of instruments was experimental in a number of his later works. In several places in the orchestral version of *A Hundred Hardanger Tunes* the strings are employed in an original way, and the piano edition occasionally calls for an unorthodox manner of playing—for example, plucking the strings. His *Piano Sonata No. 29* ("Sonata etere," Op. 129) calls for silently depressed chord clusters, the overtones of which are then made to sound by the staccato playing of notes outside the chord clusters. The resulting sound is to be manipulated dynamically by means of a microphone and amplifier. Here, then, Tveitt stood on the border of electronic music.

A number of Tveitt's compositions may be considered program music. His first symphony, for example, has the subtitle "Christmas Eve." One orchestral piece is entitled "The Water Sprite." His second Hardanger-fiddle concerto is entitled "Three Fjords" and is supposed to depict the Sognefjord, the Hardangerfjord, and the Nordfjord. Considered in conjunction with the fact that a considerable number of his compositions are in the category of dramatic music (ballets and operas), these programmatic titles seem to underscore the fact that Tveitt's artistic inspirations were often associated with visual or other non-musical impressions. Nearly all of the folk tunes that he chose for *A Hundred Hardanger Tunes* are vocal melodies with texts that seem to have struck a responsive chord in the composer's musical imagination.

Tveitt's later compositions included a "Hymn to Freedom" for Janissary band (1968) and a "Sinfonietta" for winds (1970). For his radio programs in the 1960s he composed a number of songs and ballads, many of which have become popular in Norway. They confirm Tveitt's melodic ability in the small forms.

Relatively little of Tveitt's extensive oeuvre has been published. It was therefore a tragedy that many of his manuscripts were destroyed when the house on his farm in Hardanger was destroyed by fire in 1970. A number of his compositions exist in manuscript or in copies in other places, and some badly damaged manuscripts were retrieved from the ruins. It must be assumed, however, that much of his work is irretrievably lost.

NORWEGIAN MUSIC LIFE IN THE TWENTIETH CENTURY

The Oslo Philharmonic Orchestra and the Bergen Philharmonic Orchestra are the twin cornerstones of concert life in Norway today. Other important ensembles include the Trondheim Symphony Orchestra, which has had both state and civic support since 1936, and the Norwegian State Radio Orchestra, which was started in 1946.

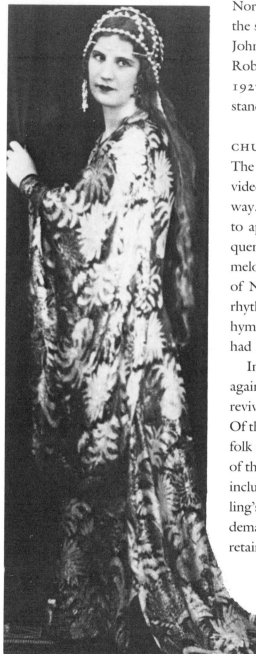

Kirsten Flagstad as Desdemona in Verdi's opera Otello. *(Universitetsbiblioteket i Oslo)*

Norway has produced many outstanding performers during the twentieth century. At the top of the list, certainly, is the famous opera singer Kirsten Flagstad (1895–1962). She was especially renowned for her Wagnerian roles and performed in most of the larger opera houses in Europe and America. Other female singers who have achieved international success are Aase Nordmo Lövberg (b. 1923) and Ingrid Bjoner (b. 1927). One of Norway's foremost pianists was Fridtjof Backer Gröndahl (1885–1959), the son of Agathe Backer Gröndahl. Other prominent pianists include Ivar Johnsen (1908–78) and the Riefling brothers, Reimar (1898–1981) and Robert (1911–88). Among the younger pianists are Eva Knardahl (b. 1927) and Kjell Baekkelund (b. 1930). Arve Tellefsen (b. 1936) is an outstanding violinist who has developed an international reputation.

CHURCH MUSIC

The publication in 1926 of the *Chorale Book for the Norwegian Church* provided a new resource for the development of congregational singing in Norway. Prior to that time the Lindeman chorale book of 1877 had continued to appear in successive editions that contained no changes of any consequence. Its strength lay not least in the large number of Lindeman's own melodies, which had become an integral part of the hymnody of the Church of Norway. Efforts by Winter-Hjelm and others to restore the original rhythmic forms of the chorales had failed, and Erik Hoff's collection of hymn tunes—including some of the old chorales in their rhythmic forms—had little influence (see p. 156).

In the new chorale book the reformist endeavors came to the fore once again. The original rhythms of several of the older chorale melodies were revived, though in most cases the isometric form was included as an option. Of the 278 melodies in the new chorale book, 39 were Norwegian religious folk songs, a type of hymn not represented in Lindeman's hymnal. Several of these were already being sung in some congregations. The folk melodies included in the 1926 chorale book were taken largely from Catharinus Elling's eleven volumes of religious folk tunes, though some came from Lindeman's collections. Fifty-one of Lindeman's original hymn tunes were also retained. It was a rich but stylistically diverse collection of melodies.

The executive secretary of the editorial committee was O. M. Sandvik. Eyvind Alnaes was responsible for the harmonizations. In general, Alnaes continued Lindeman's tradition but made somewhat more liberal use of Romantic harmonies. Despite some unevenness, one would have to say that within the confines of his chosen style most of Alnaes's harmonizations are quite good.

In 1927, just one year after the publication of the authorized chorale book, a new collection of hymns by clergyman-composer Jacob Sletten appeared under the title *A Hymnal for the Norwegian People*. Prior to this, however, Sletten had sent a number of original hymns to the hymnal committee, and eight of them had been included in the new chorale book. Among these were "The Church of Our Fathers in Norway" and "Behold, He Comes to Sinful Man." Thus his best hymn tunes were included in the chorale book of 1926 and his own collection had little practical effect.

A chorale book (containing melodies and harmonies but no texts) published some years later did have a far-reaching effect, however. It was the work of Per Steenberg (1870–1947), though it was not published until 1949, two years after Steenberg's death. It precipitated a considerable amount of discussion, for here the ideals of the reformists in the hymn controversy that had raged with such intensity in Norway during the years preceding the publication of the chorale book of 1877 (see p. 155) finally were fully expressed. Steenberg restored the old rhythmic form of several chorales as they had been sung in the fifteenth and sixteenth centuries, omitted melodies included in the authorized chorale book that he considered unsuitable for congregational singing, and included a considerable number of melodies that he himself had composed.

The biggest break with the prevailing tradition in Norwegian hymnody, however, was Steenberg's harmonizations of the chorale melodies. He provided new harmonizations for all of them, in most cases in a style similar to that used in chorales around 1600. The fact that he used similar harmonies in a number of the newer chorales, such as those by Lindeman, was severely criticized by some. Steenberg's book was never authorized for use in the Church of Norway, but it had considerable influence on Norwegian church music nonetheless—as, indeed, did the entire church-music movement (see below) of which Steenberg was the leader in Norway.

Steenberg completed his degree in organ at the music conservatory in Oslo in 1891. Thereafter he studied with Johannes Haarklou and Christian Cappelen, and later left for a period of further study in Leipzig. In 1902 he became organist in the Vaalerengen Church in Oslo, and from 1927 to 1940 he was organist at St. Mark's Church, also in Oslo. He was highly regarded as a teacher of music theory and had many pupils. In his later years he taught at the Oslo Music Conservatory.

It was only toward the end of his career that he began working with the late Renaissance choral style. His earlier compositions—e.g., *Church Cantata* (1913), *Cantata for the Dedication of a Church* (1927), and several organ compositions—were in a late Romantic style, influenced to some extent by Cappelen. Toward the end of the 1920s he became involved in the Laub

Movement, a Danish reform movement that sought a renewal of church music based on the chorales of the Reformation era. The stylistic ideals of this group were shaped partly by the writings of Thomas Laub (*Music and Church, Danish Hymnody*, and others), and partly by Knud Jeppesen's studies in the music of Palestrina. Especially influential was the latter's monograph, *The Style of Palestrina and the Dissonance* (original publication, 1923; English translation, 1927).

Steenberg's most important works after he became associated with the Laub Movement are his *Choir Songs for Divine Worship* (1930–38) and the previously mentioned chorale book. The choir anthems, consisting of motets and short arrangements of chorale melodies, are for the most part in what could almost be called a late Renaissance choral style. Several of Steenberg's original chorale melodies have become well established in Norwegian hymnody. Among them are his tunes for "Surely Thou Art King" and "Love from God," which were included in the hymnal of 1926.

Both through his own compositions and as a teacher Steenberg had a considerable influence on Norwegian church music. With respect to style, however, the leading Norwegian composers of church music who came after him have moved in quite different directions. Many Norwegian composers of this period have written church music; indeed, the chief compositions and efforts of some of them have been in this area. The oldest of these after Steenberg are Fridthjov Anderssen and Sigurd Islandsmoen, then Arild Sandvold and Ludvig Nielsen. Paul Okkenhaug and Rolf Karlsen will also be discussed here, although they might be considered among the next generation of composers.

Fridthjov Anderssen (1876–1937) received his training at the Oslo Music Conservatory in 1893–95, where his teachers included Gustav Lange and Catharinus Elling. In 1901–02 and again in 1918–19 he studied in Leipzig, with Emil Paul and Salomon Jadassohn.

Anderssen was born in northern Norway and his entire professional life was spent in that area of the country. He was organist in the Bodin Church from 1902 to 1904 and in the Bodö Church from 1904 until his death in 1937. A music teacher, choral director, and orchestral conductor as well as an organist, he played an important role in the music life of Bodö and the surrounding area. His compositions include pieces for male chorus, organ works, and a "Kyrie eleison" for mixed chorus. The last mentioned, his best-known composition in Norway, is a fugue that demonstrates sound compositional technique and fine musical sense. His organ works include several fugues, a broadly conceived fantasia based on the chorale "In Deepest Need," and a festival prelude on the chorale "From Heaven Above to Earth I Come" that provides for an optional ensemble of five brass instruments. Anderssen wrote several larger works for male chorus, including the cantatas *Ocean Wave* (text by Anders Hovden), *Song of Departure* (text by Per Sivle), *North Norway* (text by Knut Hamsun), and a cantata for the city of Bodö's centennial jubilee in 1916. He also published a number of folk-tune arrangements for male chorus. Other works include piano pieces. songs with piano accompaniment, and orchestral compositions.

Sigurd Islandsmoen (1881–1964) also received his music training at the Oslo Music Conservatory and in Leipzig, where he studied with Max Reger. While in Leipzig he was exposed to the colorful harmony of late Romanticism, and it influenced his style for the rest of his life. Stylistically, therefore, he was the opposite of the later Steenberg. Islandsmoen was an organist in Moss (south of Oslo) from 1916 to 1961, and he became an active participant in the music life of the city as well. He founded the Moss Choral Society as well as the Moss Orchestral Society, and over a period of many years presented about fifty oratorios.

The greater part of his music consists of large sacred choral works. He wrote two oratorios, *Israel in Captivity* (1931) and *Homeward from Babel* (1934), and a *Requiem* (1943). He also wrote an opera entitled *Gudrun Laugar*, a number of orchestral works (including two symphonies and a "Norwegian Overture"), chamber music, piano and organ works, and several choral pieces. His best-known composition is the choral work "Dawn in the Forest." Islandsmoen had a deep interest in folk tunes. He himself collected some in his native region of Valdres, and he also arranged several folk tunes for string orchestra. Occasionally he employed folk tunes in his own compositions. His *Requiem*, for example, contains a number of themes and motives taken from Valdres folk tunes.

Arild Sandvold (1895–1984) held a central position in Norwegian church music for many years. As both cantor and organist in Our Savior's Church in Oslo (from 1933 to 1966) and as an organ teacher at the conservatory (from 1917 to 1969), he had considerable influence on the development of sacred music. The hallmark of his work was his insistence on high standards in the music of the church. No matter what his function, whether as organist or conductor or pedagogue, his impact extended far beyond the borders of the city in which he worked.

Sandvold was yet another Norwegian musician to receive his training at the conservatories in Oslo and Leipzig. At the latter he was a pupil of Karl Straube. His first appointment as an organist in Oslo was in 1914, and in 1933 he succeeded Eyvind Alnaes at Our Savior's Church. As conductor of the Cecilia Society (1928–57) he initiated many oratorio performances. He was awarded an annual government stipend in 1956.

Sandvold wrote several cantatas, including the *Cantata for the Norwegian Mission Society's Centennial Jubilee*. It was originally written for mixed chorus, soloists, and organ, but for a performance in 1967 it was also orchestrated. This work is quite effective and probably should be ranked as his most important composition. He also wrote several smaller choral pieces and a considerable number of organ works. Worthy of special mention among the latter are *Six Improvisations on Norwegian Folk Tunes, Introduction and Passacaglia,* an *Organ Sonata* in F minor, sets of variations on "Lord, I Long to Show Thy Glory" and "I Know a Fortress in Heaven," *Fantasia and Toccata* on a theme of Haydn, and *Prelude and Double Fugue* in A minor.

Sandvold's musical style is deeply rooted in late Romanticism. His organ compositions unite a colorful harmony and timbric variety with strict Neoclassical polyphonic structures such as fugues and passacaglias. The Neoclassical influence appears to have become stronger in his later years.

Ludvig Nielsen (b. 1906) also received his music training in Oslo and Leipzig. In Oslo he studied with Arild Sandvold, in Leipzig with Karl Straube and Günter Raphael. He was an organist in Oslo for several years and from 1935 to 1976 was cantor and organist at the Nidaros cathedral in Trondheim. He was also active as a choral conductor and composer.

Like Sandvold, his background is late Romantic organ music. His own compositions reflect many of the same characteristics, perhaps with an even stronger emphasis on polyphonic devices, which he commands with great competence. He has written a number of choral works including a *Te Deum, Mass for St. Olaf's Day, Songs of Joy,* and *The Dream Ballad, a Liturgical Oratorio.* Especially noteworthy among his many organ compositions are *Concerto for Organ and Strings,* "St. Olaf's Day Fantasia," a set of variations on the hymn "None Achieve the Peace Eternal," and "Passacaglia on the Dream Ballad." He also wrote a number of fine organ chorales for *Pro Organo,* a collection that he published in collaboration with Rolf Karlsen.

Paul Okkenhaug (1908–75) received most of his music education at the Oslo Music Conservatory, where he studied organ with Sandvold and composition with Brustad and Monrad Johansen.

Okkenhaug was deeply involved in the music life in north Tröndelag, the region north of Trondheim. Among other things, he was organist in the Levanger Church from 1948 until his death. He traveled around Tröndelag, giving concerts as a pianist and organist and also taking advantage of the opportunity to collect folk tunes from the region. As a composer he is best known for his incidental music for *The Play of St. Olaf* (text by Olav Gullvaag), which is performed annually at the St. Olaf's Day celebration at Stiklestad. Orchestral works deserving mention include "Lyric Dance," "Folla," and "Soga." He also wrote a number of fine songs and piano pieces.

Rolf Karlsen (1911–82), who succeeded Arild Sandvold as cantor and organist at Our Savior's Church in Oslo in 1966, studied with both Sandvold and Steenberg. In addition to a busy career as an organist and choral director he composed a large body of music for use in the church. Among his more ambitious works are an organ sonata and a cantata, *Praise the Lord, O My Soul*, for three mixed choruses, winds, and organ. The latter was composed for a festival of sacred song held in Stavanger in 1963 and sponsored by the Church of Norway. He collaborated with Ludvig Nielsen on the publication of *Pro Organo*, and also published a collection of sacred choral pieces entitled *Hymnarium*.

12

Music Since 1950

Perhaps the most important cultural change that has occurred in the second half of the twentieth century is what might be called the internationalization of the human community. The so-called "information revolution" has created an entirely new situation for humankind, one in which—thanks to such recent technological developments as stationary earth satellites and fiber optics— news originating anywhere on earth can be communicated almost instantly to people everywhere.

Norway has shared fully in this development, and in the process has emerged as an important and responsible member of the international community. It has, for example, participated actively in the work of the United Nations; indeed, Trygve Lie, the first secretary-general of the UN, was a Norwegian statesman. Norway has also accepted a large number of refugees from third-world nations and has provided generous amounts of relief aid to the poorer countries of the world. Though it is not a member of the European Community, Norway has worked closely with that organization to forge bonds of cooperation that will likely grow progressively stronger as the EC matures. Thus, despite its geographical isolation on the northern edge of Europe, Norway's political stance as the twentieth century comes to a close is one of significant engagement in the major challenges facing the human community.

The development of oil and gas reserves in the North Sea starting in 1971 has changed Norwegian society in many ways and has further underscored the country's interdependence with the rest of the world. Norway's economy has become heavily dependent on the oil industry; thus a relatively small variation in the price of oil or in the value of the American dollar (in which oil prices are denominated worldwide) has a profound effect on the Norwegian economy. The "oil boom" has been largely responsible for transforming Norway in a single generation from a relatively poor country into one that today enjoys one of the highest standards of living in the world. Moreover, policies regarding taxation and the distribution of wealth have been such that the benefits of this newfound prosperity are widely shared among the people, including those who live in remote areas. It is not an overstatement to say that most Norwegians today have adequate food, clothing, and housing as well as access to education, medical and dental care, transportation, travel, and recreational opportunities that were unthinkable in the very recent past.

Norway's economic prosperity has had a significant impact on the arts, including music. Professional orchestras have been enlarged, new concert halls have been built in some of the larger cities, and art-music opportunities have been expanded in many rural areas. The number of composers receiving government stipends has also increased significantly.

The growing cultural diversity of this once rather insular society is also reflected in its music. No longer do nearly all aspiring young Norwegian composers go to Leipzig or Berlin for their advanced training. Many are able to complete their studies at the Norwegian State Academy of Music, where instruction in composition has been offered since the opening of the academy in 1973. Those who have studied abroad have gone to a much wider variety of places than was the case in earlier years. Paris has been a popular destination since about mid-century, but other young composers have sought advanced educational opportunities in such places as Vienna, Warsaw, Utrecht, London, and various conservatories and universities in the United States. Within the Nordic countries, Stockholm, Copenhagen, and Helsinki have also continued to draw a significant number of Norwegian music students.

PRINCIPAL TRENDS

To identify the principal trends in Norwegian music against this varied background is not an easy task. What appears is a perplexing picture, with movements in several directions at the same time. Within the constant ebb and flow of this ever-changing seascape, however, one can discern two main currents. The first is Neoexpressionism, which takes as its point of departure the principles of the Second Viennese school. Included in this category is "twelve-tone music," a term used in a rather broad sense to describe any music that fairly consistently uses all twelve tones in the octave, whether or not it employs them as a tone row. The term "serial" music is used only in cases in which several parameters of the music (i.e., not merely the pitch) are arranged in series. The twelve-tone style of music was fairly prominent in Norway (as, indeed, in all of Europe) at mid-century but has slowly declined since that time. It has, however, continued to challenge and inspire a number of composers. Serialism and electro-acoustic techniques had a strong influence on the more radical composers, but this trend has waned somewhat in recent years. Other forms of Neoexpressionism have continued to play a major role, however, with Norwegian composers having been especially influenced by the music of the Polish composers Witold Lutoslawski and Krzysztof Penderecki. Minimalism is yet another musical style that emerged during the present half-century within the context of Neoexpressionism. The term denotes music that creates the impression of being static through extensive use of repeated melodic and/or rhythmic motives. This style of music appears to have engaged the efforts of a number of American and English composers from the 1960s onward, but its influence on Norwegian composers has been only sporadic.

The other principal current, which has no generic name, emphasizes the cultivation of melody. This emphasis is evident in many recent compositions for such solo instruments as flute and oboe and also in the strong interest in polyphony that continues to characterize many Norwegian composers. The 1960s constituted a decade of great experimentation among Norwegian composers, but in the 1970s there was a shift toward a simpler and more accessible musical style as composers became fully aware of the great distance that had developed between their sophisticated language and the tastes of ordinary music lovers. Thus in the music of the 1970s we find increasingly frequent use of traditional melodic and rhythmic elements. This attempt at *rapprochement* with the public is often referred to in Norway as the *nyvennlig* ("new friendly") style—a term that may be used either as a compliment or as a reproach, depending on the speaker's attitude toward what these composers are trying to do. It is clear, in any case, that a definite change has occurred in the stance and mode of expression of a number of composers. The problem for these composers, of course, is to find ways to make use of the more familiar and traditional musical resources without falling into mere clichés and pale copies of a glorious past. The danger of this possibility is undeniable; indeed, there are cases in which it has happened. Nonetheless, the *nyvennlig* style has also produced some important and interesting works in recent years.

The term Neoromanticism has also been used to describe some *nyvennlig* music, but the two are not synonymous. The term Postmodernism is generally used to describe the stylistically more radical wing of the *nyvennlig* movement. Composers in the latter group frequently borrow easily recognizable quotations from earlier composers and more concealed stylistic conventions derived from the past. The purpose of these borrowings is to establish contact with a broader listening audience while continuing to employ the wide range of stylistic tools available to a composer in the late twentieth century. Thus these composers tend to give a complex and constantly changing stylistic impression.

The sheer number of composers active in Norway during the latter half of the twentieth century is so large that it will perhaps be helpful if we divide them into several groups—though it must be acknowledged that any such grouping is rather arbitrary and does not do justice to the rich variety in the works of many individuals. In what follows, therefore, the reader should bear in mind that these groups do not have precise boundaries and that many composers might reasonably be placed in a different category.

We will, then, discuss as a group those composers who have been especially involved in sacred music. Another group has been influenced by jazz and will be discussed under this rubric. During the 1950s and 1960s still another group of Norwegian composers was strongly influenced by the radical trends in contemporary continental music—first serialism, then Neoexpressionism. These composers can be quite clearly distinguished from their contemporaries who continued to build primarily on the Neoclassical tradition in European music and to some extent also on the nationalist tradition. All of these groups can be traced up to the time of this writing. Another group of recent composers will be discussed under the rubric Postmodernists. The boundaries between this group and the others are particularly hard to draw, however.

OPERAS AND PUBLIC CONCERTS

The most important new music institution in Norway in recent years is the Norwegian Opera Company, which opened in Oslo in 1959 with Kirsten Flagstad as director. It finally gave Norway a much-needed permanent opera company, and its national influence has grown steadily through the years. Its repertoire has consisted for the most part of standard, well-known operas, but a number of newer works have also been performed. Among the latter are several new operas by Norwegian composers, including some commissioned works. The opera ballet has also gained a secure place in Norwegian cultural life with a repertoire of both older and newer works. The opera company has taken a number of productions, both operas and ballets, on tour to various parts of the country. So far as possible, tour performances have been given in cooperation with local orchestras in the communities involved.

Professional orchestras have been maintained in the larger cities throughout this period. The Oslo Philharmonic and the Bergen Philharmonic have continued to enjoy national preeminence, while the symphony orchestras in Trondheim and Stavanger have grown in size and quality in recent years.

The construction of new concert halls in several cities has also had a stimulating cultural effect. Oslo's new concert hall (Konserthuset) opened in 1977, Bergen's (Grieghallen) in 1978, and Stavanger's (Konserthallen) in 1980. Concerts are generally well attended; regular concert series seem especially to have loyal audiences. As might be expected, symphonic programs involve a mixture of selections from the standard concert repertoire and contemporary works. Both the Oslo and the Bergen orchestras have undertaken successful international tours and released widely acclaimed recordings.

The Bergen Music Festival deserves special mention. This annual event has played a major role in acquainting foreigners with Norwegian music and music life. The festival has increased in scope and importance since its inception in 1953 and in recent years has comprised a large number of diverse events including concerts, operas, ballets, plays, and folklore and art exhibits. Other cities also have launched annual music festivals in recent years, albeit on a more modest scale. Among them are Elverum, Harstad, Kongsberg, Kristiansand, Molde, and Trondheim.

New Music (the Norwegian chapter of the International Society for Contemporary Music), after an uncertain beginning in 1938, has now risen to a respected position of national cultural importance. One of its many achievements under the leadership of its longtime chairman, Pauline Hall, was its sponsorship of the ISCM international music festival in Oslo in 1953. More recently, the association has organized regular concerts in which contemporary music of both national and international origin has been presented. Local chapters of the association have also been established in various parts of the country, and these in turn arrange concerts of contemporary music in their own communities. Since 1977 the association has published a journal named *Ballade*.

MUSIC OUTSIDE THE LARGER CITIES

Fortunately, the concerts given in the larger cities constitute only a small part of the music life of modern Norway. The major orchestras of these urban centers promote a wide dissemination of music by providing concerts throughout the country. Other concerts and various musical events, both amateur and professional, can also be found in many smaller towns and villages, and the practice of making music together in private groups continues to thrive everywhere.

An agency called the Norwegian State Concert Bureau plays an important role in facilitating public musical events. Established in 1967, it organizes and supports concerts throughout the country. Thus it is an important force for the expansion of such activity into areas of Norway that would otherwise not have such opportunities.

The 1970s saw the appointment of the first "county musicians" as part of a new effort that has great promise for the further proliferation of music and music literacy. The objective is to place in each county a group of professional musicians who will offer public concerts, give private lessons, and in other ways encourage the development of music in the community. It began on an experimental basis in 1974 with the assignment of four such musicians to each of the three northernmost counties in Norway. The arrangement has since undergone various changes and has been extended beyond the original three counties, becoming an important cultural factor particularly in the rural areas. At present, some forty groups comprising about 150 professional musicians are employed in this effort. Funds for the salaries of the musicians come from the Norwegian State Concert Bureau, from the respective counties, and from the local communities.

The Norwegian Broadcasting Company (NRK) also does much to make music available to the wider public. Because its radio and television programs reach a large percentage of the population, its responsibility is great. The NRK has a large staff and excellent broadcasting facilities. It has its own orchestra with a large repertoire of both lighter music and classical music, and it also arranges for regular broadcasts by the major Norwegian orchestras.

Happily, amateur music continues to thrive in Norway despite the many opportunities for passive entertainment offered by radio, television, cinema, and recordings. A number of institutions and associations encourage the development of opportunities for amateur music activities. Among the most important and robust of these organizations are the bands—some affiliated with schools, others operating as independent or community youth bands. The Norwegian Band Federation works effectively to enhance the quality of these ensembles through various methods of instruction. The number of choruses has declined somewhat, but local groups affiliated with the Norwegian Choral Association continue to function in many communities. Much choral activity in Norway is associated with the church and will be dealt with in connection with a more detailed discussion of church music.

Interest in Norwegian folk music has burgeoned again in recent years. *Slaatt* music and folk dancing have become very popular, but folk songs have also experienced something of a renaissance. Fiddling, singing, and dancing contests—especially the annual national events, which draw large crowds—play an important role in preserving and strengthening the folk-music tradition. Both the old *slaatt* dances and the more recent *gammeldans* ("old dance") are being widely used once again.

Opportunities for music education in Norway have been greatly expanded in recent years. The Oslo Music Conservatory was the principal institution of advanced study in music in Norway from its inception in 1883

The jazz orchestra Sixpence, which performed in the Oslo area during the 1920s. (Norsk Jazzarkiv)

until well into the twentieth century. In 1969 the conservatory was converted into a private school that continues to receive public support. Four years later the State Academy of Music was established in Oslo. Its first rector, Robert Levin (b. 1912), is also known as a distinguished accompanist who has toured Europe with a number of internationally renowned artists. The academy provides high-quality, performance-oriented music training. Similar training but with a more academic emphasis is offered by the institutes of musicology at the universities in Oslo and Trondheim.

Regional conservatories have been expanded and strengthened in recent years. There are now seven such conservatories located in Bergen, Drammen, Kristiansand, Oslo, Stavanger, Tromsö, and Trondheim. Local music schools have also been established in a number of communities, with instructional programs that vary according to local needs and interests.

JAZZ IN NORWAY

Jazz first emerged in Norway during the 1920s and gathered further momentum during the following decade. Initially, the interest in jazz was largely nourished by recordings and concerts given by visiting American jazz musicians. During the 1930s, for example, both Louis Armstrong (1934) and Jimmie Lunceford (1939) brought their orchestras to Oslo. Many Norwegian musicians with an interest in jazz took jobs on the large passenger

ships sailing regularly between Oslo and New York, and in this way heard such music as it was played in the United States.

One of the earliest jazz ensembles in Norway was an Oslo-based group called Sixpence, which was organized by the pianist Fenger Grön. It performed throughout the Oslo area during the 1920s. During the 1930s another group, Funny Boys, became the first Norwegian jazz band to perform outside of Norway. It was established in 1931 and underwent several personnel changes, but for a long time it consisted of Svein Övergaard, Karl W. Engström, Finn Westby, and Gunnar Sönstevold. In addition to playing in the Oslo area, the group made several successful tours to the continent before disbanding in 1939. In the late 1930s the leading jazz ensemble in Norway was a group called String Swing, whose members included the guitarist Robert Norman. Rowland Greenberg, a central figure in Norwegian jazz for many years, also began his career at that time. Born in 1920, he became a member of Funny Boys when he was quite young. Later he played with various other groups and became a prominent jazz trumpeter.

During World War II jazz was forbidden in Norway, so it withdrew to clandestine gatherings to survive. This situation obviously limited its development for a time, but within a few years after the end of the war jazz came to flourish again in Norway.

Norwegian jazz has always been a slightly delayed reflection of the American original. Nonetheless, the jazz milieu in Norway has at times attained considerable stature and a number of Norwegian jazz musicians have achieved international reputations. A group called Big Chief Jazzband has been an important representative of jazz both in Norway and abroad since the early 1950s. It has proven to be one of the most durable and traveled jazz groups in Norway, with three of its members—Gerhard Aspheim, Eivind Solberg, and Björn Pedersen—remaining in the group over the years. In the first decade of its existence this group became the center of renewed interest in traditional jazz. It reached the peak of its influence in the early 1960s, when it operated a jazz club called Metropol Jazz Centre. The group often performed there with great success, and it also arranged for performances by many other jazz groups, Norwegian and foreign. Metropol Jazz Centre became an internationally known mecca for jazz and jazz musicians during these years.

The 1950s saw a particularly rapid growth of interest in jazz throughout Norway. Jazz clubs were started in many cities and towns, and in 1953 the Norwegian Jazz Federation was founded. Among the jazz musicians who launched their careers in this decade are Mikkel Flagstad, Kristian Bergheim, Björn Johansen (all saxophonists), Frode Thingnaes (trombonist), Erik Amundsen (bassist), and Einar Iversen (pianist).

The annual Norwegian jazz festivals have for a number of years helped greatly in promoting interest in jazz in Norway. The first such festival was held in Molde in 1961, and in 1964 a similar series was launched in Kongsberg. "Bergen Night Jazz," which is held in connection with the music festival in that lovely city, has also become an annual event. These festivals provide an opportunity for interaction between Norwegian jazz enthusiasts and outstanding jazz bands from abroad, and they have grown rapidly in both scope and artistic importance.

The festivals managed to survive the devastating decline that struck Norwegian jazz in about 1965, as a result of which all of the jazz clubs in Norway except those in Molde and Kongsberg disbanded. The decline undoubtedly had many causes, but one important factor certainly was the ascendance of the popular music that captured the interest of the younger generation at this time. Jazz musicians responded by taking the initiative in attempting to restore interest in jazz as a living form of musical expression. The Norwegian Jazz Forum was founded in 1965, and in succeeding years it arranged for a number of concerts. It soon became apparent that jazz still had a number of faithful devotees in Norway, and little by little jazz began once again to come into its own. The renewed interest in jazz includes some who prefer the traditional jazz forms, others who favor the modern trends in jazz that have recently come to the fore.

The American jazz composer and performer George Russell, who spent a good deal of time in Norway and Sweden in the late 1960s, was an important inspiration for Norwegian jazz. He performed with Norwegian jazz musicians, established his own sextet, made recordings, and served as an example and teacher for composers, arrangers, and performers. Several of Norway's best jazz musicians were strongly influenced by him.

The medium has continued to flourish in Norway since the 1970s, with a number of individuals and groups making their mark both in Norway and abroad. One of the preeminent performers during this time has been Karin Krog, who was for many years the undisputed queen of female jazz singers in Norway. Another outstanding performer is Anne Marie Görtz, who has developed something of an international reputation as a vocalist. Norway's most outstanding jazz instrumentalists during this period are saxophonists Bjarne Nerem (b. 1923) and Jan Garbarek (b. 1947), percussionist Jo Christensen (b. 1943), bassist Arild Andersen (b. 1945), and guitarist Terje Rypdal (b. 1947). Jan Garbarek has also been active as a jazz composer. During the 1980s the jazz groups Masqualero and Ytre Sulöens Jazz Ensemble began to emerge on the international scene.

COMPOSERS WITH A BACKGROUND IN JAZZ

There are several Norwegian composers whose experience has included some involvement in jazz and whose compositions reflect this background in greater or lesser degree. The oldest of these is Gunnar Sönstevold (b. 1912), who in the 1930's was a member of the jazz group Funny Boys. A native of Elverum, Sönstevold has had a highly varied career as a composer and performer. He began as a café and jazz musician, while at the same time studying piano with Erling Westher and Nils Larsen and theory and harmony with Karl Andersen. During the war he lived in Sweden, where he studied composition with Hilding Rosenberg and participated in the so-called "Monday Group" of young Swedish composers who met regularly for conversation and discussion.

Sönstevold returned to Norway in 1945 and quickly established himself as a film composer, writing music for *Bound for England*, *Operation Swallow*, *Nine Lives*, and several other films. Later he also wrote incidental music for such dramatic works as Shakespeare's *The Tempest* (1959) and the ballet *Bendik and Aarolilja* (1960). In the former and in an "Intermezzo" for violin and soprano composed during the same period he employed electronically generated sounds, the first time this had been done by a Norwegian composer. He was not satisfied with his training in composition, however, so in 1960 he went to Vienna to study at the Academy of Music and to attend Hanns Jelinek's course in twelve-tone technique. He thereafter adopted this style in his own compositions.

Sönstevold has been a productive composer since returning from Vienna despite various other duties, such as director of the music division of Norwegian State Television from 1966–73. His works with orchestra include a saxophone concerto (1962) and a concerto for oboe and harp (1979). Two ballets, *Peer Gynt* and *Ritual*, date from 1966–67. *Litany in Atlanta*, one of his principal works, was presented at the Harstad Music Festival in 1972. Scored for speaker, children's chorus, mixed chorus, jazz band, and symphony orchestra, it is intended to include amateur performers. The text is by the American writer W. E. B. DuBois and deals with a lynching in Atlanta, Georgia in 1906. This composition is a gripping musical appeal for compassion and forgiveness.

Sönstevold's chamber music includes an early duet for flute and oboe, two string quartets from the 1960s, and *Quadri* for piano, harp, and percussion (1965). He has also composed for his own instrument, the piano. An especially original composition in this category is *The Dorian Cage* for piano six-hands. Based on the Dorian tetrachord, it consists of three movements marked Prelude, Passacaglia, and Fugue. Two preludes written in 1958 are good examples of Sönstevold's pre-Vienna style with their somewhat expanded tonality, partly polyphonic structure, and free treatment of dissonance. His later twelve-tone works display a personal style and an imaginative treatment of sound. As an experienced musician he knows the instruments well; his scoring is confident and effective, as is particularly evident in his use of percussion. In some compositions, such as "Crico," scored for percussion and keyboard instruments, jazz rhythms are combined with the twelve-tone technique.

Maj Sönstevold (b. 1917) was for several years a teacher of jazz piano in Stockholm, her native city. In 1941 she married Gunnar Sönstevold, who at that time was a refugee from German-occupied Norway, and in 1945 they moved to Oslo. The years 1960–67 were spent in Vienna, where she studied harmony with Hanns Jelinek and composition with Karl Schiske. This period was no less decisive for Maj Sönstevold's musical development than for her husband's.

Maj Sönstevold's compositions exhibit considerable variety and stylistic breadth. She first became known as a composer of film music in the 1950s; her most successful effort in this genre was her music for the children's film *Toya* (1956). She also wrote incidental music for the theater as well as for dramatic productions for radio and television. Other compositions include a number of songs and instrumental works in a popular vein.

The years in Vienna marked a turn in Maj Sönstevold's interest as a composer toward music intended for the concert hall. Employing a free twelve-tone style, she created a number of quite dissonant polyphonic works. Characteristic of her compositions from this period are three piano works: a suite (Op. 1), a theme and variations (Op. 2), and a sonata (Op. 3). Formally, these works rest squarely in the Neoclassical tradition. The free twelve-tone style used in all of them, however, points toward Neoexpressionism. This leaning is even clearer in *Neun Haiku* for alto solo, flute, and harp (Op. 5), written in 1966. These sensitive and delicate settings of German translations of nine Japanese haiku are a tribute to the composer's fine poetic sense and creative imagination.

Recent works by Maj Sönstevold include "In Nazareth" for children's chorus, Orff instruments, and recorder (1980, text by Selma Lagerlöf); "Come, Heart's Joy" for flute, harp, and speaker (1982); and "Per aspera ad astra; Thoughts on Latin America" for piano (1983). In these works, as in all of her diversified production, one can admire the deep emotional involvement and the fine sense of poetry that characterize all of her music. Perhaps these are the qualities that give her music its enduring strength.

Alfred Janson (b. 1937) took piano lessons from his mother, Margrethe Janson, from childhood until his public debut in 1962. He also studied music theory and composition with Björn Fongaard and Finn Mortensen. Until 1961 he was mainly occupied with jazz, both as a pianist and as a composer and arranger. He composes for both large and small ensembles, often with vocal components. His "Lullabye" (1963), for example, is scored for string orchestra and soprano. Other works are "Canon" (1965) for chamber orchestra and tape player; "Construction and Hymn" (1966) for orchestra; and "Theme" (1966) for mixed chorus, organ, percussion, and piano. One of his best-known works is "Nocturne" (1967), which is based on Friedrich Nietzche's poem "Midnight" and is scored for mixed chorus, two cellos, percussion, and harp.

Janson has also written incidental music for several dramatic works for both stage and television. His compositions in this category include the ballet *Toward the Sun* (1969) and the music for a television series entitled "Alberte" (1972). The latter was based on a novel by the Norwegian writer Cora Sandel. An opera, *A Mountain Escapade*, was produced in 1973. Later works include "Prelude" for violin and orchestra (1975), a string quartet (1978), "Wings" for mixed chorus and jazz ensemble (1983), "Interlude" for orchestra (1985), and "National Song" for orchestra (1988).

Janson's musical vocabulary covers a broad spectrum. Jazz elements play a role in some of his works, but his deepest roots are in Neoexpressionism. A strongly lyrical quality often asserts itself in his music, giving it human warmth and expressive power.

Terje Rypdal (b. 1947) is an internationally known jazz guitarist and composer (see p. 352). Although he started out as a pop musician in the 1960s with a group called the Vanguards, his interest eventually turned to jazz. He studied music at the University of Oslo, and pursued composition with Finn Mortensen and George Russell. He has given concerts and participated in jazz festivals in many European countries and has become well known through a number of commercial recordings. As a composer, however, Rypdal has not confined himself to jazz; his art-music compositions include four symphonies, a concerto for double bass and orchestra (1972–73), a piano concerto (1979), and a violin concerto subtitled "Undisonus" (1981). Several of these compositions combine stylistic traits derived from jazz, Neoromanticism, and Neoexpressionism.

Other composers in this category include Helge Hurum (b. 1936), Egil Kapstad (b. 1940), Björn Alterhaug (b. 1945), Terje Björklund (b. 1945), and Björn Kruse (b. 1946).

POP, ROCK, AND POPULAR SONGS

"Pop" and "rock" are somewhat ambiguous terms used to describe related types of music having broad appeal to young people. The best known of the early Norwegian groups performing such music was the Monn Keys, which became popular in the 1950s. The leader of the group, Egil Monn-Iversen

(b. 1928), has maintained his importance in Norwegian pop-music circles, as have other members of the group. Monn-Iversen is also known as a composer and arranger of light music.

Pop music came to prominence in Norway in the 1960s, when the fame of the Beatles was at its zenith. Norwegian pop groups tended to follow the examples of similar groups in England, Sweden, and North America. The most successful of the many Norwegian pop groups that sprang up at this time were the Pussycats and the Vanguards. The latter included Terje Rypdal, who near the end of the decade established a group called Dream that made a number of successful jazz/rock-style recordings. Rypdal later moved into jazz and other musical languages. Wenche Myhre, who eventually became popular in Germany, was another prominent pop musician in Norway during the 1960s.

At the end of the decade a distinction began to appear between groups performing lighter dance music and those performing more advanced concert or show music. The best-known groups performing the two types of music were, respectively, the New Jordal Swingers and Popol Ace. Jan Teigen was vocalist with the latter group until 1977. Norwegian pop groups of international note in recent years include A-HA, Bobby-Socks, and Dollie de Luxe.

Popular songs have blossomed in Norway in recent years, partly because of the influence of pop music and partly against the background of traditional Norwegian folk songs and *skillingsviser* (see p. 108). The rich Swedish song tradition has also had an impact on this development. A large number of completely new songs have been written. The undisputed leader in this area was Alf Pröysen (1914–70), who rose to instant fame in Norway with the publication in 1948 of his first volume of poems, *Bunkhouse Songs*. Pröysen also wrote short stories and plays, but it was primarily as a writer of song texts and a performer that he became known and loved both in Norway and in the other Scandinavian countries. Much of his writing, particularly his songs, was directed to children. Thorbjörn Egner (1912–90) also enjoyed international recognition as a writer of songs for children. Some of his best-known songs were composed for such children's plays as *The Singing Town*, *Wily Mouse and the Other Animals in Hakkebakk Forest*, and *The Musicians Come to Town*.

Although both Pröysen and Egner wrote melodies for some of their own texts, many more have been set to music by other composers. Christian Hartmann (1910–85) was especially prolific in this area, writing music for texts by Pröysen, Egner, Herman Wildenvey, Einar Skjaeraasen, and others. Hartmann also wrote art songs and incidental music for stage and screen. Other leading Norwegian composers of popular songs and light music in

Torbjörn Egner's own illustration for The Singing Town. *(Torbjörn Egner)*

the twentieth century have been Reidar Thommessen (1889–1986), Kristian Hauger (1905–77), Johan Öian (1915–78), and Finn Ludt (b. 1918).

A number of singers of these lighter songs have come to the fore in recent years. Among the best known of these are Birgitte Grimstad (b. 1935), Aase Kleveland (b. 1949), Lillebjörn Nilsen (b. 1950), and Lars Klevstrand (b. 1959).

THE RENEWAL IN CHURCH MUSIC

The renewal in church music, which was already under way before 1950, has continued apace since that time. An important event in this connection was the establishment in 1952 of Musica Sacra, "an association for church-music renewal" established in close association with the Laub movement in Denmark and the circle surrounding Per Steenberg (see p. 339). Musica Sacra has four stated objectives: 1) revival of the rhythmic form of the

Reformation-era chorales; 2) dissemination of new hymn tunes of high quality that will enrich the worship services; 3) understanding of and active participation in the liturgy by the congregation; and 4) revival of the Baroque organ tradition. This organization was especially active during the first twenty years of its existence.

As early as 1965 the Church of Norway began working on a new liturgy for divine worship, a new hymnal for congregational use, and a new chorale book for organists. In 1969 a liturgy reflecting many of the priorities of Musica Sacra was sent to a number of congregations on a trial basis. However, the liturgy actually adopted in 1977 did not follow these priorities as closely. The new hymnal was completed in 1984 and the new chorale book in 1985.

Musica Sacra sought not only to restore an old tradition but also to incorporate contemporary music suitable for congregational use. The latter effort has had considerable impact, for many Norwegian composers have written sacred music for both liturgical and non-liturgical use. Norway's Sacred Song Society, an association of church choirs, has also actively promoted new church music. Several premieres, including some of commissioned works, have taken place at the national song festivals held annually in various parts of the country.

Many composers have contributed to the creation of this repertoire of new sacred music in Norway. Several of them are or were active on other musical fronts as well, but their prominent identification with church music makes it appropriate that they be discussed in this context.

Conrad Baden (1908–89) was an organist as well as a prolific composer of both sacred and secular music. His compositional style ran the gamut from the late Romanticism of his earliest works to Neoclassicism to Expressionism based on a free use of tonality and, in a few works, an almost twelve-tone idiom. Throughout his career, however, the complexity of his music always varied greatly, ranging from simple pieces intended for congregational use to more complicated and sometimes extremely dissonant compositions for orchestra.

At the center of Baden's compositions for church use stand his vocal works: a Mass for choir, soloists, organ, and orchestra (1949), two cantatas, a number of motets, and other vocal works of varying length. His organ compositions were also written for use in the church. They consist of several variations on and arrangements of Norwegian religious folk tunes as well as original works. Among the latter are a three-movement *Sonatina* (1965) and *Pezzi Concertante: Preludio, Pastorale, Tema con variazioni, Fuga* (1966).

Baden wrote six symphonies at various times throughout his creative life (the first dates from 1953, the sixth from 1980), and they reveal a corresponding breadth of style. Other works with orchestra include *Fantasia breve per orchestra* (1965), *Concerto per orchestra* (1968), and a cello concerto (1986). He also composed chamber music, including four string quartets.

Baden's music is so varied that it does not lend itself to a summary characterization. Most of his compositions exhibit a keen sense for musically balanced form and a sound, polyphonically oriented compositional technique. With respect to form he was primarily dependent on Neoclassicism, though he occasionally engaged in experimentation. On the whole, when one thinks of Baden's music one tends to think first of its overall solidity.

Knut Nystedt (b. 1915), a central figure in Norwegian church music since 1950, has had wide and comprehensive experience as an organist and choir director. His first teachers were Arild Sandvold, Per Steenberg, and Bjarne Brustad. He later took several study trips to the United States, where he studied with Aaron Copland and others. He completed degrees in organ (1936) and conducting (1943) at the Oslo Music Conservatory and served as organist at the Torshov Church in Oslo until 1985. In 1950 Nystedt founded the Norwegian Soloists Choir, one of the country's leading mixed choruses, and served as its conductor until 1989. The chorus has performed an extensive repertoire, especially of newer works, and has toured extensively in many countries.

As a composer he has undergone a long development. In such early works as the orchestral suite *High Mountain* as well as his first compositions for piano, he largely continued the nationalistic tradition characteristic of the 1930s. Neoclassical features gradually came more to the fore, however, in his second and third string quartets, where the harmonic language also became freer. A significant change is evident in his works dating from about 1960. The orchestral work *The Seven Seals*, for example, exhibits a new harmonic idiom and represents a decided turn toward Neoexpressionism. With respect to form he also moved away from Neoclassical models and at the same time began occasionally using twelve-tone themes. Such themes appear in a more concentrated and artistically well integrated form in "The Moment" for soprano, cello, and percussion (1963) and in the fourth string quartet (1966).

Nystedt's most important compositions include several cyclic works for mixed chorus and orchestra. His first oratorio, *The Path of Grace*, was completed as early as 1946. *The Burnt Offering* (1954), scored for speaker, mixed chorus, and orchestra, explored new stylistic avenues. Based on the biblical account of the confrontation of the prophet Elijah with the prophets of Baal, it exhibits fine dramatic timing as it builds up to the climactic declaration: "Then the fire of the Lord fell and consumed the burnt offering." It then concludes with a stirring hymn of praise.

Lucis creator optime for soloists, mixed chorus, organ, and orchestra is one

Knut Nystedt.

of Nystedt's principal compositions. Written in 1969 for the centennial anniversary of Augsburg College in Minneapolis, it was premiered by the Augsburg Choir and the Minnesota Orchestra under the direction of Stanislaw Skrowaczewski. It is built on the old Latin hymn that gave the work its name. The five stanzas of the hymn comprise the text, and the Gregorian chant associated with the text is used in the introduction and conclusion. The main body of the work is built on constantly changing sonorities in which Nystedt employed highly advanced compositional techniques, not least in the orchestra.

An interesting twelve-tone work dating from 1970 is *Suoni* for flute, marimba, and female voices, in which the composer continued to experiment with nontraditional sonorities and tone clusters. Indeed, sonority is a key concept for the understanding of many of Nystedt's works as he constantly attempts to create new variations with which to enrich his world of sound. A stunning example of this is *De Profundis*, a motet for *a cappella* mixed chorus written in 1964. Here Nystedt skillfully blended simple chant-like melodies and tone clusters to produce an artistically unified piece whose effect is gripping.

Later works include "A Hymn of Human Rights" for mixed chorus, organ, and percussion (1982), *Sinfonia del Mare* for orchestra (1983), *For a Small Planet* for mixed chorus and instrumental ensemble (1983), *The Lamentations of Jeremiah* for *a cappella* mixed chorus (1985), a *Stabat Mater* for mixed chorus and cello solo (1986), and "O Crux" for *a cappella* mixed chorus (1987). A concerto for French horn and orchestra dates from 1987 and a fifth string quartet from 1988. *The Song of Solomon* (1990) is an elaborate work for choir, reader, instrumental ensemble, and dancers. Nystedt's more recent compositions tend to be somewhat more polyphonic and less experimental. Rarely, for example, do they incorporate twelve-tone themes in the manner of several of his works from the 1970s. In general, however, they represent a further development of his personal style.

Because his compositions for church use generally are designed for amateur musicians, Nystedt employs simpler structures and less-advanced sonic techniques in these works. His two masses *Spes mundi* (1970) and *Thanksgiving Celebration* (1972) were written for the worship service and have been performed in that context. Nystedt has written many vocal works of various lengths, most for *a cappella* mixed chorus or chorus with organ but also some for solo voice and organ. Many of these compositions have become very popular. The best known of these is "Cry Out and Shout," a work that has made Nystedt's name well known among choral directors and singers in the United States. "Blessed Be He" and "He Is Arisen" are other examples of his more widely known and frequently sung functional music.

Nystedt's mastery of the organ is evident in his many compositions for that instrument. Among the best known of these are "Toccata" (1941), "Fantasia trionfale" (1955), the twelve-tone "Pietà" (1961), "Resurrexit" (1973), and "Exultate" (1975).

In addition to the five string quartets, Nystedt's chamber-music works include *Pia memoria* (1971), a requiem scored for nine brass instruments. Once again, as he had done earlier in *De Profundis*, Nystedt skillfully combined Gregorian material (the melody from the "Lux illuxit" sequence) with contemporary elements in a work that is a fine amalgam of tradition and modernity. Among his orchestral works are the *Concerto Grosso* for three trumpets and strings (1946), *Land of Suspense* (1947), *Collocations* (1963), and *Mirage* (1974).

Nystedt's fifth string quartet is perhaps the best example of his mature style. The imaginative use of sound continues to be central, but here it is combined with a motivic/thematic technique that is clearly rooted in the Classical tradition. It is precisely this wedding of tradition and modernity together with a brilliantly imaginative use of sound that especially characterizes Nystedt as a composer.

Egil Hovland (b. 1924) is a highly versatile composer whose compositions include works of various types both sacred and secular. Stylistically, too, his music displays a range virtually unmatched by any other Norwegian composer: everything from Neoclassical works to pieces in both serial and Neoexpressionist styles.

Hovland studied organ at the Oslo Music Conservatory, where his teachers included Arild Sandvold and Per Steenberg. He later studied composition with Bjarne Brustad in Oslo, Vagn Holmboe in Copenhagen, Aaron Copland in the United States, and Luigi Dallapiccola in Italy. Since 1949 he has been organist at Glemmen church in Fredrikstad (south of Oslo). He began composing in the mid-1940s, partly as an heir of the late Romantic tradition, partly inspired by Steenberg's classes in late Renaissance polyphonic vocal music. Hovland also became interested in Gregorian chant, both as a liturgical medium and as musical material, and this interest too has left its mark on some of his music. The stylistic foundation for most of Hovland's compositions during the 1950s, however, was Neoclassicism. During this period he wrote a *Festival Overture* for orchestra, Op. 18 (1951); his first (Op. 20, 1953) and second (Op. 24, 1955) symphonies; and a "Concertino" for three trumpets and strings, Op. 23 (1955).

Hovland began to move in a new direction in 1959 with *Suite for Flute and Orchestra* (Op. 31), the first of many compositions in which he used the twelve-tone system. In some compositions that followed he moved further in the direction of serial music, in others he used a somewhat freer twelve-

Egil Hovland.

tone technique. "Motus per flauto solo" (1961) is based throughout on the use of a tone row. A more personal adaptation of the twelve-tone system is employed in *Song of Songs* (1963), a chamber-music work for soprano, violin, piano, and percussion. This powerful setting of an English translation of a biblical text aroused considerable interest at several performances in Scandinavia. The twelve-tone technique also forms the basis for the orchestral work *Lamenti*, Op. 43 (1963). The title associates the work with the Lamentations of Jeremiah, but the composition has no text. This piece also employs such techniques as tone clusters and aleatory elements. A more serialized use of the twelve-tone technique appears in *Varianti per due pianoforti*, Op. 47 (1964), but once again the style is combined with tone clusters and aleatory elements. The work consists of twenty variations, but the performers determine the order in which they shall be performed and may, if they choose, omit some altogether. The only firm structural requirement is that the variation titled "omega" is always to be played last.

Norwegian church music remained fairly conservative until the early 1960s. Neoclassicism had indeed left its stamp on some of the music written for church use, but neither the twelve-tone system nor Neoexpressionism had had any noticeable impact. In the 1960s, however, Hovland began to use more radical stylistic devices in his sacred compositions. Other composers followed his example, but he remained the leading avant-garde composer of sacred music in Norway through this decade and the next.

The twelve-tone system appears in *Magnificat* for alto solo, alto flute, and harp, Op. 44 (1964) and in *Elementa pro organo*, Op. 52 (1965). The latter also employs chance elements along with tone clusters and other Neoexpressionist techniques. Thereafter Hovland produced a number of sacred works that were fairly experimental in character. In 1967 he composed two large works of this type: *Rorate* for organ, chamber orchestra, five sopranos, and tape recorder, and *Missa Vigilate* for mixed chorus, two soloists, ballet dancers, organ, and tape recorder. *Missa Vigilate* was written for an experimental worship service held on the last Sunday of the liturgical year. The Gospel reading for that Sunday is the parable of the five wise and the five foolish maidens (Matthew 25:1–13), and the dancers are intended to represent this parable.

More large compositions for the church followed. In 1968 he wrote *Resurrection Mass* for choir, three trombones, two organs, and congregation (Op. 60), for the Uppsala (Sweden) cathedral. *All Saints' Mass* for soprano, mixed chorus, three trumpets, three trombones, tuba, and congregation (Op. 70) was composed in 1970. *Missa Verbi* (Op. 78) and *Missa Misericordia* for *a cappella* mixed chorus (Op. 80) were both written in 1973. Other sacred works include *Good Friday* (Op. 75), a liturgical Passion play, and *The Well* (Op. 77), a religious work written for a church opera group in Stockholm. Both date from 1972.

Hovland has also continued to write secular music. Among his more recent works in this category are *Rhapsody 69*, Op. 65 (1969); *Tombeau de Bach*, Op. 95 (1978); *Concerto* for piccolo and orchestra, Op. 117 (1986); and a ballet, *Danses de la morte*, Op. 127 (1983).

Symphony No. 3 for chorus, speaker, and orchestra, is one of Hovland's principal works. The texts are taken from the biblical book of Job and a poem by Odd Medböe, "Because You Made Me a Man." Hovland had begun this symphony in the late 1950s but did not complete it at that time. In 1969 he received a copy of Medböe's poem, and this together with selected passages from Job became major elements of the work, which was finished in 1970. This symphony in one movement is an effective composition in which the spoken text plays a major role.

Another work in which recitation is an element is *The Lily*, Op. 61 (1968), subtitled "A Message of Love from the Song of Solomon." A highly expressive work in a moderately contemporary idiom, its five sections reflect the varying moods of the biblical text. The orchestra creates a subtly powerful backdrop for the spoken voice, but musically the highest points are reached in two orchestral passages where the speaker is silent. The spoken voice is also used effectively in his popular *Saul* (Op. 74), a motet for speaker, mixed chorus, and organ (1971), and in *Job* (Op. 79), a suite for organ with *ad libitum* speaker (1973).

Much of Hovland's music can be characterized as solid, practical music for use in the church. He has composed many motets for soloists or for choir, some with organ accompaniment. Several of his hymn tunes and introits are often sung. He has also written a number of organ pieces for use in the worship service. These compositions are in various styles, but Hovland always takes into account the performers and the listeners for whom the music is intended. Thus much of this music is only moderately difficult and more readily accessible than many of his other works.

Hovland has had a distinguished career as a composer, organist, and activist in the work of liturgical renewal in the Church of Norway and has been a central figure in Norwegian church-music circles for many years.

Some younger composers whose primary activity is in the area of church music are also deserving of mention. Per Christian Jacobsen (b. 1940) attended the Oslo Music Conservatory, where he studied organ with Arild Sandvold and composition with Finn Mortensen. Since 1976 he has been a teacher of composition at the State Academy of Music in Oslo. As a composer he has written primarily for mixed chorus (both accompanied and *a cappella*) and organ. His choral works include "Et facta est lux" (*a cappella*) and "Logos" (with organ). Other young composers in the sacred genre are Trond Kverno (b. 1945), Kjell Mörk Karlsen (b. 1947), and Sigvald Tveit (b. 1945). Tveit has written several musicals based on sacred texts. Some of these, such as *Spring Will Surely Come* and *The Good Land*, have become quite popular. He has also composed a number of shorter vocal works and has distinguished himself as an arranger and composer of children's songs for television.

THE MODERNISTS OF THE 1950S AND 1960S

Most of the composers in this group began their careers after 1945, though some wrote their earliest works before or during the war. There was at this time a considerable distance between a) the composers who were thoroughly committed to the new trends in postwar continental music and b) those who continued to build on prewar Norwegian music traditions and were relatively untouched by avant-garde music.

The composers of the Second Viennese School had little influence on Norwegian music and musicians prior to 1950. The leading modernist in Norway during the 1950s was Finn Mortensen (1922–83), who was a vital force in Norwegian music not only as a composer but also as professor of composition at the Norwegian State Academy of Music. His principal teachers were Thorleif Eken (harmony), Klaus Egge (counterpoint), Erling Westher (piano), Reidar Furu (double bass), and Niels Viggo Bentzon (composition). As an early and fairly solitary modernist in Norway's music milieu, Mortensen found it no easy task to develop a style consistent with his musical principles. During the late 1940s he had studied the twelve-tone technique on his own, but he did not use it in his compositions at that time. His first large works—a *Trio* for violin, viola, and cello, Op. 3 (1950); a *Wind Quintet*, Op. 4 (1951); his only symphony, Op. 5 (completed in 1957); and a *Sonata* for flute (written for the late Norwegian flute virtuoso, Alf Andersen)—are all in a style in which tonality is treated with considerable liberty. One can tell that Mortensen had absorbed Hindemith's *Craft of Musical Composition*; aside from the flute sonata, where there is virtually no polyphony, his style is largely polyphonic. It is also evident in these works that he had studied with Klaus Egge and that he admired the music of Harald Lie. The symphony shows that Mortensen had high regard for Bruckner, whom Lie also admired.

Mortensen's early compositions, then, can be characterized as Neoclassical. A good example of these early works is the *Wind Quintet*, which aroused considerable interest at the International Society for Contemporary Music festival in Stockholm in 1956. Its three movements are in the customary Classical order (fast-slow-fast) and consist respectively of sonata

Finn Mortensen. (Norsk Musikkinformasjon)

form, ternary form, and double fugue. The first and third movements revolve around E-flat as the tonal center, with a fresh and lively language in sound Hindemith tradition, while a deeper lyric-elegiac character comes to the fore in the slow movement.

Mortensen's productivity ceased for a time following the completion of the flute sonata. He had reached a critical turning point in his musical development and before proceeding further found it necessary to come to grips with some very basic questions in music theory. A period of study with Niels Viggo Bentzon in Copenhagen in 1965 liberated his creative powers once again, however; that same year he completed his *Piano Sonata* (Op. 7), and a year later the *Fantasia and Fugue* (Op. 13), also for piano. He now began to take advantage of his earlier studies in twelve-tone technique and, encouraged by Bentzon, advanced to an atonal, twelve-tone musical language and fairly strict serial construction.

Several times he employed a symmetric form in which corresponding sections (one being a mirror image of the other) flank a central point or axis. This form appears, for example, in *Fantasia and Fugue*, which inaugurated his second period. The Fantasia begins in a whisper and builds to a climax that constitutes the center of the movement. At this point the first part is repeated in retrograde and the movement concludes as it began. After a bridge passage of several measures the fugue enters with a six-measure theme characterized by wide leaps and rests functioning as constitutive elements. This theme is developed through standard dodecaphonic techniques—inversion, retrograde, and inverted retrograde—and the ordered use of all these possibilities is itself also serialized. Intervals of the fourth are frequent, especially in the Fantasia. In the concluding part of the fugue Mortensen employed a pointillistic technique that appears to reflect the influence of Karlheinz Stockhausen.

Similar principles were employed in the compositions that followed. His most rigidly structured serial work, "Tone Colours" for orchestra, Op. 24 (1962), is organized symmetrically around a midpoint and includes some aleatory elements as well. In the *Sonata for Two Pianos*, Op. 26 (1964), the framework for certain improvised sections is determined by spinning two wheels that appear in the score. This aleatory feature has given the work its nickname, "Wheel of Fortune Sonata."

Mortensen made strict use of twelve-tone rows in only three compositions: "Three on the Beach," Op. 20, for women's voices (1961); *Twelve Small Twelve-tone Pieces for Children*, Op. 22, for piano (1961–64); and "Evolution," Op. 23, for orchestra (1961). He defined serial music as "athematic and aperiodic music, organized in series, developed according to principles mediating between extremes." This "mediating between extremes" is essential to Mortensen's musical language, as is clear in his *Piano Concerto*, Op. 25 (1963). The "extremes" being mediated in this case are the composite sound and the dynamics. Tight tone clusters are contrasted with widely spaced chords whose pitches are distributed over a wide register, and powerful *fortissimos* are contrasted with almost inaudible *pianissimos*. Both pitch and dynamics in this single-movement work are, with certain modifications, treated serially.

An example of Mortensen's strict use of a twelve-tone row is the "Waltz" from *Twelve Small Twelve-tone Pieces for Children* (example 59). The original and retrograde forms of the twelve-tone row are the basis of the entire work. It is in ABA form, A being built on the original form of the row and B on the retrograde. In A the right hand states the row twice, the left hand once (the latter taking some liberties in measures 2–3 and 6–7). The A and B sections overlap in that the last note of the row in A (measure 8) is the first note of the row in retrograde form in B. In B, both right and left hands state the row twice. Even within this diminutive piece one can observe the composer's expressivity in the subdued, almost lyrical dialogue between the two voices.

Mortensen's compositions from the late 1960s again approach Schoenberg's twelve-tone technique but with a relatively free use of the tone row.

Example 59. Finn Mortensen, Waltz from Twelve Small Twelve-tone Pieces *for Children.*

This characteristic is evident in two large works: *Fantasia for Piano and Orchestra*, Op. 27 (1965–66) and *Per orchestra*, Op. 30 (1967). After 1970 he advanced to a style that he called "new serialism." The "extremes" requiring mediation in this case are a melodic twelve-tone style on the one hand and a pointillistic technique on the other. He employed this style in a number of chamber-music compositions, including *New Serialism I, II, and III* (1971–73) and *Hedda—Cavalcade for Large Orchestra*, Op. 42 (1974–75).

The *Suite for Wind Quintet*, Op. 36 (1974), occupies a special place among Mortensen's works. Its five movements bear the titles "Wind Soloists," "Avant-garde," "Doubtful Dialogue," "Tango for Three," and "Wind Quintet." The composer described this composition as follows:

The first movement introduces the five soloists. In the second movement, "Avant-garde," I have tried by means of exaggeration to understand how the listeners perceived my pointillistic music from the late 1950s. In the last movement, "Wind Quintet," I am thinking about how my first wind quintet from 1951 was listened to as I let the voices go up and down rather mechanically, imitate each other in a cheerful, somewhat comical way, and suddenly stop on an E-flat chord which gives a hint that the piece is over. Astonishment over the modern composer's difficulties in establishing a point of contact with the listeners probably underlies "Doubtful Dialogue." "Tango for Three" expresses the burlesque, the grotesque, and the dissolute through such devices as using a Wagner tuba in a somewhat unaccustomed role as accompaniment for a "Jazz tango for saxophone."

It is evident from these comments that the *Suite for Wind Quintet* expresses both humor and irony; it is a work in which the composer laughs at himself but also at the listeners who have reacted in various ways to his works through the years. Bubbling with humor, it is fun to listen to and is perhaps one of his most accessible works. It is hardly typical of his total output, however. More representative of Mortensen's music vocabulary is the strong expressivity that characterizes works created at various stages in his stylistic development. An almost frenzied intensity of expression, with tremendous contrasts in dynamics, texture, and structure, are features common to many of his works.

As professor of composition at the State Academy of Music, Mortensen had a considerable influence on many young composers, not least because of his open and straightforward attitude toward all systems, theories, and trends. His pedagogical goal, he once said, was "to release what the students have within them, not to saddle them with systems." This method has borne rich fruit, as evidenced by the great stylistic breadth of the works of the many promising young composers who had the good fortune to study with him.

One of Norway's most important modernists is the Italian-born composer Antonio Bibalo (b. 1922). He was trained as a pianist at the conservatory in Trieste, graduating in 1946. Some years later he went to London, where he studied composition with Elisabeth Lutyens from 1953 to 1956. After vacationing in Norway during the summer of 1956, he decided to become a Norwegian citizen, and except for brief stays abroad he has lived there continuously to the present day.

Since his studies with Elisabeth Lutyens, Bibalo has composed in a free twelve-tone style. *Concerto allegorico* for violin and orchestra (1957), one of his first compositions in this style, is dedicated to Fartein Valen, whom Bibalo greatly admires.

Antonio Bibalo. (Norsk Komponistforening)

Bibalo has created a large and diverse body of compositions. His well-developed sense for dramatic music is evident in his operas and ballets, which constitute a considerable portion of his output. His first opera was *The Smile at the Foot of the Ladders*, (1958–62), with a libretto adapted from the Henry Miller short story by that name. Its premiere in Hamburg in 1965 was successful and brought Bibalo wide recognition as a composer. The libretto of his opera *Miss Julie* was adapted from the play by August Strindberg. Here Bibalo managed to recreate Strindberg's play as an opera with great inventiveness and fine dramatic sense. An even greater success than his first opera, it was premiered in Aarhus (Denmark) in 1975 and has since been produced at several opera houses in Europe.

Bibalo's more recent dramatic works include *The Ash Lad*, an opera for radio that was broadcast over Norwegian National Radio in 1977, and *Ghosts*, an opera based on Henrik Ibsen's famous play. The latter is undoubtedly one of this composer's principal compositions. His stirring music in conjunction with Ibsen's powerful text results in an opera of great expressive power. His first ballet, *Pinocchio*, was premiered in Hamburg in 1969. Later works in this genre include *Nocturne* (1970) and *The Flame* (1972), both of which were written for television.

Bibalo has also written a large number of purely instrumental works. His compositions for orchestra include "Pitture Astratte" (1957), "Elegy for a Space Age" (1963), "Sinfonia notturna" (1968), and "Il concerto da camera" for harpsichord, violin, and string orchestra (1974). A symphony in four movements dates from 1979. In the area of chamber music he has written *Autonale*, a concert suite for flute, vibraharp, double bass, and piano (1968); *Astrale*, a wind quintet (1972); *The Savage; Four Impressions for Six Players* (1983); and *Racconto d'una Stagione Alta* for cello and piano (1986).

Bibalo's music is marked by rich color and motivic inventiveness. It is based on the twelve-tone technique, but he uses this technique in his own way and employs tonal elements when it suits his purposes to do so. His idiom is very much his own; his attitude toward music is sometimes almost mystical. Several of his finest compositions have "nocturnal" associations of one kind or another; "Sinfonia notturna," which was inspired by Herman Wildenvey's poem "To the Night," is a good example of this. Bibalo is also interested in astronomy, so perhaps it is his sense of the infinity of the heavens that finds its artistic reflection in these works.

Arne Nordheim (b. 1931) emerged as the leading representative of avant-garde music in Norway during the 1960s. His brand of modernism should not be construed as a revolutionary break with the past, however. Even though his mode of expression at times sounds quite radical, his musical language is deeply rooted in the western European music tradition.

Arne Nordheim.

After attending the Oslo Music Conservatory, Nordheim studied with Karl Andersen, Bjarne Brustad, Conrad Baden, and Vagn Holmboe. His first large works were two string quartets, one (entitled "Epigram") written in 1954, the other in 1956. The style in both of these works appears to reflect to some degree that of Bartók. The composition that first attracted considerable attention, however, was a 1957 song cycle entitled "Evening

Land," a setting for soprano and chamber ensemble of a text by the Swedish writer Pär Lagerkvist. The music is clearly tonal, though the tonality is handled rather freely. Nordheim's first orchestral work, *Canzona per orchestra* (1960), drew international attention. The title was intended to remind the listener of the early Baroque Venetian style and especially of Giovanni Gabrieli, whom Nordheim admires. What Nordheim did in this composition was to express in a modern idiom the Venetian school's idea of combining various dynamic contrasts and related masses of sound. Even in this early work, then, Nordheim's tonal language is related to that of Neoexpressionism. As time went on he, like many other Neoexpressionists, began to make use of the tape recorder and other electronic devices. His first such composition was music written in 1961 for a reading on radio of Antoine de Saint-Exupéry's *The Little Prince*. He used the same technique the following year in a ballet score entitled *Catharsis*.

With his concentration on the elements of sound, Nordheim was well on the way to eliminating altogether the rhythmic and melodic elements from his music vocabulary. The decisive step in this direction was taken in "Epitaffio" (1963; revised in 1977), a piece written in memory of the flutist Alf Andersen. It is a work for orchestra and tape, the latter a recording of choral sounds. Melodic and rhythmic elements are reduced to a minimum in favor of a highly sensitive and sophisticated concentration of orchestral sound that is further enhanced toward the end of the piece by the electronically modified choral sounds on the tape. Melodic and rhythmic elements have played varying roles in Nordheim's later compositions, but this concentration on aspects of texture has continued to be of central importance.

Several of Nordheim's compositions dating from the late 1960s make prominent use of electronic devices. He had also originally planned to use a tape recorder in *Eco* (written in 1967–68), but later decided to score it for soprano solo, children's chorus, mixed chorus, and orchestra *sans* violins. It is a setting of two texts by the Italian poet Salvatore Quasimodo, "I Morti" and "Alle fronde dei salici." Nordheim understands these texts as a timeless protest against violence and suppression, and his setting of them is deeply felt and very powerful. The composer was awarded the Nordic prize in composition for this work in 1972.

Nordheim's interest in electronic music led in 1968 to a residency at "Studio Eksperymentalne," an electronic music studio in Warsaw, Poland. It was here that he wrote "Solitaire" and "Pace," both of which employ a taped reading of the texts. These two pieces are also associated with the so-called "Sound Sculpture" created in cooperation with the sculptor Arnold Haukeland for a center for the blind at Skjeberg (near Oslo). The music emanating from the sculpture is produced by two tape loops playing at different speeds. The resulting sound, therefore, is continually changing as the conjunction of the two tapes constantly varies in unpredictable ways. This effect is further modified electronically by devices controlled by photoelectric cells that respond to the surrounding lighting conditions.

Similar concepts were used by Nordheim in creating music for the Scandinavian exhibit at the 1970 world exhibition in Osaka, Japan. In this case the sound was produced by six tape loops playing at various speeds. (Someone has calculated that it would take 102 years of continuous playing for all of the possible combinations to be played and all of the loops to return simultaneously to their original starting points.) This work was entitled "Poly-Poly"; a concert version of the same piece has the subtitle "Lux et tenebrae." Nordheim has since used the same basic idea—i.e., of several parallel "sound tracks" proceeding at different speeds—in a number of purely orchestral works, such as "Floating" (1970) and "Greening" (1973). In these and other later works, however, the sharp dynamic and textural contrasts that appeared earlier (e.g., in *Eco*) have largely given way to great surfaces or arches of sound, with smoother transitions from one to another. The same is true of *Spur*, a concerto for electronically amplified accordion and orchestra (1976).

Nordheim also wrote a good deal of vocal and ballet music during the 1970s. "Doria," for tenor and chamber orchestra (text by Ezra Pound), was written for Peter Pears, who premiered the work at the Bergen Festival in 1975. "To one singing" (1976), for tenor and harp (text by Percy Bysshe Shelley), was also written for Peter Pears. Ballet music includes *Beaches* (1974), *Ariadne* (1977), and *The Tempest* (1979). The score for *The Tempest* calls for orchestra, chorus, two vocal soloists, and tape. In this work Nordheim made effective use of various stylistic devices as consonant chords and motivic-thematic elements appear along with sophisticated dissonant sounds. The result is a veritable aural fairyland that seems perfectly appropriate for Shakespeare's magical drama. A page from the score of this remarkable work (with nontransposed parts) is reproduced on page 373. The two vocal parts are treated instrumentally but the words come through quite clearly nonetheless. On the syllable "fear" the two voices imitate each other in contrary motion. Nordheim's cantata *Tempora Noctis* (1979) uses electronic devices in conjunction with two soprano soloists and orchestra. The central theme, taken from a portion of Ovid's *Amores*, is death. The work was premiered in 1979.

One of Nordheim's finest works is *Wirklicher Wald* for soprano, cello, mixed chorus, and orchestra (1983). The text is a combination of passages from the biblical book of Job (sung in Hebrew) and Rainer Maria Rilke's poem "Todeserfahrung" (sung in German). The musical resources are

A page from the score for Nordheim's ballet The Tempest.

Scene from Nordheim's ballet The Tempest. *(Den Norske Opera)*

welded together in such a way as to create a work that is both beautiful and powerfully expressive. Other works from the 1980s are "Tenebrae" (1982) for cello and orchestra, composed for the famous cellist Mstislav Rostropovitch; "Aurora" (1983), composed in collaboration with the English vocal quartet "Electric Phoenix" (also employing electronic devices); and "Magma" (1988), written for the centennial celebration of the founding of the distinguished Concertgebouw Orchestra of Amsterdam.

As is evident from the foregoing, much of Nordheim's music calls for orchestra, the human voice, and electronic media. His chamber-music works, in addition to those already mentioned, include "Signals" for electric guitar, accordion, and percussion (1967) and "Colorazione" for organ, percussion, tape, and other electronic devices (1968). Among his few compositions for solo instruments are two works dating from 1971: "Partita II" for electric guitar and "Listen" for piano.

In addition to being the foremost composer of avant-garde music in Norway in recent years, Nordheim is without doubt the best-known Norwegian composer of his generation internationally. The experimental element that most people associate with his music really does not convey an accurate picture of him as a composer, however. In his artistic heart of hearts he is a Romanticist and a lyricist. As he once said of himself: "I often feel like an ordinary, old-fashioned composer, a landscape painter, a *lur*-playing Romanticist who has no hidden agenda regarding either *seter* life or cultural revolution." Perhaps the Neoromantic features in his music have come more clearly to the fore in his later compositions; it certainly is the case that tonal elements appear more frequently in several works written since 1975. The foundation of his music, however, rests upon a well-developed, imaginative, and exceedingly keen ear for textural effects.

Finn Arnestad (b. 1915) also emerged after World War II as a representative of modernism in Norway. He attended the conservatory in Oslo and later studied in France, Germany, Holland, and Belgium. Arnestad's production is not extensive, but what he has written is carefully and musically executed. His style is highly personal: it can be described as basically Neoexpressionist, although Neoclassical characteristics also appear in some works. Most of his compositions are for symphony orchestra.

One of his most important works is *I.N.R.I.; A Symphonic Mystery Play* (1958). Each section bears a superscription taken from the story of the passion and resurrection of Christ. The music is strongly Expressionistic. Arnestad has indicated that the work could also be performed with pantomimed pictorial scenes. Perhaps Arnestad's best-known orchestral composition is "Aria Appassionata" (1962), a short work employing an intense, fervent musical language. He also wrote concertos for violin (1962) and piano (1976). Especially important among Arnestad's vocal compositions is "The Smith and the Baker" for baritone solo and chamber orchestra (text by Johan Herman Wessel). Written in 1966, it employs indigenous folk-dance forms as well as recitative and aria forms derived from the Baroque era, though within a style that remains distinctively his own.

Arnestad has been strongly influenced by the twelve-tone technique, but he rarely makes use of tone rows as a basic compositional principle. He has also been occupied with acoustics and has sometimes used the interference phenomenon as a basis for harmonic development in his works. The principal impression given by his music is expressivity, to which everything else is subordinate.

Edvard Hagerup Bull (b. 1922) is a Norwegian-born composer who has lived most of his professional life abroad. He began his training in Oslo, then went to Paris, where his teachers were Charles Koechlin, Darius Milhaud, and Jean Rivier, and to Berlin, where he studied with Boris Blacher and Joseph Rufer.

The preponderance of Bull's music has been instrumental, especially orchestral. His six symphonies reflect his stylistic development from 1955 to 1982. The first is bright and lively in character but contains an undercurrent of lyricism that comes more to the fore in the later symphonies. The Neoclassical influence is evident in all of them, although (uncharacteristically for symphonies following Neoclassical models) the first movements tend to be in relatively slow tempos.

Bull has written two operas and two ballets. The librettos for both operas, *The Tinderbox* (1973–74) and *The Ugly Duckling* (1977), were derived from the tales of Hans Christian Andersen. His first ballet, *The Faithful Tin Soldier*, was written in 1948–49; the other, *Münchhausen*, dates from 1961. Both ballets have also been arranged as orchestral suites. Other orchestral compositions include the overture "Sinfonia di Teatro" (1952), "Undecim Sumus pour orchestre de solistes" (1962), "Chant d'Hommage à Jean Rivier" (1975), and "Posthumous" (1976).

Bull's seven compositions for solo instruments and orchestra are also major works. A trumpet concerto written in 1950 was followed by *Divertimento pour piano et orchestra* in 1954, a concerto for trombone and chamber orchestra in 1957, a second trumpet concerto in 1960, a flute concerto in 1969, *Sonata con Spirito* for piano and orchestra in 1970, and *Concerto pour saxophone, alto et orchestra* in 1980.

Bull has been less prolific as a writer of chamber music. His works of this type include two wind quintets; *Ad Usum Amicorum* for flute, violin, cello, and piano (1957); *Duo pour clarinette et piano* (1978); *Sonata a quattro* for string quartet (1980); and *Sextet for Flute, Clarinet, Violin, Cello, Piano, and Percussion* (1985).

Bull's very personal musical style is largely independent of the various trends of the day. Neoclassicism has been an important influence, but primarily as a point of departure for his own musical language. His early works tend to be bright and cheerful in character; thereafter deeper and more inward qualities begin to emerge, sometimes combined with greater lyricism, sometimes with dramatic or tragic elements. His music has won a considerable audience in both France and Germany.

Two other modernist post-war composers worthy of mention are Björn Fongaard (1919–80) and Hallvard Johnsen (b. 1916). Fongaard developed a harmonic system using microtones, and within the confines of this system composed a large number of works, most employing electro-acoustic devices of various kinds. Johnsen's style is rooted in tonality. He has written twelve symphonies as well as an opera, *The Legend of Svein and Maria* (text by the late Norwegian writer Alfred Hauge).

One of the younger composers in this group who has created a large and varied body of works is Kaare Kolberg (b. 1936). He was among the first Norwegian composers to address the problem of widespread public alienation from modern music, and elements intended to bridge this gap with the audience began to appear in some of his early compositions. His point of departure as a composer, however, is Neoexpressionism, with frequent use of ostinato elements. Among his most important compositions are "Plym-Plym" for mixed chorus; a church ballet, *The Canaanite Woman*, for organ and two percussionists (1968); the television opera *Tivoli* (1974); *For the Time Being* for vocal quartet and tape (1984); and an orchestral work, *Aria in aria* (1983). This last work is based on material taken from Kolberg's incidental music for Ibsen's play *The Master Builder*. In its concert version it is one of Kolberg's finest works, convincing in form and poignant in expression.

John Persen (b. 1941) is a true son of northern Norway whose music reflects an almost militant determination to assert the validity of Sami culture. He was first trained as an agronomist and a teacher, but in 1968 he came to the Oslo Music Conservatory and studied composition with Finn Mortensen. He has written primarily orchestral and chamber music, although one of his principal works is an opera, *Beneath Cross and Crown*, completed in 1987. Orchestral works include "Earache," "Orchestral Work II," and "ČSV." The last of this series won first prize in a competition held to celebrate the opening of the new concert hall in Oslo in 1977. The title, which reflects the composer's deep political involvement, is Sami and means "dare to show that you are Sami." "Orchestral Work II" was originally composed for a television ballet but was written in such a way that it can also be performed independently. Persen himself has characterized this work as "naked and brutal" and has stated that it was not his intention to write "aesthetically beautiful music." "Et cetera," a chamber-music work, won the "composition of the year" award from the Society of Norwegian Composers in 1988. Persen's musical style is Neoexpressionist and postserial. In recent years he has also begun to employ electronic devices.

TRADITION AND NATIONAL ROOTS

Many Norwegian composers active since 1950 have been influenced in varying degrees by the Neoclassical tradition. This group consists not only of composers born early in the century, but of a number of younger composers as well. Nationalistic elements, derived from Norwegian folk music or from other strands of the indigenous music tradition, play an important role in the works of many of these composers. Elements drawn from Sami folk music also appear in some of these works.

Indeed, the Neoclassical trend has been and continues to be unusually strong in Norway. That this is so is owing both to historical circumstances and to the personal inclinations of some of the composers. Perhaps a certain innate conservatism in Norwegian music life has also played a role. Whatever the reasons, the composers to whom we now turn display considerable stylistic variety in their compositions—everything from relatively pure Neoromantic traits to more experimental features and occasionally some Neoexpressionist elements. The boundary between this group and the more modernistic composers discussed in the preceding section is far from clear, as is also that between this group and the Postmodernist composers to be discussed shortly. One can say, however, that most of the composers in this group have been influenced by a conscious affinity with the nationalistic tradition.

A leading composer within this group is Johan Kvandal (b. 1919). The son of David Monrad Johansen, Kvandal completed degrees in organ and conducting at the Oslo conservatory, where his teachers included Per Steenberg, Ingebjörg Gresvig, and Geirr Tveit. He also studied composition with Joseph Marx (Vienna), Nadia Boulanger (Paris), and Boris Blacher (Berlin).

In his early compositions Kvandal continued the Norwegian nationalistic music tradition of the 1930s and its association with folk music. This is evident in his "Sonatina" for piano, Op. 2 (1940), and can still be seen a decade later in "Norwegian Overture," Op. 7, portions of which reflect the Norwegian *slaatter*. His work with Nadia Boulanger was a major turning point for him, however, and since the late 1950s his music has been much more Neoclassical in character. The new style appears in a fully developed form in "Symphonic Epic," Op. 21 (1962), a large, single-movement work that displays an expressive, at times dramatic tonal language. The Neoclassical style also marks his *Concerto* for flute and string orchestra, Op. 22 (1963). The expressive Aria of this four-movement work is a fine contrast to the rapid, joyous music of the outer movements.

Kvandal has written a number of chamber-music works; one of the most important of these—indeed, one of the principal compositions in his catalogue of works—is the *String Quartet No. 2*, Op. 27 (1966). Compared to the orchestral compositions of the early 1960s, this quartet employs a more fervent manner of expression as well as a more thoroughly considered form. One senses that Bartók's quartets lurk behind this composition. The four movements, which are played without pause, are marked as follows: I. Prologue (Allegro/Lento e lugubre); II. (Lo stesso tempo/Allegretto); III.

Johan Kvandal.

Adagio/Allegro; IV. Epilogue (Lento e lugubre). The introductory Allegro employs motivic material that is also used later in the quartet. The "Lento e lugubre" sections in the first and last movements are closely related and constitute a kind of unifying foundation for the work. Both are built on the same bass ostinato motive and the first measures are completely identical. (The development in the last movement proceeds somewhat differently than that in the first, however.) A slow bridge passage leads to the second movement, an Allegretto in ABA form. The third movement also has a slow introduction preceding a scherzo-like section in somewhat free rondo form. The quartet is a strongly personal musical statement both in its treatment of form and in the intensity of its expression.

"Da lontano" for alto flute and piano, Op. 32 (1970), is relatively short, but within its concentrated ternary framework the composer created a lyrical character piece of great expressive power. The *Wind Quintet*, Op. 34 (1971) and *Quartet* for flute, violin, viola, and cello, Op. 45 (1975), are larger works. The order of movements in the quintet—Largo, Presto, Adagio ma non troppo, and Allegro—is reminiscent of a Baroque *sonata da chiesa*. Its generally polyphonic structure and fine interplay of the parts also remind one of Baroque music. Nonetheless, though the basic Neoclassical style is clear, the musical language is Kvandal's.

In the late 1960s Kvandal turned once again to folk music for inspiration and thematic material. The first result of this was *Three Slaatt Fantasias* for piano (Op. 31), a commissioned work written for the Bergen International Festival of 1969. Most of the folk tunes came from the published collections of O. M. Sandvik and some unpublished transcriptions by L. M. Lindeman, but the composer also used a folk tune from Skjaak that he himself had transcribed. This material is used with great freedom and ingenuity. The result is a suite-like work in which a slow fantasia in the middle provides a fine contrast to the quick outer movements.

Kvandal continued to employ folk-music material in several of his succeeding works, such as a partita for organ on the folk melody "How Good to Reach the Harbor," Op. 36 (1971), and *Norwegian Stev Melodies* for solo voice and piano, Op. 40 (1973–74). In the *Sonata* for solo violin, Op. 45 (1976), he used a jew's-harp *slaatt* from Gudbrandsdalen.

One of his chief works, *Antagonia* for two string orchestras and percussion, Op. 38 (1972–73), also dates from this period. The title, according to the composer, implies "opposites that really belong together." In accordance with this concept, the two orchestral groups play sometimes independently and sometimes as a single ensemble. The three movements are worked out along the lines of the Viennese Classicists, and the work as a whole is clearly symphonic in character. The slow middle movement con-

Example 60. Antagonia, Johan Kvandal,
Second movement, measures 13–20.

tains a few hints of the Neoexpressionist handling of sound, but as is always the case with Kvandal these tendencies occur only within a well-controlled thematic-rhythmic structure and tonal mooring.

Example 60 is from the second movement of *Antagonia*. Note how, in measure 18, the second group answers the statement of the first group in measure 15: the violin solo is transposed down a fifth and moved forward a half measure in relation to the beginning of the block of sound below. In measure 18 and following the second group imitates the corresponding tremolo by the first group an octave lower.

Other major compositions are Kvandal's *Violin Concerto*, Op. 52 (1979); a third string quartet, Op. 60 (1983); and *Concerto for Organ and String Orchestra*, Op. 62 (1984). The violin concerto is a three-movement work that largely follows Neoclassical models. Much emphasis is given to melodic voice leading and motivic variation, with the solo instrument as the natural focus of melodic interest. The themes are of compelling power and the overall effect is one of happy music making. The organ concerto and the Op. 60 string quartet are also in the Neoclassical tradition.

Kvandal has written some vocal music, primarily for church use. His experience as organist at Vaalerengen Church (1959–74) gave him a thorough acquaintance with the distinctive character of church music, as is evident in his compositions in this genre. The sacred aria "O Dominum Deus" (Op. 26, No. 2), a setting of a Latin text ascribed to Mary Stuart, is an expressive solo for soprano with organ accompaniment. Another work, "Benedicam Dominum," is also for soprano and organ. Other sacred works include three solo cantatas, songs for mixed chorus and organ, for *a cappella* mixed chorus, and for solo voice and organ.

Another vocal work deserving of mention is the *Ibsen Cantata*, Op. 51, written for the celebration of the 150th anniversary of the birth of the great Norwegian playwright (1978). His first effort in the area of dramatic music was that written for *Skipper Worse* (1967), a television series based on Alexander Kielland's novel by that name. Eight selections from this music were later published as an orchestral suite.

Kvandal's compositions occupy a central place in modern Norwegian music. His tonal language is solidly Neoclassical but with roots also in Norway's nationalistic music traditions. His music has a distinctively personal stamp and is highly engaging to most listeners. Not surprisingly, therefore, he is one of Norway's contemporary composers whose compositions are most frequently performed.

Öystein Sommerfeldt (b. 1919) is another important modern Norwegian composer. He attended the Oslo conservatory and briefly studied composition with Fartein Valen, but the decisive points in his training as a composer were two periods of study in Paris with Nadia Boulanger (1952–53 and 1955–56).

Sommerfeldt's catalogue of works, though varied, contains a preponderance of piano pieces and songs. His language has been significantly influenced by Norwegian folk music, especially the religious folk melodies. He regards melody as the backbone of all music, a view that he asserts more forcefully than anyone else in contemporary Norwegian music. Stylistically, the contemporary composer who stands closest to him is perhaps Johan Kvandal.

His piano music can be divided into two groups: a) relatively short character pieces in a predominantly homophonic style; and b) larger works— sonatinas and suites (*Fable Suites*)—typically written in two-voiced polyphonic style.

The form of the character pieces frequently is ternary. Those written in slow tempos generally have an elegiac tinge, thus allowing their affinity with religious folk tunes to shine through. In "Little Folk-tune Elegy" (Op. 39, No. 3), Sommerfeldt made direct use of a religious folk melody from Nordland transcribed by Catharinus Elling. The faster character pieces are brighter, often with a dash of humor as an important ingredient. Such pieces as "Little March" (Op. 7, No. 1), "The Sorehead" (Op. 7, No. 5), and "Jolly March" (Op. 42, No. 1) are of this type.

The five piano sonatinas give a somewhat different picture: not only are they much longer works, but they display a tendency toward greater tonal freedom as well. Some sections are clearly bitonal, and at times the harmonic foundation virtually disappears altogether. The fast movements of the sonatinas appear to build on the style of Klaus Egge's fantasias on Norwegian *slaatt* rhythms (see p. 331). The slow movements in these works also have an elegiac cast, but they are clearly polyphonic and less similar to the folk-tune style than the slow character pieces.

The three *Fable Suites* were published in 1963 (Op. 10), 1969 (Op. 15), and 1977 (Op. 51). The first two have no subtitles, but the three movements of the third have the titles "Gangar I," "Thoughts," and "Gangar II." Thus in this case the connection with folk music is explicit, even though it is also evident in the music—especially the rhythms. The use of rapidly shifting tonality and occasional bitonal passages creates color within the confines of a simple and largely two-voiced structure.

Two Songs (Op. 2) was Sommerfeldt's initial venture into this genre. "June Night" (text by Einar Skjaeraasen), the first song in the set, has been widely sung. The rest of his songs for voice and piano (about twenty-five in all) are spread throughout his catalogue of works. There are also occasional songs using other instruments or ensembles for accompaniment. Sommerfeldt has composed a few choral pieces and has made a stunning choral arrangement of "Snow," a song by Sigurd Lie.

Among his few orchestral endeavors are some of his most important compositions. The first works in this genre were his merry "Miniature Overture," Op. 11 (1960) and *La Betulla*, Op. 12, a symphony started in 1960 but not completed until 1973. The name, which means "the birch tree," comes from a boarding house where the composer was staying at the time he completed the work. He once wrote of this:

> "La Betulla" is situated on the southern slope of the Alps, close to the Swiss border, with a view of Lake Lugano. The grove of slender "Nordic" birch trees outside my window was constantly in view as I was working on this composition, which builds to some extent on earlier symphonic material. Concentration, clarity, and clean lines are things which in recent years I have always tried to express musically . . . The clean lines, transparent orchestration, and simple form of the "Allegro risoluto" in the first movement perhaps contain a whiff of the fragrance of a birch grove in northern Italy.

The symphony's three movements are in the standard fast-slow-fast order, though the last movement has a slow introduction. The allegro movements sparkle with life, while the middle movement is a deeply felt, elegiac adagio.

Sommerfeldt has also written three orchestral suites built on Grieg's *Norwegian Peasant Dances* and a symphonic prelude entitled "The Oak Tree" (Op. 63). "Yearning" (Op. 50) is for piano and orchestra, "Hafrsfjord" (Op. 30) for speaker and orchestra. The latter, based on a text by Alfred Hauge, was composed for the 1100-year jubilee commemorating the battle of Hafrsfjord in 872.

Sommerfeldt's catalogue of works also includes compositions for solo instruments and for various small ensembles. Among the former are "Divertimento" for flute solo (Op. 9), "Monologue" for cello solo (Op. 45), and "Fantasia for Mouth Organ on an Old Norwegian Folk Song" (Op. 52). Compositions for small ensembles include a sonatina for violin and piano (1972) and a sonata for cello and piano (1988).

Sommerfeldt's music has a clear tonal base, although one occasionally encounters bitonal passages as well as some in which the tonality is fluctuating. Both melodically and rhythmically his music often reflects the influence of Norwegian folk music. Nonetheless, he has managed to avoid an excessive dependence on these sources. In its melodic form, its rhythmic vigor, and, not least, its fine harmonic sensitivity his music reflects the individuality of the composer. It represents an independent continuation and further development of a style with a long tradition in Norway's music history.

Edvard Fliflet Braein (1924–76) was one of the most important Norwegian composers of his generation, and also one whose connection with the nationalistic musical tradition was especially strong. He grew up in a musical environment in Kristiansund, where his father was an organist, and completed a degree in organ at the Oslo Music Conservatory in 1943. Later he studied composition with Bjarne Brustad and orchestral conducting with Odd Grüner-Hegge. In 1947 he composed "The Happy Music Makers" (Op. 1), a serenade for clarinet and three strings. The following year he completed a "Concert Overture" (Op. 2), which was performed by the Oslo Philharmonic in 1949. These early works display both a playful style and a sound compositional technique. The overture in particular has maintained its popularity in Norway and is one of his most frequently performed compositions. In 1950–51 Braein went to Paris, where he studied composition with Jean Rivier. Thereafter he lived primarily in Oslo.

Braein's catalogue of works is extensive and varied. The jovial mood that pervaded his early works reappears in many later works as well, including "Serenade" for orchestra, Op. 5 (1952); "Capriccio" for piano and orchestra, Op. 9 (1958); and "Little Overture," Op. 14 (1962). Many other compositions have deeper content and somewhat darker colors, however. Among these are "Adagio" for strings, Op. 6 (1953); "Symphonic Prelude" for orchestra, Op. 11 (1960); and "Largo" for strings, Op. 12 (1962).

Braein's most important works are his three symphonies and two operas. The first two symphonies (Opuses 4 and 8) date from 1950 and 1954, respectively, and the third (Op. 16) was finished in 1968. The operas are both relatively late: *Anne Pedersdotter* (Op. 18) was finished in 1971 and premiered at the Norwegian Opera the same year; *The Busybody* (Op. 21) dates from 1975.

The symphonies follow in the mainstream of the Norwegian symphonic tradition, exhibiting both weight and depth in their musical content. Their form is Neoclassical; this appears most clearly in the first, which contains four movements, and in the second, which contains three. The third symphony is a single-movement work. Perhaps the most important of the three is the second, whose epic breadth and almost tragic character give it great power.

Anne Pedersdotter is considered the most important opera by a Norwegian composer in recent years. The libretto, by Hans Kristiansen, is adapted from a play by Hans Wiers-Jensen that in turn is based loosely on historical events. Anne Pedersdotter was burned as a witch in Bergen in 1590, and this tragedy served as the basic inspiration for the play. The historical material is handled very freely, however, within an overall fictitious plot. Braein employed the leitmotif technique to depict the struggle between good and evil forces in human beings. Each of the two main themes represents a specific domain: hate, superstition, and witchcraft versus love and reconciliation. The main characters are portrayed with fine psychological insight: one can follow Anne's struggle with the evil around her and within her until she at last succumbs to evil, wishing death upon her aged husband Absalon. The style in *Anne Pedersdotter* is clearly tonal throughout, but the harmony ranges from simple triads to sharp dissonances and is carefully adapted to the dramatic situation. Both the lyrical and the dramatic parts are worked out in a completely convincing way. The opera might be described as "popular" but with serious artistic involvement and deep human understanding.

The Busybody was adapted from Ludvig Holberg's play by the same name, again with Hans Kristiansen as the librettist. This opera displays the lighter, more jovial side of Braein's nature. It is a comedy that is full of lively antics and was well received at its premiere in 1975.

Braein also wrote a number of shorter works, primarily songs and choral pieces. They are for the most part in a lighter vein, sometimes almost sentimental. The song "Out by the Sea" has enjoyed great popularity.

In all of his compositions, Braein's strength is that he consistently maintained an intuitively musical attitude toward his material. There is no heavy theorizing here, no philosophical or epic content that might overshadow the spirited music making. He once wrote concerning his music: "The music must speak for itself, and its purpose is to reflect quite simply the joys and sorrows and moods that I find it natural to express in music." Such a goal can be a limitation, but in Braein's case it was clearly a strength.

Oddvar S. Kvam (b. 1927) received his training at the Oslo Music Conservatory. He also holds a degree in law and is a practicing lawyer, but he has nonetheless managed to compose a large number of works in several genres. Two of his compositions for orchestra won prizes at the opening of the new concert hall in Oslo in 1977: "Prologue" (Op. 13), and "Opening" (Op. 28).

Kvam has also written a large number of choral works, some *a cappella* and some with various kinds of accompaniment. It is in this category that we find what is perhaps his most important composition: *Querela pacis* for two choruses and orchestra. It is a setting of a Latin text by Erasmus of Rotterdam and has been performed many times both in Norway and elsewhere.

Ketil Vea (b. 1932) is a composer and music teacher who has made significant contributions to the music life of northern Norway. Like John

Persen (see p. 377), he has made use of elements from Sami music in his compositions—for example, in "Jiedna" (the Sami word for "sound") for orchestra and soprano solo.

Ketil Hvoslef (b. 1939), a son of Harald Saeverud, first studied viola and organ at the Bergen Music Conservatory, then went to Stockholm for further study in composition with Karl-Birger Blomdahl and Ingvar Lidholm. He later studied with Thomas Rayna and Henri Lazarof in London.

Hvoslef has been a prolific composer of primarily instrumental music. His works with orchestra include a piece entitled "Mi-Fi-Li" (1971), "Antigone" (1982), and *Symphonic Variations* for orchestra (1982) as well as concertos for piano, trumpet, double bass, cello, and bassoon. He has also written a double concerto for flute, guitar, and chamber orchestra (1977) and a concerto for violin and pop band. In the area of chamber music he has composed two string quartets, a wind quintet, and a clarinet quintet. He has written music for both stage and film productions as well as solo works for flute, trumpet, organ, and piano. "Organo solo" is based on thematic material taken from his incidental music for a play by Knut Horvei. "The Revelation to John, Chapter 12," is a composition for organ, speaker, and dancer.

Hvoslef's versatile style is determined to a large extent by the specific requirements of the task at hand and the instruments for which he is writing. For the most part his music can be characterized as freely tonal. It also builds on the Neoclassical tradition with respect to themes, motivic development, and structure. Solid technique and a thoroughly musical treatment of his material are characteristic of Hvoslef as a composer.

Trygve Madsen (b. 1940) composes in a rather conservative tonal style and his music is generally light and animated. Among his most important works are a concerto for oboe, strings, and percussion and an orchestral overture.

Folke Strömholm (b. 1941) is another composer who has made use of elements derived from Sami folk music in his compositions. His orchestral works "Sami Overture" and "Samiaednan," for example, are the first to employ Sami *joiks*. Other compositions include a piano concerto and some chamber music. Reluctant young students might appreciate the title "Farewell to the Piano" given to one of his piano pieces.

Ragnar Söderlind (b. 1945) has also drawn some of his inspiration from the Arctic region of northern Norway, though he has not made direct use of Sami materials in his compositions. He first studied in Oslo with Conrad Baden, Jenö Hukvari, and Odd Ulleberg, then went to the Sibelius Academy in Helsinki where his teachers were Erik Bergman, Joonas Kokkonen, and Ulf Söderblom. He is a prolific composer whose compositions include both orchestral and chamber music as well as vocal compositions. For orchestra he has written "Rokkomborre" (1967), "Mourning Music" (1968), "Fantasia Borealis" (1969), and "Polaris" (1970). "Mourning Music" was written in response to the Russian invasion of Czechoslovakia, while "Rokkomborre," "Fantasia Borealis," and "Polaris" reflect the influence of the sights and sounds of northern Norway. Compositions for smaller ensembles include a string quartet (1975); *La Poema Battuta* for percussion, a cyclic work whose three movements are entitled "Presentazione," "Concertante," and "Hymnus"; and the song cycle *Cherry Blossoms* (1967), five Japanese love poems set for baritone, flute, English horn, cello, and percussion. A chamber opera, *Esther and the Blue Stillness* (1972), was produced for television. Using a text adapted from a one-act play by Sigbjörn Obstfelder, Söderlind created a lyrical and genuinely romantic work.

Söderlind has written three symphonies. The first (1975) is clearly Neoromantic, whereas the second (1981), subtitled "Sinfonia breve," is dramatic in character. The third (1983–84), subtitled "Les illuminations symphoniques," makes use of a text by Arthur Rimbaud. Scored for soprano and baritone solos and orchestra, its principal strengths are the fine interplay between text and music and the colorful orchestration. "Eystradalir" (1984), which Söderlind calls his "nostalgic rhapsody," is based on Norwegian folk tunes.

Söderlind is an avowed Neoromanticist, but his musical vocabulary is broader than such a characterization might suggest. "Polaris," for example, begins with something very close to a twelve-tone style and ends with a clearly tonal section. Söderlind's studies in Helsinki gave him a foundation in the Sibelius tradition that reinforces his own strong feelings about nature. The influence of Neoclassicism is also evident in his handling of form, but he is not bound by these models. His music creates an impression of profound lyricism that finds expression in a style that is clearly his own.

Olav Berg (b. 1949) studied composition with Antonio Bibalo and with Lennox Berkeley in London. He has written orchestral music, chamber music, and music with vocal components. Among his more important compositions are "Poseidon" (1982), "Etude" (1987), and "Epilogue" (1988). Other works include a clarinet concerto (1987), "The Story" for mixed chorus and chamber orchestra, and a composition for organ entitled "Song." *The Halibut* is a work for chamber orchestra and reader based on a fairy tale by Regine Normann. Berg's music has considerable stylistic breadth and includes some postmodernist elements.

Halvor Haug (b. 1952) began his professional training in Norway, then went on to study composition at the Sibelius Academy in Helsinki and with Robert Simpson in London. He composes primarily orchestral music but has also written for chamber ensembles and solo instruments. His principal orchestral compositions to date are *Symphonic Pictures* (1976), two symphonies (1982 and 1984), and a "Sinfonietta" (1983). Chamber-music works include a string quartet and a brass quintet.

POSTMODERNISM AND OTHER RECENT TRENDS

Some recurring features in the somewhat perplexing array of styles displayed in the music of the 1980s are summed up in the term "postmodernism," which signifies a conscious new effort at *rapprochement* with the general concert-going public through the use of such things as easily recognizable quotations from earlier composers and/or conventions derived from older musical styles. On the continent this trend was already evident in the work of a number of composers during the 1970s. In Norway, as we have seen, it was Kaare Kolberg who first began to move in this direction, and others quickly followed. Postmodernist elements appeared with increasing frequency in the late 1970s and 1980s, yet without completely dominating the musical panorama. A number of Norwegian composers—some older, some younger—continue to compose works that are largely an extension of Neoclassicism, and of course modernism is still alive and well. The latter could perhaps be best characterized as a continuation of Neoexpressionism, at least with respect to its textural and structural characteristics. Minimalism has played a rather limited role in Norway, but the influence of its principles cannot be totally dismissed either; indeed, virtually everything that has been happening on the international musical scene has had some impact on Norwegian music. Not least, electronic music continued to be a factor during the 1980s, usually simply as an element in compositions otherwise written for standard orchestral instruments.

One composer who is closely identified with postmodernism is Olav Anton Thommessen (b. 1946). He began his music studies at Indiana University, where his teachers included Bernhard Heiden and Iannis Xenakis. He later studied in Poland and at the Institute of Sonology at the University of Utrecht (now part of the Royal Conservatory at the Hague) in Holland. His compositions include both instrumental and vocal works. A chamber opera, *The Hermaphrodite*, consists of six parts written at various times: "The Secret Gospel" (1976), "The Hermaphrodite" (1975), "A Concert Chamber" (1971), "Echo of an Echo" (1980), "Mutually" (1973), and "The Overtone" (1977). Another major composition is *A Glass Bead Game* for chorus and orchestra (1980), the title of which is taken from the well-known novel by Hermann Hesse. It is a large work consisting of six parts, each of which can be performed independently: "Pedagogical Overture" (with narrator), "Macrofantasia on Grieg's A-minor Concerto," "Beyond Neon,"

"Choral Symphony" (with chorus), "Through a Prism," and "Encore on Verdi's Dies Irae: Apotheosis" (with chorus). "Through a Prism," a double concerto for cello, organ, and large orchestra, was awarded the prestigious Nordic prize in composition in 1990. Thommessen has also written "Stabat mater speciosa" for mixed chorus.

Thommessen's instrumental works include two compositions for four percussionists, "Most" for school orchestra, "Staff Arabesque" for Janissary band (1974; also arranged for orchestra as "Barbaresque"), "Up-Down" for symphony orchestra (1972–73), "Scherzophonia/Scherzophrenia" for violin, cello, and piano (1982), and "The Second Creation" for trumpet and orchestra (1988). He has also written incidental music for several Shakespearean plays: *The Tempest*, *Macbeth*, *King Lear*, *The Taming of the Shrew*, and *Romeo and Juliet*.

Although Thommessen's style is an outgrowth of Neoexpressionism, postmodernist elements have gradually come to occupy an important place in his music. As a result of his keen interest in the relationship between the composer and the audience, "mediation" has become a central concept for him. He borrows from the music of an earlier day in order to make it easier for the listeners to follow the thematic and structural development in his music. A masterful orchestrator, he creates works distinguished by their imagination and rich tonal color. He has also become deeply involved in political and pedagogical issues relative to music. From 1984 to 1988 he served as professor of composition at the Norwegian State Academy of Music in Oslo, where, in cooperation with Lasse Thoresen (see below), he is also engaged in a research project in sonology. The goal of this project is to create better tools for use in music analysis, especially with regard to newer music.

Lasse Thoresen (b. 1949) cannot quite be classified as a postmodernist, although his music is not lacking in *nyvennlig* (see p. 346) characteristics. He studied composition with Finn Mortensen and Werner Kaegi and in 1988 became professor of composition at the Norwegian State Academy of Music in Oslo. Like Thommessen, he studied at the Institute of Sonology at the University of Utrecht and is one of the principal investigators in the previously mentioned research project at the music academy in Oslo.

Thoresen's compositions include the chamber-music works "The Garden" (1976), "Interplay" for flute and piano (1981), and "Bird of the Heart" for violin, cello, and piano (1982). For piano solo he has written *Four Inventions: In Memory of Fartein Valen* (1968) and *Stages of the Inner Dialogue*. Thoresen has composed for chorus and for various other solo instruments, and has occasionally employed electronic devices in such works as the television ballet *Creations*. In recent years he has composed a number of colorful orchestral works, including "The Sun of Justice" (1982), *Symphonic Concerto* for violin and orchestra (1984; revised in 1986), *Concerto* for two cellos and orchestra, subtitled "Illuminations" (1986), and "Hymnic Dance" (1987). Many of these titles reflect the composer's affiliation with the Bahai religion.

Postmodernist elements also appear in some of the compositions of Magne Hegdal (b. 1944). Hegdal received his music training in Oslo, where he studied piano with Nicolai Dirdal and Erling Westher, and composition with Conrad Baden and Finn Mortensen. He made his debut as a pianist in 1969. Many of his compositions are for piano, but he has also written for orchestra and smaller ensembles. His catalogue of works includes a two-movement *Sinfonia* for orchestra (1972); *Übung*, a concerto for two pianos and orchestra (1977); and three concertos for various instrumental ensembles (1978–79). Among his vocal works are "Credo" for mixed chorus and "Air: To a Gothic Cathedral" for soprano, piano, and percussion. In 1987 he wrote a multimedia work entitled *Concerto*. Piano works include *Three Saccharine Pieces: Salon Music for Piano*, *Herbarium* (forty-five short pieces), *Birds*, and *Études*.

Hegdal's point of departure stylistically is the serialism of the Second Viennese School, but he has proceeded beyond this to the use of the aleatory principle, which plays an important role in his music. Hegdal is fascinated by the relationship between the prescribed and the chance elements in music, with all of the opportunities for variation that are thus created. Concerning *Herbarium*, for example, he has said: "Neither the individual parts nor the composition as a whole should be perceived as something that develops through time. The pieces stand here—awaiting attention, one could almost say—and the totality is a result of ever-new ways of regarding them."

Synne Skouen (b. 1950) received her professional training at the Music Academy in Vienna and the State Academy of Music in Oslo; her teacher in composition at the latter was Finn Mortensen. She has been deeply involved in political issues relative to music, especially regarding the position of female composers. She was editor of the music periodical *Ballade* from its inception in 1977 to 1986. Her catalogue of works to date includes a mini-cabaret for speaker and instrumental ensemble called *What Did Schopenhauer Say . . . ?*; ballet music, including *Evergreen* (a television ballet, 1979) and *The Prophetess* (1988); and incidental music for several theater productions. Among her more recent orchestral compositions are "Night Piece" (1987) and "Intonazione—Quasi una fantasia" (1988). Other compositions worthy of note are the video opera *Shower* (1984), "Angrboda's Daughter" for chamber ensemble (1986), and a piano piece, "Greet Domitila."

Skouen's compositions exhibit considerable variety—everything from the grotesque humor of *What Did Schopenhauer Say . . . ?* to the tenderness and emotion of such compositions as "Angrboda's Daughter" and "Night Piece." Throughout this range, however, her music is generally engaging and absorbing.

Cecilie Ore (b. 1954) attended the Norwegian State Academy of Music in Oslo and later studied in Paris, Utrecht, and Amsterdam. Among her compositions to date are "Carnatus" for mixed chorus (1982); "Helices," a wind quintet (1984); and an orchestral work entitled "Porphyry" (1986). "Carnatus" was performed at the International Society for Contemporary Music festival in Canada in 1984. Ore has also aroused interest abroad with some of her electro-acoustic works. Her compositions are characterized by an imaginative use of sound within the confines of a tightly organized form.

Rolf Walin (b. 1957) stands out as one of Norway's promising young composers. He has a varied musical background, having performed with jazz and rock groups as well as with ensembles playing medieval and avant-garde music. He studied composition at the Norwegian State Academy of Music and in the United States. His compositions include an orchestral work entitled "ID" (1982); "Mandala" for two pianos and percussion (1985); "Zur Psychopathologie des Alltagsleben" for female voice and instrumental ensemble; and a concerto for timpani and orchestra (1988). Elements derived from jazz appear in some of his compositions, and he occasionally employs electronic devices.

A FINAL WORD

Our study of the music of Norway has now carried us from the mist-enshrouded days of the Stone and Bronze Ages to the present time, from crude instruments made of bone and bark and wood to the latest products of electronic wizardry. It is hoped that in the course of this study, readers will have caught a glimpse of the vitality and individuality of the music tradition of this land that lies astride the Arctic circle in the northernmost part of Europe.

These qualities are most evident, perhaps, in Norwegian folk music, the pervasive influence of which has been traced through many periods. They are also manifest, however, in countless other ways that may be less obvious to an outside observer. They are clearly present in the rich choral tradition that has flourished in Norway for many years. They are discernible in the best works of such early masters as Waldemar Thrane, L. M. Lindeman, and Halfdan Kjerulf. They are even more evident in the words as well as the works of those two great firebrands of Norwegian music, Ole Bull and Rikard Nordraak. And they found expression in the rich outpouring of distinctive works during the so-called "golden age" of Norwegian music in the latter half of the nineteenth century, attracting the attention of music lovers the world over.

We trust that our concluding chapter has demonstrated that Norwegian music today is no less vital than that of the past. Ours is a time of ferment, of experimentation, of groping for new sounds and new forms that are the appropriate next steps on the pathway from the past to the future. A goodly number of talented composers are diligently and enthusiastically at work along this pathway. Only time will tell whether from their ranks will emerge the great master or masters who will lead us all toward the music of to-morrow.

Glossary

gangar: a Norwegian folk dance ("walking dance"); a folk-dance tune in 6/8 time (or in 2/4 time with triplets) used for such a dance.

halling: a vigorous Norwegian folk dance, most often performed as a male solo dance; a folk-dance tune in 2/4 time used for such a dance.

joik: the traditional folk music of the Sami people.

kulokk: the most prominent and complex type of Norwegian herding music. Literally, "cow call."

langeleik: an ancient stringed instrument of the zither type, with one fretted melody string and from three to seven drone strings. This instrument is still played in the Valdres region of Norway.

lur: an ancient wind instrument fashioned from wood and birch bark and played like a trumpet. The name is also used for an instrument made of bronze that produces a sound similar to that of a modern trombone.

nynorsk: "new Norwegian." An alternate form of the Norwegian language derived from local dialects.

seter: a dairy farm in the mountains used only during the summer months.

skillingsvise (pl. *skillingsviser*): a song text published in pamphlet form during the early nineteenth century. Also called a "street song." A number of such songs became intertwined with the folk-music tradition and are sometimes regarded as folk ballads.

slaatt (pl. *slaatter*): a Norwegian dance tune of instrumental character. The principal types of *slaatter* are the *gangar*, the *halling*, and the *springar*, though other names are used for these subtypes in various regions of the country (see details in chapter 6).

slaattestev: *stev* (see below) that are associated in the folk-music tradition with certain *slaatt* melodies.

springar: a lively Norwegian folk dance; a folk-dance tune in 3/4 time used for such a dance. In western Norway, *springars* are performed with three almost equal beats, but in the valleys of central Norway the three beats in each measure are of unequal duration. In Telemark, for example, they are long-medium- short, while in Valdres they are short-long-medium.

springleik: the name commonly used in the Gudbrandsdalen region of Norway for the type of dance tune more commonly known as a *springar*.

stev: a type of monostrophic folk poetry in specific metrical patterns ("old *stev*" or "new *stev*"), sung to traditional and mostly very old *stev* tunes. Still practiced in the Telemark and Setesdal regions of Norway.

Selected Bibliography

Aksdal, Björn. *Med Piber og Basuner, Skalmeye og Fiol.* Trondheim, 1982.

Benestad, Finn and Dag Schjelderup-Ebbe. *Edvard Grieg: The Man and the Artist.* Norwegian edition Oslo, 1980. English translation by William H. Halverson and Leland B. Sateren. Lincoln and London, 1988.

Blanc, Tarald Höyerup. *Christiania Theaters Historie 1827–1877.* Christiania (Oslo), 1899.

Brock, Hella. *Edvard Grieg.* Leipzig, 1990.

Broholm, H. C., W. P. Larsen, and Godtfred Skjerne. *The Lures of the Bronze Age.* Copenhagen, 1949.

Dahm, Cecilie. *Kvinner komponerer. Ni portretter av norske kvinnelige komponister i tiden 1840–1930.* Oslo, 1987.

Dorfmüller, Joachim. *Studien zur norwegischen Klaviermusik der ersten Hälften des zwanzigsten Jahrhunderts.* Marburg, 1969.

Eggen, Erik. "The sequences of the Archbishopric of Nidaros." *Bibliotheca Arnamagnaeana* 21–22 (1968).

Finck, H. Th. *Grieg and his Music.* London, 1910; reprint New York, 1971.

Foster, Beryl. *The Songs of Edvard Grieg.* Brookfield, Scolar Press, 1990.

Gaukstad, Öystein. *Norsk folkemusikk. Ein bibliografi.* Oslo, 1951.

Gaukstad, Öystein (ed.). *Edvard Grieg. Artikler og taler.* Oslo, 1957.

Grieg, Edvard. *Complete Works*, ed. Finn Benestad, Dan Fog, Nils Grinde, Hampus Huldt-Nyström, and Dag Schjelderup-Ebbe. 20 vols. Frankfurt, London, and New York, 1977–.

Haugen, Einar and Camilla Cai. *Ole Bornemann Bull (1810–1880): Romantic Musician and Cosmopolitan Norwegian.* University of Wisconsin Press, 1992 (projected).

Hernes, Asbjörn. *Impuls og tradisjon i norsk musikk 1500–1800.* Oslo, 1952.

Herresthal, Harald. *Norwegische Musik von den Anfängen bis zur Gegenwart.* 2d ed. Oslo, 1987.

Horton, John. *Edvard Grieg.* London, 1950. (In English)

Huitfeldt, Henrik Jörgen. *Christiania Theaterhistorie.* Copenhagen, 1876.

Huldt-Nystrom, Hampus. *Fra Munkekor til symfoniorkester.* Oslo, 1969.

Johansen, David Monrad. *Edvard Grieg.* Oslo, 1934. English translation by Madge Robertson. Princeton, 1938.

Kindem, Ingeborg Eckhoff. *Den norske operas historie.* Oslo, 1941.

Kjerulf, Halfdan. *Samlede Verker*, ed.

Nils Grinde. 3 vols. Oslo, 1977–80.

Kortsen, Bjarne. *Contemporary Norwegian Chamber Music*. Bergen, 1971.

——. *Contemporary Norwegian Orchestral Music*. Bergen, 1969.

——. *Contemporary Norwegian Piano Music*. 4th ed. Bergen, 1976.

——. *Fartein Valen: Life and Music*. 3 vols. Oslo, 1965.

——. *J. H. Freithoff (1713–67) Man and Music*. Bergen, 1974.

——. *Modern Norwegian Chamber Music*. Haugesund, 1965.

Kortsen, Bjarne (ed.). *Grieg the Writer*. 2 vols. Bergen, 1972.

Lange, Kristian. *Norwegian Music. A Survey*. Oslo, 1971.

Lange, Kristian and Arne Östvedt. *Norwegian Music*. London, 1958.

Nordraak, Rikard. *Rikard Nordraaks Samlede Verker*. Oslo, 1945.

Norwegian Folk Music. Series I: The Hardanger-fiddle Slaatter. Vols. 1–5 ed. Olav Gurvin, vols. 6–7 ed. Jan Petter Blom, Sven Nyhus, and Reidar Sevaag. Olso, 1958–81.

Norwegian Music Institutions and Music Life. A Survey. Oslo, 1981.

Sandvik, Ole Mörk. *Norwegian Religious Folk Tunes*. 2 vols. Oslo, 1960–64.

——. *"Springleikar." Norwegian Country Dances*. Oslo, 1967.

Sandvik, Ole Mörk and Gerhard Schjelderup. *Norges Musikhistorie*. 2 vols. Kristiania, 1921.

Schjelderup-Ebbe, Dag. *Edvard Grieg. 1858–1867*. Oslo and London, 1967. (In English)

——. "Modality in Halfdan Kjerulf's music." *Music and Letters* 38 (1957): 238–46.

——. "Neuere norwegische musikwissenschaftliche Arbeiten." *Acta Musicologica* 44 (1972): 25–29.

——. "Norwegische musikwissenschaftliche Arbeiten 1972–1979." *Acta Musicologica* 52 (1980): 68–73.

——. *A Study of Grieg's Harmony*. Oslo, 1953.

Schlotel, Brian. *Grieg*. London, 1986.

Searle, Humphrey and Robert Layton. *Twentieth Century Composers. Vol. 3, Britain, Scandinavia and The Netherlands*. London, 1972.

Sevaag, Reidar. *Det gjallar og det laet*. Oslo, 1973.

——. *Geige und Geigenmusik in Norwegen. Vol. 1, Die Geige in der Europäischen Volksmusik*. Vienna, 1975.

Skyllstad, Kjell. "Thematic structure in relation to form in Edvard Grieg's Cyclic Works." *Studia Musicologica Norvegica* 3 (1977): 75–94.

Stendahl, Björn. *Jazz Hot and Swing. Jazz i Norge 1920–1940*. Oslo, 1987.

Wallner, Bo. *Vaar tids musik i Norden*. Stockholm, 1968.

Yoell, John H. *The Nordic Sound*. Boston, 1974.

Music Institutions and Agencies in Norway

Readers desiring further information about specific aspects of Norwegian music are encouraged to call or write to one or more of the organizations listed below. The professional associations will also be pleased to facilitate communication with individual composers or performers.

A. *Archives*

Norwegian Music Information Center
Toftesgate 69
N-0552 Oslo 5, Norway
Tel. (02) 37 09 09

This is the principal clearinghouse for information regarding contemporary music life in Norway. It houses both scores and recordings of a large body of new Norwegian music. The Norwegian Jazz Archive and the Norwegian Archives for Folk and Popular Songs are also located at this address.

B. *Professional Associations*

Society of Norwegian Composers
Klingenberggate 5
0161 Oslo 1, Norway
Tel. (02) 42 56 78

Most contemporary composers are members of this society, which is pleased to facilitate contact with its members as appropriate.

Norwegian Musicians' Union
Youngsgate 11
0181 Oslo 1, Norway
Tel. (02) 40 10 50

C. *Collections of Primary Materials*

Norwegian Folk Music Collection
Post Boks 1017, Blindern
0371 Oslo 3, Norway
Tel. (02) 45 47 48

University of Oslo Library
Att: Norwegian Music Collection
Drammensveien 42
0255 Oslo 2, Norway
Tel. (02) 55 36 30

This extensive collection is a valuable source of information concerning Norwegian music life past and present.

Bergen Public Library
Att: Music Division
Strömgate 6
5000 Bergen, Norway
Tel. (05) 31 97 50

This is the principal repository of original Grieg manuscripts, letters, and other documents. Its holdings include the rich collection of Grieg manuscripts and letters discovered in New York City and purchased by the Norwegian government in 1986.

D. *Institutions of Advanced Music Education and Research*

Norwegian State Academy of Music
Gydasvei 6
Post Boks 5190 Majorstua
0302 Oslo 3, Norway
Tel. (02) 46 40 55

The academy is pleased to receive inquiries concerning advanced music education in Norway and will also assist interested parties in establishing contact with any of the seven regional music conservatories located in Oslo, Drammen, Kristiansand, Stavanger, Bergen, Trondheim, and Tromsö.

Institute of Musicology
University of Oslo
Post Boks 1017 Blindern
0371 Oslo 3, Norway
Tel. (02) 45 47 50

Musicological Institute
University of Trondheim
7055 Dragvoll, Norway
Tel. (07) 59 65 57

Norwegian Council for Scientific Research
Sandakerveien 99
0371 Oslo 3, Norway

The council provides support for research in the humanities, including music.

Norwegian Arts Council
Grev Wedels Plass
0151 Oslo 1, Norway
Tel. (02) 42 39 19

This agency supports various enterprises involving music and other art forms.

E. *Associations with Specialized Interests*

New Music
Toftesgate 69
0552 Oslo 5, Norway
Tel. (02) 37 08 10

This is the Norwegian section of the International Society for Contemporary Music (ISCM).

Norwegian Rock Music Federation
Toftesgate 69
0552 Oslo 5, Norway
Tel. (02) 37 08 10

Hövikodden Art Center
1311 Hövikodden, Norway
Tel. (02) 54 30 50

This center seeks to promote appreciation of contemporary art and music.

F. *Major Organizations Concerned with Public Performances*

Bergen International Music Festival
Lars Hillesgate 3 A
5000 Bergen, Norway
Tel. (05) 32 04 00

The festival, held each year during the last week of May and the first week of June, presents performances of a wide variety of traditional and modern music by Norwegian and non-Norwegian artists and groups.

Norwegian Broadcasting Corporation
Bj. Björnsons Plass 1
0340 Oslo 3, Norway
Tel. (02) 45 90 50

Oslo Philharmonic Orchestra
Munkedamsveien 14
0250 Oslo 2, Norway
Tel. (02) 41 60 65

Bergen Philharmonic Orchestra
Lars Hillesgate 3 A
5000 Bergen, Norway
Tel. (05) 32 04 00

Norwegian National Opera
Storgate 21
0184 Oslo 1, Norway
Tel. (02) 42 94 75

Music Index

This index includes most of the arrangements, collections, original compositions, folk tunes, and hymns cited in the text. It does not include (a) compositions with generic titles (cantata, concerto, quartet, requiem, symphony, sonata, allegro, etc.) or (b) incidental music for dramatic productions except when such music exists in the form of a piano or orchestral suite. Numbers in italics denote items represented by a music example on the page(s) indicated.

General Index

(Numbers in italics refer to text accompanying a visual illustration or music example.)

This book was designed by
Jungsun Whang and set in
Galliard by A-R Editions, Inc.
It was printed by Edwards
Brothers, Inc., using 60 lb.
Finch Opaque.